The
ENJOYMENT
of THEATRE

The
ENJOYMENT

of THEATRE

Third Edition

KENNETH M. CAMERON
PATTI P. GILLESPIE

MACMILLAN PUBLISHING COMPANY
NEW YORK

MAXWELL MACMILLAN CANADA, INC.
TORONTO

MAXWELL MACMILLAN INTERNATIONAL
NEW YORK   OXFORD   SINGAPORE   SYDNEY

Editor: David Chodoff
Production Supervisor: J. Edward Neve
Production Manager: Muriel Underwood
Text & Cover Designer: Sheree L. Goodman
Cover photograph: Richard M. Feldman
Photo Researcher: Chris Migdol

This book was set in Goudy old style by Ruttle, Shaw & Wetherill, Inc.,
printed by R. R. Donnelley, and bound by R. R. Donnelley.
The cover was printed by Phoenix Color.

Macmillan Publishing Company
866 Third Avenue, New York, New York 10022

Macmillan Publishing Company is part of the Maxwell Communication
Group of Companies.

Maxwell Macmillan Canada, Inc.
1200 Englinton Avenue, East
Suite 200
Don Mills, Ontario M3C 3N1

Library of Congress Cataloging in Publication Data

Cameron, Kenneth M. (date)
  The enjoyment of theatre / Kenneth M. Cameron, Patti P. Gillespie.
  —3rd ed.
      p.   cm.
  Includes index.
  ISBN 0-02-318430-2
    1. Theater.   I. Gillespie, Patti P.   II. Title.
PN2037.C27   1992
792—dc20   91-12251
                                                                            CIP

Printing 1 2 3 4 5 6 7 8   Year: 2 3 4 5 6 7 8 9 0 1

PREFACE

Revising a successful book can be difficult, as the authors try to steer between keeping what is best and identifying what is something less than that. Preparing a third edition of a successful book is downright daunting. On the other hand, it is not enough merely to add what is new since the last edition: the book cannot grow longer and longer.

We have, therefore, prepared this third edition with three goals in mind—goals defined within the parameters of preserving what readers have told us works best in the previous editions:

UP-TO-DATE KNOWLEDGE—Current scholarship and practice have guided our revisions. For example, exciting new discoveries of Shakespeare's own theatre, tantalizing new approaches to understanding performance offered by the new theories of semiotics and deconstruction, and troubling new understandings about our world and our art emerging from new feminist scholarship have enriched this third edition. The tumultuous changes in the political landscape since 1988 have resulted in a complete rewriting of what is now Chapter 16, "Changing World, Eclectic Theatre: 1960s–1990".

FLEXIBILITY—Aware that instructors should not be locked into a book's structure or a single set of plays, we have continued to make sure that parts, chapters, and sub-sections can be assigned in orders other than that of the table of contents. As in earlier editions, our aim has been a book flexible enough for a wide variety of plays, course structures, and teachers. Ours is a book that allows teachers to teach *their* course, not ours.

DIVERSITY—Convinced that pluralism is an outstanding feature of today's world, we have tried to revise the book to celebrate diversity. We have expanded Chapter 17, "World Theatre"; we have tried to suggest the contributions of African-Americans and women to drama and theatre; we have sought out visual materials that show diversity.

At the same time, we have kept many features of a book that has been very well received in two previous editions. Our highly praised treatments of the nature of theatre and of audience (Chapters 1 and 2) have been kept but have been enhanced by a consideration of ritual. Our effective chapters on reading and seeing plays (Chapters 3 and 4) have been maintained, with additional materials devoted to play analysis. Our chapters on theatre makers have been kept more or less intact, although new material has been added on aspects of technical theatre and public relations. Our chapters on theatre history, always a notable feature of the book, remain authoritative yet understandable by the introductory student; revisions here include additional materials on Shakespeare and contemporary theatre, and updated scholarship in other sections.

We have replaced as many as three-quarters of the book's illustrations without losing either the appropriateness or the careful captioning of earlier editions. THE ENJOYMENT OF THEATRE has always been unusual for its inclusion of historically important illustrations, and it continues to be so: in the historical chapters, our goal has been to use illustrations contemporary with the period under study. In the non-historical chapters, on the other hand, we have continued to use mostly photographs, selecting among New York, regional, and educational theatres, with the greatest emphasis on university and college productions. We believe that students are best served by seeing many examples of college and university theatre—the theatre that is closest to them, that they are likeliest to work in themselves, and that is the career choice of their teachers. We have featured color photographs of such theatres in one of our color sections, photographs that show the sophistication and elegance of much contemporary educational theatre.

THE ENJOYMENT OF THEATRE continues to be a text for the introductory course in the theatre. It continues to relate art to life, the theatre to the world. Its very first sections continue to define theatre in terms of other activities the introductory student knows (athletics, television, movies). It continues to build on this with two major approaches that instructors may emphasize or order as they think best: understanding the theatre through the ways it is made; and understanding the theatre through its past.

Students now live in a world where events happen with dazzling speed. The world beyond the theatre has seen wrenching change since our last edition: the Berlin Wall came down; an individual tried to face down a tank in Tiananmen Square; the American savings and loan industry collapsed. At the same time, the theatre showed changes that might, on the surface, seem unrelated but that understanding would show to be linked: performance art gained new emphasis; a formerly supressed playwright became president of post-Cold War Czechoslovakia; the number of new productions on Broadway continued to decline. We have tried, in this edition as in earlier ones, to show how the world and the theatre interact. We hope, therefore, that the student being introduced to the theatre by this book will come to understand how the theatre works, what it is and what it has been, and how it interacts with and clarifies that real world that now moves so fast.

CONTENTS

The
ENJOYMENT
of THEATRE

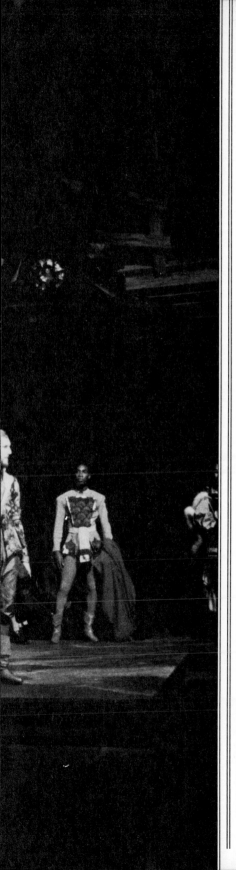

PART ONE

THEATRE
and
ITS
AUDIENCE

CHAPTER ONE

THEATRE AS A PERFORMING ART

Shakespeare at Ashland, Oregon . . . *Carousel* at a high school in Iowa . . . a student-written play at the American College Theatre Festival in Washington, D.C. . . . *Il Trovatore* at New York's Metropolitan Opera . . . rock concerts . . . an African dance-opera in Philadelphia. But—an urban drunk performing before ten people? A child of nine performing for herself? An actor rehearsing on an empty stage?

Performing arts are many things, but things that have in common *performance* and *art*.

Performance involves the body and/or the voice in doing something for somebody's enjoyment.

Art is an activity that makes its product for its own ends. It is also an activity that is self-contained and artificial: it does not need to have any immediate use in the world. (For example, sign painting is an application of some of the techniques of an art, painting; however, sign painting is an activity devoted almost exclusively to its usefulness—making signs—whereas painting is an art that has no *useful* product at all, although its product is often very expensive and much sought after.)

So, the performing arts are human activities that make or make up stories or movements or sounds or combinations of those things for people's enjoyment. They are highly diverse, each appealing in very different ways to different responses.

FIGURE 1-1. **Performance.** The performing arts have in common the human performer. *Dance and the Railroad,* by David H. Hwang, directed by Roberta Uno Thelwell, designed by Sarah Stauderman. (*Courtesy New WORLD Theater of the University of Massachusetts, Amherst.*)

Yet what is to be prized about the performing arts is their very diversity, their variety, and their many mutual contradictions, because human beings thrive on artistic diversity. A healthy culture (like a healthy ecosystem) is one that encourages such variety; a culturally healthy individual is one who can enjoy a variety of these seemingly polarized activities—going to a movie one night, a ballet another, a baseball game on Saturday afternoon, a symphony concert on Sunday.

This book will try to separate the theatre from the other performing arts. The separation is partly artificial, however, because one of the outstanding qualities of the theatre is the extent to which it contributes to and draws from other activities. Even for the individual theatre artist, such contributions and borrowings are valuable: actors dance and sing as well as act; they play baseball and create films; they are often themselves members of the audience. Theatre artists—playwrights, actors, directors, designers—move from film to theatre to opera to spectacles like political events and pageants.

Because a healthy society welcomes diversity, healthy arts are themselves diverse; because artists create in diverse ways, audiences must be able to respond in diverse ways. The performing arts, it must be emphasized, are not competitors but relatives, and audiences need to learn to appreciate the entire family. Because each member of the family is complex, however, the study of any one of them takes care and time.

MAJOR PERFORMING ARTS AND RELATED ACTIVITIES

Enormous overlap exists among the performing arts, so much so that one of them—the theatre—has sometimes been seen as an amalgam of the others; in that view, theatre itself would be the umbrella that covers the performing arts. Although this idea fails as a definition of theatre, it serves as a reminder that the theatre uses elements of other arts and that without them it would be a less compelling art.

We can include other arts *with* the word *theatre*—theatre dance, theatre music—so long as we remember that each art has its own special characteristics. We must not pretend that film, television, dance, opera, staged plays, and mime, for example, are all "theatre" in a vague and general way, or we will lose the crucial distinctions among them. The performing arts have much in common, but what they have in common does not make them identical. To talk about them and appreciate them, we must know both what they share and what they do *not* share; then, when we understand some of their similarities and their differences, we will be able to look at one of them more closely.

What Is Film?

In the movie films, he said, we only look at what is there already. Life shines on the shadow screen, as from the darkness of one's mind. It is a big business.

E. L. DOCTOROW, *Ragtime*

Soft music. Low lights. People taking their seats, whispering, chuckling. Popcorn. Rattle of candy papers. The music ends; the lights go to black. "Exit" signs glow. A bright image appears on a slightly concave screen: names. Images of people and places, real people, real places, their images big, colorful. The images move at the same rate as real people. Loud music. Voices—the people talk. The images embody a story about people. At rare times, the speed of the images slows; once, they even freeze like a still photograph. The way that these images are presented changes, sometimes giving us very close-in pictures, sometimes very distant ones. Sometimes we are presented with images of only part of what the human eye would really see—a hand, a flower, a road. Sometimes we do not even see what the human eye might look at in the same situation; the machine that makes the images is looking at something else, and that something else becomes of great importance to us. The story continues, the images flash on.

Film is a complex form of communication relying on putting things together simultaneously and sequentially.

JOHN HARRINGTON, *The Rhetoric of Film*

Film:

1. Uses a projected image of events, places, and people and not the events, places, and people themselves.

2. Usually presents a story and characterization.

3. Gathers its audiences into special places ("theatres") but does not allow any interplay between the audience and the images because the images have no sensitivities of their own.

4. Can be repeated identically any number of times until the film itself breaks down—but the film can be reprinted and thus saved from any sign of deterioration whatsoever.

It was René Clair who pointed out that if two or three people were together on a stage, the dramatist must ceaselessly motivate their being there at all. But the film audience accepts mere sequence as rational. Whatever the camera turns to, the audience accepts.

MARSHALL MCLUHAN, *Understanding Media*

What Is Television?

The audience for American television is what may be called a mass society [that] has somewhat different values and social controls from the traditional western society. In the traditional society, the upper classes set the standards of the culture and the lower classes followed along.

DAVID POTTER, in *"The Historical Perspective"*

A living-room. Few lights. Sounds from the rest of the house, from the street. Somebody passing through the room to the kitchen. A screen, twenty inches or so in its long dimension; slightly distorted sound with poor treble values. Images of real people and places, the visual quality of the images rather poor in comparison with the real people and the real places, these images being made up of moving dots. Saturated colors in rather oversimple, slightly unreal values. The images of the people are playing out a story, but one of the people in the living room does not like the story and presses a switch, and another story appears. This story seems to be preferable, but it stops and other people appear and begin to talk about automobiles. Nobody in the living room seems to care much that the images are talking about automobiles, but one of the real people leaves the room and comes back with a can of beer. The images stop talking about automobiles and the other images appear and begin to act out their story again. It is a funny story, and there is loud laughter with the funny parts, as if a big audience were sitting with the people in the living room. There is an image of a living room in the story, and it looks remarkably like the living room in which the people are sitting to watch the story. In the story living room, they even have a screen of

FIGURE 1-2. **Film.** From its earliest days, film—movies, motion pictures—captured movement and took it to millions through easily replicated, machine-made imagery. *The Animated Picture Studio,* c. 1912. *(Courtesy of the Library of Congress Motion Picture Collection.)*

the same sort, on which other images are being shown. They are images of a news story about a real disaster of a year before.

Time was when a person went to the movies and surrendered, knowingly, to a few hours of fantasy, the walk from home to cinema marking the transfer from world of fact to world of fiction. Now the unreal filters from the "tube" into the home along with the real.

DANIEL SHORR, "The National Seance," in *Review* Magazine

Television:

1. Uses an image made up of dots on a cathode-ray-tube "screen" to create a record of events, places, and people.

2. Presents both stories with characterization and precise records of actual events, or "news."

3. Does not gather its audience but locates its outlets (the screens) in informal living spaces (living rooms, bedrooms, bars) and allows no interplay between audience and images because the images have no sensitivities of their own.

4. Can be repeated identically any number of times if recorded on film or tape; however, the commercial structure of the industry that presents television in the United States makes the frequent repetition of most programs unlikely.

The cool TV medium provides depth structure in art and entertainment alike, and creates audience involvement in depth as well.

MARSHALL McLUHAN, *Understanding Media*

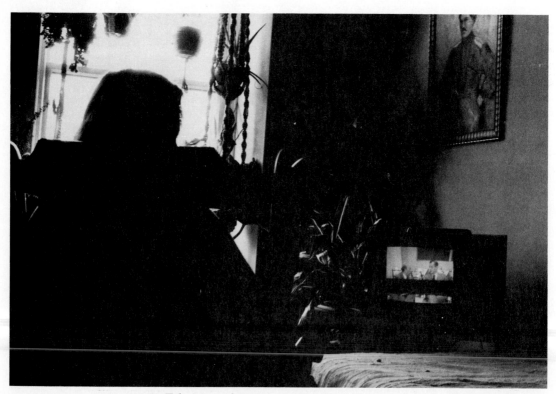

FIGURE 1-3. Television. Alone or in very small groups, the television audience watches imagery that can be captured and replayed through modern VCR technology. *(Photo by Augustin Aldrete.)*

What Is Opera?

Without music, opera is not opera.

J. MERILL KNAPP, *The Magic of Opera*

A huge theatre. Elegance of decor, elegant dress on many of the audience. An entire orchestra in a pit between the audience and the stage. The lights dim; the orchestra plays—melodies, promises of what the performance to come will hold. Darkness, then stage light. A crowd in Renaissance costume, gathered before the gates of a Renaissance palace. They sing. An officer strolls among them. He sings. Everybody sings—nobody talks. The scene changes to a palace courtyard on a huge scale. Two women sing— glorious, soaring melodies that fill the large theatre with their voices. The audience applauds and the performance stops while the applause continues. Then the singers continue, performing a story of high passion and extreme situations—revenge, coin- cidence, violence. They sing in Italian, a language the audience does not understand. The story is printed in the program so that the audience will know what is going on, but most of them know the opera so well that they do not need the notes.

Our inner life . . . provides music with the form through which music expresses that life. Every contradiction ceases from the moment that the form and the object of the expression are identical.

ADOLPHE APPIA, *Music and the Art of the Theatre*

Opera:

1. Uses live performers on a real stage in artificial (i.e., made-for-the-purpose) settings.

2. Uses story and characterization.

3. Gathers its audience into theatres that allow the audience to influence the performance through their reactions.

4. Can be repeated, but with the inevitable variations natural to any human endeavor: because of the production structure of commercial opera compa- nies worldwide, however, it is extremely rare that the same singers will repeat the same opera frequently for a long time in the same theatre, and most singers take a day or two between performances.

5. Uses an orchestra, typically located between the stage and the audience, and uses music as the dominant means of communication, both actor-to- actor and actor-to-audience.

Opera may be a museum piece in the contemporary world, but the true opera lover is not daunted. He is always seeking an amalgam in performance [that] will produce a miraculous result—that moment when drama, orchestra, singing, and spectacle unite to achieve what is promised by a composer and librettist of genius.

J. MERILL KNAPP, *The Magic of Opera*

What Is Dance?

Dancing employs rhythm in both spheres—audible and visual. It is a time-space art, and the only one.

AGNES DE MILLE, *The Book of the Dance*

A theatre, a stage. Low house lights. Loudspeakers for sound. Lights to black and stage lights up: an intense blue, like sky, a picket fence, a suggestion of beach or country road or moor. Two women in very long skirts. Music through the loudspeakers. The women move to the music, their movements rhythmic, stately, visually beautiful, yet not like the movement of ordinary human beings. Their movement is to ordinary human movement what the voice of the opera singer is to the speaking voice—an extension of it, virtually another kind of reality with one foot in the mundane world. The women's bodies are disciplined and trained, even athletic. Slowly, the women grow, become ten feet tall. We understand that it must be that they are carried by other dancers who are hidden by the long skirts, but our understanding does not much change the strange and wonderful effect of their height. Two men appear. They move in the same rhythmic and beautiful way as the women, but they do not increase their height. Dwarfed by the women, they dance with and around them. There is the suggestion of a story—there is interaction among the dancers, clear suggestions that they see and respond to each other. Their actions suggest familiar human events— meeting, wooing, rejecting, loving. The men collapse; perhaps they are dead. The women's height changes. They dance together in "virtual spontaneous gesture."

The primary illusion of dance is a virtual realm of Power—not actual, physically exerted power, but appearances of influence and agency created by virtual gesture.

SUZANNE LANGER, *Feeling and Form*

Dance:

1. Uses live performers in a real space with artificial settings.

2. Sometimes presents stories and characters.

3. Gathers its audience into theatres and allows the audience to interact with the performance; audiences can influence the performance through their reactions.

4. Can be repeated, with the inevitable variations natural to any human endeavor.

5. Movement—both aesthetic and symbolic—is the principal means of communication, usually to musical accompaniment.

The symbol of the world, the balletic realm of forces, is the world and dancing is the human spirit's participation in it.

SUZANNE LANGER, *Feeling and Form*

FIGURE 1-4. **Dance.** Classical and modern dance have become among the most popular of performing arts. *The Firebird* at the University of Wyoming, choreographed by Patricia Tate, designed by Ron Steger.

Just as these performing arts can be seen to have some common characteristics without being identical, so certain *non*-arts can be seen to share elements of performance:

What Are Athletic Events?

The battle of Waterloo was won on the playing fields of Eton.

THE DUKE OF WELLINGTON

A brisk October afternoon. Bright sunlight, the air cool enough for sweaters and wool jackets. An oval stadium that seats thirty thousand people; in its center, the green and grassy stretch of a football field. Food and some alcohol in the audience; color in the stands and on the field—pom-poms, pennants, young men and women in cheerleaders' uniforms, two uniformed marching bands. Two teams in differently colored uniforms. Four people in striped shirts on the field; one blows a whistle, and a ball is kicked from one end of the field toward the other. A player in blue catches the ball and begins to run; players in red wrestle him to the ground. The blue players gather together, then line up on each side of and behind the ball. One of them passes the ball backward. Players charge in all directions, blue and red mingling in fierce, violent contact. The audience cheers. The cheerleaders do somersaults and hand-springs, and they exhort the audience to more noise. The blue players kick the ball to the red, who move it back up the field with skill and determination. The audience becomes noisier. The red cross a white line with the ball, and a larger part of the audience makes more noise than ever, tooting horns and ringing bells and shouting. Two men dressed in a horse costume canter onto the field and cavort about. The players line up again and prepare for the red team to kick the ball to the blues again.

When the One Great Scorer comes to write against your name—He marks—not that you won or lost—but how you played the game.

GRANTLAND RICE, *Alumnus Football*

Athletics:

1. Use live performers in a real performing place.

2. Use competition instead of story; have no characterization. (However, sports audiences often create near-mythic "characters" around sports heroes.)

3. Gather their audiences into prepared—and often very large—spaces and allow the audience reaction to influence the event.

4. Can never be repeated in an identical way. The rules of sports guarantee that the *form* will be repeated, but it is in the nature of games and competitions that the outcome will always be different and will always be in doubt until the very end.

Anyone who doesn't know how to play is illiterate. . . . Sport is where an entire life can be compressed into a few hours, where the emotions of a lifetime can be felt on an acre or two of ground, where a person can suffer and die and rise again on six miles of trails. . . .Sport is a theatre where sinner can turn saint and a common man can become an uncommon hero.

GEORGE SHEEHAN, in *On the Run*

What Is Ritual?

Anthropologists are not unanimous in their definition of ritual, but there is general agreement that, in the view of those who enact and watch it, ritual produces results that lie beyond the termination of the performance.

ANTHONY GRAHAM-WHITE, "Ritual in Contemporary Theatre and Criticism"

The interior of an Iroquois long house in the seventeenth century: a sick woman lies in a cubicle. Inhabitants of the house talk in low voices, cook, warm themselves at the central row of fires. A hand lifts the hangings of the door and a face appears — red, distorted, framed in black hair. The face is a mask, the wearer a member of the

FIGURE 1-5. Athletics. Organized sports have audiences, defined spaces, rules, and limited times, and they elicit some of the same responses as performing arts. *(Photograph courtesy of the Sports Information Office, Athletics Department, University of Maryland.)*

False Face Society. The False Face enters, dancing. Another follows, the face black, the mouth shaped as if blowing. Another enters, the mask this time with a grotesquely bent nose, eyes of pounded copper. They shake rattles made from turtle shells. They sing. They dance into the corners of the house, into the sick woman's cubicle. The people of the house look on; some sing. They give the dancers tobacco. The False Face dancers circle the sick woman and dance out into the winter night.

The claim of ritual to authenticity is set against the artifice of theatre and its definition as entertainment.

EDITH TURNER, "Philip Kabwitha, Ghost Doctor"

CHASING OUT PESTILENCE

This Picture Depicts the Great False Face Society in the Act of getting Rid of All Sickness from the Village. This is done at the Mid-Winter Festival. The False Face Members come into each home and shake their Medicine Rattles into every dark corner of the house, even under the beds. They will chase all evil spirits and Bad sickness out into the cold to Freeze.

The Picture shows the different Types of Medicine Masks of the Society. There is the Spoon Mouth, the Whistler, Buffalo Mask and the Doorkeeper.

The Doorkeeper always stays at the door, it is his job to see that the evil spirits do not sneak back in once they are outside. Then of course you must give each False Face Member his dole of Indian To-bacco, but first you must have the singer sing their favorite song so they can Dance for their To-bacco, for that is their Creed. Then they will Go on their happy way knowing they have done the Earth People a world of Good.

FIGURE 1-6. Ritual. Using some aspects of performing art (e.g., mask, music), ritual has the additional characteristic of *efficacy*, the desire to effect some purpose (e.g., healing). Here, the ceremony of the Iroquois False Face Society, as recreated by artist Ernest Smith, with his description of the ritual. (*Courtesy of Donald G. Cameron. Photograph by Rochester Museum of Arts and Sciences.*)

Ritual:

1. Has live participants, some of whom may be specially masked or costumed.

2. Need not have a script but has fixed features (song, dance, sacrifice), which do not necessarily follow a rigid order.

3. Has a goal: to cure the sick, to guarantee a good harvest, to please a god.

4. Does not define an "audience"; everyone is a participant so long as he or she is part of the culture. An "audience" would be defined by nonparticipation.

5. Can be repeated, although with variations typical of live human activities; however, attempts at exact repetition may be part of the ritual's efficacy.

The difference between animal and human ritual is that animals are always performing what they are, while humans can choose to perform what/who they are not.

RICHARD SCHECHNER, *Between Theatre and Anthropology*

Certain arts, then, and some non-arts share characteristics but are not identical. All share, as well, certain elements with theatre:

What Is Theatre?

The theatre is the home of the Now.

A theatre. An audience, waiting, expectant in the half-light. The accents of New York mingle with those of the Midwest and the South. Many people are carefully dressed, some informally. Between audience and stage there is an orchestra pit, but there is no orchestra visible; instead, loudspeakers flank the stage opening. Darkness. Stage light. A voice, music; an authoritative man is counting a rhythm for a group of dancers. He begins to teach them a simple dance routine, then withdraws into the audience part of the theatre and directs the others through a loudspeaker. There are characterizations and a story, but the characters both talk and sing their emotions and their experiences. We learn that they are trying out for the chorus of a Broadway show. They dance. They sing. They make the audience laugh, listen, sit still with attentiveness. The sexual attractiveness of several of the women onstage is emphasized by their costumes and is part of what is sung and talked about. The language and the subject matter, by the standards of many communities, is frank, even a little shocking. But the audience responds with joyous laughter, noisy applause.

"Is this a theatre?" whispered Smike, in amazement; "I thought it was a blaze of light and finery."

"Why, so it is," replied Nicholas, hardly less surprised: "but not by day, Smike—not by day."

CHARLES DICKENS, *Nicholas Nickleby*

FIGURE 1-7. **Theatre.** One of the world's greatest playwrights continues to challenge and inspire theatre artists: William Shakespeare's *The Tempest* at Center Stage, Baltimore. Directed by Stan Wojewodski, Jr. *(Photograph by Richard Anderson, courtesy of Center Stage.)*

Theatre:

1. Uses live actors on a real stage with artificial settings.

2. Uses story and characterization.

3. Gathers its audiences into defined spaces and allows the audience reaction to affect the performance.

4. Can be repeated, but with the inevitable variations natural to any live activity.

. . . can this cockpit hold
The vasty fields of France? or may we cram
Within this Wooden O the very casques
That did affright the air at Agincourt?
. . . let us, ciphers to this great accompt,
On your imaginative forces work.
Suppose within the girdle of these walls
Are now confin'd two mighty monarchies. . . .
Think when we talk of horses that you see them
Printing their proud hoofs i' the receiving earth;
For 'tis your thoughts that now must deck our kings. . . .

WILLIAM SHAKESPEARE, *The Life of King Henry the Fifth*

Some Aspects of Theatre

There is so much overlap among these activities that we might think that only some mechanical differences separate them—that, for example, theatre is simply opera without the music, or that film is merely theatre recorded on strips of acetate, or that television is nothing but film made visible with electronic impulses. Such a view, however, is woefully inaccurate. It is not entirely false—the mechanical differences do have significance—but it does not begin to touch on other differences.

When an important element in a performing art changes, the art itself changes. That is, a composer who sets a play to music does not automatically create an opera. When, however, a story from one performing art is transferred to another—as, for example, when George Bernard Shaw's play was made the basis of the musical My *Fair Lady*— it is clear that, although the superficial elements of the versions are similar (basically the same story, the same characters, and many of the same audience–actor elements that play and musical share), the end products are different. My *Fair Lady* is not simply Shaw's play sung. Its internal structure is different; its emphases are different; its audience's expectations are different. Where one audience draws its pleasure from story suspense, brilliance of language, and acting performance, the other draws its principal pleasure from the glory of melody and the performance of the singers and dancers.

In fact, the differences that seem to separate dance from theatre, theatre from opera, opera from film, and so on create other and more profound differences. The *fact* of film defines the difference between movies and theatre; but the *art* of film is made possible by camera work, by editing, by a juxtaposition of images that is impossible in the theatre, by a disjunction (sometimes) between sound and image that is unlikely in the theatre, and so on.

The very structure of a film script—the way the action moves forward—is vastly different from that of a play because film gives its information differently. Indeed, it is not too much to say that *the basic differences among the performing arts are founded on their differing means of communication.* Thus, it is possible to have the same story at the center of a performance in each performing art, but to have the performances themselves turn out to be markedly different because of the differences in the arts. For example, Shakespeare's *Romeo and Juliet* has been a staged play, a ballet, an opera, several films, and *West Side Story*, a Broadway musical. All are significantly different, even though the Shakespearean text itself is the basis for much of the script in the film and opera versions. Artists make decisions that select from Shakespeare's story—those elements that will best be communicated by their art, the opera composer selecting those moments and events that are best communicated musically, the choreographer those moments and events that are best communicated in structured and pleasing movement.

Another thing that happens is that each art focuses its audience's attention in a different way. The production of Shakespeare's play may lead us to watch and listen to the actor, the richness of his or her voice, and the poetic beauty of Shakespeare's verse; the opera may lead us to listen to the music instead of watching the singer or following the dramatic development of the story; the dance may ask us to watch and to respond sympathetically with our own bodies, almost forgetting story and character, which become a pretext for the movement.

FIGURE 1-8. **Change of Element.** When an important element in a performing art changes, the art itself changes: Samuel Beckett's *Endgame,* top, in its theatrical form; bottom, as dance. Top, the University of Rochester, directed by Kenneth M. Cameron; bottom, IMPROVISATIONS UNLIMITED, choreographed by Lillo Way. (*Bottom photo by Anderson Associates.*)

Art and Life

After reading these discussions of artistic and athletic events, someone might be tempted to look at still other activities and say, "But what about rock concerts? Or the circus? Or church services? Aren't they related, too?"

Of course they are. So are many unplanned events that draw a crowd and that are then affected by that crowd—an argument between two drivers whose bumpers have locked, for example, or a street demonstration, or a political rally, or even a classroom with a teacher and students. Are not these in some sense theatre, too—or at least performance? Wasn't the "Goddess of Liberty" that students created during China's 1989 protests in some way theatrical?

The answer, of course, is yes—but a qualified yes. In order to talk about the theatre, in order to understand the *art* of the theatre, we must distinguish somehow between that art and life. We must define *theatre* to give it a separate identity despite its many spillovers elsewhere. (Notice our basic assumption here: *art and life are different.* Some theorists disagree.)

An older definition of *theatre* included qualities like the separation of actors and audience, the shape and structure of the building in which theatre was done, the kinds of things that actors performed, and the aesthetics of the art. On the other hand, a radically modern definition would reject those elements and would try to include recent movements into the streets and fields ("street theatre," "guerrilla theatre"), as well as group therapy, parades, and many other activities; it might not distinguish between actors and audience; it might have difficulty identifying the things that the actors performed.

In this book, we distinguish between theatre as an artistic event and the appearance of some elements of theatre in life. For this reason, the argument between the two angry drivers is excluded from our idea of theatre—because it lacks the single characteristic that most separates the art of the theatre from theatrical events in life: *artistic self-awareness,* the intention to create art; as well, it lacks the two elements that are part of self-awareness: *preparation* and *discipline.*

By *self-awareness,* we mean the performer's awareness that what is done is meant to accomplish certain ends and to have certain effects on the audience.

By *preparation,* we mean the anticipation of performing, with all the necessary training, psychological orientation, and talent.

By *discipline,* we mean the admission that performance exists for both audience and performer, and that the performer lives life so that the performance (whether by actor, playwright, director, or designer) will be at optimum level every time it is undertaken.

Artistic self-awareness does not guarantee that every performance will be good. It does try to guarantee that what is done will, in fact, be a performance and not an accident and that it will aspire to be art.

To define *performance,* then, so that it will exist within the definition of *theatre,* it should have, besides self-awareness or intention, three other elements; the *actor,* the *audience,* and the *action.*

By *actor,* we mean a performer who impersonates—that is, somebody who uses the pronoun *I* and means somebody else.

FIGURE 1-9. The Home of the Now. Theatre's immediacy, its nonrecoverability, is perhaps its greatest strength—and its greatest disadvantage: once completed, a gesture or a performance ceases to exist. *On the Verge,* directed by Marcy Gamzon, scene design by P. Gibson Ralph. University of Rochester Summer Theatre. *(Richard Russell Photo.)*

By *audience,* we mean a group of people separate from the actor who are gathered together for the specific purpose of attending the event.

By *action,* we mean an invented human development within which the actor's impersonation functions—*not an action that is told about, but one that is embodied by the actor and seen by the audience.*

The theatre, then, is an art in which performers, by impersonating, represent or embody imitations of people in a story that is shown to an audience.

The theatre is not better or worse than other performing arts because of its special nature; it has its special attributes, from which both advantages and disadvantages inevitably spring. Its greatest advantage is *immediacy,* the sense of "nowness" that arises from theatre's *showing* of human actions rather than telling about them. The theatre has been called "the home of the Now"; the person who said that meant that the theatre is a unique art because, in it, fictional events happen with convincing truthfulness even as we watch, and they happen and are gone even as a moment exists and is gone, never to be recaptured. The audience for this "home of the Now" must pay close attention because the Now will vanish; the playwright must work with great skill to make the Now so important that audiences *must* pay attention; the actors must perform brilliantly so that the Now will be arresting, vibrant, more memorable than life. Tomorrow night, the actors will perform a little differently because they are humans and not machines; tomorrow, the audience will be different, and the interaction between actors and audience will change.

Because of the physical presence of the actor, the theatre presents a more immediate image of human behavior than any other art. We are human beings; we are touched, aroused, dazzled by the immediacy of other human beings. Neither the heightened intensity of portrait painting nor the close-up intensity of film can equal the impact of live performers because we are in the theatre with those living human beings who present their stories so convincingly and entertainingly.

We remain fascinated by the humanness of being human. Theatre is the art that brings us up close to a human activity that is rivetingly like life in its immediacy but satisfyingly unlike life in its artistic separation.

The other side of the virtue of immediacy is the partial disadvantage of *nonrecoverability*. As we have seen, film and television performances can be recovered exactly as they were made; the theatrical performance cannot. When the moment is gone, it is entirely gone. We cannot play it over as we play a videotape, except in memory. Nor can we fast-forward to see how a performance will come out; nor can we put the performance aside for a while and pick it up later; nor can we interrupt it (as we could, for example, a tape) and start it up again later, or run part of it over.

Each theatrical performance is unique. The actor is quite right to say, "You should have seen me last night!" Or, as one critic wrote, "What I love is that at any moment I may see the leading man suffer a heart attack!"

Thus, *the theatre performance proceeds at its own pace and must be followed at that pace,* and for better or for worse, *it can be neither replicated nor repeated.*

The theatre's immediacy gives it an inherent *intensity.* Good art gives an intensity far greater than most of life. To say, however, that a great moment in the theatre is more intense than one in opera or dance is not true; it is best to say that they are different. Dance and opera cannot match the illusion of a great comic or tragic scene greatly played, when it is neither movement nor music that we follow, but convincing and immediate human action.

Another aspect of theatre that can work both for and against its effectiveness is its *scenic and spatial limitation.* Film, for example, can take us anywhere and show us actual images of distant places, even on a vast scale (the Grand Canyon, the city of Hong Kong, outer space). The theatre can give us replicas of such places but can give them only on a scale appropriate to the actors working in or in front of the scene. Also, many kinds of activity are difficult or impossible to bring on the stage—car chases, elephant stampedes, and chariot races among them. Film and television not only show such things, they also show selective close-ups that will heighten our awareness and enjoyment of the events: speeding hooves, snorting nostrils, whirling wheels.

If the theatre tried to rival such scenes, it would have to offer compromises, as it did, for example, near the end of the nineteenth century when chariot races *were* shown onstage by putting the horses on treadmills. Common sense told the audience that the treadmills were there, or else the horses would have dashed off into the wings and there would have been no race to see. Yet audiences loved the scenes, even though they were seeing a rather obvious trick—and their enjoyment emphasizes a paradox in the theatre's problems with scenic space: the very restrictions on space

FIGURE 1-10. **Space and Scene.** Theatrical space is always limited, however big the theatre, but technology allows creation within that space of all kinds of "reality." Scenery from *The Merchant of Venice,* late nineteenth century.

and locale increase the audience's enjoyment *because they know the illusion is an illusion.* Put another way, this means that *the artificial nature of theatre gives everything put on the stage a paradoxically heightened reality.* It is a curious thing, but an audience will applaud a scene in which real food is really cooked on a real stove, exactly as if they had never seen food cooking on stoves, much less been able to see such things in their own kitchens.

Thus, the spatial and scenic limitations of the theatre are a seeming disadvantage that can most potently be turned to a remarkable advantage. Compromises, often in the form of symbolic representations, are the essence of theatre: the "wooden O" must be made to hold both France and England; six men must be made to represent an army; a platform must be made to represent a throne.

The real art of the theatre lies, then, not in presenting life, but in presenting heightened visions of life within the special conditions of immediacy, intensity, and symbolic representation.

CHAPTER TWO

THEATRE AND THE PERFORMING AUDIENCE

A close connection exists between an art and its society: art is either an expression of society or a response to it. The theatre is both: it directly expresses social structures and ideas, and it responds to social pressures to cause changes in itself. The expression and the response happen because of two groups: theatre artists and theatre audiences.

WHAT IS AN AUDIENCE?

An audience is people at an event.

But is it one person? Or ten? Ten thousand? Ten million?

One answer would be that the size of an audience depends on the artistic medium. Ten million people could easily make up the "audience" for a television production; however, to have an audience of ten million for even the most successful of stage plays or musicals, we would have to fill the largest theatre every night for years. An "audience" of ten or twenty million people for a film is possible, if the film is shown often enough; ten or twenty million as the "audience" for an opera or ballet would require changing the way that most ballet and opera companies work, because they do not present the same things night after night after night for years and years.

To speak of an "audience" of millions for a play or an opera or a dance perfor-

FIGURE 2-1. **Gathering or Audience?** Groups gathered for a specific purpose are not necessarily audiences, although they share many qualities with audiences: here, a ceremony for peace at the start of the Persian Gulf War.

mance, however, is fruitless for two reasons: first, the performance is different on different nights; second, the millions who watch a television show or who see a film over a period of months in many different movie houses are not an "audience" in the way that the people gathered to see a single performance in a theatre are an audience. The television "audience," in fact, disintegrates into many smaller ones in living rooms and bedrooms and bars, just as the "audience" for a film disintegrates into many smaller groups who see it in many different places on many different occasions. In the sense that we use the word for the theatre, then, *an audience is a group drawn together by a theatrical event, at a certain time and place, that is aware of itself as a group.*

This group self-awareness is very important. The sense of belonging to the group and of contributing to its size is one of the remarkable aspects of theatre, the rich and exciting consciousness of a shared experience in which each individual's response is heightened by those sharing it and by the awareness that one's own response heightens that of others. Although television comedy often uses a "laugh track" or plays the laughter of a live audience to simulate the experience of the theatregoer, the experience simply is not the same for the individual sitting in a living room. In the theatre, the individual's laughter is buoyed up, expanded, made more joyous by other laughter, or the individual's solemn understanding of a serious play is made richer because other people are responding in the same way. Both kinds of response are tied into the idea of *permission*, the agreement common to the members of the social group—the audience—that it is all right to laugh at these events or to be solemnly moved by them. This *permission* is an extension of the very nature of theatre art: theatre as art tells its audience that what is being embodied is *not* life and that it is permissible to respond to it in sometimes unusual ways (laughing out loud, for example, at a character who is weeping in a comedy). Permission is a *social* phenomenon, carried over from the outer society into the temporary society of the audience itself.

The theatre is a social as well as an artistic experience then, and *a theatre audience is a social entity, however temporary.* Its members are drawn together by the event and by the "appetite for art" that makes them want to enjoy the event. They enter into a relationship with the event and with each other.

To join a theatre audience is to enter willingly into two remarkable relationships, one with the artistic event on the stage and one with the other people in the audience. The audience's goal is *to share.*

WHAT DETERMINES AUDIENCE SIZE?

It would be difficult, it seems, for one person to be an audience. Still, royalty used to have plays performed especially for them, and "theatres royal" had special boxes for the king or queen or duke. Anyone who has gone to a movie in the early afternoon has been a member of a very small audience, and frequently we sit alone to watch television. We have to admit, therefore, that the group is not essential to the idea of audience in every medium, but *where the group is lacking, the medium will make up for the difference by saturating the viewer or by providing an artificial group* (by using a laugh track, for example, or backing much dramatic action with appropriate music), or else *the medium, lacking a group audience, will be unsatisfying.*

But how large a group is an effective audience? Twenty? Two thousand?

Two forces are at work, and they often work against each other. One is the force of the group, partly unconscious but very strong. "Groupness" needs a number of people in a confined space, or at least a *defined* space; it is no accident that theatre interiors are designed, when possible, without empty spaces along the sides, because people who sit there feel "cold"; they are left out. In the same way, theatres that host events that draw small audiences frequently have movable walls or screens to enclose the small audience—to give it a defined space in which it feels enclosed and comfortable.

A group in too big a space loses track of itself and stops behaving like an audience. It grows uneasy. It becomes self-conscious. Sometimes it becomes a mob. Schools that use their gymnasiums as theatres, for example, sometimes suffer because the huge, echoing gym space, with wide and empty gaps along the sides, encourages people to belong to a mob and not an audience.

The economics of the theatre is the force that is sometimes opposed to "groupness." It demands that the audience be big enough to pay the investors, the actors, the rent on the building, the author's royalties, the heat and light and maintenance of the space. Thus, groupness may sense that three hundred people is the right audience size; economics may demand three thousand.

Some people would say that economics is a false force and should be ignored. "An audience is people," the argument would go, "and people are more important than money." However, actors are people, too, and so are authors and maintenance persons and those who sell heat and light. A theatre ignores economics at its peril; when it

FIGURE 2-2. **Audience Size and Space.** The too-small audience remains only scattered individuals, without group awareness.

does, it will have to survive with actors who do not care about being paid, authors who do not collect royalties, and so on. Such theatres certainly exist and have existed off and on for a very long time. The tension between group sense and economics has been partly responsible for the waves of "group theatres" and "little theatres" that have appeared in every age since at least the democratic revolutions at the end of the eighteenth century.

From the varying points of view of different audience members and different theatre artists, there is no perfect audience size and no perfect audience space. Most theatres are compromises in this respect, and sometimes not very good compromises, especially when theatres have become physically huge (accommodating several thousand) in order simply to hold more people. In those cases particularly, the little theatres and the free theatres become the conscience of the time.

Again, variety and diversity must be allowed.

WHO GOES TO WHAT?

Few people are so committed to a single performing art or even to a single activity that they pursue it to the exclusion of all others. Devoted theatregoers are also members of audiences for ballet, baseball, television, and opera. Still, there are preferences among audience members, and there are tendencies toward alignments of audiences that are significant for theatre artists and theatre businesspeople.

One survey gave an idea of who the people are who make up North America's huge audience and of what they go to see. The audience is fairly young, with the majority under forty; it has more women than men, although other figures suggest that the male–female imbalance is changing. There are very few blue-collar occupations among this audience, but a large proportion of "professional and managerial" workers. Thus, for performing arts audiences, the mainstream of middle-class society is best represented: fairly young, affluent, mixed in gender.

Overlap from one performing art to another is significant. Breadth of taste typifies theatregoers. Shakespeare and baseball, Beethoven and Molière—audiences are able to love them all.

The theatre audience is a social group, but it is a group only of the moment. Just as the performance is Now, so, too, is its audience. For all their sharing and their common experience, the people in a theatre audience may never come together again.

WHY DO THEY COME?

What brings an audience into a theatre in the first place? It is easy enough to say that people come to the theatre for entertainment. But *entertainment* has many meanings: some people are "entertained" by computer games, others by pornography. People are "entertained" by television, baseball games, and rock concerts.

Why is it that on a given night, people go to the *theatre* instead of staying home or going to a ball game or a movie or a rock concert?

Three things can be cited.

The Stirring of the Imagination

All art stirs the imagination, sends it on inward journeys, that, perhaps, only dreams and madness offer it otherwise. The theatre does this with enormous visual potency and tremendous immediacy; the theatre is *now*. Only contemporary film, with its intense color and its saturated, heightened sound, is a serious rival in the presentation of fictions, or "stories." The opera and the dance offer other qualities: superb, soaring vocal music in one and astonishing physical athleticism and gorgeous movement in the other.

The theatre, however, has traditionally stirred its audience's imagination by giving *less* rather than *more* stimulation—not by saturating it, but by tantalizing and catalyzing it with hints. It has often put a mask on the actor's face, taking away facial mobility; it has used symbolic or suggestive scenery, or even no scenery at all, to create a richer imaginative *idea* of reality than any imitation reality could give; it has taken its stories from dreams and myth and fantasy and has thus touched levels of the mind and heart below the purely rational.

FIGURE 2-3. **Imagination.** Often using less rather than more stimulation, theatre creates by causing the audience's imagination to create, as with this nonrepresentational setting by Emil Pirchan in the 1920s.

The Revelation of the Familiar

Perhaps because mirrors fascinate people, visions of themselves and of their own real world have fascinated audiences. "It's so real!" is sometimes a compliment for a theatre piece. Are we entranced with our own image? Or is it that humankind is a very complex species worthy of its own deep examinings?

Reality surrounds us: Look out the window; there is reality. Watch the man next door, the woman behind the desk, the child in the playground; they are reality. Do we build special structures to house them, pay money to watch them? Hardly.

Theatregoing is a paradox. People buy tickets, travel distances, go through great difficulty to see images of themselves and their surroundings "in play," in something that is "just like life." But it is *like* life, not life itself, and it is *like* life in a very special way: compressed, focused, made magical.

Part of the magic lies in the "safety" of what happens within the playing space. What happens there is insulated from causing anything to happen in the outer world; when the play is over, it is truly over, finished, completed, and it sends nothing out into the streets except its own memory. If a man is shot onstage, he will not have to be taken to a real hospital; if a woman is widowed, she will not have to stand in a real welfare line or suffer real anguish tomorrow when she wakes up. The play is truly "play," as children's make-believe is play. So, too, with the theatre: *as art, it is harmless.*

Now, some critics of the theatre would take it to task for being harmless; they would argue that even an art should affect events in the real world. George Bernard Shaw spoke of the play "doing its work in the world," but he was referring to the *ideas* that a play generates in the minds of its audience. The fact remains, however, that *as art* theatre is "harmless"—*and that is one of its attractions.* Many people speak of theatre as "escape," and, although the idea is a weak one to describe what really attracts an audience, "escaping the consequences" is an important element in the theatre's pull. We can watch horrifying or electrifying events; we can behave as we are not allowed to behave in life, guffawing at a human being's suffering or applauding murder—because those events are harmless.

The Revelation of the Exotic

Here is another theatrical paradox: on the one hand, the theatre attracts people by dealing in the familiar and the comfortable; but, on the other hand, it also draws them with the new and the strange.

Thus, there is a three-way tension among three kinds of appeal to the audience: the stirring of the imagination, the satisfaction of the desire for the familiar, and the arousing of the appetite for the exotic.

The tension between the familiar and the exotic is greatly affected by the passage of time. To a considerable extent, those elements that stir the imagination persist, but *familiar* and *exotic* are rather relative terms, and it is sometimes difficult to understand which of these attractions was at work in a play from the past. What is familiar to one generation may be foreign to another; what it exotic to one may be familiar or even boring to a later generation. Science fiction is an example, for technology is always making yesterday's fantasies wrong or silly. Nevertheless, exoticism is an attraction. Before the world was thoroughly explored, foreign locales were a great draw. At the beginning of the industrial revolution, factories were popular settings. The theatre makes the exotic known to the audience—and thus, in a way, demystifies it and makes it safe.

HOW DOES AN AUDIENCE PERCEIVE?

If an audience goes to the theatre to be imaginatively stirred through a perception of the familiar or the exotic, how does it perceive what is going on?

Three general attitudes of the theatre greatly affect the way that the audience perceives a performance: convention, innovation, and style.

Convention

Conventions could be called *contracts*. Conventions are shortcuts between what is meant and what is done. To the actor, a convention may be a gesture that, through continued repetition, has come to convey great meaning—a hand raised to the forehead, palm out, the eyes turned up, to indicate suffering. To a scene designer, a convention may be the placing of a scenic house so that only part of it is actually onstage, the rest of it seeming to lie outside the audience's vision at one or both sides of the stage. The onstage part that the audience sees may be a strict imitation of reality; *convention* allows the scenic designer to mean that the entire house is there, although common sense says that it is not. The very fact that both audience and actors accept the idea that there is *anywhere* offstage is a convention, instead of their insisting on the commonsense reality that *offstage* is simply a slightly dirty area in a theatre.

A convention is a contract between the audience and the theatre artists, an agreement to do things this way for the good of all. In the modern theatre, the acceptance of the idea that days or months or years pass between scenes or acts is a convention; the acceptance of taped music during dramatic action is a convention;

FIGURE 2-4. The Exotic. The new, the unusual, and the unknown (even the nonexistent) have audience appeal: one of the most important productions of the early twentieth century, *Sumurun*, with designs by Ernst Stern.

the acceptance in many theatres of actors in partial undress is a convention for total nudity.

Innovation

Pulling against convention is innovation. It is the introduction of new ways of giving meaning. It is novelty, "originality."

Theatre artists and audiences both demand innovation—up to a point. That point, however, is not easy to define. Many outside factors affect people's willingness to accept a convention or to demand innovation in its place.

Usually, innovation comes from the artists' side of the theatre. Audiences do not "demand" a change, at least not in the way that we are accustomed to having people demand things. Audiences, after all, do not have a real voice. Their voice is in their hands and their pocketbooks. Their "demands" may best be seen in their enthusiastic welcoming of an innovation, or a change in the way a convention is used.

Technology is itself the parent of much innovation. The coming of movies at the end of the nineteenth century quickly drew a large audience; what it saw was much the same thematically as what it saw in the theatre of the day, and the acting conventions were identical, but the technology was innovative. Ballet dancing on the toe—"en point"—was developed about 1825, perhaps in combination with the invention of the shoe needed to perform such a feat; it was an innovation that paralleled technology. Presumably, it was a response to a demand for greater displays of virtuosity.

Still other innovation may come from the acquisition of new information. Historically accurate costumes were possible only when historical knowledge was broadened by people working outside the theatre, and period costuming was accepted as something other than an exotic rarity only when that knowledge was disseminated through the theatre audience by historically accurate books and pictures.

FIGURE 2-5. **Innovation.** Although much theatrical innovation comes as new form or new content, some comes as adoption of new technology: here, an early use of the railroad for the melodrama *Under the Gaslight. (From Stanley Appelbaum,* Advertising Woodcuts from the Nineteenth Century Stage. *New York: Dover, 1977.)*

Style

Style is the result of interaction among convention, innovation, and the life of the times. The word *style* is one of the most useful, and yet one of the most confusing, that is applied in the performing arts. Each group of performers in each age has its own artistic style: a mixture of inherited tradition, of meaningful convention and innovation, and of their own aesthetic sense of what is pleasing and beautiful. Clothes are said to be "stylish"; there is a "New Orleans style" of jazz as compared with a "Chicago style"; there are "kosher-style" dill pickles. Some performers are said to have a "personal style" that distinguishes them from other performers.

Plays from the past are sometimes said to be produced in "period style," and sometimes productions are even labeled "style" productions. In the sense that we will mean it here, however, *style refers to the particular characteristics of a performance that the audience sees and hears that set it off from all other performances.*

Some characteristics that go to make up a production's style are the following:

Level of Abstraction

Abstraction is removal from observable reality. Thus, theatre artists can reproduce observable reality, abstract parts of it to generalized but understandable shapes, or contradict it almost entirely: scenic designers can make see-through walls or open space punctuated with geometric forms; costumers can design contemporary clothes or rigid nonclothes that change the shape of the human body; lighting designers can imitate sunlight or flood the acting space with red or blue.

Amount of Detail

In most areas of theatre, it is possible to vary the amount of information from almost none to an overwhelming amount: the actor may speak in a monotone, stand still, make no attempt to imitate life or to interpret text (little detail); or the actor may busily imitate behavior or create symbols with a thousand moves and gestures and turns of voice (much detail). The setting may be the blank wall of the theatre (little detail) or the meticulous imitation of a real place—even the real place itself (much detail). The costume may be a black leotard (little detail) or a rich silk dress covered with dollar signs sewn in brilliants (much detail).

FIGURE 2-6. **Style.** These two drawings of ships suggest how, by changed uses of line and shadow, and by varied amounts of detail, different styles result: that is, the depicted ships would look different even if the actual ships were identical.

Social Class

In class-conscious societies, mannerisms of speech, clothes, and body movement, as well as personal effects, furniture, decor, and almost every other aspect of life, reflect class and money or the lack of them. A French peasant of 1670 looked, acted, and spoke very differently from Louis XIV, the French king. In the same way, a stockbroker of our own day probably sounds and dresses and moves differently from a trucker. Actors playing peasants and kings show the same degree of difference, although it must be remembered that *the style of the theatre is different from the style of life.*

Given Circumstances

Sex, race, state of health, age, and profession create stylistic differences. A minister's sermon does not sound like a teacher's lecture; a disco dancer does not move like a golfer. A sick man neither sounds nor moves like a healthy one; men and women have noticeably different styles of dress, speech, and movement *in certain ages.*

Historical Period

The way people talk and move, the kind of clothes they wear, and the way their living spaces are shaped and decorated are different from period to period. Theatrical speech and movement, costumes and hairstyle, and settings reflect aspects of their historical period.

When theatre artists choose to produce a work from the past, they have a great range of styles to choose from. In doing a French comedy of 1670, for example, they might choose to do it "authentically," that is, in as close a reconstruction as is possible of the original scenery, costumes, acting, movement, and so on. Or they might decide that, the essence of the play being comic, it is most important to make stylistic decisions in terms of such comic values as brightness, color, and symmetry. Again, they might decide to work at a level of abstraction rather different from the original, so that the costumes might have large areas of pure color without detail and the setting might be very simple and even painted like a cartoon. On the other hand, the decision might be made to change the historical period entirely in order to make the play easier for a modern audience to grasp, and so it might be put squarely into contemporary clothes and settings, and contemporary references might even be inserted into the script. In each case, *consistency* of style would be sought.

It should be pointed out that *historical period* usually refers to social and not theatrical history. As a general rule, *revivals of past works seek to imitate the style of the life of the period and not the style of the theatre of the period.* An audience will accept a copy of the styles of a period if it is convinced that the copy is a reasonably good one of the life of the times; it generally will not accept a copy of the theatrical style of a past period because conventions and theatrical styles of the past, having been supplanted by successive waves of innovation, may well look foreign or even ridiculous. A modern audience seeing a meticulous copy of the acting style, settings, and theatre costumes of 1670 might respond that the style is "not accurate." They would mean that the acting, settings, and costumes were not like the modern idea of seventeenth-century life, forgetting that life and the theatre are sometimes far from identical.

When an audience does not understand a style, it will be annoyed, for the very good reason that it cannot go beyond the style to the real business of the theatre, the stirring of the imagination, and it will give up its own imaginative participation in order to try to cope with stylistic effects. When, however, an audience has a very strong concept of a style of the past (a theatrical style, not a lifestyle) and theatre artists choose to play on that concept, the result can be "camp"—using a past style for its own sake, most often to make fun of it. Nowhere is such a "camp" approach so common as in productions of what are loosely called nineteenth-century melodramas. The curious fact is that the dramatic style being made fun of never actually existed in precisely the way that either audience or most theatre people seem to think—but no matter: it has become a style of its own, and audiences are pleased by it, for all its howling inaccuracy.

FIGURE 2-7. **Theatrical Style.** These two productions of *Hamlet* show how different amounts of detail and different uses of line create different styles for the same play. *(Top design by Claude Bragdon, courtesy of the Department of Rare Books and Special Collections of the University of Rochester Libraries, and of Peter W. Bragdon.)*

DO AUDIENCES HAVE STYLES?

Insofar as an audience represents an age and a social class, it, too, will show a style, probably the same style that influences the theatre. But the question does not mean "Do they have distinctive ways of moving and dressing and speaking?" because these elements are unimportant *to their role as audience*. It means "Do different audiences react in different ways that will affect the performance?"

The answer, of course, is yes. The social level of an audience greatly affects its response. The "gallery gods" of the nineteenth-century theatres or the audiences of the penny theatres of the same period were notorious for their raucous behavior when they were displeased, their applause when they were pleased. They were noisy, sometimes obstreperous; they interrupted plays, drowned out bad performances, and cheered their favorites to a standstill. Upper-class audiences, because of their supposed aesthetic sophistication, may put different, special demands on performers; much of the abstraction of the late-eighteenth-century French Neoclassical theatre came, for example, from its audience's insistence on a "propriety" that reflected an unreal concept of aristocratic behavior.

And the psychology of groups, as it varies from age to age, greatly affects the "style" of an audience. Our own is an age—in the theatre, opera, and dance—of restraint. Nobody throws ripe tomatoes at the performers anymore; nobody has rioted in an American theatre in decades. Our audiences for athletic events and rock concerts, on the other hand, are far more boisterous than our theatre audiences. Rock audiences sometimes weep, laugh, get high, sing, dance, fight. Athletic events at all levels are noisy.

The factors that determine audience style are very complex. First, probably, is *group self-image*—the customs and manners of a certain group, defined by social and sometimes economic factors, as well as by gender, level of education, and the group's own sense of social place. Sometimes, an audience forms *because* it wants to assert its idea of social place—the black-tie audience at opera, for example, or the quite different, but equally self-confident, audience at Country and Western.

Of almost equal importance is *sense of place*—that is, the behavior appropriate to an opera house is very different from that appropriate to a comedy club. *Preparation for the event* depends partly on sense of place. It is one thing to flop into a chair in pajamas to watch television and another to dress formally, travel miles, pay a hundred dollars a ticket, and eat a special meal before a special trip to Broadway.

DOES AN AUDIENCE WORK?

If audience and theatre makers interact, then it must follow that the audience itself has a responsibility in the system that we call theatre. A performance cannot be seen as the product of the work done on only one side of the curtain. Nor can it properly be seen as something "given" from one kind of person (the theatre maker) to another kind of person (the audience). It is, instead, something that exists in the very complex *interaction* between them; and it follows, therefore, that the audience has a task for which it should prepare.

FIGURE 2-8. **Audience Style.** What audiences bring with them to the theatre—as shown here, assumptions about proper behavior, pleasure, and official censorship—are important determinants of both how they will behave and how they will perceive the performance.

FIGURE 2-9. **Preparation.** Advertising is only one of the means by which audiences prepare for performance. Here, a nineteenth-century poster that should have been read properly as preparing for visual spectacle and eroticism.

Ideas of "comfort" and "escape" sometimes appeal to the audience. Theatre people, however, object to audiences who want to behave passively. "They sat on their hands" is a theatre saying. But slumping into a seat and waiting to be entertained is not the proper posture of the theatre audience, because it is too limiting, both to the audience's own pleasure and to the potential of the theatre itself. "Entertain me" is like a child's "Tell me a story" in its passivity, and its end result in an audience is childish performance—the sort of mindless mush that sometimes turns up on television (where audiences are of necessity more passive) and that, regrettably, turns up in the theatre whenever the audience lets itself get complacent and lazy.

Performance is based on an unspoken agreement between artists and audience. The basic clause for the performers is "I will not hurt you." The basic clause for the audience is "I will work to enjoy you."

A good audience fulfills its part of the agreement in two ways: first, by *making its imagination work* when that imagination is stirred by the performance; and second, by *remaining open* to new ways of being moved, entertained, and excited, by remaining open to having its imagination stirred in surprising ways. It does no good for Shakespeare's Chorus in *Henry V* to say,

Suppose within the girdle of these walls
Are now confin'd two mighty monarchies. . . .
Think when we talk of horses that you see them,
Printing their proud hoofs i' the receiving earth;
For 'tis your thoughts that now must deck our kings. . . .

if the audience will refuse to do these things. The Chorus speaks of the audience's "imaginative forces." Forces *work*. The audience must "suppose" and "think." It is "your thoughts" that dress the actors. If the audience for such a play simply lay back in its easy chairs and said, "Ho-hum, I'm tired; entertain me," there would be no entertainment at all. Curiously, the more an audience causes its imagination to work, and the more open it forces itself to be to new imaginative stimulation, the more entertained it will be.

In addition to its imaginative responsibilities, the audience can also heighten its own pleasure through *preparation for the performance*. Its preparation falls into two categories: an *understanding of the theatre* and a *sympathy for the work*. Understanding of the theatre means a basic mastery of the how's and why's of what theatre people do, an appreciation of the arts of the performers that is distinct from the specific value of any performance. That is, it is not appropriate for an audience to say merely, "I didn't like it" or "I thought it was wonderful." Both statements say much about the speaker, little about the performance. Instead, it is the spectrum of appreciative statements that is revealing: one actor was excellent because of the understanding of the role, the way body and voice were used; the playwright created a stunning scene for two actors in Act I but didn't quite bring off a climactic speech in Act III; the set designer not only created a first-rate acting space but also created a visually beautiful treat for the audience; and so on. Through such understanding of the arts of the theatre will come greater audience pleasure; that, in turn, will contribute to an increased ability to let the imagination work.

Sympathy for the work is developed through an absorption of material available about the performance before going to see it. This means familiarizing oneself with *mediation*—reviews and advertisements, the program. It seems a small point, but a theatre program does give essential information about where a scene is taking place and when it is happening, and it is mere laziness if an audience does not take that information in.

Sympathy for the work means going to the theatre with a general idea of what sort of event one is going to see—so that, for example, somebody who wants to see a comedy does not leave the theatre because *Cat on a Hot Tin Roof* sounded like a funny title; or somebody who wants to introduce children to the theatre does not become enraged because *Who's Afraid of Virginia Woolf?* is not a children's play. It is fairly commonplace for someone to say, "I never read reviews or criticism; I don't want to be told how to think." But there is no reason at all why criticism should tell anybody how or what to think; it serves, instead, as a prod and a guide, leading potential audience members away from some works and toward others.

An audience cannot afford to be lazy. Its own response depends on its taking part; one can no more enjoy the theatre as a nonparticipant than one can enjoy playing tennis that way. Audience laziness leads to mindlessness, limitation of scope, and stagnation. As A. Nicholas Vardac wrote in *Stage to Screen*, "From the mid-nineteenth century to the [mid-twentieth] is a period of imaginative laziness—a laziness not on the part of the artists of the theatre, but rather on the part of their audiences. They had not come into the theatre to participate imaginatively. . . . They had come to be shown."

CHAPTER THREE

HOW TO READ A PLAY

Seeing a play and reading a play are different experiences. They require different tools and different approaches.

Seeing the play in the theatre is the complete theatrical experience. Reading the play in a book means making the effort—and knowing how to make the effort—to understand the play as it will appear in the theatre.

Reading the play is not the same kind of activity as reading a novel or a story. The novel and the story are complete in themselves; their language fills them out completely. A play, on the other hand, is a part—a vital and important part—of a different kind of artistic experience.

The aesthetician Suzanne Langer defined certain kinds of art as having "discursive form"—form apprehended across real time, a kind of apprehension that dictates the order in which the audience perceives the work. The drama and the novel both fall into this category, which distinguishes them from painting, for example. They are still quite different from each other. The *staged* play has a rigid link to the real time of the audience: it must be understood *as it takes place.* The novel, on the other hand, has a rigid internal time, a "pastness" that Langer called "virtual history." Virtual history is quite different from the reader's real time; the reader's real time can vary (when the reader puts the book down, for example) without changing the "virtual history."

Reading a play seems to put it into the aesthetic category of the novel. However, other differences of form make the play incomplete as a readable form: above all, the play text has broad areas left blank, which the reader must learn to fill in through clues that are actually clues to performance, not elements of the art of a distinct aesthetic form (as paragraphs of description, for example, are valid elements of the art of the novel). Usually, we read plays "as if" we are seeing them. (A kind of play meant only for reading is called *closet drama;* it is a special case, and in fact its form, although superficially that of plays meant to be staged, is different, generally including far more information in the speeches so as to fill in the blanks of the stageable play. Closet dramas are not usually stageable.)

Some modern theatre artists have called the playscript "not a text but a pretext" for production—that is, not a complete, self-sufficient work of art. Others have talked of the playscript as "notation" for production.

The written play seems like a contradiction: it is one part of an art form and is not self-sufficient, and yet it can be read with pleasure *as if* it were complete and self-sufficient.

The reader, then, approaches the reading of the play differently from the reading of a novel. The principal goals are *understanding the first reading of the play, analyzing the play and its parts,* and *organizing a response to the play.*

FIRST READING

Reading begins at the beginning—with the title, the first piece of information. The author believed it said something important about the play; therefore, it is a clue to at least one important part of the play—perhaps a central idea, perhaps a central character. A title like *Cats* is very straightforward; on the other hand, a title like *Top Girls* is mysterious until well into the play.

Reading continues with the cast of characters, which gives information on the size of the cast and its makeup by age, sex, and so on; the characters' names and their relationships; and, sometimes, what the characters look and sound like.

The opening stage directions usually describe the setting and the play's opening moments. In the scripts of plays that have been produced, these stage directions often reflect the actual Broadway or London production; in other plays, they give the playwright's vision of the setting. Sounds may be described as well. It is now possible to visualize, and perhaps to listen to, the play's opening.

However, the reader must ask some questions: *What kind of theatre is being used? What is the historical period of the play?* Can the reader carry this period into the imaginary production—in costumes and setting, for example? *What is the opening mood?* Somber or happy? Tense or relaxed? *How do characters get on and off the stage?* Is the setting inside or outdoors? Are there doors? Where? Where do the characters enter from?

Then, with the beginning as strongly visualized as possible, the reader begins to read the play, underlining and making notes on:

- What happens in the play.

- Who makes things happen and who tries to stop things from happening; also, what is the relative importance of the characters.

- What key words, images, and ideas run through the play (and, probably, what the relevance of the title is).

FIGURE 3-1. **The Mind's Eye.** Early reading editions of plays often included woodcut illustrations that showed the audience the story, but not necessarily the staging. What are the clues here, if any, to staging? What clues suggest this is an artist's invention?

After this first careful reading, the reader is familiar with the play and has a sense of what it is about and of what happens in it, as well as of who its characters are.

The later readings of a play aim at orderly, informed analysis of the play. Analysis may result in a judgment about the play.

PLAY ANALYSIS

The Greek critic Aristotle (see p. 221) created a theory of play analysis that others have modified. What follows is based on interpretations of Aristotle but is not strictly Aristotelian.

Aristotle said there were six parts to a play. A modern interpretation of them gives the following:

1. Plot

2. Character

3. Idea

4. Language

5. Music

6. Spectacle

This breakdown is still useful. We can go through most plays and show how every aspect—every speech, every movement, every activity—fits these categories.

In Aristotle's analysis, these six parts are closely linked and are *causes* of each other: that is, each "comes from" or "is the product of" the parts listed below it. Plot is at the top because it is most important. In the theatre, audiences follow plot and understand other things through plot. Plot is also first because it is "caused" by all the other parts, most immediately by character (characters *do* things), whereas a character is "caused" by what he or she believes and wants (idea) and by what he or she says (language), and so on.

Plot

Plot is *the ordering of the incidents* in the play. This means that it is not only *what happens* in the play; it is also the *order* in which things are made to happen and the *reasons* why things are put in that order *by the playwright.*

Kinds of Plot

We can identify two kinds of plot:

1. Causal plot (also known as *linear,* or *antecedent-consequent,* or *climactic*). The incidents of linear plot can be seen to lie along a line of causality from beginning to end. The word *climactic* is sometimes used because such plots build to a *climax,* the most exciting moment of the plot for the audience. (Note that the term refers to the response to the plot, not to the plot itself.) Causal plots are of two major types:

- Single line of development, with no subordinate lines (for example, Sophocles' *Oedipus Rex*).

- Multiple lines of development, consisting of a major line and various subordinate ones ("subplots") (for example, Shakespeare's *Hamlet*).

2. Episodic (also known as *contextual* or *thematic*) plot. The incidents (episodes) of episodic plot do not follow each other because of causality; rather, they are ordered by the exploration of an idea or a character. Social-problem plays have often used this kind of plot, with each scene exploring a new aspect of the social problem or enlarging the study made to that point. An extreme example is a nineteenth-century play (Georg Buechner's *Woyzeck*) for which the author never settled on a final ordering of the scenes.

Parts of Plot

Plot is itself made up of parts. Aristotle and later critics have identified the major parts of plot:

EXPOSITION —the giving of information about past events. The greatest amount of exposition often comes at the beginning of the play, when the audience knows least

FIGURE 3-2. Kinds of Plot.

about plot and character. In some plays, however, important exposition is delayed until late; in a murder mystery, for example, the most important facts about past events ("whodunit") come at the end.

POINT OF ATTACK —the place in the *story* where the dramatist begins the *plot*. Greek playwrights tend to begin their plots late in the story and so are said to have a late point of attack; Shakespeare tends to begin his plots toward the beginning of his stories and so is said to use an early point of attack.

ACTION —the central chain of events in the play, particularly as those events are the central character's attempt to achieve an important goal. Action and character are tightly bound to each other and are understood through each other, so that an answer to the question, "What is the play's action?" always requires inclusion of the character.

Successful action in a linear plot is a *whole* action; that is, it has a beginning, a middle, and an end. *Beginning* means that nothing relevant comes before (and nothing irrelevant is included); *end* means that nothing relevant is still to come. If the action is not a whole action, the play will not be understandable to its audience as a work of art.

Wholeness is fundamental. It is one of the most important aspects that distinguish art from life, which art imitates. Unlike a play, a life is not perceivable as a whole,

FIGURE 3-3. **Rising Action.** The killing of Caesar from a late nineteenth-century production of *Julius Caesar*. Although an important and exciting event, this is part of the play's complication, not its high point.

especially while it is being lived. Our lives are diverse and complicated; we carry on several "actions," of which we perceive only dimly (and often incorrectly) the beginnings; the ends are always over our life's horizon.

People say they do not understand their lives; they are confused or they have lost control or they have identity crises. In the work of art (the play), on the other hand, wholeness allows us to understand, and so to learn. A dramatic character may be confused or out of control or in an identity crisis, but the audience sees the entirety of that situation: beginning, middle, and end.

It is important to remember that drama is able to reveal life to us *because* it is an invention and not "real life."

Suffering—awareness; a passive state of undergoing emotion, of allowing emotion to work on.

Discovery—the passing from ignorance to knowledge. When characters discover, they usually are led to decide (act). Discovery therefore propels action.

Reversal—any change in the direction of the action, usually occasioned by a discovery that is contrary to a character's expectations.

COMPLICATION —the opposing or entangling of the action. Often, at the beginning of the play, the action seems simple—for example, a character desires to accomplish something. It becomes complicated by obstacles, particularly by the efforts of other characters to frustrate the action, even to destroy the central character.

Most plots have many complications. Each complication changes the action as the character must deal with the complication before pursuing the original goal or must pursue that goal in terms of knowledge gained from dealing with the complication.

Two important kinds of complication are

- Caused complication, that is, complication through the agency of another character, a god, or a force.

- Accidental or coincidental complication—for example, from a storm, a flood, or a chance meeting of characters.

RISING ACTION —action of increasing complication.

CRISIS —a point in the action where complication forces the character to make a decision; a turning point. Derived from the Greek for "decision," *crisis* means "decisive moment." We expect to find rising action from complication to crisis.

RESOLUTION, FALLING ACTION, OR DENOUEMENT —from the French, "the untying"—the unraveling of complication, the decline as crisis is passed and complication is resolved.

Dramatic Structure

Structure is sometimes used as a metaphor for the internal nature of a plot, as we might talk of the structure of steel I-beams that are the skeleton of a building. To clarify, dramatic structures are sometimes put in visual terms: linear plot is shown as a line rising from beginning to crisis, then falling rapidly. Sometimes, this structure is pictured as a sawtooth of minor rising and falling actions along the major line of rise and fall. Discussions of structure focus on the parts of plot as structural members of the whole.

Character

A dramatic character and a real human being are not the same thing. Dramatic character is an invention. The fact that a dramatic character pursues human goals, speaks human words, and embodies human responses means only that the dramatic character is part of a human artistic creation that is about life, not that it is life itself. Dramatic character is, at best, an imitation of selected aspects of humanity.

Dramatic characters have no existence before the play and no future after the play is over. They are no more than what the playwright has given us.

Dramatic characters are performed by actors to create a convincing imitation of real people.

FIGURE 3-4. **Character and Action.** Brutus' oration over the corpse of Caesar, from a late nineteenth-century production of *Julius Caesar:* character perceived by what he says, by what he does, by what others say about him. (Compare for visual details and staging with Figure 3-1, showing the same scene.)

Character and Function

Because characters are inventions in a work of art, they can be seen as both imitations of human beings and as *functions* within the work. *Function,* in this case, means the dramatic task that the character performs. *Good character always has function; character without function is bad character.*

Every character can be analyzed in every scene for its function in terms of the play's parts: for example, to further the plot, to express idea, to contribute to spectacle. Reading to understand the function at each moment illuminates how the play works and how well it works.

Character and Conflict

A hundred years ago, it was common to say that "drama is conflict." Nowadays, we are inclined to say that conflict is central to many dramas but not to all of them.

Character conflict—the opposition of another character to the central character—

reveals both characters and is "dramatic" in its intensity and in its potential for complication. Conflict between opposed characters may provide an easily understandable moral or philosophical opposition (good versus evil).

Some plays contain conflicts between the central character and an impersonal force: for example, fate, the gods, or society. Frequently in these plays, the impersonal forces are personified by a humanlike character.

Continuing Kinds of Character

Critics and scholars have come to designate certain kinds of character that repeat themselves in many plays:

- Protagonist—the central figure of the main action.

- Confidant(e)—a character in whom the protagonist or another important character confides.

- Antagonist—in a play with character conflict around the main action, the one who opposes the protagonist.

- Author character or *raisonneur*—one who speaks for the author, directly giving the author's moral or philosophical ideas; usually not the protagonist.

- Foil—one who sets off another character by contrast—comic where the other is serious, stupid where intelligent, shrewd where naive.

- Sympathetic and unsympathetic characters—those created by the playwright so as either to appeal to the audience or to repel it.

Perceiving Character

In reading the play, we perceive dramatic character in several ways:

- Through the stage directions, although some playwrights do not discuss character in the stage directions.

- Through what other characters say. However, we have to understand these other characters before we can know how to interpret what they say.

- Through what the characters themselves say about themselves, with the same problem of interpreting what they say.

- Through what the characters do—their *acts*.

- Through relationships among characters. Under the increasing pressure of the complicated action, the real nature of relationships—hate, love, friendship, dependence, forgiveness—shows more clearly.

- Through the plot itself. Character is understood through many parts of the plot. For example, decision reveals character; complication forces character to decision. And characters often change as the plot develops. Many plays have central characters who behave and think differently at the end of the play from at its beginning; they have "learned." Studying and accounting for

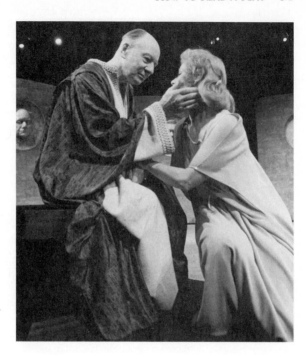

FIGURE 3-5. **Character.** The great British actor John Gielgud as Julius Caesar at the National Theatre, London. (*Courtesy of the British Tourist Authority.*)

such changes helps one gain understanding of both character and play. Some critics even say that "the play is understood by its ending," a great oversimplification but often a useful notion.

Idea

No play is without meanings. Even the lightest comedy has meaning because it imitates human action and because it expresses a time and a society. A play does not have to be full of intellectual speeches to offer meanings, and the careful reader of the play learns how to find these meanings and understand them.

Plays seldom offer single, simple meanings. The best plays offer many meanings; an attempt to reduce these to "the idea of the play" or "the theme of the play" oversimplifies the play.

The kinds of meanings fall generally into two categories: *idea*—meanings contained entirely within the play; and *extrinsic meaning*—those meanings in the society and the period of which the play is an expression. We are concerned here with idea.

The play's idea comes in part from its plot. We tend to generalize from example, and the playwright, by choosing and ordering events, has created an example. We then may generalize from that example (the play), seeing that (in this playwright's view) certain causes lead to certain (good or bad) events.

Idea comes also from character. In a good play, the play's major ideas are embodied in the character of the protagonist and the protagonist's action. If the character is positive (approved by the author, "good"), then the protagonist embodies a good.

FIGURE 3-6. **Idea and Character.** The use of painted white masks extends the idea of Doug-las Turner Ward's *Day of Absence*—a visual heightening not available to the play-reader. Directed by Rochelle Calhoun and Lauren Price, designed by Eugene Warner. *(Courtesy of New WORLD Theatre, University of Massachusetts, Amherst. Edward Cohen Photo.)*

These "goods" and "bads"—the defining elements of the play's moral world—are best understood through the system of rewards and punishments in the play.

Thus, in plays with conflict, the victor in the conflict represents a positive way of acting, a "good." The loser represents a "bad." Rewards and punishments may take other forms, like money, love, promotion, or pardon for a supposed crime.

For example, the critic Northrup Frye saw some denouements as creating a new society, different from the one at the beginning, and in his critical approach, many of the play's ideas can be understood from who is included in the new society and who is left out. Often, such society-making takes the specific form of a party, even a wedding. Analyzing the new society will reveal idea by answering questions like, What kind of people qualify? What are the human qualities that cause people to be shut out?

Typically, the protagonist explains his or her own idea (ethical attitude) near a crisis; rewards and punishments come in the denouement.

Some ideas, or statements of these ideas, will be found in the words of the play. Certain sections of dialogue are especially likely to reveal ideas:

- Important characters' speeches before and after crises. Such speeches often explore the crisis and the author's reasons for having the characters act (make decisions) as they do.

- Important characters' speeches when alone onstage or when with a confidant.

- Author characters' speeches about complications and crises.

- Speeches in the denouement that themselves tie up questions or issues raised in the play.

Language

Language is an important carrier of meaning in the play text. However, language can be studied apart from its meaning. As an "act" separate from the meaning of the words, language is one of the most revealing clues to character.

Language, of itself, tells the reader the given circumstances of character (through social level of usage, vocabulary, dialect) and emotional state (through kind and amount of words and through rhythm).

The kind and use of language are important carriers of idea. Most important are:

- Key language. Careful reading often reveals words that are used again and again in important contexts. The frequent appearance of the word *death,* for example, in a play about love would suggest that the play's idea is probably not "Love conquers all."

- Key figures of speech. Critics sometimes speak of "image clusters," especially in poetic plays. Repeated images or metaphors are much more evident to the play reader than to the playgoer; they are a very subtle (sometimes unconscious) carrier of meaning. Many analysts have pointed out, for example, the many images of weeds in Shakespeare's *Hamlet;* the image cluster supports an idea about the protagonist as fighting against an evil, choking, destructive environment.

Music

In musical plays, the importance of music to character, mood, and rhythm is clear. In nonmusical plays, the reader must see the language itself as embodying music. The language of drama is language for the human voice, not for the page: it is meant to be listened to. Even in prose plays, such language has rhythms and the beauty of sounds.

The difference between prose and poetry should be obvious to the reader; shifts from one poetic form to another (as in some of Shakespeare, for example) or from prose to verse must be watched for. Prose, rhythmic prose, blank verse, rhymed verse, and other musical uses of language should always be noted and questioned: Why has the playwright used these? What is the effect?

Primary effects of the musical use of language are mood, level of abstraction, and level of seriousness. Regular, slow rhythms create very different moods from sharp, staccato ones; verse, especially rhymed verse, is usually more abstract and, in serious plays, more serious than prose. In comedy, the rhymed couplet, although artificial, enhances the witty line by providing an extra accentuation, the rhyme.

FIGURE 3-7. **Spectacle.** In reading the play, scenes such as this must be imagined, a difficult process for the reader with no theatrical experience. (*From Stanley Appelbaum,* Advertising Woodcuts from the Nineteenth Century. *New York: Dover, 1977.*)

Spectacle

In reading, it is important to try to visualize so as to understand spectacle. Much of spectacle in the modern theatre, to be sure, is the work of designers whose genius cannot be predicted from the page. The cues for their work are there, however, in the same text that the reader uses. The imagination must work.

Spectacle, like language, embodies idea in its use of symbols. In many ways, however, it addresses the audience at a level different from language and intellect—that is, at the level of the graphic arts. Spectacle—which, on the stage, is always working on the sense of sight—is the hardest of the six parts to understand from the text. It is necessary to imagine it as fully as possible, but the imagined spectacle of the reader will probably prove quite different from the actual spectacle of performance.

ORGANIZING A RESPONSE

The result of a play analysis should be an organized response to the text. An organized response should be:

- Informed—that is, based on a knowledge of drama and theatre.
- Orderly—that is, consistent and well reasoned.

■ Defensible—that is, capable of explanation to somebody else (in a written paper, for example).

This kind of response is systematic. This means that it is made not because of individual likes and dislikes, but because of the nature of the play and the reader's ability to understand it.

Some people try to explain their attitude toward a play by saying, "My opinion is as good as yours." The trouble with this explanation is that understanding is not a matter of opinion. Opinion is a statement of feeling. It belongs in the same category as the old line, "I don't know anything about art, but I know what I like." The trouble with not knowing anything is that it actually prevents response; all it allows is gut reaction, which is quite a different matter. Part of the enjoyment of theatre does depend on gut reaction—but only part.

One way of organizing a response is to determine the play's *genre*.

Genre

Generic criticism is a major branch of dramatic criticism, and whole books have been devoted to the definition of tragedy (for example). Such definitions sometimes change under historical pressure, so that a more specific genre like Neoclassical tragedy comes into being. Here, therefore, it is possible to give only the broadest definitions of four major genres:

1. Tragedy—a work of the highest seriousness, with a serious protagonist in a serious action with serious consequences. Usually, as well, human decision is important to the idea of tragic action.

2. Comedy—a work whose issues are usually social and mundane, not concerned with ultimate (spiritual or moral) matters, with a protagonist involved in an action without deeply serious consequences. Usually, as well, human decision is limited, comic character being comic because it is locked into types or into intense self-interest.

3. Melodrama—a work of apparent seriousness with issues cast in terms of extremes (black and white), the actual issues being much less profound than the language suggests and often sparse in idea. "Happy endings" are frequent, although not inevitable. Character is much closer to comic character—locked into types and seldom driven to deep decisions. Threats to the protagonist are often physical and play on audience sympathy.

4. Farce—a comic work whose aim is laughter, from a non-English word meaning "to stuff," because farce is stuffed with laughter-producing elements. The protagonist pursues a mundane, often trivial action, and the characters are often devoid of decision or thought. Both the characters and the plots of farce are called *mechanical*, and it is, in fact, in the working out of its machinery that farce often finds its best laughter.

FIGURE 3-8. **Genre.** Melodrama, with its extreme highs and lows, is still one of the most popular of genres; it often seems to deal with important ideas while only using them as springboard (a common device, for example, in TV soap opera).

Response and the Parts of a Play

Analysis allows us to understand the parts of the play and how they work. Our responses to the play should be able to determine if:

- Plot is internally consistent, interesting, and appropriate to the genre.
- Character is active, interesting, and consistent and has function throughout.
- Idea is important and is embodied in character and plot.

- Language is interesting and expressive.

- Music (including the music of language) supports and enriches the other parts.

- Spectacle is interesting and appropriate, and if it supports rather than overpowers the other parts.

CHAPTER FOUR

HOW TO SEE A PLAY

As we said at the beginning of Chapter 3, reading a play and seeing a play are different activities. They use different tools and they give different results: reading gives analytical knowledge and the aesthetic and intellectual responses possible with an incomplete artwork; seeing gives a wide range of responses, appropriate to a complete artwork but much affected by the transitory nature of the form (the "Nowness" of performance).

Some critics and scholars have dealt only with the written play and have said that they preferred reading the play to seeing it in the theatre; however, theirs is a different activity from theatregoing and is not part of the enjoyment of theatre.

The enjoyment of theatre takes place in the theatre. Theatre is an art that exists in performance, and it is as an audience at a performance that we must approach it.

TOOLS FOR SEEING

To understand these two chapters on reading and seeing a play, it is necessary to understand that we are treating these activities as different in kind. We have treated reading a play as an analytical act—as a critical experience instead of an aesthetic one. We will now treat seeing a play as an aesthetic experience, not a critical one. This distinction is justified by the difference between the play text and the performance.

The "parts of the performance" are not the same as the parts of the play—and,

FIGURE 4-1. Theatre, Performance, Audience.
The actuality of the theatre, the presence of the
audience, the immediacy of performance, make
seeing the play very different from reading it.

in fact, the new critical dimension called *performance criticism* is still trying to define
the "parts" of theatrical performance.

Aristotelian Analysis and Performance

The analysis discussed in Chapter 3, "How To Read a Play," based on Aristotle, is
appropriate to study of the play *text*. When we come to performance, however, that
analysis is inadequate.

Consider the emphasis of the six parts of the play. Of the six, four—plot, character,
idea, and language—belong to the text. Music and spectacle, although described in
the text, belong to performance.

Yet, when we see a play in performance, plot, character, idea, and language are,
in fact, submerged in a greater whole, and they do not appear to us as "parts" called
plot, character, and so on, but as elements in that organic whole. Even more important, that organic whole has utterly different qualities: aspects of art that, by their
very nature, cause us to understand them in a new way.

For example, character in performance is not merely written words and intellectual
constructs called *decisions*. It is a very complicated creation that is mostly in the work
of the actor, for whom the play text (and its six parts) is the foundation of the
artistic creation, but not the artistic creation itself.

In addition, the nature of the theatre radically alters the significance of spectacle.
Theatre is primarily visual. Suddenly, spectacle is primary. It is the "cause" of much

of the performance. Modern theatre has endowed spectacle with great meaning—in light's capacity to focus attention, to create mood; in setting's and costume's capacity to give information about time, place, personality, and society; and so on.

Performance also introduces entirely new questions of art—the art of the actor above all, but the art of other theatre makers, as well. Analysis of the play text ("reading a play") raises only the question of the art of the playwright, and then considered only as the writing of text. The writing of text is a great art, but it is not the art of performance, and the formal analysis (via the parts of the play) that allows us to appreciate the text is inadequate for the appreciation of performance.

Finally, performance is complex and *synergistic:* many elements happen simultaneously and reinforce each other. At the same time, the "Nowness" of performance prevents our holding on to a moment so as to analyze it. Thus, seeing a play requires our responding to many stimuli and fusing them to form a whole, moment by moment, while we quickly compare each moment (unconsciously or semiconsciously) with the moments of the performance that have already passed. One critic has called this process "electronic" to contrast it with the linear process of reading the play.

Aristotelian theory remains the bedrock of dramatic analysis. It is unrivaled for understanding the play, even the play as remembered *after* performance. However, to understand performance itself, a different (or at least a supplemental) approach is needed.

FIGURE 4-2. **Synergism of Values.** In performance, qualities that are only potentials in the text are realized, and they interact to heighten each other. *Anerca* by Figures of Speech Theatre. *(Rose Marasco photo.)*

THE VALUES OF PERFORMANCE

Performance acts on an audience from several directions simultaneously, so that each audience member is receiving a complicated blend of stimuli at each moment of the performance. For purposes of analysis and discussion, these stimuli can be separated into four main groupings. They are *sensory stimulation* (sight and sound); *human values* (story and character); *artistic excellence;* and *intellectual value.* All these stimuli can act on us *simultaneously* and *synergistically,* meaning that in the best performances they not only harmonize with each other but also support and enrich each other.

After World War II, the great English actor Laurence Olivier played Oedipus in Sophocles' tragedy. His performance is generally conceded to have been the greatest interpretation of that role in modern times. At the moment when Oedipus appeared, having just gouged out his eyes, the audience response was so intense that people gasped, and many of those who saw the performance still remember the moment as a high point in a lifetime of theatregoing. (See Figure 7-16.) Because the bloody effects of the eye gouging were visual, we could say that the moment was an example of intense *sensory stimulation:* however, because the horror of the moment depended on an understanding of story and character, the moment also sprang from an appreciation of the *human values* in the performance; yet again, it was Olivier's superb performance —his *artistic excellence*—that dazzled those in the audience who appreciated the art of acting. And finally, the symbolism and meanings of the eye gouging itself were the springboard for *intellectual value* in this classic tragedy of rich meanings. All four kinds of stimuli were at work, then, and it was the four, working *together,* that made the moment.

Of the four categories of stimuli, two are inherent in *production* (sensory values and artistic excellence), and two are inherent in *text* (human values and intellectual values). This distinction lets us understand at least a few of the reasons that theatregoers see the same play many times over a lifetime without feeling bored. The text does not change (or changes very little), but the performance does, and, because of the synergistic effect of factors like acting and audience response, the total impact of the performance then changes.

It is important to understand this point, for what it emphasizes is the enormous difference between *reading a play* and *participating as audience in a performance.* To read a play is to engage in an appreciation of half its potential (and then only if the reader is trained in such reading); to see the play in performance is to approach its full potential.

It will be helpful to look at each of the categories in more detail.

PRODUCTION

Sensory Values

Theatre comes from the Greek word meaning "seeing place." The Latin *auditorium* means "hearing place." We often speak of a performance as a "show." Thus, the vocabulary of the theatre acknowledges its remarkable visual and auditory power.

The audience relies on two senses: seeing and hearing. (Rarely, plays and movies have tried to appeal to other senses—Smell-o-vision, vibrating seats, physical contact with the performers—but the attempts are oddities.) Everything the audience understands about the performance comes through those two senses. The brain processes the information and uses it in several ways, but seeing and hearing remain the root senses of the theatre.

Spectacle

Of the two senses, vision is the more powerful. We believe what we see. When an actor says one thing with words but another with gestures, we believe the gesture. Our language acknowledges this power. "I see," we say when we understand something; having met a friend we say, "I saw so-and-so." Doctors "see" us; people "see" ghosts (a much more frightening experience than hearing one). "Seeing is believing."

Our eyes believe. *Spectacle*—that which is seen—rules.

So potent was spectacle in the Greek theatre that a story is told of one of Aeschylus' plays in which the chorus appeared as the Furies (avenging beings): "When, at the performance of the *Eumenides*, Aeschylus introduced the chorus in wild disorder into the orchestra, he so terrified the crowd that children died and women suffered miscarriage." *Seeing* the Furies was the shock, supported by the sense of hearing and tremendously strengthened by the play itself. Until the moment when they entered "in wild disorder," the Furies had existed as creatures of the mind's eye; suddenly, they were visible to the physical eye: they existed.

A modern audience might laugh at these very same Furies. Most of us, no longer sharing or even understanding the ancient Greek religious system, might find such

FIGURE 4-3. **Sensory Values: Sight.** The visual is often the most potent of human senses. *Electra* at Trinity University, San Antonio, Texas.

figures interesting or quaint or even comical, but we would not have the "mind's eye" vision to prepare us for the horror of the seen. Thus, spectacle does not mean merely "what is seen" in a purely objective sense; it means "what is seen" in the context of the seer. The physical eye sees merely what is there; it is a physical system—lens, retina, optic nerve—for receiving physical stimuli. The mind, on the other hand, sees in the context of a rich and complicated mixture of symbolism, association, and meaning.

Spectacle is not merely the horrifying or the symbolic, however. It is also the beautiful and the impossible. Most of us respond strongly to the sheer visual appeal of beauty. A parade is a "show" because of its visual beauty: the colors of flags and uniforms, the arranged mass of floats and drill teams, the pleasing movement of synchronization. Football halftime shows, circus performances, laser-light shows, and rock concerts are all great appeals to our love of visual beauty.

And perhaps of greatest importance to certain forms is the value of "seeing the impossible." Magic shows are spectacles of the impossible; so is circus trapeze work. So is much of dance, for example, the dazzling tap work of Broadway show dancing and the defiance of gravity that is classical ballet. We are greatly excited and moved by this "spectacle of the impossible"; through our vision, we come to understand that a certain artist is doing what we thought unlikely or undo-able. And we must *see* it "live." Notice how much weaker the value is, for example, of a magic show seen on television or a dance performance seen on film.

No wonder that our expression for going to the theatre is going "to see a show."

Sound

Hearing is the other of the audience senses. It makes possible the beauty and excitement of a great actor's voice. Some of the audience's richest moments in theatre have come about because of this sound.

Sound is not merely orchestral music or individual noises; it is the whole rich world of the ear. Perhaps it is most important in the theatre because of the actors' voices and the words they say. Voices are "orchestrated," and directors cast actors so that their voices will blend and match. There is an analogy to opera here. Each actor develops the voice to attain maximum range and flexibility. Moreover, the playwright supplies words, sentences, and overlapping lines so that voices still "sing" together, and the words and sentences and voices themselves have beauty *distinct from the meaning of the words* (an aspect of Aristotle's "music"). We are very much in the habit of listening to what actors say rather than listening to the aesthetic values of voice and language, but it is possible to do both; in opera, where the language is often not English, the reverse is true, and the meaning of the language is ignored so that one may concentrate on the glory of the voice. Actors' voices can be effective in the same way, though audiences may not appreciate them with quite the same conscious understanding. Certain actors have voices whose unusual qualities are by themselves effective—a flexible contralto; a husky, breaking voice. Other actors use their voices in surprising ways: vocal swoops, controlled tremolo, meticulous rhythm. The very sound of language, too, is part of the sensory value of the theatre, whether in obvious examples like rhyme or in more subtle poetic language.

Artistic Excellence

Beyond and behind the appeal of theatrical imitation, of "embodied narrative," there is an element of artistry by which all other things are given value and are heightened: the skill of the actor, the designers, the director, and others. Audience response to the actor is probably the easiest to understand and is the response we most often sense. *Understanding of the art of the theatre* makes such a response possible, and that response greatly enriches all the others. A knowledgeable audience member does not applaud merely the *fact* that the actor created a brilliant character (which the indifferent audience member may confuse with the playwright's creation of character) but also applauds the *artistry* with which the actor did it. (Not only *what* but also *how*.) In the same way, the knowledgeable audience member is able to respond to the artistry of the director, because knowledge allows an understanding of the contribution that the director made.

This kind of response is possible when the audience member is knowledgeable and when the audience member enjoys and critiques the performance simultaneously. This is not to suggest that the audience member holds back and does not participate in the performance; rather, it suggests that the perceptive audience member is able both to participate and to process information about the performance. "Aesthetic distance"—the separation of audience from performance through art—is set up, as if the audience member were watching the audience watch the play. Perceptions are divided between a subjective participation in the experience and an objective understanding of how the performance came about.

Above all, an appreciation of the artistic element of the theatre requires an understanding of how theatre artists work and of why they make the choices that become the performance. Why did the actor drop his voice to a whisper instead of raising it when the character was angry? Why did the costumer dress the leading character in blue instead of red? Why was only part of the house shown instead of the whole thing? The ability to perceive these choices and to understand how they were made comes from gathering knowledge about how theatre artists work, and such knowledge comes from going to the theatre, from working in the theatre, and from studying about the theatre (as in this book).

In part, an appreciation of the element of artistry comes from an awareness of potentials and possibilities—of the human voice and body; of the use of space; of light as a plastic entity; and of pictorial composition.

At its best, the theatre should make us gasp, and one of the elements at which we will gasp is the ability of artists to transcend what we think are human limits.

TEXT

Human Values

Drama is the imitation of human action; theatre embodies that imitation in performance. As audience, we generalize from the particular imitation to human truths. The nature of imaginative art focuses attention so that invented lives are more significant than most real ones. For many people, the memory of Hamlet is more powerful than the memory of many acquaintances.

The human values of such human imitations are many. They include *human understanding,* the increased awareness of what it is to be a human being; *emotional sympathy,* the participation through art in suffering and joy; *arousal* of pleasure, including a wide range of pleasures from the laughable to the erotic; and *psychic perception,* the observation of mythic patterns, as in dreams.

Audience response to human values comes from two principal factors: story and character. (*Not* Aristotelian plot—the ordering of incidents and the reasons for that ordering: neither order nor reasons can be perceived clearly in performance.)

Story

Stories are seemingly as old as human language. Some are complicated and long; some are short and simple. Stories are made up of incidents and have "coherence"; that is, each one is held together by a strong internal force. This force may be causality, but it can be chance or the oddity of the happening.

Stories serve the audience in two ways. First, they are compelling in themselves. Second, they serve as the framework for the other values of character, humor, and so on. In a sense, we understand the other values through our understanding of the story. As individuals, we tend to believe that people are understood by their behavior; behavior, focused by art, is story.

It is possible to watch a performance for the value of story alone. Many of the action series on television, for example, offer story as their most important value.

The response to a story comes from *suspense* and *surprise.*

Suspense is the unfolding of events at the pace created by the theatre itself in an artfully crafted structure that will best ask and answer the question "And then what happened?" We must note that a question is *both* asked and answered; that is, the art of suspense lies in manipulating events and time so that the audience will understand *what* story it is to anticipate and *how* that story is progressing through time. A critic said some years ago that art is the creation and satisfaction of appetite,

FIGURE 4-4. Suspense. All plot is suspenseful if the plot is good, although we commonly think of suspense as very highly charged, often with physical danger. A scene from *The River Niger,* directed by Elliott C. Moffitt, designed by Frank Whaley, at Fayetteville State University.

and the definition is not at all inaccurate for suspense, because its two parts—creation and satisfaction—catch the necessary parts of both good suspense-making and good audience response to it. We cannot have story suspense without preparation for it (creation of appetite); that is, we cannot have a haphazard succession of events and call their sequence *suspense*. Who would care if we began a play by showing John, then shifted to Maria, then to Robert, then to Dana, and so on all evening? This would be all preparation and no story; there could be no "And then what happened?" because *then* would be meaningless. Therefore, to have story suspense that will arouse pleasurable audience response, we must have preparation, connectedness, and resolution (the answer to the question "And then what happened?").

Surprises—changes of direction, reversal, dashing of expectations—these sound like the opposite of suspense, because they suggest that instead of having the question answered, we are being sent off in a different direction or being sent all the way back to the beginning. Not so, however; effective surprise is one of the principal pleasures of story, for it puts us through a pleasing imitation of real experience, which is full of surprises and setbacks; yet the surprise of the theatre is "safe" and therefore pleasurable instead of painful, for it happens only within the contract between performers and audience.

Surprise, like other story elements, must be prepared for. There can only rarely be surprise that is outside the world that the performance creates. That is, it would be "surprising" to have a flying saucer land onstage and carry off the leading character when he got into a terrible mess in Act III, but unless the play had prepared us for flying saucers, this surprise would not truly be a surprise at all; it would be a violation of the contract. It would give us, as audience, not pleasure but annoyance.

Surprise can take several forms. There can be the surprise of the unexpected; the surprise of reversal; the surprise of the prepared-for but unpredictable, when the event (often the high point of a play) astonishes us despite the fact that we know something of the sort must happen. In *Oedipus Rex,* for example, Oedipus' blinding of himself is effective because it is so horrible and shocking. We know that he will do something almost unthinkable to himself, but we do not know what. Related to this sort of surprise is the "least likely" of several choices, a necessity in murder mystery plays. Such plays rely heavily on story for their success, and the basic question that they pose ("Who did it?") makes surprise of choice essential in the last act. Like other sorts of surprise, this will work only if the surprise is carefully prepared for—if, in fact, we can say in retrospect, "Of course! That was inevitable!" (That is, it was set up for us.)

The Aristotelian parts of plot, like plot itself, are not adequately understandable in performance. Sometimes they can be perceived after the performance is over.

Character

Representations of human beings move through the patterns we have called stories. Their behavior in those stories reveals them to us. They are not mere stick figures, mere zeros. They are *characters*.

A *character* is the representation of a human being in a theatrical performance. A character is not a living human being, nor is it ever a completely rounded imitation of a living human being (nor is a character in performance the same as the Aristotelian part, character.) A character in performance is a detailed representation of a human being *insofar as the audience needs to know that person in the work of art.* The aspects of character that the audience understands are often clearer than similar aspects of people in real life; we may come to know theatrical characters better than our closest relatives. Great characters become part of the common image of "what it is to be a man and woman"; they are quoted, discussed, and made examples of as few real human beings ever are.

Characters and story (like character and plot) are interlocked. We understand each through the other. Nevertheless, they remain a little independent of each other, so that we may have different characters move through the same basic story. The same sequence of events can be used in several ways. "Boy meets girl, boy loses girl, boy gets girl" was a formula for stories of the 1920s and 1930s that could be dramatized around characters as different as classical divinities and factory workers. Incidents, then, allow us to understand characters within a rough framework, but the context and the place of the incident in the story let us perceive characters more fully; when Fred hits Tyrone with a baseball bat, if we know that Tyrone was messing around with Fred's wife and that Fred has never recovered from his experiences in the Vietnam war, we can form a much better idea of the characters than we ever could from the event itself.

Responses to a character may come from several impulses: identification, subconscious reference, and association.

"Like me" is a common positive response. "It's my story" or "He could be me" are sources of pleasure or suffering. We like to see the mirror held up so that we can watch ourselves. Connected with this idea is the idea of universality of character, the character with whose theatrical experiences everyone can connect.

Subconscious reference is another kind of identification, but so different that it needs to be talked about separately. This is a response to something that is like us, perhaps, but that we recognize as being like us at a level below the conscious—as in our dreams or our fantasies. We watch *Hamlet* because there are aspects of Hamlet that we can identify with, true, but we watch it also because the Prince of Denmark is the main character in an action that partakes of dreams and of myth, something we fantasize about living through—or fear living through. Frankenstein's monster is not at all "like me," but he may be terrifyingly like our nightmares. Such characters are also a mirror, but not one in which we see our superficial selves; we see the selves we carry, hidden.

Historical names and famous people have their own appeal. Shakespeare's histories were, in their own day, effective character plays for this reason. The musical *Evita* gains from its association with a real woman; in the nineteenth century, a semidocumentary treatment of such notorious events as real murders and trials created successful theatre. All such plays depend in part for their impact on convincing us that we are seeing "truth"—although the farther the real-life people on whom they are modeled are from us (in time and occasionally in culture), the less "truth" matters. To take advantage of the associative response, the play must choose people with whom the audience has strong ties, and it must present them in a convincing

FIGURE 4-5. **Historical Character.** Showing actual people as dramatic characters both celebrates those people and gives importance to the performance; many of Shakespeare's plays, for example, are "histories." Here, the real Harriet Tubman and a dramatization of her life, Paul Morse's *Harriet Tubman*, directed by Johnny Saldana. *(Right photo by Lyle Beitman, courtesy of Arizona State University.)*

fashion (that is, by casting actors who look like the real people or by using effective makeup, and by hewing closely to known events and not violating the "facts" of history).

Intellectual Values

Generally, ideas are given least thought while we sit in the theatre but are the things that we talk about most after we have left. There is a good reason for this seeming contradiction: the theatre is "the place of the Now." Performance is transitory. When it is behind us, preserved only in our memories, the vividness of the sensory and artistic pleasure fades, and we are left with the intellectual content, which remains sharp and fresh because of the sharpness of our minds. Ideas, in fact, become more acute with time, if we allow ourselves to be interested in them. As well, ideas are

FIGURE 4-6. **Intellectual Values.** This photograph shows a moment rich in spectacle, yet one also rich in visually communicated intellectual value: the play is Anouilh's *Antigone,* itself an ideological text, shifted in period from World War II to 1990, with clear images of rock and game show. Directed by Catherine Schuler at the University of Maryland.

frequently the element of theatre that reviewers and critics talk about because, being intellectual and capable of verbalization, ideas are far easier to put into words than the brilliance of an actor's gesture or the beauty of a lighting effect.

There are ideas behind or embodied in every play, to be sure, but some ideas are more interesting and more important than others. As well, some ideas are more interesting and important to certain people, less so to others.

Questions of importance and relevance are highly debatable, and more often than not, a debate about relevance and importance is really a debate about "what I like" or "what I believe." In the area of theatrical idea, however, the audience member errs by making a personal judgment. It is far better to ask, at least, why the idea was important to the theatre people who created the performances than to say unthinkingly, "That idea is not important (to me)" or "That idea is irrelevant (to me)."

The artistry of performance is best comprehended not by the intellect but by the body and the heart and the receptive self. Pure idea, which is dealt with directly by the intellect, belongs not in the theatre but in the lecture hall. Theatrical idea, which reaches the intellect through the medium of performance, is entirely integrated into the other elements and neither manipulates them nor obscures them.

Too, idea is not the element that the performer cares most about. There is an old theatre adage: "If you have a message, send a telegram." Directors only rarely talk to actors about the "idea of the play"; designers do not try to express idea but try, instead, to provide good acting spaces and aesthetically pleasing spaces. A playwright may talk about "what my play means," and director, designer, and actors will work with the playwright to enhance these ideas; however, they will work through the other values—for they know that *in performance it is those values that must succeed.*

This is not to say that ideas do not belong in the theatre. Nor does it mean that performers have contempt for ideas or that ideas are themselves an intellectual, after-the-fact invention. What it does mean is that idea is not a be-all and end-all in the theatre. In a sense, idea is the most important element in making a serious judgment about the importance of a play, but that judgment is made only if the play succeeds brilliantly with the other values. *Hamlet* is a great play both because it is a stunning experience to see *and* because it is rich in complex ideas. A less important play, effective as it may be in performance, has less complex ideas that are less central to the culture, less tantalizing on the largest scale of human concerns.

RESPONSES OF THE AUDIENCE

To discuss now the responses of audience members to performance is to delve into an area as complex and mysterious as human psychology itself. No one can say for certain how an audience will respond; no one can say for certain how an individual in an audience is responding at any moment. Performances differ from each other; audiences differ from each other; individuals in an audience differ from each other.

Individual postures toward a performance vary from extreme involvement (identification) to extreme objectivity. At any point along this spectrum, individuals bring such vastly different psyches to the experience that two people, sitting side by side at the same performance, may have quite different experiences and may behave outwardly in entirely different ways. Thus, any observations made about audience response are generalizations to which there must always be many exceptions.

Exterior behaviors that indicate audience responses are covered in the following sections.

Laughter

Laughter is the actor's reward in comedy, the actor's torment in serious drama. In general, audiences seem to laugh for two widely different reasons: because they are truly amused and because they are uneasy. The laughter of amusement is largely a response to human values—that is, to an understanding of story and character—although there is considerable intellectual involvement in our laughter at satire, for example. The laughter of amusement may range from enormous belly laughs at wit or pratfalls ("We had them rolling in the aisles?") to low chuckles of appreciation that reflect warmth and approval.

The laughter of unease can be shattering for the actor, who may find the audience laughing uproariously at completely improper moments. Such laughter springs not

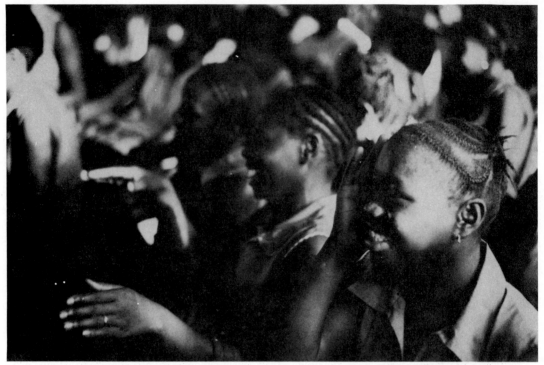

FIGURE 4-7. **Audience Response.** Laughter at comedy is a positive response to human values. (*Photo courtesy of Martin Banham.*)

from amusement but from stress; it is not the laughter of an understanding of human values but the laughter of rejection of the experience represented by the performance. "Nervous laughter" is familiar in life; it has its counterpart in the theatre. Inevitably, it means that the performance has failed (but the failure may be the fault of the audience and not of the performers).

Silence

"You could hear a pin drop!" The silence of rapt attention is familiar. Although we associate applause with the theatre, it is silence that is often the surest key to the effective response of an audience. Silence means attentiveness, for the body is being held still. The body at rest is not necessarily still; it shifts position, coughs, taps its fingers. A thousand people who do not make a single sound are remarkable, then. The performance has them in a very tight grip.

Such silence cannot be preserved for an entire evening. Like the pauses between movements of a symphony, when voices hum, coughs resound, and programs rattle, performances of even the most compelling sort must provide occasional release. Normally, such release points are built into the text of the play.

Applause

"Ours be your patience then, and yours our parts;/Your gentle hands lend us, and take our hearts" (Shakespeare's *All's Well That Ends Well*). The performers' request for applause dates to classical times. Clapping is still the way of signaling approval of performances in North America, from athletics to music to political speeches. It signals gratitude, approval, sometimes a request for more, an encore. In some instances, an audience will rise to applaud—the "standing ovation" that signals special favor.

Actors take their bows so long as applause lasts. "Milking" applause for more bows is considered bad form; contrarily, repeated bows at the curtain are the result of extended applause.

It is, perhaps, an oddity of theatrical convention that there is no audience behavior to signal positive response to serious or even tragic performance. In comedy, laughter follows comic events; in tragedy, profound silence is often the most significant response. Even at the end of many serious performances, silence will be the audience's behavior, as if even applause were too frivolous for the moment. Applause, then, is the usual sign of approval, but silence may be a sign of the deepest effect.

Tears

People do still weep in the theatre, although the copious waterworks of years ago are seldom seen. Such shedding of tears today may be—in fact, usually is—silent; it may be only the tear in the eye, the lump in the throat. In either case, it is an outward sign of "empathy," the "believing with" an emotional moment. It is human value that stirs empathy, often at a far less than tragic level. Fictional deaths of animals and children, the parting of lovers, and similar human events can provoke tears.

We live in an age (in the United States) when public weeping is discouraged. Public laughter is approved; public tears are not. We still have such expressions as "having a good cry," and a certain kind of dated, highly empathetic movie is still called a "four-handkerchief picture." By and large, however, the taboo against public crying is almost too strong even for the "allowed behavior" of the darkened theatre. When we are moved, we try to hide our tears and keep our sniffles silent.

Unease

Audiences have several negative behaviors (most of them unconscious) that reflect negative responses to performances. The most obvious of these is *noise:* coughing, shuffling of feet, whispering, shifting positions. When a thousand or more people begin to do these things at once, the noise level can get quite high, and the actor will believe that it is deafening. All the sounds that are suppressed when an audience is attentive become noticeable the moment that the attention wanes. Coughs resound like gunshots; programs rattle like so many sails in the wind; feet scrape on the floor like coffins being dragged over a pavement. Bodies, tensed to watch and listen, are working off nervous energy. Each individual believes that he or she is being quiet, but the cumulative effect is loud—and horribly revealing.

More conscious negative behaviors include comments about the performance and getting up and walking out of the theatre. Rarely, nowadays, do they include catcalls, boos, remarks to the actors, or thrown objects. However, new theatregoers accustomed to television may talk back to the actors or make comments without realizing that as spectators they are being rude and destructive.

Negative behaviors reflect negative responses; negative responses reflect a failure of communication between performance and audience. *Either* the performance *or* the audience—or *both* of them—may be responsible. Bad performances can cause negative responses, but *bad audiences can have negative responses to a good performance.*

BAD AUDIENCES

What is a bad audience? It is an audience that is unable or unwilling to respond to the performance before it under the conditions of the theatre. Thus, bad audiences are of two kinds: (1) the *unprepared audience,* which does not understand the nature of theatre art and so responds to performance as it does to life; and (2) the *unwilling audience,* which refuses to accept the nature of the performance before it.

FIGURE 4-8. **The Prepared Audience.** It understands the theatre and has prepared itself for the play it is about to see.

The Unprepared Audience

The unprepared audience is usually new, or fairly new, to the theatre. It confuses art and life. It shows inappropriate responses because the intensity of theatre acutely embarrasses it; it may laugh at scenes of suffering, love, or nobility; it may, in extreme cases, try to interrupt the performance to prevent what, in life, would be offensive behavior.

The Unwilling Audience

The unwilling audience can be any audience alienated from the performance by poor mediation or by personal stubbornness. Some people simply dislike musicals; others hate comedy. They should stay away from the forms they dislike; if trapped into them by accident or mistake, they show an extreme of unease. Less obvious, but far more common, are audiences who are shocked or dismayed by elements of performance—usually intellectual value, sometimes human value or sensory value—that they are unaccustomed to. These elements run a wide spectrum from nudity to religion. Again, as with the unprepared audience, there is an ignorance of the nature of art and the "harmlessness" of the theatre; in the case of the unwilling audience, however, the ignorance exists despite considerable theatre experience. The unwilling audience should know better but refuses to.

We all begin as the unprepared audience. We all have a potential for being the unwilling audience. We grow away from the first with experience and knowledge; we avoid the second with alertness to the theatre's essential nature and to the role of the audience in performance.

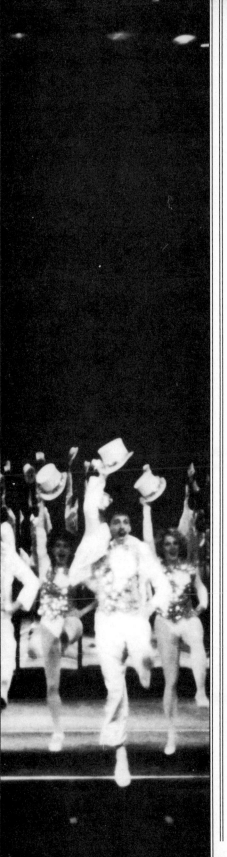

PART TWO

TODAY'S THEATRE *and* ITS MAKERS

CHAPTER FIVE

MAKING THEATRE TODAY: THE CONTEXT

Before studying the people who make theatre happen, we need to examine the contexts in which they work in the United States. In what kinds of spaces can they make their plays? Are some arrangements of actors and audiences better than others for certain sorts of plays? What kinds of producing arrangements are available, and what are their strengths and weaknesses? Finally, how can theatre productions be financed, and what are some implications of the different funding sources?

THEATRE SPACES

Given the diversity of theatre groups around the country, it should not be surprising that they choose different sorts of physical spaces in which to work. With various elaborations, three basic theatre spaces now dominate: proscenium, thrust, and arena stages. In addition to these three, a few less common arrangements can be named and briefly described.

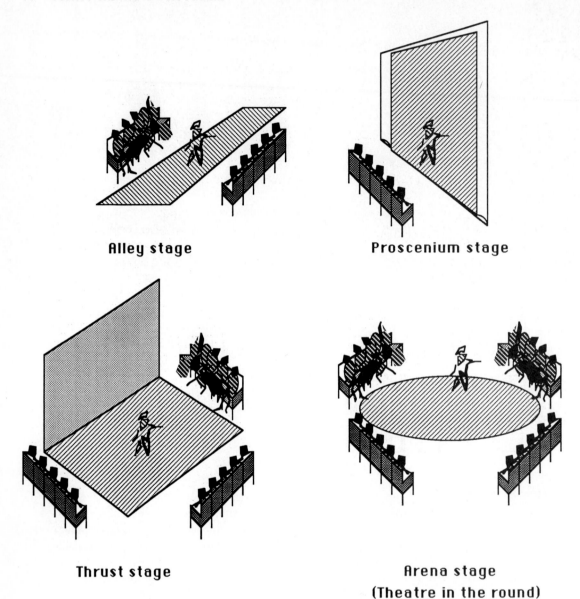

Alley stage

Proscenium stage

Thrust stage

**Arena stage
(Theatre in the round)**

FIGURE 5-1. **Basic Theatre Spaces.** The diagram highlights the relationship between actors and audience in four common spatial configurations: proscenium (actor faces audience); alley (audience on two sides of actor); thrust (audience on three sides of actor); arena (audience surrounds actor).

Proscenium Stages

The most popular theatre shape in Western Europe and America since the seventeenth century, proscenium theatres are marked by a proscenium arch that separates the stage and the auditorium.

The stage behind the proscenium arch is typically equipped with a rigging system, which allows scenic pieces to be "flown" (lifted out of sight above the stage floor), and a trap system, which allows objects and people to sink below the stage floor or to rise from it. Some are equipped with wagons or "slip stages" that allow scenery to be moved into place from the *wings*, the spaces on each side of the stage. In most proscenium theatres, there is an area that extends a few feet in front of the arch, an area called the *apron* or *forestage*.

The auditorium is arranged so that almost all seats face the stage. Ground level seats are *orchestra seats*. Above them are *balconies* (also called *galleries*), which may curve around at least part of the side wall. Older proscenium houses have small, separate balconies, called *boxes*, usually on the side walls of the theatre near the stage. These boxes were at one time the most prized seats in the theatre, but they are now usually avoided because of their bad angle for viewing the stage (bad *sight lines*).

Thrust Stages

Some plays, especially those of Shakespeare and his contemporaries, were not written for production in a proscenium theatre. For this reason, several theatre companies, especially those whose repertory stresses plays from the past, have sought a variation of the theatre used in Shakespeare's day. Such groups have built theatres with thrust (also called Elizabethan, or Shakespearean, or three-quarter-round) stages.

In such theatres, there is no arch separating the actors from the audience. Instead, audience members are placed on three sides of the action, usually on a raked (slanted) floor to improve sight lines, and in balconies. Actors enter the playing area from the back or through *vomitories* (passages that run through and under the audience and open near the stage itself). Because in this theatre elaborate stage machinery cannot be concealed behind a proscenium arch and because, too, of the close physical relationship between the actors and the audiences, thrust stages tend to rely on acting, costumes, and properties rather than complex scenic effects. Indeed, in such theatres, without a front curtain and proscenium arch to mask them, all scene changes and all actors' entrances must be made in full view of the audience.

Of the many thrust theatres, perhaps the best known are those at the Festival Theatre in Stratford, Ontario, Canada, and at the Guthrie Theatre in Minneapolis, Minnesota, both of whose repertories stress revivals of masterpieces from the past.

Arena Stages

The audience in the arena theatre surrounds the playing area, hence its other name: *theatre in the round.* Many people prize the closeness of actors and audiences in arena staging, an intimacy especially well suited to many plays in the modern repertory.

FIGURE 5-2. **Thrust Stage.** The thrust stage (also called the Shakespearean or Elizabethan stage) and the proscenium stage are the two most widely used configurations today. Shown here, Indiana University (Pennsylvania). (*Photograph courtesy of Lynn Lockrow, Auburn University, whose setting for* Tartuffe *is shown.*)

With neither a proscenium arch nor a back wall to mask movements, all property and scenic shifts and all actors' entrances must be done either in blackout or in full view of the audience. Perhaps for this reason, arena stages tend to avoid elaborate scenic effects in favor of close attention to the details of costumes, properties, and acting.

Although less common than either proscenium or thrust stages, arena stages exist throughout the country, most notably at the Arena Stage, Washington, D.C., and the original Alley Theatre, Houston, Texas.

Other Configurations

Sometimes from choice and sometimes from necessity, acting companies may take their performances to audiences instead of having audiences come to them. For such performances, a wide assortment of spatial arrangements must be found or created.

The booth stage has long been a popular solution. Here, actors erect a curtain before which they play, either on a raised platform or in a cleared area. The result is very much like the thrust stage, with the curtain serving both as a place from which to make entrances and as a background against which to perform. Because it meets the basic needs of performance and can be quickly erected and dismantled, the booth stage has long been the favorite of traveling companies.

Alley stages place the audience on two sides, with the actors performing between them, and often with scenic units at each end. In some countries, such arrangements are found in regular theatres; in the United States, however, they are used mostly by actors who find it necessary to perform in school gymnasiums.

Finally, only the imagination limits the space in which actors perform for audiences. In the United States, we have records of theatre taking place in streets, parks, factories, and even elevators—again, an index of the great diversity of our theatre.

PRODUCING SITUATIONS IN THE UNITED STATES

Its center is still New York City, but American theatre now touches most cities throughout the country. Although its diversity makes classification difficult, we can divide American theatre first into *professional* and *amateur* (each with several subcategories). Because some theatres resist these categories, we have a third group: *theatres for special audiences.*

Professional Theatre

Broadway

Say the word *theatre* to an average American, and he or she will probably think immediately of New York's Broadway. The word, in fact, has several different meanings. *Broadway* is, first of all, the name of a street in New York that runs the length of Manhattan. But the word *Broadway* also designates the whole area around Times Square (Broadway and several streets adjacent to it), where most of New York's commercial theatres are located. The word was once used in various union contracts to specify a certain kind of theatre in which only union members could work, and then only for a fee or salary that met or exceeded the negotiated union minimums for that kind of theatre. And the word *Broadway* refers to a whole complex of qualities that people associated with the glamorous, glittering world of the legitimate theatre:

FIGURE 5-3. Broadway. The heart of the commercial theatre in the United States features a statue of George M. Cohan ("Give My Regards to Broadway") and a TKTS booth where theatregoers can pay reduced prices for shows not sold out.

elaborate settings, rich costumes, distinguished stars, polished performances, and sophisticated musicals and plays.

Although New Yorkers attend the Broadway theatre in large numbers, tourists also make up a sizable part of its audiences. From across the country, people flock into its theatres as part of "seeing New York." They expect to see plays written by the best-known playwrights, performed by the best actors, and designed by the best artists available, for which they are willing to pay—in the 1990s—about $50 a ticket (up from about $25 in the 1970s). At such prices, Broadway audiences comprise mostly the affluent: a social group that tends to be middle-class or above, white, mature, and somewhat conservative in taste and politics.

Broadway is best known for its musicals, where spectacle, rather than intellectual value, is prized. Situation comedies somewhat like those seen on television vie with musicals for popular acceptance. The remaining repertory consists of occasional serious dramas, mysteries, biographies, and one-person shows. Because of the high costs of producing on Broadway, its theatres seldom offer untried plays; they feature instead revivals of successful plays from past Broadway seasons or recently written plays transferred from successful runs elsewhere, most often London, Off-Broadway, or the regional theatres.

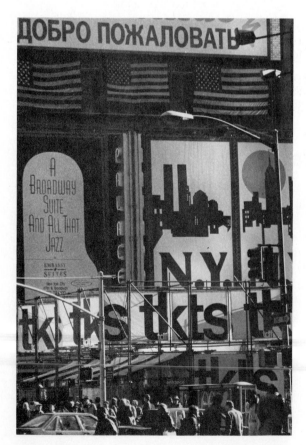

FIGURE 5-4. **Broadway.** The vitality of New York's theatre scene is captured by this photograph. Notice the number of people visiting the TKTS booth, the advertisements plastered on adjacent buildings, and the conjunction of U.S. and Soviet emblems, visual evidence of the political situation in the early 1990s.

Broadway's reputation today rests in large part on the high quality of its productions rather than on the literary merit of its drama. Because many theatre professionals believe that they have not established themselves until they have succeeded on Broadway, Broadway sets the standards of American acting, directing, and design. Broadway artists command among the highest salaries paid in the American theatre, and unions protect them by establishing minimum salaries and controlling working conditions. The major theatrical organizations are the Dramatists Guild (for writers), the Actors Equity Association (for performers), the Society of Stage Directors and Choreographers, United Scenic Artists (for designers), and IATSE (for technicians).

Much of Broadway's appeal, and also many of its problems, stem from money. Its costs of producing continue to climb, for several reasons. As real-estate prices in Manhattan soar, so do the costs of renting theatre space. Personnel costs rise with the demands of the unions. Costs of the goods and services needed to open a show— lumber for scenery, fabrics for costumes, advertising in newspapers and on television— have become almost prohibitive; and then, there is the money needed to keep the show running once it has opened. Costs are now so high that even a fairly modest show must run months (rather than weeks) in order to recapture its original investment, a situation that has made the *long run* a regular feature of the Broadway theatre.

Accelerating production costs have also produced the "hit-or-flop" syndrome. A play can make big money (*Godspell* returned over 20,000 percent to its investors) or it can go bust (*Hellzapoppin* lost $1.2 million for its investors). Boom or bust: "You can make a killing in the American theatre but you can't make a living there."

Another result of high costs has been to limit the potential audience for Broadway shows and to increase the power of certain New York reviewers. As ticket prices rise, the number of people able (or willing) to afford the Broadway theatre declines, as does the willingness of audiences to risk an unpleasant evening in the theatre. Audiences therefore look to a reviewer to steer them toward plays they will like and away from plays that they will not like. In so doing, audiences invest certain New York reviewers with enormous power over the fate of shows. And this audience affects the repertory in other ways as well, for producers actively seek productions to appeal to its tastes. Thus, the cycle of depending on tried-and-true plays, playwrights, and artists is reinforced. Simultaneously, opportunities for original plays, untested actors, and unknown directors are further constricted.

Broadway has tried to solve some of its money problems. For example, two low-priced ticket sources, the Times Square TKTS booth and the Lower Manhattan Theatre Center, sell tickets at half price on the day of performance for shows not sold to capacity. The computerization of ticket sales allows out-of-towners to compete with New Yorkers for good seats, and credit card payments by phone eliminate the need to write for tickets or to stand in lines to purchase them. The Theatre Development Fund, established in 1967, supports commercial productions of special artistic merit; and New York City offers incentives for the construction of new theatre buildings. The success of these efforts to make Broadway more accessible cannot yet be gauged.

Although detractors of Broadway have long deplored the grip that big business seems to have on it and have predicted its death many times, Broadway continues to be the model of much professional theatre in America. A testament to its authority

FIGURE 5-5. **Broadway.** This Sunday matinee finds theatre patrons clustered in Shubert Alley, where the marquee for the Booth theatre promises a musical play, and posters on the wall just beneath it advertise major shows offered by theatres on the two adjoining streets.

in matters theatrical is that some other professional theatres, like road shows and dinner theatres, strive to imitate it.

The Road

Many communities regularly import recent Broadway hits by booking the touring theatrical companies (road shows) that each year criss-cross the country. Although such road shows originate in New York, they seldom employ the original Broadway cast; but they do use professionals. Because road companies travel with complete sets and costumes, they are usually able to offer polished performances of recent hits to audiences outside the major cities, who would otherwise be unable to see them. Business is best for big name musicals, good for plays with well-known stars, risky for everything else. And the road is big business, grossing over $350,000,000 in 1990 (up 43 + % from the preceding year).

Dinner Theatres

Throughout the United States, dinner theatres offer successful Broadway plays of past seasons as the mainstay of their repertories. The quality of such companies varies widely. Some use union personnel, and their quality tends to be higher than those that rely on pick-up personnel.

Restrictions of space and budget cause almost all dinner theatres to simplify the lavish scenery and costumes of the originals in favor of smaller casts, smaller orchestras, and fewer sets; but, like Broadway, most seek to entertain rather than to elevate or instruct their audiences. In addition to the play itself, they add the sociability of drinks and dinner, so that an evening in the theatre is a festive occasion, not unlike going out for dinner before seeing a show on Broadway.

THEATRE MAKERS

C-1. **Acting.**
She Stoops to Conquer,
Trinity University.

C-2. **Acting.** *A Chorus Line,*
Wright State University.

C-3. Makeup.
A *jing* actor in China.
Courtesy of People's Republic of China.

C-4. Design: Scenic Rendering.
The Memorandum, by Vaclav Havel. Designer,
Robert Groff, Bowling Green State University.

C-5. Design: Scenic Rendering and Completed Setting.
The Servant of Two Masters. Designer, Lewis A. Crickard, Dartmouth College.

C-6. **Playwrights: The New Play.**
The Emir's Secret by Yahaya S. Dangana, in production in Nigeria.

C-7. **Design: Costume Rendering.**
School for Wives, designed by
Helen Huang, USAA.

C-8. **Design: Costume Rendering.**
Anything Goes, designed by
Dennis A. Parker, USAA.

C-9. **Design: Costume Rendering.**
Cabaret,
designed by Dennis A. Parker,
USAA.

C-10. **Directing.**
The Alchemist, directed by Eric Forsythe,
University of Iowa (designs by Dan Menteanu,
Lisa LoCurto, Marie Angele).

C-11. **Directing.** *The Misanthrope,* directed by David P. Karsten,
Western Michigan University (designed by Greg Roehrick).

FIGURE 5-6. Off-Broadway. Two of several small theatres just east of 9th Avenue are among those opened during the 1970s and 1980s to serve as tryout spaces for unproven works. Notice that they are named for a major French author and a major American director/critic. Comparing with Figure 5-5 can suggest the more elaborate nature of the Broadway theatrical experience.

Off-Broadway

The name *Off-Broadway* derives from the location of its theatres, which lie outside the Times Square theatre district. In addition to location, Off-Broadway houses were once contractually defined by their limited capacity (no more than 299 seats) and by their lower-than-Broadway salaries (as negotiated with the major unions).

Originally, the goals of Off-Broadway differed from those of Broadway. Off-Broadway sought to serve as a showcase for new talents: untried artists could work; established artists could experiment with new techniques; new plays could find production. Off-Broadway artists hoped to remain aloof from both threats of censorship and the problems of high-risk commercialism.

Although Off-Broadway continues to offer employment to actors, directors, and playwrights (producing three or more shows for every one of Broadway's by the mid 1980s), its production costs have risen and, with them, its need to succeed at the box office. As risk has become less practical, Off-Broadway has become a rather less expensive version of Broadway, for which it now serves regularly as a tryout space. Shows that succeed Off-Broadway may move to Broadway, often with the same casts, directors, and designers, but with much larger budgets.

Even though Off-Broadway and Broadway overlap in several respects, the lower ticket prices Off-Broadway attract a more diverse audience and thus allow a somewhat more varied repertory. In addition to small musicals and situation comedies, Off-

Broadway produces some serious works, even those that are potentially controversial. For about half of what it costs to see Broadway shows, Off-Broadway audiences can choose among revivals from the classical repertory, recent successes, and original plays. Some of the productions are very good; some are not. But modest risk-taking is part of attending the Off-Broadway theatre and, for those who support it, remains a major part of its attraction.

Off-Off-Broadway

As Off-Broadway moved closer to Broadway—in practice, if not in location—some artists felt the need for an alternative theatre where authors, directors, and actors could work closely together to produce plays in an artistic, rather than a commercial, environment. Thus, Off-Off-Broadway grew up in the late 1950s as a place dedicated to the process of creating art and exploring the possibilities of the theatre. It did not want to become a tryout space for Broadway or to succumb to Broadway's or Off-Broadway's commercialism.

Productions feature imaginative, but seldom elaborate, sets and costumes. Although the casts and designers in such spaces are not necessarily union members and are seldom paid even their expenses, they continue to work, exploring the limits of a vision that is often socially, politically, or artistically alien to current American values. Lower ticket prices encourage attendance by people priced out of the Broadway theatre, and the excitement caused by unknown plays and artists draws adventurous patrons to coffeehouses, lofts, cellars, churches, and small theatres tucked away all over Manhattan and even some of the other New York City boroughs, where they watch artists perform plays that stimulate them.

Although sometimes amateurish and often controversial, the offerings of Off-Off-Broadway provide a genuine alternative to the commercialism of both Broadway and Off-Broadway. Off-Off-Broadway remains the focus of much of the truly experimental and political theatre in America.

Regional Theatres

The vitality of regional professional theatres is one of the most heartening developments in the American theatre. In more than fifty major cities throughout the United States and Canada, more than sixty professional theatres bring art to their audiences. Unlike the commercial Broadway theatre, these groups are usually organized as not-for-profit enterprises and so can be more adventurous with play selection, production style, and personnel decisions. They contribute to theatre throughout America by diversifying and enriching its repertory, developing new audiences, training and revitalizing theatrical artists, and providing employment opportunities. Perhaps for this reason, regional theatres have been called "the conscience of the American theatre."

Regional theatres offer five major benefits:

1. *A forum where new plays and classics can coexist and provide an alternative to the comedies and musicals that are now the mainstays of Broadway.* Some, like the Guthrie

FIGURE 5-7. Regional Theatre. The Folger Theatre, Washington, D.C., associated with the Folger Shakespeare Library, specializes in reviving works of Shakespeare. Its stage incorporates features that permit a dramatic action uninterrupted by changes of scenery and encourages a close relationship between actors and audience. *(Photograph by Julie Ainsworth, by permission of the Folger Shakespeare Library.)*

Theatre in Minneapolis, have earned reputations through the excellence of their classical revivals. Others, like the Dallas Theatre Center and the Actors Theatre of Louisville, have been especially successful in sponsoring new plays. Such theatres have reversed the tradition of plays' beginning in New York and then trickling down slowly to the rest of the country. Much new drama now appears first around the country, where it is nurtured and tested. The best of it moves beyond its local area and throughout the country, often ending in New York.

2. *A source of new audiences for live theatre.* The art of theatre suffers without knowledgeable audiences, because theatre artists become complacent, accepting the ordinary or the mediocre rather than demanding the excellent. With the growth of regional professional companies, audiences across the country have come to appreciate live theatre as an art form and a cultural resource.

3. *A training ground and an energizing center for theatrical artists.* Colleges and universities begin the training of many young artists; the professional regional companies serve to introduce young artists to the profession, allowing them to work intensively with experienced artists. Today, many of our best talents in acting, directing, and designing begin their careers at one of these regional companies—and some elect to stay there throughout their careers.

4. *An important opportunity for the seasoned professional.* Commercial theatre can dull an artist's creativity and vitality because its repertory is restricted and because its productions, when successful, can run for months or years, a numbing experience for an artist. Moreover, the commercial theatre seldom offers those roles from the classical repertory that stretch the actor's craft. For these reasons, the best actors are often anxious to spend time with a resident theatre, where they can play a wide variety of roles from many of history's best plays. The exchanges between the regional and the New York theatres seem to be raising the standards of the whole profession.

5. *More jobs.* In New York City, job opportunities are dismal. There are at least five times as many professionals as there are jobs. Regional theatres offer an alternative to New York. For several years, more professional actors have been working outside than inside New York; and designers, few of whom get more than *one* show per season in New York, are now shuttling back and forth across the country, providing scenery, lighting, and costumes for professional productions.

The network of regional professional companies is large and growing. Both in quantity and quality, they are a major force in the American theatre. They may be, when taken together, what so many critics and scholars have long sought: America's National Theatre.

Amateur Theatre

Amateur theatre is theatre performed and produced by people who do not earn their living in the theatre. The two major kinds of amateur theatres in America are educational theatres and community theatres.

Educational Theatres

Theatre existed in American colleges and universities even before there were professional theatres here. Theatre and drama were at first extracurricular, performed at special events like commencements. They were later included within the curriculum of departments like classics or English. Drama and theatre became college subjects in their own right only early in this century, when George Pierce Baker (1866–1935) instituted classes in playwriting (and later play production) at Radcliffe College (1903), Harvard (1913), and Yale (1925). By 1914, Carnegie Institute of Technology was offering the first theatre degree. Shortly after World War II, most colleges and universities organized departments of drama (often in combination with speech) and offered, in addition to coursework, both undergraduate and graduate degrees.

Although differing in principal emphases, the functions of educational theatres now closely parallel those of the regional professional companies: training future

FIGURE 5-8. **Educational Theatre.** More than two thousand college and university theatre programs across the United States have active production programs of great diversity. Shown here, *Adam and the Experts*, at National Technical Institute for the Deaf, Rochester Institute of Technology. *(Directed by James Graves.)*

artists, developing new audiences, expanding the theatrical repertory, and providing jobs.

Obviously, the major goal of academic programs is the education and training of students. With the demise of the resident stock companies, training in acting, directing, playwriting, design, and technical production has been largely assumed by the academic institutions. Although many persons complain of the limitations placed on such training because of the basically conservative, even stultifying atmosphere of many academic organizations, the fact remains that most training for the profession now takes place in this world. Although each program is unique, the general pattern of instruction involves some combination of formal classroom work and public performances of selected plays.

The number of educational theatre programs alone is sufficient to render their influence strong. Whereas America now boasts more than sixty professional regional companies, it supports more than two thousand theatre programs in colleges and universities. In small cities without resident professional companies, theatre productions at the college are the best for miles around, and in smaller towns, such productions may be the citizen's only opportunity to view live performances. Through introductory classes and small touring companies, college and university theatres introduce thousands of students at all levels of education to a variety of plays. For many students, these are the first brush with live theatre. Thus, the role of educational theatre in building new audiences can scarcely be overestimated.

FIGURE 5-9. **Educational Theatre.** Training in musical theatre constitutes a part of many programs in colleges and universities. Shown here, a production of *Broadway Musical Memories*, a revue from Western Michigan University. *(Directed by Randy Bernhard, designed by Kevin Abbott and Jill Lyons.)*

Happily, because education is a primary goal, such theatres usually display a strong commitment to a wide range of plays and production styles. Alongside standard musicals, comedies, and domestic dramas, collegiate seasons are likely to include significant works from the past and experimental works for the future. Consequently, audiences for university theatre productions often enjoy far richer fare than would normally be possible in community or dinner theatres.

Too, the number of people required to maintain theatre in an academic setting has given the employment potential of the profession a healthy boost. At the college and university level alone, more than ten thousand productions are mounted each year and more than four thousand teachers are employed. When the growing number of high school drama classes, elementary programs in creative drama, and producing groups devoted to children's theatre are considered, it becomes clear that the academic complex is a major source of jobs. Indeed, educational theatre, considered at all levels, is probably the largest employer of theatre artists and scholars in the United States at the present time.

Community Theatres

Community theatres exist throughout the country. Cities with one or two regional professional companies may have a dozen community theatres. In towns with neither professional nor educational theatre (except, perhaps, the annual high-school play), a community group may produce plays in a school, a church, or a civic auditorium, providing entertainment and recreation for both participants and audiences.

Community theatres vary enormously. Some pay none of their participants, drawing directors, actors, and office personnel from volunteers in the community; others pay a skeleton staff—a technical director, box-office manager, and an artistic director—who work for a governing board of community volunteers. Almost no community theatres pay their actors or stage crew except under very special circumstances.

In communities without professional companies, community theatres fill the important role of introducing new audiences to the theatre and of keeping live theatre a part of the cultural life of a community. Where professional companies do exist, community theatres serve important recreational needs of people for whom participation in theatre is a greater pleasure than sitting in an audience. In their constant search for volunteers to help with production, such theatres regularly introduce many new people—especially young people—to the world of the theatre. Community theatres are, in fact, the first theatre experience for many people who later enter the profession. Finally, the relatively modest ticket prices of most community theatres bring into their theatres many who might not at first pay the price of a regional professional company. Some of these newcomers will become lifelong supporters, not only of their local community theatre but also of the regional professional companies and, when in New York, of its commercial theatres.

Theatres for Special Audiences

Some theatres cannot be categorized according to our earlier scheme, for they have both professional and amateur companies. Such theatres define themselves not by their financial structure but by the specific audiences that they aim to serve.

Children's Theatre

Among the most long-lasting of such groups are the children's theatres. Whether an established professional company, a university program, or an amateur group composed of community volunteers, whether using adult or child actors, a children's theatre aims to produce plays with special appeal to young audiences in order to instill in such audiences a love of the theatre.

The repertory usually consists of plays specially written for youth, using stories and issues of interest to that age group. Their range is great—from imaginative retellings of popular fairy stories, myths, and legends to sensitive treatments of contemporary social problems like drugs and divorce. Production styles vary, but most avoid domestic realism in favor of less literal presentations. With relatively

FIGURE 5-10. **Children's Theatre.** Some colleges and universities have major programs in creative dramatics and children's theatre, as does Arizona State University, whose production of *Wiley and the Hairy Man* is shown here. *(Directed by Donald Doyle. Photograph by Lyle Beitman.)*

modest ticket prices (adults often get in at reduced rates when accompanied by a child) and an unusually high commitment to their audiences, children's theatres introduce many young people to the art of the theatre and, from this large group, recruit some as lifelong supporters of all kinds of theatre.

Political Theatres

In another kind of theatre for special audiences, the goals are openly political: black theatre, Chicano theatre, feminist (or women's) theatre, and gay theatre. These groups note (correctly) that theatre through the ages has been controlled by middle- or upper-class white males. Although their individual aims vary, they share common assumptions:

- That the interests of middle-class white males are not their own.

- That group awareness can be heightened by art. They seek, therefore, a theatre that can display their group's experiences and explore its problems.

These theatres serve their audiences in very different ways. Some favor intense political statements; others avoid polemical works altogether. Many urge a continued separation of their theatres from those of the mainstream; others work to integrate their own art and artists into the commercial theatre as quickly as possible. Some of the theatres produce works with high production values and traditional dramatic texts; others disregard accepted production values and work largely through improvisation. Some seek modest social change; others advocate revolution. Some have budgets of hundreds of thousands of dollars; others have no budgets at all. Some charge audiences to attend; others perform in the streets and parks—wherever people congregate—and charge nothing.

Whatever their techniques, these theatres for special audiences strive to offer an alternative to the traditional theatre, which they believe has either demeaned them or ignored them.

THEATRE FUNDING

From its beginnings, American theatre has been organized as a profit-making business: businesspeople invest money in a theatre company or a production and hope to recover their investment, with interest, from box-office receipts. This same pattern persists today on Broadway and Off-Broadway, though now the stakes are higher and the sale of film, television, and video rights joins the box office as a likely source of revenue. Dinner theatres adapt this basic pattern by adding income from the sale of food and drink; community theatres, by relying on volunteers for donations of time, money, and goods.

Educational theatres are subsidized. Although the out-of-pocket costs of their productions must often be defrayed by the sale of tickets and program advertisements, the salaries of the faculty (who usually direct, design, manage, and mount the productions) are almost always paid by the university. Because the students who act and crew the productions are seldom paid, the majority of the labor costs associated with producing plays is charged to the university, not to the production. This substantial subsidy allows such theatres to be somewhat adventurous in their selection of plays.

With an occasional exception, government funding for theatre in this country has been conspicuously absent. Thus, one closely watched development was the establishment in 1965 of the National Endowment for the Arts (NEA), whose purpose was to encourage the development of the arts throughout the country. It did so in two major ways: by establishing state arts councils as coordinating and funding units and by subsidizing some existing performance groups. To receive grants, theatres must be organized as not-for-profit theatres, a radical departure from the Broadway model.

The NEA continues to be controversial. Not all citizens agree that government should fund art when urgent social problems remain unsolved and unfunded: the homeless, for example, remain on the streets of many U.S. cities. Not all citizens agree that taxpayers should pay for art that some find offensive. The latter issue led to a threatened cutoff of the NEA's funding in 1990. Both issues promise to be debated for some time yet.

The precedent set by the NEA may help account for a relatively new phenomenon: cities and counties, through their parks and recreation departments, are supporting

FIGURE 5-11. **Government Funding.** The fight against drugs included some government funds for theatre companies dedicated to educating audiences about the dangers of abuse. Shown here is one such company, Anstie's Limit, performing *Edge of Death,* whose junk sets and costumes were emblems for other kinds of junk and waste. *(Written and directed by Kenneth M. Cameron.)*

theatre as a form of recreation, for citizens who seek an alternative to their well-established programs in sports and crafts. Through both advice and money, recreation departments strive to improve the work of local community theatres, which they view as an important resource for the participants and their audiences.

Some people are encouraged that new patterns of funding may be emerging in America, patterns that will make it possible to produce theatre freed from the hit-or-flop syndrome, from the drudgery of the long run, and from an unemployment rate of more than 90 percent among Actors Equity members.

CHAPTER SIX

THE PLAYWRIGHT

Wright means "maker." As a wheelwright is a maker of wheels and a shipwright is a maker of ships, so the play*wright* is a "maker of plays"—not a *writer* of plays. At least, not basically and primarily. (Yet, we call what a play*wright* does, play*writing*—so the art consists of both making and writing.)

It is partly an accident that what the playwright does looks like what the poet does and like what the novelist does—setting down words on paper. If playwrights had a set of symbols like mathematical notation or musical notation, we might be less tempted to think of them as mostly *literary* artists. (Nobody thinks of mathematicians or composers as literary artists gone wrong.) In addition to the use of language to describe dramatic action, of course, the playwright also deals in the language of the characters, and, because they speak with the same words in which poems and books are written, the playwright "writes" dialogue for them, and so is a "writer."

It is a common misconception that any writer who writes good conversation "ought to write a play." Novelists and short-story writers often write excellent conversation in their works. Is this talent a clue to their potential to write plays? Not really. The connection between fictional conversation and stage dialogue is a very thin one, more one of accidental resemblance than of real substance. The novelist's conversation is praised for its truth to life, for example; so is the playwright's sometimes—but the playwright's dialogue is a much more terse, loaded, *active* thing than the novelist's, because it has to serve the needs of the stage and not of the page, and those needs are different, involving character motivation, density of information, and rhythm.

To say categorically that playwrights are not "writers" would be foolish. To say that they are not literary artists would be silly. Playwrights join novelists and poets in various academies of arts and letters; their works are studied in literature courses; literary scholars write books about them. They are not, however, *primarily* literary artists; they are primarily artists of the theatre who leave a literary record (the play) of their work behind. In trying to remember this distinction, we should keep in mind a critic's observation that "Molière saved French comedy from literature"—that the theatre artist triumphed over the purely literary artist.

This is not to say that writing plays somehow disables one from writing other things. On the contrary, some poets and novelists have been excellent playwrights. However, relatively few people have been artistically successful with other forms as well as the play. Usually, then, the playwright is an artist related to literary artists but separable from them—by the nature of the thing created, by the nature of the materials, and probably by temperament and impulse. What the playwright shares with all artists is the need to create: art is a way of knowing oneself and the world, of expressing ideas and feelings about oneself and the world.

WHY A PLAYWRIGHT?

Why somebody becomes a playwright instead of a novelist or a poet is something of a mystery. There is a germ of truth in the idea that playwrights often start out to be something else. But then, many theatre people start out as something else—directors as actors or stage managers, agents as designers or actors. Perhaps there is a difference in that so often playwrights start out to be something quite outside the theatre. It has often been observed that much of the vitality of new movements in theatre comes from the entry into it of people from entirely outside the theatre who then write a play or plays. The germ of the mystery is why they decide to write that play.

The answer lies in the nature of the playwright's craft: creating replicas of human action rather than records of it (novels) or responses to it (poems).

Outside the mainstream, the theatre has been very tolerant of forms, length of plays, and styles radically different from those in vogue in the mainstream; that is, what would be "bad plays" by mainstream definition may be welcome outside the mainstream. In fact, a case can be made for saying that the newcomer's strength lies in ignorance; lacking knowledge of the "rules" of mainstream playwriting, the new-comer writes in a new and refreshing way. The first plays of playwrights as widely different as Molière and Edward Albee illustrate this "strength of ignorance," and it is no accident that in both cases the early plays were very short, for the newcomer is unwittingly innovative when creating what is there to be created and then stopping, without regard for the so-called full-length entertainment of mainstream practice. It is when, then, a newcomer has an idea for what we have called a "replica of human action," however slight and however short, that a playwright is in the making. When

FIGURE 6-1. The Playwright as Player: Molière. Like Shakespeare, Molière was an actor as well as a playwright. Many scholars believe that his acting was an important contributor to his playwriting.

the newcomer is brought by luck or design into contact with a theatre and theatre people, plays get written.

It is not an accident that new playwrights often appear in bunches. Whether they are the University Wits of the Elizabethan period or the Off-Off-Broadway playwrights of the early 1960s, they are drawn to playwriting by the same theatrical conditions at the same time—in the case of the University Wits, the explosion of theatrical interest in Oxford and London; in the case of the Off-Off-Broadway playwrights, the explosion of theatrical excitement in the cafés of New York City.

Other factors are, of course, important. A dying or dead theatre rarely attracts new playwrights; a vital one does—and, paradoxically, a vital commercial one attracts them both to itself and to its avant-garde opposite. Money is often an important factor, as is social status. It is sometimes argued, for example, that the English theatre did not attract would-be playwrights in the eighteenth century because the licensing laws made the craft financially unattractive, and many turned to the novel instead. When, on the other hand, a theatre offers large financial rewards, as the American theatre did from the 1920s to the 1950s, many new writers are drawn to it.

A theatre's ability to attract new playwrights is one measure of its own health. The American theatre of the last twenty years, by this standard, has not been a healthy one. Despite several attempts to attract new talent—including, most of all, university playwriting degree programs—results have not been impressive.

FIGURE 6-2. **The Playwright and the Play: Friedrich Schiller.** Below, a sketch for the Romantic
playwright's *Maria Stuart* by the important early
producer, the Duke of Saxe-Meiningen.

TRAINING AND THE CRAFT

Playwrights are neither born nor made; they happen. Unlike actors and directors, they do not, as a rule, go through structured periods of formal training to perfect their art. To be sure, there are playwriting programs in American universities, but their record of producing playwrights who write plays of recognized quality is not comparable with the impressive records in acting, direction, and design. Courses in playwriting often familiarize theatre students with the problems of the playwright and give an enriching new slant on the other areas of theatre work; advanced degrees in playwriting are frequently combined with scholarly work in such a way that play-writing becomes an adjunct of critical study. Playwriting as an academic discipline, however, suffers from the same problems as creative writing in general, and when it seems to produce results it is because the same factors are at work: teachers who are themselves artists and who teach as much by example as by precept; constant encouragement of creativity itself, so that the student is surrounded by other writers and playwrights; and strong professional links with agents, producers, and publishers, so that entry into the mainstream is greatly eased.

This is not to say that playwriting can be neither learned nor taught. Certain supposed "rules" can always be taught. And when a theatrical style remains in vogue for a long period, playwrights can be "taught" the hallmarks of that style, meaning really that they can be taught how to imitate the plays that have already succeeded in that style. Thus, in the realistic theatre, would-be playwrights could be taught to put exposition into the mouths of characters who had a reason for explaining things; they could be taught to prepare for the third-act resolution by planting information about it in Act I; they could be taught that taxi drivers and duchesses do not speak in the same way; and so on. Insofar, then, as playwriting is a craft, such teaching was and still can be effective. Its limitations lie in the difference between the craft and the art of writing for the theatre and between the imitation of an existing style and the innovation of a new one (the newcomer's "gift of ignorance").

As well, when imitation of an existing style has been wanted, playwrights have frequently come from within the theatre. They are "people of the theatre" who are "theatre-wise." What is really meant is that they have familiarity with a particular style. Thus, the actor Molière could become a playwright when he wanted a vehicle for himself in the mode of the day.

When imitation of an existing style has not been the principal object, however, playwrights have often come from totally unexpected directions, and their practice of the craft has been radically different (and has been much pounded by critics; indeed, the work of such newcomers is most often called "not really a play" by reviewers, which is often a way of saying that the work in question is not an imitation of the dominant style). Most often, when newcomers have a very strong impulse to say something in the theatre, however, they do not take kindly to an imitation of the existing style, because styles that have dominated for a long time become increasingly drained of their potential for saying something new. Consequently, we sometimes find newcomers doing really remarkable things—flying in the face of established practice, writing "nonplays," being viewed with derision by mainstream professional and critic alike.

FIGURE 6-3. **The Playwright and the Play: Eliza Anderson.** Anderson won the playwriting award at the 1990 American College Theatre Festival in Washington; below, a scene from her play, *The Lower Rooms. (Courtesy of ACTF and Brown University.)*

In our own time, this separation has been spectacularly true of both black and feminist playwrights. Both groups have been deeply committed to a view that by its very nature has rejected some aspects of mainstream practice, and both groups have been made up of people who feel personally rejected and who, more often than not, *are* rejected by the mainstream. The black plays of the 1960s, therefore, were called "crude," "naive," and so on, just as were the feminist plays of the 1970s. Both groups of playwrights found audiences, however—obviously an essential for any new playwright—and their successes with those audiences, being noted by the mainstream, caused some of the playwrights to be adopted or co-opted into the mainstream. As a result, what had been "crude" and "naive" and "not a play" became "experimental" and "new." In such a way are some playwrights' careers shaped; others find success by careful adherence to tradition and established form.

Since the 1960s, new playwrights have increasingly come from outside the dominant (white, middle-class, male) culture. What we have called "existing style" is, after all, the acceptable expression of a dominant culture. As American society encouraged pluralism (through, for example, antidiscrimination laws), the theatre accepted more pluralism of subject matter (feminism, black and Latino issues) but has accepted little change in the existing style of its commercial mainstream.

PLAYWRIGHT AND AUDIENCE

"The drama's laws/The drama's patrons give," Samuel Johnson wrote in the eighteenth century. The remark illustrates the uneasy relationship between the playwright and the audience, for, to the playwright, the audience is a fickle monster that can make the artist either rich and loved or humiliated and poor. Between playwright and audience exists a relationship that is often ambivalent in the extreme.

Johnson's remark should remind us, too, that the playwright and the critic not only take a quite different view of the "laws" of the drama but also are frequently indifferent to each other. Not all critics, to be sure, set about to define the "laws" of the drama, but many do; yet while they are doing so, the playwrights are listening not to them but to themselves or to the audience. In fact, innovative playwrights frequently work apart from or even in opposition to the "laws" of the moment, and what they write is written according to a set of "laws" that are yet to be discovered. Thus, it is a mistake to think that playwrights pursue their craft by listening to critics. Very few do. Probably they often should, but most do not. Many playwrights would insist that they do not because they are themselves the makers of the drama's laws. In fact, they are not. They are artists, who neither make rules nor observe them; they make windows, as it were, through which the landscape of dramatic law can be glimpsed.

The relationship between playwright and audience is rather different. Audiences do not care for the laws of drama either. They care for their own responses. They are, however, often conservative and cautious. When they go to a theatre, they want to get their money's worth, and they seldom want to be lectured at, shocked, frightened, or bored. They do not want to suffer either heart attacks or fits of yawning.

FIGURE 6-4. The Playwright and the Play: Royall Tyler. America's first successful professional playwright was a Vermonter; below, a musical version of his play *The Contrast* at the University of Vermont, directed by Edward J. Feidner, designed by Nancy J. Haynes. (*Portrait courtesy of the Vermont Historical Society.*)

As a result, they look with enthusiasm on any novelty that imitates what they are familiar with.

This attitude leaves many playwrights in a quandary. They are all right if they are content to do hackwork—but few are, and even those who are successful hacks dream of one day having an artistic hit. Consequently, the majority of playwrights find themselves caught between their own urge to create and their audience's demand that they imitate what has already been done.

The new playwright may at first write plays that attract only a small audience, but the playwright will be encouraged if even a small audience is supportive, finding that it responds to the newness of the work. After a small initial success, the playwright may move toward the mainstream; an audience may be moving toward the playwright at the same time, both being the product of historical change. Sometimes, audiences accept new language, new ideas, and new forms with a speed that is startling. If the moment is not right, however, the playwright may not find an audience, may not even find production, and then will stop writing.

Once established, the American playwright enjoys one or more years of acceptance and then, more often than not, begins to lose the audience. Yesterday's innovator becomes tomorrow's has-been. Rare is the contemporary playwright who is a lifelong success, even a lifelong presence in the theatre; most reach a plateau and then seem to imitate themselves or to decline. One American playwright estimated that an Off-Broadway or Broadway career lasts ten years.

A few playwrights, however, hold their audiences and grow with them. They are the masters of their theatres—playwrights of lasting and secure power.

THE PLAYWRIGHT'S COMPROMISE

In the realistic theatre, playwrights have had to strike a balance between their own impulse to expand meaning and the stage's impulse to limit meaning to the same role that it plays in life. For earlier playwrights, language was a primary means of theatrical communication, and realistic plays about upper-class life could be heavily verbal because the people they were about were (or so it was believed) articulate and literate. However, as the theatre focused more on inarticulate protagonists in a democratized theatre, verbalism became a less useful tool and playwrights found themselves trying to find a compromise between their own impulse to "say" things and their characters' inability to say much of anything.

This example illustrates the kind of compromise that playwrights have always made. In the early nineteenth century, it was a compromise with the pyrotechnical needs of Romantic acting and the needs of Romantic scenery; for Molière, it was a compromise with the moral and literary proprieties of an autocratic society; for Euripides, it was a compromise with tradition and established, even ritualized, form. No playwright escapes the awareness that there must be a compromise between the creative impulse and the conditions of the theatre of the time (i.e., the culture of the dominant audience).

The theatre has two characteristics that do not belong to other arts (except, perhaps, film—whose compromises are often even more severe). First, it is an art in which the need to provide a frame for the arts of acting and design must be met;

and second, it is a public art, subject to both a legal and a social censorship that the novel, the poem, and the essay do not know. Satisfying the first of these requirements—providing a structure for actor and designer—is not a compromise but a basic quality in writing plays. Satisfying the second—whether it is meeting the stylistic demands of realism or the moralistic demands of censorship—requires a compromise that playwrights make only with reluctance. Pressures of censorship, however, seem to be on the rise—to temper language, to avoid certain subjects (AIDS, abortion), to offend no one.

THE PLAYWRIGHT IN THE REAL WORLD

Plays begin as a great variety of things: a story overhead, a chance remark, a note jotted down on a slip of paper. There are as many beginnings of plays, probably, as there are playwrights: some begin with an idea, some with a character, some with a situation, some with a story. And from that beginning, different playwrights take widely different tracks: some write detailed outlines, some write none: some write hundreds of pages of dialogue, some put down on paper no more than will appear in the finished play. One way or another, however, the play is written—over a period of days, months, or even years—and then its real life begins, for a play on paper is only a long step toward a theatre performance, holding the promise of life instead of life itself.

Getting the Play Produced

In recent years, the number of theatres in which new plays can be produced in the United States and Canada has increased noticeably. Many plays now begin their lives in regional theatres; in addition, organizations like the National Playwright's Conference of the O'Neill Theatre Center give first productions to a wide spectrum of scripts, many of which are later produced elsewhere. New York, however, remains the goal of most playwrights. There are two reasons: money and status. Broadway royalties are far higher than anywhere else, and Broadway production is subject to the best reviewing and is the most prestigious.

Plays are not produced at any of these theatres by accident. Nor are many new plays that attract widespread attention (except at an institution like the O'Neill Center) scripts that come out of nowhere. Most are submitted to regional theatres or Broadway or Off-Broadway producers by agents. Far less often, a play may reach a producer by way of an actor or a director. In any case, the playwright's first high hurdle is finding that first production, whatever the medium used to reach a producing organization.

The Playwright and the Theatre

Producers have readers who read scripts and make comments. When a script is accepted for production, it already has an accompanying list of such comments as well as the producer's own views; added to these will be the ideas of the director when one is chosen. Each principal actor will add ideas, and each of these people—producer, director, actors—may have still other ideas that have come from friends, wives, lovers, and relatives. The playwright having a first play done is tempted to try to please everybody. By the time several plays have been done, however, the playwright may be downright rude about suggestions coming from any source at all. Between these two extremes lies the kernel of the playwright's work during the production period: accepting ideas for changes that are wisely based in the unique circumstances of the production. Perhaps regrettably, in the modern American theatre the director is assumed to have considerable critical skill and to be an expert in everything from dramatic structure to dialogue. Changes in a script, however, are rarely simple; as the Broadway playwright William Gibson said some years ago, altering a play is like taking bricks out of a wall: for every one that is taken out, half a dozen others have to be put back. At times, the playwright wonders what it was about the play that ever caused people to want to do it, because they have asked for so many changes that nothing seems to be left of the original. Confronted with this situation, the playwright may throw a temper tantrum, go home, or say, as more than one successful Broadway playwright has, "Do it as it is!"

The Economics of Playwriting

A few playwrights do make livings, especially as the number of regional theatres has multiplied, but the hit-or-flop life of Broadway still prevails; the playwright can still make only a killing, rarely a living. Standard Broadway contracts, under the aegis of the Dramatists Guild, give the playwright a percentage of the theatre's weekly gross, a percentage that climbs as the gross climbs past certain plateaus. On a hit, these figures can be impressive—thousands of dollars a week. On a modest success, they can be a thousand a week or less. On a flop, nothing. Considering that few playwrights have a successful play every year, we can easily see that the income from even a hit

FIGURE 6-5. The Playwright's Profession: Making a Living. This "author's benefit" ticket for an eighteenth-century play gave admission to a performance from which the author got a share of the profit.

must be spread over several years, and that after an agent's commission and professional expenses and taxes are taken out, the prorated remainder may be less than many businesspeople take home. There are, of course, the significant additional income of film and television sales—and perhaps most importantly, there is the secondary income of amateur and stock production.

Amateur rights are handled mostly by two organizations, the Dramatists Play Service and Samuel French, Incorporated. They collect royalties on productions by amateurs (community, school, and university theatres) for the life of the play's copyright—since the Copyright Law of 1977, the author's life plus fifty years. Although the royalty on a single performance of a play is small, the collective royalty per year on a play that is popular with the nation's several thousand community and college theatres can be large, and even plays that fail on Broadway can become staples of amateur theatre and go on providing income for decades.

Yet, with all this, relatively few people make a living as playwrights. It is a difficult craft that requires special talent, and it is made far more difficult by the conditions under which plays must find production. Many potential playwrights now move to television and film, and there is some question whether —despite grants, theatres, and organizations that encourage new plays—playwrights may continue to decline in number until the theatre itself recovers its vigor.

CHAPTER SEVEN

THE ACTOR

The actor stands at the center of the theatre. The actor is its linchpin, its keystone; witout him or her, there is nothing—an empty building, a hollow space. Directors cannot direct nor designers design without actors; the playwright can create only works to be read like novels.

The actor alone can make theatre without the help of other artists. The plays that the actor invents may not be very good, it is true, and they may even be merely stories told well (as in oral cultures, when the storyteller is an actor-narrator). The actor can make costumes, can build a theatre, and can provide at least crude scenery for it. At a level of development that can be identified in several periods, we see just such an actor and just such a primitive theatre: the plays improvised or crudely crafted, the costumes emblematic of the craft of acting rather than of a character (as a circus clown's is, for example), the stage a platform with a curtain behind it instead of elaborate scenery. Out of such an actor-intensive theatre may occasionally grow a sophisticated one, such as the *commedia dell'arte* of Renaissance Italy (see p. 275). More often, however, such an actors' theatre changes in the direction of the theatre that we know, adding playwright, designer, and director. No matter how far this theatre develops, however, it remains the descendant of that primal theatre—actor-centered.

We often identify the greatness of certain ages in the theatre with the names of plays and playwrights, when in fact what we are doing is identifying great ages not of theatre but of drama. Plays survive and are easier to recapture than that ephemeral Now, the actor's performance. The existence of great plays from fifth-century B.C.

Greece, Elizabethan England, or seventeenth-century France should not cause us to forget that these were also great ages of acting. It is no accident that Sophocles, Shakespeare, and Molière were actors as well as dramatists.

We cannot have great plays without actors, but we can have great acting without plays.

THE PARADOX OF THE ACTOR

The French theorist Denis Diderot (1713–1784) used the expression "the paradox of the actor" as the title for an essay on acting, in which he tried to capture what seems to be an essential contradiction in the art: in order to appear natural, the actor must be artificial.

This contradiction takes several forms, whose language and whose specifics change from age to age; nevertheless, the paradox remains at the center of most thinking about the art.

Natural Versus Artificial

One of the things to be learned from a study of the history of acting is that almost every change in acting for the mainstream theatre has been seen as an improvement of the "natural" or the "real." Partly, changes in philosophy are at work, for the idea of "natural" and "real" human behavior is one of the root concerns of philosophy. When an age's idea of "what it is to be human" changes, the manner of depicting human beings on the stage changes as well, and what is typical of the older concept is viewed as outdated and "nonhuman"—that is, artificial.

However, there is a distinction to be made as well between the idea of what humanity is and the idea of what humans might or should be. Certain ages and certain forms of theatre have prized an idea of humanity that was sometimes rigidly defined in its behaviors; such an idea of humanity sets up many "proprieties"—rules based on the ideal—that must be observed. On the stage, elegance of diction, grace of movement, and limitation of gesture may become almost moral issues, and we find such extremes of stage propriety as the "rule" that the left hand must never be used for an important gesture. Such a strictly limited kind of acting will seem highly "artificial" to anybody who believes that the stage must imitate life explicitly, and what will seem "natural" will then be a kind of acting that does not stay within the proprieties. Much of the conflict between French and English acting in the eighteenth century and between Neoclassical and Romantic acting in the early nineteenth century arose from precisely this difference. The "artificial" actor in such a dispute would see the greatest allegiance to the rules of the theatre, based on an ideal and not on a literal concept of "what it is to be human"; the "natural" actor would see the greatest allegiance as being to life—or to an interpretation of life. Neither idea is better than the other, although bitter battles have been fought over their differences.

FIGURE 7-1. **Early Greek Actors.** This copy of a Greek original seems to show both chorus and actors with masks and costumes for a satyr play.

Technique Versus Inspiration

Our own age is one whose theatrical heritage is primarily a "natural" one, at least in the realistic theatre. Modern American actors sometimes speak disparagingly of an actor who is "technical," meaning one who builds character out of careful, conscious use of body and voice—meticulously rehearsed inflections, carefully chosen poses and gestures, and so on. Their belief is that "technical" actors work mechanically and so fail to bring imagination and life to their work. The technical actor is seen as "full of tricks." Again, there is a strong belief that "technique" is somehow an enemy of the convincing, the lifelike, the believable.

At the far extreme from the technical actor is the "inspirational" one, whose work, although carefully rehearsed, is not assembled from external behaviors but is created through application of mental and emotional techniques that supposedly work to reach the actor's emotional and mental center and then somehow push outward into onstage movement and vocalization. In theory, the character created by the inspirational actor will be more "real," more "natural" because it does not rise from conscious intellectual work but from the inner sources that also give rise to music and poetry. To the inspirational actor, the approach is fresh and the creation original and not stereotyped.

Inner and Outer

Technical and inspirational acting have their direct counterparts in "outer" and "inner" acting. As one actor put it some years ago, "I like to build my house first—then I start to live in it." She meant that she liked to create the "outer" part of the role; then, comfortable with that—voice, posture, costume, gesture—she could move inward toward emotional intensity and conviction, believably "living in" the shell she had created.

Other actors work from the inside out. All of their early work will be devoted to mental, emotional, and spiritual exploration. Only when that work is completed do they feel that an outer structure can be built. In the cases of both the "inner" and the "outer" actor, truth to the character is being sought, and the difference is really a difference of emphasis and of sequence. The "inner–outer" distinction is not quite the same as the "technical–inspirational" one; the "technical" actor's work begins and ends with externals, whereas the "outer" actor's work finally leads inward, and the "inner" actor's work leads toward externals in a way that the "inspirational" actor's does not. Inspiration supposedly gives rise to externals through a nonintellectual leap, and, as Diderot suggested, those externals can vary from performance to performance and may supply only an occasional "sublime moment."

Being and Pretending

To reach emotional truth, it has been said, the actor must *be* the character; on the contrary, another point of view insists, the actor must always stand aloof from the character and *pretend*. Here is precisely the paradox that Diderot observed. If an actor were really to be the character, how would he or she control onstage behavior? What would keep the actor from becoming inaudible at times? What would keep the actor, as Othello, from actually killing the actor who plays Desdemona? What would cause the actor to modulate the voice, control the tempo of a performance, listen to other actors? And, contrarily, if the actor always pretends, what will he or she be but a lifeless imitation of humanity, a puppet, a windup toy? How will the actor keep the speeches from sounding like empty nonsense? How will gestures be anything but graceful hand-waving?

Because the actor is at the center of the theatre, this paradox is the paradox of the theatre itself: in order to be convincing, one must lie. The actor both "is" *and* "pretends," exploiting both inner and outer, both technique and inspiration. It is never enough for the *actor* to be satisfied that a sigh or a smile is perfectly truthful; the sigh or smile must also have the carrying power and the communicative value to be perfectly truthful *to the audience*.

The two halves of the paradox of the actor are always in tension. Their relative strengths vary from actor to actor and from age to age. It is only rarely that a really good actor will be found at either extreme.

THE ACTOR AND THE ROLE

It should now be clear that actors do not create real human beings, on the one hand, nor do they somehow transform themselves and erase their own personalities utterly. Instead they engage in a creative act whose end product is a *construct*, that is, an entity made by human agency for a particular purpose. Both the actor and the audience must be very careful to remember that the creation *is* a construct and not a full-fleshed, living human being, for all that actors and audiences may speak of the construct by its name, just as if it were a real person named Hamlet. The construct remains an invention, and one actor's construct may be quite different from another's construct of the same name—Laurence Olivier's from Kevin Kline's Hamlet, for example. In the literary sense, character is a construct that represents human personality and that expresses itself through *action*. In the sense of the word used by Aristotle, the effectiveness of a character depends on how well it fits into the narrative

Charlotte and Susan Cushman.

FIGURE 7-2. **The Actor and the Role: Charlotte Cushman.** The greatest of American actors in the nineteenth century, Cushman often played male roles (here, Romeo, with her sister Susan as Juliet). This suppression of gender was one of the prices of stardom, where her competitors at the top were all men.

whole and affects plot. This idea has an important implication for the actor: we define character on the basis of the function within the artistic whole and *not merely on the basis of how well it imitates a human being.* Therefore, a dramatic construct may be a convincing imitation of human being in its superficial attributes—it may talk like one and may have preferences in clothes and food and entertainment like one— and yet it may be a "bad" character in that it makes no important contribution to the artistic whole and the action. An actor who concentrates on mannerisms of the character and fails to grasp the character's function as contributor to the action will fail and will be guilty of what the Russian actor and theorist Stanislavski called "tendencies."

For the actor, *character* means something like "the imitation of a human being as it expresses itself through the words and the decisions created by the author, *in relation to the other characters in the play and their decisions and words.*" The actor's character exists on the stage (only) and has no life off the stage; the actor's character exists in an artificial time scheme that is quite different from the time scheme of real life. It is helpful for the actor to figure out where the character is coming from when it walks on the stage, what it has been doing, and so on, but such analysis has to be limited strictly to conclusions relevant to onstage action and onstage time or it will lead to sideshows and tendencies, or even to the creation of a play that the author never wrote (and one that, regrettably for the audience, takes place offstage).

The actor is a person; the character is a construct. In order for the character to *seem* to be a person during the two or three hours of performance, the actor must use parts of his or her own real self, observations of other people, and sheer invention and imagination.

The Whole Actor

In approaching character, actors bring three aspects of themselves to the task. We can identify these three parts of the actor's creative self as:

1. *The actor's consciousness.* Several components of successful acting are conscious. Primary among these are *concentration, selectivity,* and *analysis.* Without *concentration,* the actor might at times dissolve into neurotic collapse, haunted by personal problems that would destroy the work. What can be noted about successful actors is the astonishing degree of concentration that they bring to their task. "The show must go on" is a cliché, but it does describe the good actor's tenacious ability to continue when the physical or emotional self is hurt or threatened.

Selectivity is the ability to discriminate among possible solutions to an acting problem. (The process is more or less conscious in different actors.) Choices may be as simple as between two qualities of voice for a word or line or as complex as identification of a memory, among many memories, from which an emotion springs. Often, there is no one correct answer in such a selection; there is one that may work best for a particular actor in trying to illuminate a certain moment of a performance. It is because of this selectivity that actors so often experiment, trying, rejecting, and trying again with different voices, gestures, and rhythms. To an outsider, an actor's process in creating a character often seems slow, repetitive, and aimless. Even in

FIGURE 7-3. **The Actor's Life.** Professional photographs and a resume of the actor Ruth Ann Phimister. In postcard sizes, with a telephone answering-service number, the photos are sent to agents, producers, and casting directors as reminders; page-size photos, usually with the resume on the back, are sent whenever a role is being sought or the actor wants to introduce herself. Actors need hundreds, sometimes thousands of them—a significant professional expense.

RUTH ANN PHIMISTER
AEA/SAG/AFTRA

5'7"   126 lbs.
Hair & Eyes: Brown

REGIONAL THEATRE/DINNER THEATRE

LIFE WITH FATHER	Carousel Dinner Theatre	*Cora (u.s. Vinnie)*
CRIMES OF THE HEART	Florida Studio Theatre	*Meg*
ABSENT FRIENDS		*Evelyn*
THE HEIRESS	Clarence Brown Company	*Mrs. Montgomery*
A STREETCAR NAMED DESIRE	South Carolina Summer Rep.	*Blanche*
TARTUFFE		*Elmire*
MOTHER GOOSE ON THE LOOSE		*Mother Goose*
THE CRACKER FACTORY	Anstie's Limit, S.C.	*Cassie*
EDGE OF DEATH		*Emily*
TWO WOMEN/FURNITURE		*Woman*
PRIVATE LIVES	Hiers Dinner Theatre, S.C.	*Amanda*
THE ODD COUPLE	Plaza Dinner Theatre, Tx.	*Cecily*

NEW YORK THEATRE COMPANIES

THE LAST SUPPER	Northern Lights Theatre Co.	*Monica*
ON THE ROCKS	The Shaw Project	*Lady Chavender*
SIX OF CALAIS		*Philippa*
DOMESTICITY OF FRANKLIN BARNABAS		*Clara*
MACHINAL	Roundabout Ensemble Company	*Multi-characters*
LIONS OF THE HILL		*Bridget*
A-BOMB BEAUTIES	Playmarket	*Helen*
EMERGENCY EXIT		*Nightingale*
COMRADES	American Folk Theatre	*Karen*
BABIES		*Irene*
INTELLIGENCE	American Place Theatre	*Shelley*
THE JAR	Manhattan Plaza	*Louise*
JUST THINK IT OVER, GIACOMINO	Theatre of the Ethical Culture	*Rosario*
MORNING'S AT SEVEN (Bus&Truck)	Edgewood Organization	*Myrtle, Arry (u.s.)*

FILM/TELEVISION/RADIO

NEW YORK STORIES	Woody Allen Segment	*Stand-in for Julie Kavner*
FILM ON COUNTY GOVERNMENT	University of S.C. ITV	*Susan*
FEELINGS	PBS Pilot for Dr. Lee Salk	*Teacher*
THE CUSTOMER IS ALWAYS RIGHT	South Carolina Educational TV	*Runner*
A DOLL'S HOUSE	South Carolina Educational TV	*Kristine*
CRIME TO COURT		*D.A.*
HERE WE ARE		*She*
REQUIEM FOR A NUN	South Carolina Educational Radio	*Temple*

COMMERCIALS: On camera and voiceover experience on request.
  SOUNDS LIKE RUTH ANN: Voiceover tape on request.

their conscious work, however, actors do not proceed as scientists might proceed, and often they are still trying to frame a creative question while already searching for the answer, because the conscious process is so highly complex. The guidance of the director is of enormous importance here, of course, and the same outside observer who wondered why the actor seemed to work so slowly might also wonder why the director asked the actor so many questions; the answer is that the director is trying to help the actor to frame questions and to select the best answers to them.

Analysis is the element of the actor's consciousness that deals with the reading of the dramatic text on its first level—breaking it into units and understanding its complex inner relationships. The analytic element is exercised throughout the pre-rehearsal, rehearsal, and performance periods by actors who are determined to perfect their understanding and interpretation of the script and of their characters.

2. *The actor's instrument.* By the *instrument* we mean the entire physical self that the actor uses in playing a character; it is conveniently separated into body and voice. Whereas the audience does not see or hear the work of the consciousness or the imagination directly, it always sees and hears the instrument, for the instrument is the medium through which the others express themselves.

The "external" or "artificial" or "technical" actor might appear, at first glance, to be the one who makes the most conscious use of the instrument. However, this association of the instrument with the externals of acting is at least partly an appearance and not a reality. The properly trained actor of any method will make the maximum use of body and voice, because without them the consciousness and the imagination are strangled. What the bad actor of any method will do, however, is use *learned* instrumentation—"tricks," clichés, personal mannerisms—rather than instrumentation that springs from creative understanding of the character and the play.

The instrument is given to the actor. What is given can be developed, and good teaching can do wonderful things to improve voices and the use of bodies; the fact remains that the size and shape of bones, the delicate tuning of vocal mechanisms, and the size and shape of the body are in large part given at birth. "Talent" does not consist of having a beautiful face or a beautiful voice, or even of having a body and voice that are flexible and expressive without training. Insofar as "talent" applies to the instrument, it consists of making maximum use of what is given and of recognizing its strengths and its limitations.

3. *The actor's imagination.* Within the actor's mental and emotional self lies the wellspring of creativity: the imagination. It is the force that impels all creativity, working often in images rather than in rational discourse, surfacing into the consciousness unpredictably, frequently working while the rest of the organism sleeps. In all fields, including science, great and original ideas and creations have come while the conscious mind rested or actually slept: "I woke up with the problem solved," or "It came to me in a dream," has been a common story for millennia. Sometimes the imagination works while the conscious mind is "at rest" because of a condition other than sleep; the disassociation used in marathon running, for example, has given rise to the solutions to problems, and other such irrational "leaps" have come through yoga and other meditative disciplines.

FIGURE 7-4. **Instrument and Imagination.** Only through training and experience can the actor express the full range of movements and sounds inspired by the imagination. *Angel Street*, directed by Laurence Carr, designed by P. Gibson Ralph, at the University of Rochester Summer Theatre.

Contemporary psychology and physiology now suggest that the "lateral hemispheric specialization" of the brain may play a large part in what we call the actor's imagination. Recent findings indicate that the right and left halves of the normal brain have separate but interconnected functions, the left dealing with logic and language, and the right with image, metaphor, pictures, and music. Early training "teaches" the brain to mute the signals coming into the consciousness from the right half (probably because language and logic are vitally important to European and American culture); it may be this muting that causes us to see the imagination as irrational, mysterious, and hidden. The muted or "hidden" quality is also the reason for the many exercises used in actor training and rehearsal to penetrate years of habit in order to help the actor to work directly with the imagination. It is as if, in early life, we learned to erect shields around the imagination—the work of the right half of the brain—and to lower those shields only in sleep and altered states of consciousness; then, as adults, we must learn new techniques to penetrate them or to lower them for creative work.

Imagination is the key that opens the door to memory, itself a rich source of the actor's understanding and playing of character. Imagination is also the function that processes nonrational data (from such sources as the text, the creative work of other actors and the director, the setting and costumes) and that gives back new understanding of play and character. It is the function that gives the actor an understanding of stage space and the body's relation to it. It is the source of whatever is new, particular, and magical in performance, for it is unique to the individual actor, and its nonrational "leaps" are like the working of magic. Yet, because it comes from a part of the brain that does not process data rationally, it is held suspect by purely rational people; in an age that considers itself rational, imagination in acting is suspect and is made to give way to the more understandable, visible process of analysis. Conversely, when a society permits extensive inner searching and is familiar with such searching through its own religion and thought, an acting that relies perhaps excessively on the imagination may result, and such acting may, like the workings of the right half of the brain, lack the logical, communicable links to the external world that make most performances understandable to the audience. The result in such a case might be a performance that could be called "novel" or "original" but that is beyond comprehension.

The successful actor, then, effectively uses consciousness, imagination, and instrument in balance. The conscious mind analyzes the playscript and the "conditions of performance" and translates that information into a form usable by both the instrument and the imagination. Even as they work, however, the consciousness continues to analyze and to shape and change its findings; at the same time, the decisions and findings of the imagination are communicated directly, along with the decisions of the consciousness, to the instrument. The complexity of the process is virtually beyond description—and, in fact, it is not adequately understood by either scientists or artists. Perhaps it is enough for our purposes to suggest that if we seek

FIGURE 7-5. **Imagination.** The compelling but artificial "truth" of the stage is a product, in part, of the actor's imagination. David H. Hwang's *Dance and the Railroad*, directed by Roberta Uno Thelwell, designed by Sarah Stauderman. (*Courtesy of New WORLD Theatre, the University of Massachusetts, Amherst.*)

to define the word *talent* in acting, we do so by looking at this three-way, continuing, constantly shifting interchange. Talent, we may be able to say, is the ability of the consciousness to inspire in the imagination a set of actions and sounds that the instrument can express to an audience as theatrical character, excitingly and brilliantly.

Acting and Performing

A full-fledged talent for acting cannot be thought of merely as an ability to entertain well in public—to clown at parties or to tell jokes superbly. The latter are parts of a talent for *performing*—that is, for reaching and delighting an audience without regard to character or theatrical action. As we have already tried to suggest, there is more to acting than this. A good actor, of course, is also a good performer; a good performer, however, may not be a very good actor.

Some kinds of theatre or the related arts put a higher premium on performing than on acting; circus high-wire work, for example, requires great performers and has no use for actors. Musical comedy, on the other hand, requires both acting and performing, but the ability to "sell" a song requires performing of a high level. Because performers must often play themselves, strong performers who act theatrical roles sometimes have difficulty, or they so overpower the dramatic character that it is obscured. In star-oriented theatres, productions are sometimes thrown out of balance by the casting of famous performers who are so habituated to playing themselves that they cannot or will not break out of that pattern.

Performing must not be confused with external or artificial acting, which may seem like performing because of its planned and deliberate gestures, and its sometimes exaggerated vocal effects. External acting, however, focuses on communicating an idea of character in theatrical action; performing focuses on communicating the performer.

The performer plays *to* the audience; the actor plays the character *for* the audience.

THE PERSONALITY OF THE ACTOR

The personality of men and women who act has been a source of fascination for centuries. The actor has long been seen as a special sort of person; even before the Romantic interest in odd and exotic individuals, actors were studied because of their ability to interpret human psychology and because of their apparent ability to balance both halves of the "paradox of the actor." Too, a number of traditions came to surround the acting profession, and if they were not always accurate, they came to seem accurate as actors themselves believed in them: "all actors have to be crazy"; "all actors are immoral"; "the theatre attracts misfits and oddballs"; "actors like to show off"; and so on. Such ideas are no better than gossip until they are proved by objective standards, and for every immoral actor and show-off, there is an opposite to disprove the stereotype. Nonetheless, some of these old ideas persist.

Because of a lack of hard data and the persistence of stereotypes, we cannot

FIGURE 7-6. **The Actor's Life.** The great nine-teenth-century American actor Ira Aldrich, who, because he was black, spent most of his professional life in Europe and had a limited choice of roles. Here, as Aaron in Shakespeare's *Titus Andronicus.*

describe accurately the "personality of the actor." We might note the following, however:

The actor's profession puts him or her outside the mainstream of most lives, because actors work odd hours, work at a very high level of energy and concentration, and live a life of extreme professional and financial peril.

Part of the actor's reward is applause and other forms of audience approval, and a personality geared toward applause may be an insecure one; yet, to face tryout after tryout, opening after opening, show after show takes stamina and a courage unknown to men and women in secure careers.

The actor's personal relationships are easily threatened by unusual hours, job insecurity, and the need to be able to move geographically on short notice.

Because theirs is a high-stress life, actors are as subject to the allure of drugs and alcohol as the rest of the population, and perhaps more so.

The ability and desire to act, like all creative work, is "different," and the committed actor may be judged an outsider by the rest of society.

Thus, although we cannot draw a profile of a typical actor, we can point out some qualities that frequently occur. What must be clearly understood, however, is that the qualities that make a good actor—creativity, concentration, determination, stam-

FIGURE 7-7. **The Actor and His Culture.** The nineteenth-century American actor Thomas D. Rice as "Jim Crow," a black stereotype that gave a name to Southern segregation. Rice was white and played in blackface. In the case of Rice and Aldrich (Figure 7-6), it is easy to see how the theatre, both in roles and in the actors' lives, expresses its society—in this case, racialism.

ina, access to the imagination, playfulness, the ability to cope with rejection, non-rational thinking, and detailed emotional memory—should be kept separate from qualities that may appear because of the *profession* of acting and its stresses; in other words, the nature of the profession in our society may bring out behavior that is not typical of the art of acting but of our society's use of it. Thus, the "personality of the actor" has to be a composite of those qualities that make up talent and those qualities that appear in response to the environment in which talent is used.

ACTOR TRAINING

Although there are supposedly actors who are "born," and although there have been young children who were talented actors, it is a fact of theatrical life that all actors must train long and hard and must refresh that training throughout their careers.

Actor training does not refer to a specific kind of study or to a set period of time. Acting is taught in hundreds of colleges and universities, for example, and degrees in acting are granted by many of them, but the chronological length of such programs and the granting of degrees does not mean that the actors are through training when the degrees are given. In the final analysis, every actor's training is special to him or her, and its length will be different from the training periods of other actors.

There are a number of actor-training systems. The most influential in the United States and Canada are those based on the ideas of Konstantin Stanislavski. Other systems have very different foundations, such as the psychological theory of transactional analysis or the theory of games and improvisations. Different as these are, they are helpful in varying degrees to different actors. *No one system is best for everybody.* The important thing about these systems is that they organize the work of the actor's consciousness, instrument, and imagination. Without a workable system, the would-be actor makes progress only randomly, repeating mistakes and often making bad habits worse. With a workable system, the actor finds the way out of this self-destructive cycle. A good system trains all three parts of the actor.

Preliminary Training

There was a time when would-be actors "came up" through a provincial and repertory system, moving from small roles in minor companies to larger roles and more important theatres. They learned by imitation and they learned by taking hints from experienced actors. Nowadays, most professional actors have formal training, either in a college or in one or more private studios. Each such institution uses a system, but most of them require some kind of preliminary training. Many young actors have trouble recognizing this preliminary work as part of acting, although it is essential. (In a college, such work usually comes in the freshman year.) Without it, most actors would not succeed. Partly, it is a process of *unlearning* mistaken notions and bad habits, and partly it is a process of training mind and body to adapt to the conditions of the theatre instead of the conditions of life (by learning, for example, that behavior that is considered ridiculous in life is sometimes essential in rehearsal and performance.)

It is usually thought to be unwise for beginning actors to go directly into the rehearsal and performance of plays or parts of plays—so-called scene work. Instead they are given preliminary training in the following areas:

Relaxation

Surprisingly, many people who want to learn to act are so tense that they are quite literally unable to act; that is, muscle tension inhibits or totally prohibits any creative use of the instrument. Physical tension causes sudden, random, or pathological movement (shaking, trembling) and dangerous misuse of the vocal mechanism. Tense actors may think of themselves as *intense* and not tense; without training, they have no way of telling the difference. They see themselves as "really into" a role, when the teacher or the audience sees nervous, confusing, and uncontrolled movement.

Relaxation exercises cover a broad range from disciplines as different as modern dance and yoga. All are intended to cause the consciousness to let go of the body, to return it to its natural state of receptiveness and awareness, and to make the body itself supple and loose.

Contact or Awareness

The relaxed body, freed from the tyranny of tension, becomes aware of itself and its environment. The consciousness no longer hurries it along toward some rigid goal; it has time, as it were, to stop and enjoy the scenery (including its own internal scenery). The coming and going of the breath, the comfortable positions of the body in standing, sitting, kneeling and lying, the sense of the nearness and farness of objects and people—these things and many more can be explored. Sensory awareness is raised, and exercises are given that can be repeated (throughout the actor's life, if necessary) to maintain or renew that awareness.

Contact with others can also be taught so that the beginning actor learns to relate to other people, to help them, and to accept the help that they offer. The accepting of such help is, perhaps surprisingly, very difficult for many beginners, probably because not asking for or accepting help is a habit brought in from life. Most of us are taught to be "self-reliant" and "independent," and our society prizes these qualities. However, the *self*-reliant actor is a menace. *Taking* and *giving* are the bases of good performance.

Centering

Many disciplines, among them Eastern meditative religions and some schools of modern dance, emphasize exercises that focus on a bodily center—that is, a core of balance and physical alignment, a place from which all movement and energy seem to spring. This idea of a center concerns both the body (balance, weight, and placement) and the voice (breathing and sound making). In yoga, the abdomen below the diaphragm is such a center; in the dance of Martha Graham, the center is slightly above the pelvis.

Centering leads the beginning actor away from the mistaken idea that the physical self is located in the head and the face, that the voice is located in the mouth and the throat, and that the physical relationship to the rest of the world is located, through gravity, in the feet; rather, the actor finds the center somewhere near the crossing point of an X of arms and legs—a center of gravity, a center of balance, a center of diaphragmatic breathing.

Play

Dramas are "plays"; actors are "players." Yet beginners are often anything but playful. A terrible intensity and a terrible seriousness rule the work. To counter this tendency, much of early training is spent reteaching people how to play, in the sense both of teaching them to play games and of teaching them to approach the creative act joyously. Because children often have this sense of playful theatricality in their own pastimes ("Let's pretend"), many theatre games are versions of children's games or of adult "parlor" games that are noncompetitive fun.

Training the Instrument

"Stage movement" and "voice production for the stage" sound like titles of academic courses. They suggest that the subject matter can be learned and that then, like familiarity with Shakespeare's plays or a knowledge of the calculus, they can be

FIGURE 7-8. **Training the Actor.** These early nineteenth-century illustrations show rather standardized poses and gestures, usually learned by apprenticeship or imitation, for communicating standardized emotional states: despair, painful recollection, sublime adoration. Modern actors would look upon them as "playing attitudes"—imitating a general state (despair) rather than playing a specific character in despair of a specific kind for specific reasons.

forgotten or assimilated. In actuality, the training of the instrument is a lifelong process.

Both body and voice use complicated sets of muscles put into action by the brain, sometimes consciously, sometimes unconsciously and habitually (for example, few of us have to remember to breathe). The actor has to be made aware of the muscles being used, has to improve the condition of the muscles, has to unlearn or relearn or learn a pattern of use of those muscles, has to repeat such patterns so often that they become habits, has to learn precisely what muscular actions will produce what results (sounds or movements), has to learn what combinations of commands and muscular sets will provide new, unusual, and effective sounds or movements. As well, the actor has to learn the "proper" application of certain kinds of voice (singing) and movement (fencing and dancing).

Body and Movement

The actor's body need not be heavily muscled, but it should be flexible, strong, and responsive. The actor does not train as an athlete does (one set of muscles would be developed at the expense of others); instead, the goal is *resistance to fatigue, quick responsiveness,* and *adaptive ability* (that is, the ability to imitate other kinds of posture and movement or to adapt movement to, for example, aged posture and movement or the posture and movement of a body much heavier). The actor also learns the following:

1. *Body language and nonverbal communication.* We all express our emotional states and our basic psychic orientations through *body language.* The actor learns to "move" the physical center to match that of the character. The actor also learns how all of

FIGURE 7-9. Movement. Fencing and various kinds of fighting are only a small part of the movement training of the complete actor. Aphra Behn's *The Feigned Courtesans, or A Night's Intrigue* at Macalester College, directed by Cynthia Goatley, designed by Daniel R. Keyser. *(Tom Nelson photo.)*

us communicate without words, through such simple gestures as the waving of a hand ("hello" or "come here" or "no thank you") to complex "statements" of posture and gesture that say things completely different from the words that pass our lips. Such training takes two forms: study of the subject (much of it still in the fields of psychology and anthropology) and application to the actor's body.

2. *Rhythmic movement.* Ballroom dancing, simple modern dance, disco dancing, and the like have the double advantage of being enjoyable and of helping the actor to move to an external rhythm.

3. *Period movement and use of properties.* Historically accurate, and theatrically effective, use of fans, canes, swords, shawls—the list is endless.

4. *Movement in costume.* Theatrically effective movement and gesture in wigs, capes, hoop-skirts, boots—again, the list is a long one.

5. *Movement onstage.* Traditional interior settings do not have walls that meet at the same angles as rooms, and so stage furniture in such settings is rarely angled as real furniture is. As a result, "crosses" (movements from one point onstage to another) take unreal routes. On the proscenium stage, actors must learn to "curve" crosses so that they end up on a line parallel to the curtain line with another actor (in this way, neither winds up speaking upstage into an acoustical well). On thrust and arena stages, the actor learns to play to all of the audience, to adapt posture and movement so that each section of the audience is treated fairly. Too, there are ways of bending, sitting, and standing that are appropriate to the stage in that they are not awkward or comical, although training in these "correct" ways of doing things is becoming more appropriate to training in period movement.

Voice Production

The human voice is a product of controlled muscular work and chamber resonance (head and chest). Its shaping and control are not simple. Nonetheless, we make sounds and shape them all the time—only to find that our everyday sounds are inadequate for the theatre because they cannot be heard, they cannot be understood, and they are unpleasant. Unlearning and relearning are necessary for most actors.

The human voice is produced when air is forced over the *vocal folds* or *cords*, causing them to vibrate and to set a column of air vibrating, producing sound. This sound induces vibrations in cavities in the head and in *bones* in the head and chest. The sound is shaped in the throat and mouth, primarily with the jaws and tongue and is further shaped into the sounds we call words by initiation of sound; interruption of sound by the interaction of lips, tongue, and teeth; and placement of sound through action of the lower jaw and of the tongue.

The actor trains the vocal mechanism for maximum control of *every word that is uttered*, as well as for the production of sounds that are not words.

Other voice and voice-production training covers:

1. *Breath control.* The principal source of the pressure that pushes air over the vocal folds is the *diaphragm*, a large muscle curved up under the lungs. When it flattens (downward), air is pulled in; when it releases (upward), air is pushed out.

Lesser muscles along the ribs and upper chest are not so important to proper breathing; many untrained people, however, are "chest breathers" whose diaphragms are little used. Chest breathing, without effective use of the diaphragm, limits capacity and control and, under the stress of making loud and extended sounds in a theatre, often tenses muscles and transmits that tension into the throat. *Diaphragmatic breathing* is as essential for the actor as for the singer, giving increased capacity and maximum control.

2. *Throat relaxation.* Tightness in the throat and the lower jaw is a source of common and severe voice problems. Muscular tightness there "chokes" the sound, restricting the vocal folds and closing up the resonating chambers. The actor learns to produce enormous volumes of sound without ever allowing the muscular effort in voice production to affect throat and jaw.

3. *Tongue and lip dexterity.* "Lazy tongue" is a common ailment; it produces slurred consonants and sloppy speech. Tongue twisters and other exercises tone the muscles and force actors to listen to the sounds they make.

4. *Sound placement.* Like singers, actors learn to "aim" sound at different reson-ating elements in their heads. Sounds may be more or less nasalized; they may make more or less use of deep "chest resonance."

5. *Correction of habits and defects.* Few actors come to training without such vocal defects as adenoids (which cause denasalized sound), poor dental structure (lateral lisp), vocal nodes (hoarseness of voice). Some problems are the result of habit or acculturation, such as nasality, regional accents, and lazy tongue.

6. *Dialects.* The idea of a "stage speech" that is radically different from "standard English" is disappearing, and the day of the actor who talks like an English aristocrat is past. Nonetheless, accurate knowledge of how different ethnic and regional groups speak is essential. In learning the specific characteristics of each variety of speech, the actor will probably make use of the *phonetic alphabet*, a system for recording sounds rather than spellings.

Training the Imagination

The word *training* may be inaccurate. Actors go through a process in a training atmosphere and are *encouraged* to discover their imaginations. Whether or not the imagination itself can be "trained" remains open to question, and many psychological data suggest that what we have called *imagination* is a capacity of the brain and the mental-emotional self that is always at work but that rarely surfaces. Still, if one can teach the rational brain mathematics, perhaps one can teach the nonrational brain imagination. Most certainly, one can try to encourage the nonrational brain to speak up and make itself heard.

Creative Exercise

In the belief that all people have imaginations and that all are "creative" (as children are creative), teachers devise exercises to free actors from both embarrassment and inhibition. Writing down dreams as a regular part of daily preparation can help many,

FIGURE 7-10. **Imagination.** The nineteenth-century German actor Ludwig Devrient as Shylock.

especially those who insist that they "never dream" or "dream nothing interesting." The very fact of causing themselves to remember and write down dreams leads to an acceptance of the idea of dreaming and hence to a greater willingness to "listen to" their dreams, which demonstrate imaginative elements—images, metaphors, and puns. Dreams are often playful in their structure and their language, and they have both content and form that our rational minds would never think of.

Childhood memory can be turned to good account in the same way. An exercise in memory becomes an exercise in imagination as the actor finds how much detail the mind is capable of holding and of using.

Other exercises in sensitivity or creativity use group participation in building a story or a moment. Each actor in turn builds on the story. Student actors have earlier gone through work in relaxation and contact, so that they will have got rid of any fear of participation.

Image Exercises

The creative mind probably works, at least a good deal of the time, in images rather than in words (although many words are themselves images). Image exercises encourage the actor to grasp the mental pictures that the brain offers. For example, simple character-creation around pictures, objects, or sounds can be beneficial. An actor is given an object and told to perform a related character for the group: a knife is set out; the actor bends forward, walks with difficulty, the body held to protect its center greedily. From "knife," the actor went to "sharp," sharp in business, a miser, then added the element of "a cutting wind."

Visualization

Group exercises build a scene, each member contributing details and working to *see* the scene. Such an exercise is useful in touching the actor's sense of creativity, in sharpening concentration and sense of detail, and in preparing for those times in rehearsal and performance when the actor must "see" for the audience:

> HORATIO: But look, the morn in russet mantel clad
> Walks o'er the dew of yon high eastward hill.
>
> *Hamlet*

Sense Memory

Like group storytelling, individual recounting of the "picture" around a memory encourages a sense of detail and of visual memory. As many senses as possible are incorporated. Such memories need not come from childhood; they may come from the day before, even moments before. The purpose is to cause actors to capture a sensory moment in all its fullness and, through both remembering it *and* recounting it, to cause them to be able to create such sensory reality around moments that come not from memory but from the theatre.

Improvisation

No single word and no single tool has been more used and misused in the last several decades than *improvisation*. Improvisation—the creation of quasi-theatrical characters or scenes or plays without the givens of drama—has been used to create theatre (without a playwright), to enlighten an actor about a character (the so-called *étude*, or improvisation based on material in a dramatic script), to structure theatre games, and to teach many aspects of acting. As a tool for training the imagination, it is an application of the techniques already mastered. In a sense, it is the basis of some of the other techniques; having an actor create a character around an image is such a use of improvisation. It can be used to apply the imagination, to stimulate it, or to supply raw materials not within the actor's experience. (That is, an improvisation focused on a frightening event may help the actor who has never experienced fear.)

In order to work, improvisation is kept simple and is carefully focused by the instructor. Improvisations can quickly develop along unwanted lines, especially with actors who want to "tell stories" (create theatrically interesting situations); when that happens, there are often so many processes going on that student actors do not understand what they are doing. For the purposes of the imagination, it may be enough to create, for example, a scene of the sort discussed under "Visualization" and then to have the group improvise their participation in the scene—feeling the air, wading into the water, and setting up a picnic on the beach. To do more would risk complete loss of the imagined setting and a departure into other areas altogether.

Training the Consciousness

Certain areas of the actor's conscious work can be taught through example and through guided participation in production work. These include discipline, concentration, theatrical analysis, observation, and script analysis.

Discipline

Actors are taught to be *prompt, alert,* and *ready to work*—to get enough sleep, to avoid alcohol and drugs when working, and to come in a frame of mind and a set of clothes that will permit maximum work. Actors *prepare:* they do bring the script and a pencil; they have done whatever homework on the play has been requested. Actors are *constructive,* not destructive: they do not make comments about other actors, do not break out of character while another actor is working, and do not indicate in any way that another actor's experiment with a character is wrong or comical or foolish. Actors are *respectful:* they talk to the director about problems, not to other actors or the costume designer or the playwright.

Concentration

The habit of concentration comes from work. In many cases, student actors whose acquaintance with mental work has been limited to the classroom will have difficulty at first with the level of concentration that is needed. Not only the length of time but also the depth of the concentration that is required may seem unreasonable. Yet, it is only through remarkable efforts of concentration that progress is made. An actor who cannot attain such concentration may need to return to exercises in relaxation and contact to find out what is distracting the mind. Where a severe problem continues to exist, there may be a psychological difficulty that a nontheatrical expert will be needed to resolve.

Theatrical Analysis

It should be a goal of actors' training to make them aware of their place in the theatre in each production. This does not mean merely that actors must understand their roles; it means that actors must grasp how they relate to the entire complex of the performance, including:

1. *Spatial understanding,* which includes an awareness of each setting in which the actor appears, its shapes and proportions, as well as an understanding of the relationship of the setting to the size and shape of the theatre and its audience. To reach this goal, actors in many theatre training programs are required to study design, lighting, and costume and to work on productions in nonacting jobs.

2. *Research resources,* for which the best preparation is usually a study of the history of the theatre. Knowledge becomes a resource, and formal study in this discipline will include a working knowledge of resources in the field.

3. *Dramatic appreciation,* for which the best preparation is usually a study of dramatic literature and a broad reading in the field. Every actor is expected to know the classics of each period.

FIGURE 7-11. The Actor and the Instrument.
The early nineteenth-century Anglo-American actor Junius Brutus Booth in several roles. These are worth studying to try to determine how role and body interact: for example, what sort of actor does he seem to be? How does his instrument—his eyes, for example, or the vigor of his gesture—help or hinder him in certain kinds of roles? What about the relationship between body and costume?

Observation

As distinct from imagination and visualization, *observation* is a conscious perceiving and recording of sensory data. For the actor's purpose, it is limited mostly to the seen and the heard. Observation can be taught through a variety of devices that require attention to detail, such as talking through or writing highly detailed descriptions of objects (a specific chair, a dead fish). It can be encouraged by requiring the keeping of a notebook with daily or weekly entries of sounds and sights (people). The goal is to cause actors to build a "library" of people on which they can draw in building character.

Script Analysis

The dramatic script is the foundation of the actor's work. *Imagination* and *instrument* are the means through which the script is embodied. Training in script analysis has three principal goals:

1. An *understanding of the entire drama*. On the first reading, the actor will be making judgments and sorting out impressions. Trained in the theatre, the actor will read the script as a "notation" for a performance: the potential for production will be grasped, at least in general. Likes and dislikes (sometimes vague ones) will form. An awareness of the play's *totality* will take shape. Of particular importance to the actor on first reading will be the *style* of the play, its main *impact* on its audience, and its overall *shape*. Under style, the actor will understand the degree of abstraction of the script; the kind of language, whether poetic or mundane; and the historical period. The *impact* will be comic or serious and will be expressed most importantly through language or action, through idea or spectacle. The *shape* will describe the play's gross structure and its overall rhythms, whether it builds slowly or quickly to crises, whether it relaxes gradually from them or drops abruptly. This first contact with the totality of the play will also indicate what demands it will put on its actors— the size of the cast, special requirements of their instruments, the size of the major roles, and the relative degree of intensity of the emotions to be embodied.

2. An *understanding of the place of the character in the whole drama*. The actor is trained to resist one question—*What makes my character stand out?*—and to ask another one instead—*How does my character contribute to the whole?*

Dramatic action means change; when a character is offstage, changes are taking place, and when the character returns, those changes must be noted. The actor balances two lines of development: the character's and the play's.

3. An *understanding of the details that make up the character*. A deeper understanding of the play and the character's part in it emerges from repeated readings, as does a detailed sense of just what the character is. The actor keeps a notebook in which ideas about the character are written down, as well as all those things in the script that indicate the nature of the character. These include those things discussed under "Character" in "How To Read a Play," especially action and decision, with character traits as they appear in the stage directions, the character's own speeches, and the speeches of others. All must be evaluated in terms of the production and should be discussed with the director and the other actors. For example, one character says to

FIGURE 7-12. **Stock Character.** The nineteenth-century actor F. S. Chanfrau, who specialized in playing "Mose, the Bowery Boy." Stock character, consisting often of set routines and tried-and-true "shtick" (clichés), may ease the actor's task, but it may also take over the actor and make creativity impossible.

another that she shows "facial contortions" and her voice goes up "two octaves." The actor playing the character described must know whether these things are true (that is, whether the other character's description is accurate) and then work out when and where to use these traits.

It is essential for actors, as for all theatre makers, to look at the play in terms of its theatricality, that is, its artistic, sensory, intellectual, and human values. Such a breakdown gives them a grasp of the play's entirety and of its theatrical potential. It should not, however, dictate character. Grasping a play's idea, for example, must never suggest to the actor the reason for the character's existence, nor should the actor worry about how to "play the idea," or, worse yet, how to *be* the idea. The actor who says something like "In this play, I represent goodness" simply has not done the proper homework. Except in pure allegory, characters do not represent abstract ideas; they represent persons (who may embody or apply certain ideas).

In the same way, script analysis should help the actor to avoid moral value judgments. Characters in a play are not "good" or "bad" *to themselves.* Few real persons say, "I am a villain." The actor does not, then, play a villain; the actor plays the representation of a person whose actions may be judged, after the fact, as villainous—by others.

Put most simply, training in script analysis is training *to read*. It is training to understand what is *on the page*—not what might have been put on the page but was not, and not what the actor might prefer to find on the page. Script analysis deals with a very limited amount of information and tries to squeeze every drop from it; it neither invents nor guesses. Most of all, it requires that the actor read *every* word and understand it in clear detail; from that clarity and that detail will come an objective understanding of the script that can be returned to again and again when acting problems arise.

The American Stanislavski System

The specific details gained from analysis are usually applied to modern realistic acting, which continues to dominate the work of most American actors. Basically, these are ideas originated or articulated by Konstantin Stanislavski, modified by the American Method and subsequent theories.

The actor is trained to analyze character for:

1. *Given circumstances.* These are the undeniable givens that the actor must accept: age, sex, state of health, social status, educational level, and so on. Often they are contained within the script, either in stage directions or in dialogue; sometimes they must be deduced or even invented. (How old is Hamlet? Was he a good scholar at the university? Is he physically strong or weak?)

2. *Motivation.* Realistic theatre believes in a world of connectedness and cause. All human actions in such a world are caused or motivated. To play a character in such a world, the actor looks for the motivation behind each action.

Some teachers have their students make notebooks for each character with a column in which a motivation can be noted after each line or each gesture. It is important that the student actor understand that, in this system, *all* behavior is

FIGURE 7-13. **Actor Training.** In private studio or university classroom, the actor must work at the craft: here, physical exercises to relax and stretch the body.

motivated—every word, every movement, every inflection. *All action results from choice.*

3. *Objective.* Like motivation, the objective is part of a system of causality. It is the goal toward which an action strives. Motivation leads to action; action tries to lead to objective.

4. *Superobjective.* "Life goal" might be an equivalent of the superobjective if a dramatic character were a real person. The superobjective includes all objectives pursued by a character and excludes all improperly defined objectives. For example, we might say that Hamlet's superobjective is "to set the world right again"; his objective in the first scene with his father's ghost might be "to listen to this creature from Hell and put it to rest" (thus setting the world right by quieting the ghosts in it). In this case, the objective and the superobjective agree. If, however, the super-objective was defined as "to take my father's place in the world," and the objective in the ghost scene was defined as "to listen to the ghost out of love for my father," there would be a severe problem, and the two would have to be brought into sympathy. By defining the superobjective, the actor is able to check on the validity of all the character's objectives.

Both the objective and the superobjective must be active. We have expressed them here as infinitives—"to set," "to listen"—but the actor does better to express them in active terms beginning with "I want," so that their strength and vitality are clearly visible.

5. *Through line.* If motivations and objectives are seen as beads, they can be strung on a *through line* that runs consistently through the character's entire presence in the play. The through line (sometimes called the *spine*) may also be seen as the line that runs through all objectives toward the superobjective. The actor learns to recognize that something is wrong when a motivated action does not fit on the through line. Such an action was what Stanislavski called a "tendency." It leads to poor acting because it takes the character away from the pursuit of correct objectives and into vagueness and contradiction, which an audience finds confusing and finally annoying. Much of what we call bad acting is, in fact, the playing of tendencies rather than the playing of a strong through line.

AUDITION, REHEARSAL, AND PERFORMANCE

Actor training goes on long after actors begin to take an active part in performance. Most actors continue to work on their instruments throughout their careers, and many return to professional workshops to refresh and sharpen their inner work. After the initial period of actor training, however—college, sometimes graduate school, an independent studio or teacher—the actor begins to look for roles and, having found one, begins the work of building and performing a character. Each step in the process has its special conditions, and for the professional actor these steps will be repeated over and over throughout his or her life.

FIGURE 7-14. **The Actor's Life: the Star.** The nineteenth-century American actor Edwin Forrest in two of his roles, early and late in his career. Forrest was a big, athletic man who specialized in muscular roles, for which he was less and less suited as he aged. He was a bitter rival of Charlotte Cushman (see Figure 7-2) and of the English star William Macready; fans of Macready and Forrest fought, and people were killed (the "Astor Place Riot").

Audition

Most actors get roles through auditions ("tryouts"). Stars are the exception; sometimes productions are built around them.

Most auditions are done for the director of the production. Usually, the stage manager is there as well, along with someone representing the producer, if there is one. Somebody is there, as well, to read with the actor if a scene with another character is being read. (Usually, the stage manager does this.) At many auditions, actors are expected to bring prepared monologues.

The most important things an actor can show in an audition are basic abilities and the capacity to work creatively with the director and other actors. One of the director's problems in auditions is to try to sort out the creative actors from the "radio actors"—those who have the knack of reading well on sight but who lack the ability to create. Therefore, actors are often asked to improvise as part of auditions and to work with other people. Thus, cleverness in a first reading is not necessarily an advantage for the actor. What may count more is the capacity to work creatively and interpersonally.

Unfortunately, auditions cannot always be a good indicator of how well an actor will perform, and they can have heartbreaking results. Imperfect as they are, however, auditions will remain one of the most important elements of casting until a more objective, less flawed device is invented.

Rehearsal

The actor will undoubtedly arrive at the first rehearsal with many questions. One of the functions of rehearsal is to answer those questions and to turn the answers into an exciting performance.

Actors often work very slowly in rehearsal. An outsider coming into a rehearsal after, let us say, two weeks of work might well be dismayed by the apparent lack of progress. Actors may still be reading some lines in flat voices, and, except for bursts of excitement, the play may seem dull and lifeless. This situation is, in part, intentional, however. Many actors "hold back" until they are sure that things are right. They do not want to waste energy on a temporary solution to a character problem. Temporary solutions have a way of taking on a life of their own: other actors become accustomed to hearing certain lines delivered in certain ways and to seeing certain movements and gestures; they begin to adapt their own characters to them. The actors begin to commit themselves to a pattern. To avoid this, many find it productive to withhold commitment for a good part of the rehearsal period.

The actor experiments. Some of this experimenting is done away from the rehearsals; homework takes up a lot of the actor's time. Much of it takes place in rehearsals. Again and again, an actor will say, "May I try something?" Or the director will say, "Try it my way." Try is the important word—experiment, test. The good actor has to be willing to try things that may seem wrong, absurd, or embarrassing.

Most important, the rehearsal period is a time for building with other actors. Actors use the word give a lot: "You're not giving me enough to react to," or "Will it help you if I give you more to play against?" Such giving (and taking) symbolizes the group creation of most performance.

At some point during rehearsals, the creative and lucky actor may have a "breakthrough." This is the moment when the character snaps into focus. Motivations and actions that have been talked about and worked on for weeks may suddenly become clear and coherent. The breakthrough may be partly a psychological trick, but its reality for the actor is very important: the creative imagination has made the necessary

FIGURE 7-15. **Rehearsal.** A late nineteenth-century engraving, "The Pain of Rehearsal."

connections and has given usable instructions to the instrument. The character is formed.

The rehearsal period, then, is not merely a time of learning lines and repeating movement. It is a time of creative problem-solving, one in which the solving of one problem often results in the discovery of a new one. It is a time that requires give and take, patience, physical stamina, and determination. It frays nerves and wearies bodies. The intensity of the work may cause personal problems. Nonetheless, many professional actors love rehearsal more than performance because of its creativity.

Performance

Society has an overblown image of "opening night" and "being in the spotlight" that makes the first performance unnaturally stressful. The fantasy of instant stardom, rave reviews, the actor's name in lights, and standing ovations makes performances still more stressful. Few actors, in fact, achieve stardom or standing ovations, and it is a sad mistake for any actor to think that such things are the only reward for performing.

Performance causes emotional and physical changes in the actor that are associated with stress. Some change, of course, is helpful; it gets the actor "up" so that energy is at a peak, ready for the concentrated expenditure that rehearsal has made possible. Too much stress, however, cripples the actor. "Stage fright" and psychosomatic voice loss are very real problems for some. Ideally, good training and effective rehearsal will have turned the actor away from the root cause of stress (dependence on outside approval of the performance); where this does not happen, the actor may have to return to relaxation work or find outside therapeutic help.

Opening nights raise energy levels because of stress and excitement. As a result, second nights are often dispirited and dull, because when the tension of opening is removed and the energy has been expended, a feeling of dullness, even of depression, often results. The wise actor expects this pattern. Again, preparation is a help—complete understanding of the role and the total performance, creative rehearsal work, open lines between consciousness and imagination. Before the second and subsequent performances, the prepared actor reviews all character work, goes over notes, reaffirms motivations and objectives. The good actor does not say, "Well, we got through the opening; the rest will take care of itself."

Once in performance in an extended run, actors continue to be aware of a three-pronged responsibility: to themselves, to the other actors, and to the audience. Those responsibilities cannot end with the reading of the reviews.

In developing his system of acting, Stanislavski was interested both in actor training and in the problems of performance. His work cannot be viewed as merely a study of how the actor prepares; rather, it is also a prescription for the continuing refreshment of the performing actor. His system allows the actor to create what has been called the "illusion of the first time" again and again. Put most simply, this means that the actor is able to capture the freshness and immediacy of the "first time" (both for the character and for the audience) by going back each time to the mental and emotional roots of the truthfulness of the performance. This process is possible only if performance is grounded in truth discovered during rehearsal—or, in some cases, during performance itself.

Continued performance for the trained actor, then, is not merely a matter of repeating rehearsed sounds and gestures night after night; it is a matter of returning to or discovering internally satisfying truths (motivations and objectives) and satisfyingly effective externalizations of them. Such a system may not be perfect, but it is far better than the repeated performance that grows tired and dull with repetition and that leaves the actor disliking both the performance and the audience because of boredom.

Audience response to performance sometimes suggests where a performance is effective or poor, and the actor works at correcting errors as the performance period continues. Thus the creation of a character must seem completed by opening night, and yet it is never truly finished.

WHAT IS GOOD ACTING?

Understanding the art of the actor depends, first, on the ability to separate the actor from the role. An attractive or well-written role can obscure the actor's lack of imagination; a poorly written role can hide the actor's excellence; an unsympathetic role can make the actor seem unsympathetic. By learning to read and see plays, we learn to distinguish the character from the actor, then to see what kind of material the actor had to cope with. For example:

FIGURE 7-16. **The Great Actor.** The late Laurence Olivier as Oedipus. (*John Vickers photo.*)

- Was the character fully realized by the playwright? Or did it have internal contradictions? Or large blanks?

- Was the character rewarding to perform, or was it "thankless"?

- Was it merely a function, or was it a character? Did it have progression, or was it unchanging? Varied or monotonous?

Answers to such questions tell us how difficult the actor's job was. Once we understand that, we can begin to talk about what the actor did and how well the job was done.

Good acting fulfills the technical requirements of the theatre:

- The voice is clear and interesting; every word is understandable.

- Movements are complete and definite; any incompleteness or clumsiness is of the character, not the actor.

Good acting is believable—within the style.

Good acting overcomes the inherent difficulties of the role and capitalizes on the strengths of the role. It does not call attention to the actor; it creates the character fully within the context of the entire performance.

Good acting has detail and "texture" (variety and human truth), but it is not merely a collection of details; it has what one artist calls a "center," another a "through line"—a common bond tying all details together and making the whole greater than the sum of its parts.

Good acting has the capacity to surprise. Its truth is recognizable, but it goes beyond imitation to revelation.

Good acting, then, has technical proficiency, truth, a through line, and creativity; bad acting calls attention to itself, lacks technical control, dissolves into mere details because of its lack of a through line, and never surprises with its creation.

CHAPTER EIGHT

THE DIRECTOR

There have always been theatre people who exercised a strong, central influence on productions, but in the sense that the word has been used for the last hundred years, *directing* is a phenomenon of the nineteenth and twentieth centuries.

We may be able to deduce something about directing by recognizing that it appeared when illusionistic detail became important in the theatre and when industrialism was important in Western society. The era of the director is also the era of the pictorial illusionist and of the industrial manager, and we may deduce that directing is concerned with illusionism and picture making, and with management and organization, in a way or ways that had not concerned the theatre before.

Directing, like any artistic practice, has changed since its beginnings. Directing may continue to change, but we cannot say with any certainty in what direction; what we can say is that two hundred years after their first important appearance, directors are the dominant figures in theatrical production. One critic in 1990 even described a kind of musical as "a toy built by its director." (Lloyd Rose, *Washington Post*.)

A few theatres now function without directors, most notably those organized around cooperative or communal principles (see p. 369). With those exceptions, however, theatres at every level now have directors: in high schools and colleges, it is the director who organizes and oversees all productions; in many community theatres, it is the director who oversees the selection and mounting of plays; and in the professional theatre, in Europe as in North America, it is the director whose stamp goes most clearly on every production.

In essence, the director now does things that either were done by several people before the modern period or were not done at all. Put more briefly, it may be said that what the director does is to *unify*. Thus, if a single difference could be noted between a modern and an older performance, all question of styles aside, it would be this binding of all the elements of performance into a unity—a unity of meaning in the interpretation, of visual effect in the designs and staging. Because of our way of looking at things, we tend to see this unity as desirable and even inevitable, and we would find the *pluralism* (multiplicity of effects) of an older performance confusing or even comical. A theatregoer in another age, however, would accept pluralism as quite natural to the theatre and might find modern directorial unity puzzling, or even oversimple and boring.

THE FUNCTION OF THE DIRECTOR

The director unifies within two main categories, *interpretation* and *presentation*. By *interpretation*, we mean not only the analysis of the dramatic text but also the evaluation of the nature of the audience and the assessment of the abilities and potentials of the other theatre artists. By *presentation*, we mean the whole process of embodying the interpretation in the form that will be most effective for the audience. The director, then, is the crucial person who stands between the theatre's potential and the audience's enjoyment; the director is the person who is most responsible for realizing that potential.

Before the appearance of the director, interpretation was done by the other theatre artists themselves: the dramatic text by the playwright, the roles by the actors, the scenes and spectacle by a painter or machinist. Presentation was done by actors and technicians who were organized by a manager or a theatre owner, but without that artistic unity that we now almost take for granted; that is, there was always somebody to "put the show together," but in the eras before the director appeared, that someone was a troupe leader or a merchant or a religious or civic leader (as in classical Greece or medieval Europe), and the goal was not aesthetic unity but efficiency. Of course, there were people in those earlier eras who selected plays, cast the actors, rehearsed them, and made sure that everything was ready by opening night (or day); however, those jobs were often parceled out among several people, and none of them was profoundly concerned with making the finished product all of a piece.

In doing the jobs that formerly may have been done by many people, as well as in doing a job that had only rarely been done before—unifying the performance— the modern director must be effective in more than one area. Of primary importance are skills in *organization*, *human relations*, and *decision making*. Organization includes the director's ability to put ideas into order and to combine them with the ideas of other people, as well as the ability to order rehearsals, schedules, and budgets; human relations includes both the ability to inspire other artists and the ability to work directly with people of quite different kinds, imposing the director's own wishes only when absolutely necessary and working creatively with other people on group solutions to complicated problems; and decision making requires the clearheadedness to

LE MISANTROPE

FIGURE 8-1. **The Undirected Production.** Until the end of the eighteenth century, staging seems to have been worked out by actors and playwright. Here, a seventeenth-century view of Molière's *The Misanthrope.*

define problems and to see the conditions under which they must be solved (including limitations of budget, time, available talent, and so on), as well as the self-knowledge that will allow the director to make decisions (or to postpone certain decisions), often under stressful conditions. To put these skills to the greatest effective use, the director needs *stamina* and *concentration* as well as artistic talent.

In some theatre organizations, of course, some of the director's jobs are done by another person, especially in the professional theatre. Overall artistic unity may be decided by a producer. Many aspects of production will be handled by a production stage manager. Business matters will fall to a business manager or producer; however, as one moves away from the high-powered organization of Broadway, more and more responsibilities fall into the director's lap, until, in many community, school, and university theatres, it is safe to assume that the director is aware of and actively engaged in every aspect of production.

The following, then, comprise the director's functions and responsibilities (some of which may be delegated to others in some situations): the *artistic* functions of (1) script selection or approval (including work with the playwright on an original script); (2) script interpretation; (3) design approval and coordination (sets, lighting, sound, and costumes); (4) actor coaching; and (5) staging (including pictorial creation, orchestration of voices, stage movement, and performance rhythm), as well as the *managerial* functions of (1) production coordination and planning; (2) casting; (3) rehearsal scheduling and conduct; (4) performance coordination, including timing; and (5) liaison among management, actors, and designers.

FIGURE 8-2. **Pioneering Directors.** Vladimir Nemirovich-Danchenko and André Antoine, two leading directors of 1890–1920.

PLAY SELECTION

Directors in community, school, and university theatres most often select the plays they direct; in the professional theatre, they at least approve the scripts (if they are staff directors) or find themselves "matched" to a new play by a producer. Never, if at all possible, does a director take on a play he or she does not like. The demands are too great, the depth of involvement too extreme; the dislike would ruin the production.

Directors choose to do plays because the plays excite them; idea and spectacle are probably the most common elements to prompt directorial interest. Ego certainly enters in, as does the desire to exercise artistry. However, if theatrical elements conflict, directors sometimes find that they have made a bad choice; that is, they may love the idea of the play but may not know how to make the music of the language exciting or how to compensate for a lack of spectacle. As directors gain self-knowledge through experience, they learn what they do well or badly, and they learn to make wise script choices. Most important, perhaps, is the acquired knowledge of learning to study the script in great depth—not to be led astray by enthusiasm for a single element, only to find to one's sorrow later that serious problems were overlooked.

With the script chosen, the director begins to translate that early enthusiasm into the stuff of performance. To do so, the director needs a "springboard," a taking-off place from which to make a creative leap. The terms *concept* and *directorial image* are also used, but *concept* implies rational thought, and *image* implies picture making, and the director's process at this stage may be neither rational nor pictorial. Certainly, very few directors *begin* their creative work with a reasoned, easily stated idea, and those who are drawn to a script because of (for example) its music or because of the opportunity it gives to display the artistry of an actor will probably not *begin* with images. On the contrary, what many directors begin with is a seemingly random, sometimes conflicting medley of ideas, impressions, and half-formed thoughts whose rational connections may still be hidden. It is then the director's task—and the exercise of a special talent—to sort all these out and to find their connections and to see which can be given theatrical life and which cannot. Thus, much of the director's early work is not the definition and application of a "concept," but the establishment of a jumping-off place, the sorting out of raw materials from a whirlwind of impressions.

Seldom—perhaps never, except in the most perfunctory sort of work—is the springboard merely "to do the play." A director who sets out merely "to do the play" is like the actor who sets out to learn the lines and not bump into the furniture—going through the motions without ever confronting the real task. This is as true of a classic play as of the most avant-garde script. It might seem that classic plays would be an exception because, supposedly, so much is known about them and so many other productions can be drawn on—the director would simply stage the play's established greatness. Such an approach is a guarantee of dullness, at best. A play will not be exciting in performance simply because other audiences have found other productions of it exciting; it must be made exciting all over again every time it is staged.

A good director takes nothing for granted—least of all the presence of the audience. Everything that is tried will be measured against an idea of how the anticipated audience will react—with the qualification that every director knows that mere reaction is not in itself a good thing; the *proper* reaction is what is wanted.

In early readings, the director usually has both positive and negative thoughts about the play and its audience impact. Two lists could be made, one of strengths and one of weaknesses. These two lists *taken together* would show how the director's ideas were forming. It is important to remember that weaknesses as well as strengths are included. Just as artists in any form are inspired by obstacles, so the director is inspired by script problems (as, for example, the poet finds inspiration in the problem of rhyme).

Let us suppose that the director is considering Ibsen's *A Doll's House,* a realistic nineteenth-century play. The play is a classic of its kind and so has established merit; on the other hand, it is also old enough to seem dated to a modern audience in language and some plot devices. Thus, after early readings, the director could list some strengths and weaknesses:

Plus	Minus
Strong subject matter	Creaky structure—melodramatic
Excellent central character	Dated language
Great third-act climax	Some "serious" stuff now funny
Good potential for probing Victorian attitudes	Soliloquies, set speeches very hard to make convincing today

To the director who is excited by the play and is setting out to do it, these two columns might better be titled "Potentials" and "Challenges." From the realization of the one and the solution of the other will come the director's best work.

The Director and the Play: Text or Pretext?

The play is chosen; the first identification of strengths and weaknesses is made. The work of interpretation begins. It is an open-ended process, and, like the actor's, it never really finishes; it merely stops. A director who does more than one production of the same play may create quite a different production the second time: the process of interpretation has gone on and has changed as the director and the world have changed.

But a serious question arises: What is the director's responsibility to the dramatic text? Is it the director's job to put the play on the stage with utmost fidelity, or is it the director's job to create a theatrical event to which the script is merely a contributing part? Can the director cut lines or scenes, transpose scenes, alter characters? Can the director "improve" the play, or must it be treated as a sacred object?

Directors vary widely in the way they answer such questions. Their views range from veneration of the text to near indifference; the play is seen as a holy object on the one hand and as a merely useful artifact on the other.

The Worshipful Director's Approach

A director who venerates the text might say: "The play is the only permanent art object in performance; it is a work of art in its own right, to be treated with respect and love. Because it has stood the test of time, it has intrinsic value. By examining it, we can know its creator's intentions—what meanings the playwright meant to convey, what experiences the audience was meant to have, what theatrical values were being celebrated. The playwright is a literary artist and a thinker, and the playwright's work is the foundation of theatrical art. It is the director's job to mount the playwright's work as faithfully and correctly as is humanly possible.

"Historical research and literary criticism are useful tools for the director; they illuminate the classic play. Quirky modern interpretations are suspect, however: to show Hamlet as a homosexual in love with Rosencrantz and/or Guildenstern would be absurd and wrong because we know that such a relationship would never have been included in the tragic view that Shakespeare held.

FIGURE 8-3. **The Worshipful Director.** *Julius Caesar* in a French production, c. 1900. Note the creative use of levels, the importance of the central costume's brightness and draping.

"The director's job is not primarily to create theatre; it is to cause the play to create theatre. The difference is crucial. The director says quite properly, 'I must allow the play to speak for itself and not get in the way.' To do otherwise is to betray the play, and I will not do it *even if the 'betrayal' is great theatre.*"

The worshipful director views a different approach with something like horror; at best, such productions cause regret. Most often, a single word is used by the worshipful director to describe such productions: *wrong*. Because they are not faithful to their classic originals, they are *wrong*.

The Heretical Director's Approach

A director who does not venerate the text might say: *"Interpreting the text means making a theatrical entity of it for an audience."* Not making *the* theatrical entity of it, and not 'finding its meaning' or 'doing it correctly.' There is no single interpretation of a play that is 'correct.' There are only interpretations that are right for a given set of performers under a given set of conditions for a given audience.

"How, then, can a director judge the rightness of the production? The director does not, any more than a painter judges the rightness of a painting. The director's final criterion is the satisfaction of an overall goal: Is it good theatre?

"It is foolish to think that the director's task is to stage the play according to some other standard. Fidelity to some 'authorized' or time-honored view of the play is not, simply in and of itself, a good thing. It is foolish to say that the director did the play 'wrong' unless what the director did was to make bad or dull theatre. The director

FIGURE 8-4. **The Heretical Director.** Shaw's *Saint Joan* at the Kamerny, Moscow, c. 1924. As written, the play is a realistic one, but it has been reconceived here in very unrealistic staging. *(Theatre Arts)*

has to be faithful to a vision, not to tradition or academic scholarship or propriety; only when that vision fails can the director be said to be wrong.

"Does this mean, then, that the director has no responsibility to the 'meaning' of the play? Yes, in the sense that the director's responsibility is to the meaning of the performance, of which the play is only a part. Are we, then, to have homosexual Hamlets? Yes, if such extreme interpretations are necessary to make the plays into effective theatre and if they are entirely consistent within their productions. Are we, then, to have productions of classics that are directly opposite to their creators' intentions? Yes, because it is finally impossible to know what somebody else's intentions were and because an intention that was dynamite in 1600 may be as dull as dishwater in 1995; and anyway, theatre people have always altered classics to suit themselves: *Macbeth* was turned into an 'opera' as early as 1670, and *King Lear* had a happy ending in the eighteenth century."

The extremes of the heretical director's views can lead to results that many people find offensive or meaningless; on the other hand, those views can also lead to innovative and truly exciting productions. Generally both sorts take a risk: the heretical director takes the chance of being ridiculous, the worshipful director of being vapid. At their best, however, both can create productions that thrill audiences, the one with revelations of familiar material, the other with a brilliant rendition of the strong points of the classic.

SCRIPT INTERPRETATION

No matter what the orientation toward the text, the director must now work to analyze it: take it apart, reduce it to its smallest components, "understand" it. (To *understand* does not mean to "turn the script into a rational description of itself"; it means, rather, to make the director's consciousness capable of staging it.) The job of interpretation has many aspects, which are often explored simultaneously, both before and during rehearsals.

Tone and Audience Impact

Funny/serious, cheerful/sad, light/heavy—the possibilities are many and must be identified for each act, each scene, and each line, as well as for the entire play. The director looks both for the play's effects—funny lines, frightening moments, spectacular events—and opportunities to exercise invention. Neither laughter nor powerful emotion necessarily belongs unchangeably to parts of many scripts, especially when realistic acting and the concept of *subtext* (action implied but not stated in the text) are applied; the director will spend a good deal of time deciding what to do. Even when the proper tone is found for the play, the lines alone will not deliver that tone to an audience. Laugh lines must be carefully set up and "pointed," with both business (small activities performed by actors) and timing; moments that have a wonderful potential for powerful emotion can easily be lost without careful, intense study and work by the director.

Of particular interest in this aspect of interpretation is *mood*—the emotional "feel" that determines tempo and pictorial composition—and *key*—(as in "high key" and "low key"), the degree to which effects are played against each other or against a norm for contrast. High-key scenes may even go to *chiaroscuro* ("light/dark") effects that use the darkest darks and the lightest lights, as in dramatic painting; such a technique is of great value in setting the mood for a play like *Dracula*.

Relative Importance of Elements

Modern directors try to work carefully with all elements of theatre. The director must study the play to find which elements are most important and which can be used most creatively to serve the play. Spectacle (including lighting, costume, the pictures created by the actors' movement, and scenery) and sound (including music, sound effects, and language) are often elements that the director can manipulate and can bring to the play as "extras" that the playwright has not included. Character, idea, and story, on the other hand, are usually integral to the script itself, although subject to considerable interpretation and "bending" by director and actors. Many directors annotate their scripts in great detail for these three elements, some marking every line of dialogue for its contribution to character, idea, or story. Such annotations give the director both an overall sense of the play's thrust and specific instances of that thrust at work.

This area of interpretation is critical. An element misunderstood at this stage can mean a moment lost in performance, or even an important thread through the whole play; to miss a major emphasis can mean a failed production. For example, a play that depends heavily on the beauty and intricacy of its language (sound) will usually suffer if directed to emphasize story or character, with the language overlooked or ignored (a not infrequent problem in productions of Shakespeare's plays); a play of character, if directed for its story, often has incomprehensible spots and long stretches

FIGURE 8-5. **Bad Direction.** The actors are all in a line; the set is mere background; gestures are false. *Uncle Tom's Cabin* in a French production, c. 1900. (The posing of the actors may have been done by the photographer.)

where nothing seems to happen. Thus, the director must not only pick the element or elements that can be given theatrical life, but *must also pick the element or elements that the script gives theatrical life.* This means knowing *which* element(s) is most important; *where* in the play each has its heights and depths; and *how* the director will give theatrical excitement to each.

Action and Progression

Performance is active and most plays have progressive actions; that is, they occur through time (audience time and their own time), and they must at least seem to increase in intensity as time passes (as, that is, the audience is led from preparation through complication to crisis and resolution). There is a trap here for every director, however, in that it is the very nature of audience perception to need greater stimulation as time passes—a familiar enough situation to all of us, who can become bored after a time with something that entertained us at the beginning. Thus, it is part of the director's problem to counter the apparent drop in intensity that occurs as time passes by using every device possible to *increase* intensity, that is, to support theatrically the progressive intensity of the script. When it enjoys a performance, an audience's responses may be compared to a parabola: they start at a low point, rise higher and higher as time passes, and usually fall off after the climax. The director wisely structures the performance to serve this perceptual structure (or another equally satisfying one.) *The director cannot allow a performance to become static,* or it will seem to fall off rather than to remain still.

It is not enough, then, to find the important elements and to know where the script emphasizes them. The director must now find how each element grows in interest as the performance progresses. The word *progression* must be used again and again: What is this character's progression? What is the progression of the story? Is there progression in the spectacle?

If the progression is missed, the audience will become confused or bored. They may say things like "It went downhill," or "It got dull after the first act," or "It went nowhere." Theatre people seeing such a performance often say that "They played the last act first," which is a way of saying that the climactic points of the important elements were so much in the director's mind that the entire play was directed to emphasize them, and the progression was thus destroyed.

The reverse of the question "What is the progression?" is "What can I save for the climax?" In other words, how can the director emphasize the highest point of the performance (usually toward the end, coincident with the story's climax) by contrast or by saving effects for that moment? Preparation and contrast are important; equally important is *saving* something—the final high pitch of emotion, the most exciting tempo, the loveliest visual effect.

Environment

As the actor determines "given circumstances," so the director determines environment: place, time of day, historical period. Much is given in the script, although if it is given only in the stage directions, the director may choose to ignore it. Some directors cross out the stage directions before ever reading them, believing that they were written either for some other director's production (e.g., for Broadway) or for readability for armchair theatregoers. Classic plays often have no stage directions at all.

It has become common directorial practice to change the period of classic plays. Shakespeare's *Troilus and Cressida,* for example, has been done in the costumes and accents of the American Civil War. The play is about the Trojan War, but the director may have wanted to stay away from classical Greek costumes and settings because of what they say to the modern mind or may have wanted to stay away from Shakespearean costume and setting because they say something quite different (and something that might seem more comic than anything else). Setting the play in the American Civil War, then, not only had the advantage of novelty, it also identified the play with a conflict real to Americans and yet slightly distant, one that is viewed both romantically and cynically (applicable to a play that is both romantic and cynical), and it had the added advantage of separating the often confusing warriors of the opposing sides by their Americanized accents (northern and southern).

Questions of tone, mood, and key influence the director's thinking about environment. There are excellent reasons for putting a murder mystery in a country house on a stormy night, just as there are excellent reasons for putting a brittle comedy in a bright, handsome city apartment. It is not only the rightness of the environment

FIGURE 8-6. Environment. A richly textured scene that gains much from the director's exploitation of stage and setting. *Marat/Sade* at the University of South Carolina, directed by Richard Jennings.

for the characters that the director thinks of (i.e., if they are rich they should have a rich environment, if Russians they should have something Russian, and so on) but the rightness for the indefinable subtleties of mood: the laziness of a warm day, the tension of an electric storm, the depressing gloom of an ancient palace.

Idea

As we have already pointed out, idea is the element of theatre that gets the most attention after the audience has left the theatre and the least while it is enjoying the performance. Paradoxically, idea is an important criterion in play selection, many directors being committed to plays because of enthusiasm for their subject or approach. Idea may continue to influence their interpretation and their work; however, they are careful *not* to direct the play so that it is "about the idea." The other elements will usually determine the shape of the production, and idea will inhere in all of them but be blatant in none. Even an impassioned "idea" speech at the most thrilling moment of the play must spring from action and character and must exist *because* of action and character. If it exists because the playwright or the director wants to make a statement, it will leap out of the performance, and the performance will suffer.

Idea, in fact, does not inhere in individual speeches or in literal statements that can be neatly extracted from the play. The very word *idea* describes not a single, literal statement but a body of matter that we call *meanings*. It is woven into the texture of the performance, embodied in the actors' creation of their roles and the director's creation of mood, among other things. The director does not spell out the meanings for the audience; where meanings excite the director, they become something to be embedded in the entire performance.

DESIGN OVERSIGHT AND INSPIRATION

After beginning the work of interpretation, and well before rehearsals begin, the director meets with the several designers. When feasible, this process may actually begin months before rehearsals, but the practicality of production in many theatres means sometimes that it comes within short weeks or even days of casting. Communication with the designers is best started early. Many directors have approval of the hiring of designers and so can begin almost as soon as they agree to direct.

Depending on the theatre, the director and the designers (sometimes with producer, playwright, stage manager, technical director, costumer, and so on) hold *production meetings* weeks or months before the actors are cast. These meetings have three principal goals: *artistic coordination,* so that direction and designs are in harmony; *managerial efficiency,* to coordinate budgets, schedules, and personnel assignments; and *communication,* to encourage the complete exchange of creative ideas.

Within this framework, the director works on the following areas:

Design Mood and Meaning

The director is rarely a designer but knows the practical needs and the aesthetic values of both play and production. Communicating feelings and ideas about play and production to designers is an important directorial skill, especially when it is done without insisting on restrictions. The designers will have made their own interpretations of the play, which will sometimes be different from the director's. Bringing them all into a single focus is the director's task.

The director has to be careful at this stage not to be so rigid or so narrow as to cause the designers to make a single statement over and over. Unity *and* variety (or variety within unity) must be stimulated, and the potential for progression must always be inspired in the designs.

The visual potency of lighting, set, and costume is a very important determinant of mood. The director must be clear about the interpretation and must be sure that the designers share that vision. Inconsistency here will lead to a severe weakening of the performance.

Ground Plan

The ground plan is a "map" of the playing area for a scene, with doors, furniture, walls, and so on indicated to scale. In a realistic interior, the director may almost design the entire acting space simply by setting down directorial needs in detail. The number and location of entrances, the number and location of seating elements, the number and location of objects that will motivate behavior and movement (for

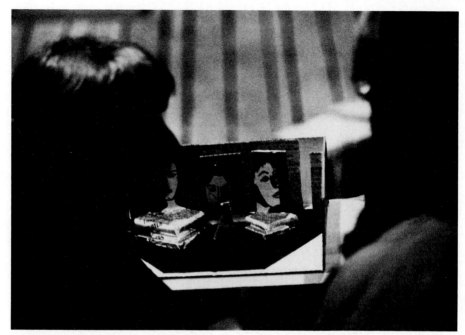

FIGURE 8-7. **The Director and the Design.** The director and the designer, silhouetted, confer about the model of the set (center) for Caryl Churchill's *Top Girls*.

example, stoves and refrigerators, fireplaces, closets, and bookcases) are important to the way many directors think about realistic plays and may be determined by such directors even before they meet with their designers. Some directors even give their set designer a ground plan, complete except for minute matters of dimension. Others may remain open until the designer has created a ground plan around a more general statement of needs.

In the nonrealistic play, or sometimes in the realistic play with exterior scenes, directors may have less rigorous requirements. Still, for variety, mood, and emphasis, the director will probably specify differences in level, separation of playing areas, the location of seating elements, and so on. An effect created by the director may strictly require certain things: one director's production of *Macbeth*, for example, had the witches shift magically from a ledge far above the stage to stage level (two sets of actors were used to play the witches); here, obviously, the designer had to provide precisely the levels demanded by the director.

As well, other design elements may be suggested or required by the director; for example, the size and shape of the space where a crowd is used, or where a sense of the isolation of a single figure is wanted, or where a feeling of cramped oppression is sought.

Once ground plans are established, they become the basis for all staging. Drawn to scale, they can be used with scale cutouts of furniture and actors to plan movement and picturization. They are also the basis for the three-dimensional model of each setting that the designer usually provides, and they are also useful to the director in planning the staging.

Costumes, Lights, and Sound

As with the ground plan, so with the other design areas: both the practical and the aesthetic must be considered. The kind and amount of movement wanted by the director influences costume design; the costume designer's work influences movement (as when, for example, the tight corset of the late nineteenth century or the very broad skirts of the eighteenth century are used). So, too, with colors: bright pastels may be suitable for a comedy; dull colors and heavy fabrics under gloomy light may match a serious interpretation. Practical considerations influence other decisions: certain areas will have to be brightly lighted so that the action can be seen; certain actors will have to be in strong colors or outstanding costumes so that they will gain focus. Lighting colors must be carefully coordinated with the colors of sets and costumes so that lights do not wash out or change other colors; the location of lighting instruments has to be coordinated with the location of set pieces and rigging to avoid casting shadows or creating physical interference.

As the production meetings continue and rehearsals near, these and many other matters will have been considered: budget, shifting of scenery, time for costume changes, location of offstage storage space. As decisions are made final, each designer provides the director with a detailed plan in the most appropriate form: color renderings and fabric swatches for costumes; ground plans, scale drawings, renderings, and models for sets; light plots with gel colors for lights. The sound designer (where one exists) may work with an annotated script and lists of sound materials (music, sound effects). These renderings, plans, and other materials represent the culmination of the designers' work with the director: detailed, readable plans for a total production, all in harmony with each other and with the director's interpretation of the text

Where a director works with a strong, creative designer, he or she may find that the design style is so powerful that the style of the entire production, even down to the movements of the actors, is determined by it. (See Figure 8-8.) Usually, a director will work with such a designer only when they already agree on the style and interpretation, before any designs are put on paper. Historically, such collaborations have created some of our most outstanding productions.

ACTOR COACHING

Most modern directors involve themselves closely in their actors' creation of their roles. It is a very rare director who does not. The influence of Stanislavski, in particular, has led to a collaboration between actor and director that has developed, in some cases, into a great dependency on the director, a dependency that is sometimes fostered by the teacher–student relationship at universities. Just as there are now playwrights who expect to have their plays "fixed" by the director (a relationship that grew primarily from the Broadway playwright–director collaborations

FIGURE 8-8. Binding Design. A designer can tie a director's hands with a powerful style— or, as here, the designer (Emil Pirchan) can work so closely with the director (Leopold Jessner) that the design's style expresses both of them. (*The Marquis of Keith*, c. 1920.) Note how rigorously this design would control the production— amount of detail in movement and costume, for example, and even in the acting style. (*Theatre Arts.*)

of the twentieth century), so there are actors who expect to have their interpretations "fixed" or even given to them whole by their directors. Particularly in educational and community theatres, great trust is put in the director by the actors, and many interpretations are virtually handed down entire from director to actor.

When the actor–director relationship works as a productive collaboration, however, the director functions as a coach who advises, inspires, and encourages the actor. Significantly, the director works in such a relationship with questions rather than with statements ("Why do you think the character says it just that way?" instead of "What the character means is . . ."). The director will have mastered the actor's vocabulary and, using it, can ask those questions that the actor may not yet be able to phrase. The director is the sounding board and the artistic conscience of the actor —mentor and interpreter, bringing to the actor's work another dimension, another voice, another view of the whole play and all the characters.

The Director–Actor Relationship

The director and the actor have had to learn to need each other, for there is no reason to suppose that early directors were warmly welcomed by actors, who, until then, had been independent. There is still much in the relationship to make it difficult for both. The actor is worried about one role, the director about the entire performance; the actor works from a narrow slice through the play, the director from the whole thing; the actor risks everything in front of an audience, the director does not; the actor naturally resents commands, the director sometimes has to give them. Add to these differences the natural indifference or apathy of people brought into a working situation by professional accident rather than affinity, plus the stressful atmosphere of rehearsals, and the relationship can be strained.

Perhaps surprisingly, then, most directors and actors work quite well together. Credit for much of this goes to the director's human skills, although some of it must

FIGURE 8-9. The Result of Good Direction. Working with the actor is probably the most important part of directing, resulting in performances that are compelling and truthful. Here, *Breaking the Code*, directed by Jim Patterson at the University of South Carolina. *(Photo by Keith McGraw, Instructional Services Center.)*

go to the patience and determination of the actor. The most potent factor may be, in the end, the knowledge that both are engaged in a creative enterprise whose success benefits both.

The director–actor relationship takes several forms:

The Director as Parent

"Do it my way because I say so." The authoritarian director gets results early and keeps control of the production. He or she risks alienating or stifling the creative actor and often lectures at considerable length and takes the role of a professor with students.

The Director as Guru

"If you do it my way, it will demonstrate our spiritual sympathies." A product of the 1960s, the guru is as much spiritual cult leader as stage director. The vision is a vision of existence, not merely of performance, and the actors are acolytes and members of a spiritual community. Brilliant work sometimes comes from devoted followers—innovative, revealing, revolutionary. The uncommitted may find it puzzling or silly.

The Director as Therapist

"Trust me; tell me your problems." In the psychologically oriented theatre of the 1940s and 1950s, the director-therapist functioned well. This director is still effective with actors trained in that tradition, especially when the actor's self and the character are made to dovetail. The director-therapist is somewhat of a mystery, if not a nosy busybody, however, to actors who work in another way.

The Director as Seducer

"You're wonderful; we're going to do great things together." Sexual seduction is not really a directorial technique, although it is not unheard of; rather, emotional attachment and even dependency are the object. This approach often succeeds in binding the actors to the director with great affection and loyalty. The difficulty lies in the lack of correspondence between affection and creative work, in the loss of perspective through noncritical, "global" attitudes on both sides.

The Director as Victim

"Do I have to do *everything?*" The director-victim suffers a lot. The weight of the production, the stress of rehearsals, the emotional demands of each scene seem draining. This director pleads, begs, cajoles, often gets remarkable results from sympathetic actors, and succeeds in touching their own emotional selves but suffers from a loss of authority.

The Director as Playground Director

"Let's have *fun* with this show!" Buoyant and youthful, the playground director tries to make everything fun, funny, cute, or touching. Much of theatre is work, however, and many plays have other qualities. This kind of director is good with children and probably an inspiration to beginners and amateurs but is too one-sided for serious actors.

The Director as Green Thumb

"I think we have something growing here." Totally organic, this director puts little or nothing down on paper, seldom seems to prepare, and always waits for things "to develop." Such directors, if inexperienced, have been known to ask when the actors were going to start to move around. With gifted and experienced actors, the director-gardener can build a profoundly creative situation, but the method—or lack of it—causes frustration and anger in many actors.

The Director as Lump

"Be better." He or she mostly sits there, a lump in the rehearsal hall, occasionally complaining to the stage manager. Directions are so vague that the actors despair: "Sort of drift to the left a little way" or "Kind of give him a love–hate look." The actors, forced to shift for themselves, may either work it out or quit.

The Director as Director

This director is an amalgam of all the above—occasionally authoritarian, sometimes seductive, organic when prepared solutions do not work, fun-loving when there is genuine fun in a scene or a situation. The complete director is multifaceted, even many-faced, all things to all people and all plays. What the good director tries to avoid is being limited, because a strictly limited approach inevitably antagonizes at least some of the actors.

Actors depend on their director. Therefore, the more precise and sure the director can be, the better. Precision and sureness come from *preparation,* and so the basis of the most productive actor–director relationships is the director's own work in advance of rehearsals.

The Director and the Characters

Many directors are themselves actors and/or acting teachers. They understand actors' approaches and vocabularies. Only rarely do they try to impose a new system on their actors, and then only if they are gurus or director-teachers. Thus, their work on character will be adapted to the system used by the actor playing the role.

Basically, the director does the same character homework as the actor, keeping a notebook, with pages or columns for each character. The director focuses, however, not on the objectives and motivations of a single character (except when working with the actor playing that character) but on shifting patterns of objectives that conflict, part, run parallel, and conflict again. It is not merely that the director maintains an overview of the terrain that the actors travel; it is that the director finds the heart of the play in the coexistence and conflict of character lines.

Too, the director is profoundly concerned with the "outside" of the performance. The director is a master communicator, interested almost obsessively in *things that signal to the audience.* This is the art of external signals, both visual and auditory. The actor devotes time and energy to the inner reasons for giving signals; the director works on those inner reasons only to help the actor, saving creative energy for the signals themselves.

As the director plans the schedule, attention is given to how each actor will build character. Some actors make great progress early, but one or two may never do so. Still, the director knows that by a certain date, "inner" work must be well under way. By some later date, the director must let go and "sit farther back," working more externally and more comprehensively. The closer the date of the first performance, the less attention the director will be able to give to detailed actor-coaching, which is only one aspect of the modern director's total job.

STAGING

"Blocking," "staging," or "traffic direction," as some people wryly call it, is one of the director's inescapable responsibilities. No matter how much the actors and even the director are devoted to inner truth and to characterization, the time must come when the director must shape the actors' moves and timing and must give careful attention to *picturization* and *composition* and to *movement*. It is in the very nature of theatre that the visual details of the stage have significance, and the director must make that significance jibe with interpretation.

Rich. II/163

What says King Bolingbroke? Will his majesty
give Richard leave to live, till Richard die?
~~You make a leg, and Bolingbroke says aye.~~

NORTHUMBERLAND

My Lord, in the base court he doth attend
To speak with you; may it please you to come down?

RICHARD

Down, down I come like glistering Phaeton,
Wanting the manage of unruly jades.
In the base court? base court, where kings grow base,
To come at traitors' calls. and do them grace.
~~In the base court come down.~~ Down court, down king!
For nightowls shriek, where mounting larks should sing.

BOLINGBROKE

What says his majesty?

NORTHUMBERLAND

Sorrow and grief of heart
Makes him speak fondly, like a frantic man——
Yet is he come.

BOLINGBROKE

Stand all apart,
And show fair duty to his majesty.

My gracious lord.

RICHARD

Fair cousin,
You debase your princely knee,
To make the base earth proud with kissing it.

FIGURE 8-10. Director's Script. Among the materials that may go into the director's book
are staging marks, often put in the margins of the playscript; notes to actors; and notes to
the director herself. This page shows staging notes for the scene discussed on page 164. For
many directors, such staging notes are the *result* of rehearsal, not the precursor to rehearsal.

Significance is the crux of the matter. We live in a world where movement and visual arrangement signify: they give signals. In the realistic theatre, the same things signify that do in life; in the nonrealistic theatre, these things can be kept from signifying or can be made to signify differently only with careful control and effort.

Before the appearance of the director, audiences seemingly found less significance in stage movement, gesture, and picture—or, more accurately, they found a *theatrical* significance in them: the star took center stage, facing front, with other actors flanking and balancing; a hero's movement pattern and posture were heroic; the heroine moved so as to show herself off and to divide or punctuate her speeches. Modern staging, with its meticulous attention to visual symbolism (picturization), beauty (composition), and movement was probably not seen before the nineteenth century except in special cases.

Much of what is taught about directing today is devoted to these matters. By and large, what is taught has been established by tradition and extended by popular theory, little of it having been tested objectively. Much of the theory of picturization—especially the supposed "meanings" of various stage areas—derives from the traditional use of the proscenium stage and probably has less relevance to thrust and arena staging. Indeed, as realistic plays exert less influence on the theatre, and as new theories of theatre evolve, many of these traditional theories of directing will probably fade.

Movement

As actors are aware of and exploit "body language," so the director is aware of and uses "movement language." Stage movement is more abundant than real-life movement; in a real situation, people often sit for a very long time to talk, for example, whereas on a stage characters in the same situation will be seen to stand, walk, change chairs, and move a good deal. Partly, this abundance of movement results from the physical distance of the audience—small movements of eyes and facial muscles do not carry the length of a theatre; and, partly, it results from the director's need for variety, for punctuation of action and lines, for the symbolic values of movement itself, and for the changing symbolic values of picturization.

Stage movement is based partly on the received wisdom of the movement implied by statements like "Face up to it," "She turned her back on it," "He rose to the occasion." Too, it serves to get characters into positions with which we have similar associations—"at the center of things," "way off in the blue," "out in left field."

The director is concerned with *direction*, *speed*, and *amount* of movement. Direction reveals both motivation and human interaction; speed shows strength of desire or strength of involvement (impassioned haste, for example, or ambling indifference); amount is perhaps most useful for contrast (a character making a very long movement after several short ones or in contrast with the small moves of several other characters).

Movement also *punctuates* the lines. It introduces speech: the character moves, catches our attention, stops and speaks. It breaks up speech: the character speaks, moves, speaks again, or moves while speaking and breaks the lines with turns or about-faces. (Pacing is frequently used for this reason. In life, we associate pacing with thought, and so a pacing character may seem thoughtful, but the turns are carefully timed by the director to mark changes in the speech itself.)

Movement *patterns* have a symbolic value much like that of individual movements and can be derived from the same figures of speech: "twisting him around her finger," "winding her in," "going in circles," "following like sheep," "on patrol," and many others suggest patterns for characters or groups. They are used, of course, to underscore a pattern already perceived in the play or the scene.

Pictorialism

Pictorialism—the exploitation of the stage's potential for displaying pictures—is not entirely limited to the proscenium theatre but has its greatest use there. From the late nineteenth century through the middle of the twentieth, the proscenium was seen literally as a picture frame, and the audience sat in locations that allowed it to look through the frame at its contents. With the advent of thrust and round stages, however, this "framing" became impossible, and audiences were located on three or all four sides of the stage, so that each segment of the audience saw quite a different picture. Thus, only certain aspects of pictorialism have universal application, and of these the most important by far is picturization.

Of considerably less importance, except on the proscenium stage, is the symbolic value of *stage areas*. These areas (on the proscenium stage) are Down Center, Right, and Left (*Down* meaning toward the audience, *Right* meaning to the actor's right and thus the audience's left) and Up Center, Right, and Left. Down Center is unques-

FIGURE 8-11. **Pictorial Overdirection.** Directors can easily overdo such aspects of pictorialism as focus and composition. After all, pictorialism is a style based on nineteenth-century painting, and styles change. Here, *The Christian*, c. 1910.

tionably the most important (or "strongest") area, followed by Down Right and Down Left. Traditional wisdom has it that Down Right is more important than Down Left and that it has a "warmth" that Down Left lacks. The Upper areas are weaker, and Up Left is supposed to be the "coldest." The real value of identifying the stage areas is in creating *variety* and *identification,* variety because it is tedious if the audience has to watch scene after scene played in the same area, and identification because the association of an area with a character or a feeling is an important tool for conveying emotional meaning to the audience. And, unquestionably, the matter of "strength" does have some importance, if only because common sense tells us that the downstage areas are stronger because we can see the actors more clearly there—and, as a result, we want to play our most important (but not all) scenes there.

Picturization

Puns and traditional sayings give us a clue to how picturization works—and also suggest to us how the mind of the director works as it creates visual images of the sort that communicate to us in dreams. "Caught in the middle," "one up on him," and "odd man out" all suggest strong pictorial arrangements of actors. When a director combines them with area identification, for example, they become richer and more complex. The additional use of symbolic properties or set pieces—a fireplace, associated with the idea of home ("hearth and family"), for example—gives still greater force to the picture. Thus, a character who "moves in" on the hearth of a setting while also moving physically between a husband and wife ("coming between them") and sitting in the husband's armchair ("taking his place") has told the audience a complicated story without saying a word.

Sometimes, as in Shakespeare's *Richard II* (Act III, Scene iii), the playwright's own symbolism creates a rich texture of both picture and movement.

["King Richard appeareth on the walls" (First Quarto); "Enter on the walls" (First Folio)]:

NORTH: My lord, in the base court he doth attend
               To speak with you; may it please you to come down?

RICHARD: Down, down I come, like glist'ring Phaeton . . . ,
               Wanting the manage of unruly jades.
               Is this the base court? Base court, where kings grow base

[Richard comes down to stage level; the usurper Bolingbroke kneels to him, as is evident from omitted material]

BOLINGBROKE: Stand all apart,
               And show fair duty to his Majesty.

["He kneels downe." First Quarto.]
               My gracious lord.

RICHARD: Fair cousin, you debase your princely knee
               To make the base earth proud with kissing it. . . .
               Up, cousin, up; your heart is up, I know,
               Thus high at least, although your knee be low.

Upstage

UR	UC	UL
DR	DC	DL

Downstage

◄──────── **Stage Right**   **Stage Left** ────────►

AUDIENCE

FIGURE 8-12. **Stage Areas on the Proscenium Stage.** "Up" and "down" are away from or toward the front of the stage; "left" and "right" are the actors' left and right when facing the audience. Areas and movements are different on arena, thrust, and alley stages.

The scene begins with Richard "on high" while his enemies are in the "base court" at stage level. (A base court was a part of a castle, but *base* means "common" or "unworthy," as well as "low" in both the physical and the social sense.) Richard says he will come "down, like glist'ring Phaeton," that is, like the young man who drove the chariot of the sun too near the earth because he could not control the horses that pulled it ("wanting the manage of unruly jades"). But the audience already knows (from earlier reference) that the sun is Richard's emblem, and the director has probably made sure that it is visible on Richard's costume and may even be suggested by the shape of his crown, so the sun is being *debased,* brought down, even as Richard physically moves down to stage level. There, the usurper tells everyone else to "stand apart," that is, to give them room, but the word *stand* may be ironic and the director may use it to make an ironic picture, because they should kneel to the king. Bolingbroke himself does kneel (stage direction, First Quarto), but the gesture is a mockery, as Richard notes, "You debase your princely knee/To make the base earth proud. . . ./Up, cousin, up . . . ," reminding the audience that Richard himself was, only moments ago, "up" on the higher level. And Richard goes on: touching his crown (a traditional bit of business), he says, "Up, cousin, up/Thus high at least. . . ." That is, he will raise himself high enough in the presence of his king (though he should be kneeling) to seize the crown.

Thus, in a quick sequence of moves and gestures, the symbolic flow of the scene is given to the audience. With a scene of this richness and detail, the director need only follow its lead; few modern scenes are this explicitly symbolic, however, and directors usually have to create their own picturization to match the interpretation.

Focus

A stage is a visually busy place, with many things to look at; therefore, the audience's eyes must be directed to the important point at each moment. A number of devices achieve *focus: framing* (in a doorway, between other actors, and so on); *isolating* (one character against a crowd, one character on a higher or lower level); *elevating* (standing while others sit, or the reverse, or getting on a higher level); *enlarging* (with costume, properties, or the mass of a piece of furniture); *illuminating* (in a pool of light or with a brighter costume); and *indicating* (putting the focal character at the intersection of "pointers"—pointing arms, swords, eyes, and so on).

Focus is largely a mechanical matter, but it is an important one that affects both movement and picturization.

Composition and Balance

Most stage pictures are rather well *composed,* or good to look at, but directors are often careful to study the production with an eye to improving the aesthetic quality of the scenes. What is *not* wanted is easier to say than what is: straight lines, lines parallel to the stage front, evenly spaced figures like ducks in a shooting gallery, and so on. *Balance* is also sought so that the stage does not seem heavy with characters on one side, light on the other. Composition is, finally, an irrational matter and a highly subjective one; directors who concern themselves with it in depth learn much from the other visual arts, especially traditional painting.

Mood

Mood is established most readily with lighting and sound and with the behavior of the characters. However, certain visual effects of character arrangement contribute, as well: horizontals, perhaps, for a quiet, resigned scene; looming verticals and skewed lines for a suspense melodrama. Mood values are as subjective and irrational as those of composition, however, and as hard to describe. In reality, what the director remains watchful for are clashes of mood, where movement and picturization conflict with other mood establishers.

Directorial Rhythm

Rhythm is repetition at regular intervals. The elements of rhythm in the theatre are those things that regularly mark the passage of time: scenes, movements, speeches, words. For the director, rhythm includes *tempo* and *timing,* as well as one aspect of *progression.* The director is concerned, then, not only with the interpretation of character and the visual signals of interpretation but also with *the rate(s) at which things happen.*

We have seen that speed of movement is important to movement meaning. Now we may say that it is also important to intensity and rhythm. We associate quickness with urgency, slowness with relaxation; change in speed is most important of all. We may compare this phenomenon with the beating of a heart: once the normal heartbeat (base rhythm) is established, any change becomes significant. The director establishes the base rhythm with the opening scenes of the play and then creates variations on it, and the shortening of the time (cues) between moves, between

FIGURE 8-13. **Focus.** The photograph is worth studying to determine the kinds of focus and the instances of counter-focus, as well as the balance and variety contributed by the single figure with the pistol. The landmark production of *Armored Train 14-69* at the Moscow Art Theatre, 1927, directed by Ilya Sudakov. *(From P. A. Markov,* The Soviet Theatre, *G. P. Putnam's Sons.)*

lines, and between entrances and exits becomes a rhythmic acceleration that gives the audience the same feeling of increased intensity as would a quickening of the pulse.

Pace is the professional's term for "tempo," but it is not a matter of mechanical tempo. Much of what is meant by *pace* is, in fact, emotional intensity and energy, and the director who tries to create a feeling of intensity by telling the actors to "pick up the pace" or "move it along" will probably succeed only in getting the actors to speak so fast that they cannot be understood. Tempo has to grow naturally out of understanding and rehearsal of a scene, not out of a decision to force things along. Indeed, the scornful dismissal of such an attempt as "forcing the pace" and "pumping it up" suggests how futile it is.

Timing is complicated and difficult, something felt rather than thought out. *Comic timing* is the delivery of the laugh-getter—a line or a piece of business—after exactly the right preparation and at just that moment when it will most satisfy the tension created by a pause before it; it also describes the actor's awareness of the timing that has produced previous laughs and of how each builds on those before. The timing of serious plays is rather different and depends far more on the setting of (usually) slow rhythms from which either a quickening tempo will increase tension or a slowing will enhance a feeling of ponderousness or doom. For example, at the end of *Hamlet,* Fortinbras has the following speech (Act V, Scene ii):

Let four captains
Bear Hamlet, like a soldier to the stage;

FIGURE 8-14. Focus, Picturization, Balance. The very full use of visual focus is nicely balanced by the variety in body positions and the differences in level; the picturization of "majesty among subjects" is easily comprehensible, with a counterpart, "something's not quite right here"; and the rather full stage is adequately balanced. However, what would focus and picturization be without the by-play among the figures at center and stage right? (The Emperor's New Clothes, directed by Frank Mundy, at South Carolina State College.)

For he was likely, had he been put on,
To have prov'd most royally; and, for his passage,
The soldier's music and the rights of war
Speak loudly for him.
Take up the bodies: such a sight as this
Becomes the field, but here shows much amiss.
Go, bid th' soldiers shoot.

[A dead march. Exeunt, bearing off the bodies; after which a peal of ordnance is shot off.]

This follows an active scene of dueling, argument, and violence, and a short, less active scene of Hamlet's and Horatio's final words to each other, with the arrivals of ambassadors and Fortinbras. Fortinbras' speech is jumpy and uneven, effective because it *lacks* regular rhythm, but it finally settles down into the firm, regular rhymed couplet, "Take up the bodies . . ." that sets the final rhythm of the play. The rest could be timed on a metronome, taking the base rate (the pulse) from the couplet. *Go* is a long sound, followed (in one director's view) by a pause of two beats. The words that remain have but a single stress among them, on *shoot.* After this one-beat word, there is another pause of as long as three beats (in the major rhythm of which

Go and *shoot* are major units). Then, the drum ("a dead march") starts its slow beating on the same tempo; a measured number of beats later comes the cannon sound ("a peal of ordnance"); another measured number of beats later, the lights begin to dim or the curtain to close, still on units of the original rhythm.

This control of a scene may seem unnecessarily rigid, and controlled rhythm of this kind works only when it is carefully planned and rehearsed because there is no such thing as a timing that is "almost rhythmic." The rhythm is either exact or it is nonexistent, and it is in stage effects like the drum and the cannon that the director can most carefully control it. (It is partly because of the need for control of such effects, in fact, that the director came into being.)

THE DIRECTOR AS MANAGER

Although we have separated the artistic from the managerial functions of the director so that we could talk about them, no clear line exists between the two. A strong element of the manager is needed in the execution of all artistic decisions, and managerial abilities are always needed in the director's work with people. Directors have to be both artists and managers in almost all of their work, and they are unique among professionals precisely because of this unusual combination of traits: on the one hand, the often solitary consciousness of the artist, and on the other, the gregarious organizational intellect of the manager. Within the same person, then, the artist proposes and the manager disposes, sometimes at widely different times and sometimes simultaneously.

Insofar as the director-as-manager can be separated, however, he or she will work in the following areas:

Production Preparation and Coordination

In a Broadway production, many managerial functions are performed by the producer or the producer's office; in community and school theatres, the director performs most or all of them: *scheduling, budgeting, personnel selection, research,* and some aspects of *public relations* all fall to the director's lot. Scheduling includes the overall flow of production work from inception to performance, including production meetings, rehearsals, and the coordination of design and technical schedules, at least for purposes of information (including costume fittings for actors, clearing of the stage for construction work, and so on). These schedules are kept by the director or the stage manager on some easily read form like an oversized calendar.

Budgets are rarely initiated by a director, who does not hold the purse strings of the theatre, but the director must be able to keep a staff budget and to understand and honor costume, setting, and other budgets. In many college and university theatres, the director functions as producer and has budget control over the design areas (that is, the production money is budgeted as a single figure, which can be carved up as the director wishes).

Personnel selection (not including that of the actors) covers the director's own staff, most particularly the stage manager and assistants. In many situations, it will extend to the choreographer and the music director, with whom the director must work closely; it may include selection or at least approval of designers.

Research is carried out by a director on virtually any aspect of the production. Designers do their own research, to be sure, but such matters as the actors' accents, social mores, manners and mannerisms, the traditions surrounding the staging of a classic, the historical conventions associated with it, critical comments on it, and the work of other actors and directors in other productions of it concern many directors. It is not their aim to steal ideas from other productions; rather, it is their aim to learn from them, to honor traditions, and to build on what has been done before. This is particularly true in the staging of something like the operettas of Gilbert and Sullivan, for example, where audiences are familiar with the work and the traditions of performance are strong. In some theatres, directors have the help of a dramaturg in this task.

Public relations is not usually a directorial responsibility, but as a matter of taste and even of self-protection, the director often wants at least advisory approval of graphic and written material. Staging publicity photos, providing historical material from research, and appearing on interview shows to publicize the production are only a few of the things that a director may do.

Casting

"Style is casting," the late director Alan Schneider said some years ago. The remark underlines the enormous importance of casting to the director; its success or failure indelibly stamps the production.

The producer or director puts out a *casting call* and schedules *auditions* or *tryouts*. In New York, much casting is done through agents and private contacts. In university and community theatres, almost the opposite situation holds true, because maximum participation is wanted and closed or private auditions are frowned on. In repertory theatres, of course, where the company members are under contract, the director must work rather differently to make the company and the plays mesh, and casting and play selection have a good deal of influence on each other.

The director's conduct of a casting session is a trial of tact, patience, and humanity. Auditions exist for the director, but would-be actors often believe that the sessions exist for them, and directors disabuse them of this error as gently as possible. Both good and bad actors try out, including good actors who are wrong for the play and poor actors who may have a quality that somehow seems right. The director wants to hear and see each one but wants to see and hear only enough of each one to know what each can do. Directors learn to make sound preliminary judgments on the basis of less than a minute's audition. It remains the director's task, however, to be considerate, positive, and polite. The goal is to relax tense actors, to help rid them of nerves that obscure talent by strangling good voices and tensing flexible bodies.

The director or an assistant keeps notes on each aspirant, often in the form of a checklist with headings for physical characteristics, voice, and so on. "Type" may also be indicated—the range of given circumstances that the individual's voice and body would suggest in the realistic theatre. Abilities and outstanding characteristics

FIGURE 8-15. **Casting.** The tormented process of casting is the basis of one of America's greatest musicals, *A Chorus Line.* Here, from a production at Wright State University, directed by Mark Olsen.

are noted in enough detail so that the notes themselves will both recall the individual to mind and serve as a basis for later judgment.

In a tryout, the director is looking not for a finished performance but for a display of potential. Script readings, performance of prepared materials, and improvisation and theatre games may be used. Aspirants may be asked to work singly or together or with a stage manager. Some will be called back one or more times because the director feels that they have more potential than was shown the first time or because more information is needed; and, as a final decision nears, the director will want to compare the "finalists" very carefully.

The actual selection of a cast is complicated and, finally, irrational. It is a creative act—the creation of the artistic unit that will bring life to the play. Feelings and hunches are important; so, unfortunately, are personal prejudices. Above all, the director wants to be sure, for replacing an actor after rehearsals have started severely upsets the creative process.

After the director chooses the cast, actors are notified. In university theatres, a cast list is posted. In other situations, the director notifies actors personally or has them notified through agents. Each person who tried out but was not cast should be thanked. If the whole process has been conducted well, there will be inevitable disappointment among those not cast, but no sense of bitterness or injustice.

Rehearsals

Every director has a rehearsal pattern, and every pattern has to be adaptable to the special needs of each cast and each play. In general, however, a structure like the following is used:

First Rehearsal

The cast gathers, a trifle nervous and unsure. Many are strangers to each other. The director plays the role of host—making introductions, breaking the ice, moving these individuals toward cohesion. (Even when the playwright sits in, it is the director who is the "host.") The play will probably be discussed at some length, the director explaining general ideas and the overall direction; the designers may be asked to show and discuss models and sketches. Certain practical matters are got out of the way by the director or the stage manager (the signing of necessary forms, the resolving of individual schedule conflicts, and so on).

Then the play is read, either by the entire cast or by the director or the playwright. Some directors interrupt this first reading often, even on every line, to explain and define; others like to proceed without interruption so that the actors may hear each other. Either way, once the books are open and the lines are read, the rehearsal period is truly under way.

Rehearsal by Units

Rehearsing entire acts is often not the way to do detailed work, and so the acts are further broken down into *French scenes* (between the entrance and exit of a major character) or *scenes* (between curtains or blackouts), and then further into *beats* or *units* (between the initiation and end of an objective). These short elements are

FIGURE 8-16. **First Rehearsal.** The director, Sharon Ammen (right), flanked by her stage manager and her designer, leads her cast through their first reading together.

numbered in such a way that, for example, all the appearances of a major character can be called by listing a series of numbers, for example, 12, 13, 15, 17, meaning scenes 2, 3, 5, and 7 of the first act. By scheduling detailed rehearsals this way, the director often avoids keeping actors waiting. Or this same number system can be used to call scenes that need extra rehearsal.

As a very general pattern, it can be said that many directors move from the general rehearsal of early readings into increasingly detailed rehearsals of smaller and smaller units, and then into rehearsals of much longer sections when the units are put back together.

Run-Throughs

A *run-through* is a rehearsal of an entire act or an entire play; it gives the director (and the actors) insight into the large movements and progressions of the play. After run-throughs, the director will probably return to rehearsal of certain small units, but, as performance nears, more and more run-throughs are held.

Technical and Dress Rehearsals

As production coordinator, the director cannot forget the integration of lights, costumes, sound, and scenery into the performance. *Technical rehearsals* are devoted to any or all of these elements, normally done with the actors but sometimes without them (when "cue-to-cue" or "dry-run" technical rehearsals are held). In either case, the stage manager usually takes over the management of the script and the cues in preparation for running the show during performance; the director makes the decisions affecting the look and sound of the production and conveys them to the stage manager.

Dress rehearsals incorporate costumes into the other technical elements, and final dress rehearsals are virtually performances in all but their lack of an audience. Nothing is now left to chance: actors must be in place for every entrance well in advance of their cues; properties must be in place, with none of the rehearsal substitutes now tolerated; costumes must seem as natural to the actors as their own clothes (achieved by giving them, weeks earlier, rehearsal costumes of cheap materials); every scene shift and light cue must be smooth, timed as the director wants it.

And then, for the director, it is over. To be sure, polishing rehearsals may be called even after opening night, or full rehearsals if the play is a new one that has gone into *previews* (full performances with audiences in advance of the official opening) and needs fixing; but, as a rule, when the play opens, it belongs to the actors and the stage manager, and the director is a vestige of another era in its life. The director may continue to check the production regularly, even for months or years if it is a Broadway success, but in effect, after opening night, the director is a fifth wheel. Until the next play, of course.

More than one director has compared directing to being a parent, the child being the production. The director rears it from birth to maturity and then pushes it out into the world. It is a paradox of the craft—as it is, perhaps, of parenting—that the proof of one's success is the loss of one's function.

FIGURE 8-17. **The Director and the Production.**
The American director Walt Witcover. An acting
teacher as well as director, Witcover gets truthfulness by creating detailed, complex life onstage.
The scene from *The Miser,* at the University of
Maryland, shows the result: variety and believabil-
ity, the student actors utterly at ease with period
costumes, the life of the play's action embedded in
the life of the times.

WHAT IS GOOD DIRECTING?

To understand directing, we must be able to assess what the director has brought to the play and what the play presented to the director as strengths and weaknesses. Our evaluation of the direction will then depend on answers to questions like:

- How well did the director analyze and interpret the script?

- How well did the director solve the problems presented?

It is important to separate the *production* being studied from the *play* being studied. The production is not necessarily bad because it fails to stage the "playwright's intentions"; nor is it necessarily good because it either stages the "playwright's intentions" precisely or turns them upside down. As we have seen, different kinds of directors take different approaches; we must try to understand the approach and then evaluate it for what it is.

Good directing is seen in an internally consistent, exciting production. It deals

FIGURE 8-18. **Performance.** The director is gone; his work remains. The final moments of *A Chorus Line*, at the Cockpit-in-Court at Essex Community College, directed by Todd Pearthree, designed by Paul Sullivan. (*Norman McCullough photo.*)

with the play's problems and exploits the play's strengths in the terms of the director's approach.

Good directing shows most of all in the work of the actors. If the actors are good and are working in a theatrically compelling whole, the director has laid a good foundation. If the actors have not been unified, if they seem to hang in space when not speaking, if they perform mechanically, if they lack motivation at any point, if they do not perform with each other, they have been poorly directed.

Good directing has technical polish—smooth cues, precise timing, and a perfect blending of all elements—that radiates "authority," the artists' confidence in their work.

Good directing creates compelling pictures and movement, but only when they expand the work of actors and playwright, never when they contradict—and never when they exist for their own sake.

Good directing gives the performance tempo without giving it mechanical speed; there is no sense of too-fast or too-slow, but the organic tempo of a living entity.

Good directing combines all elements into a whole; there is no sense of good ideas left over or of things unfinished. Everything belongs; everything is carried to its proper full development; nothing is overdone.

The good director, then, understands the play and takes a consistent approach to it, bringing the actors to life in a complete production; the bad director does not fully understand the play, often failing to ask detailed questions; does not coach the actors or coaches them only incompletely, or directs them mechanically in postures and positions and movements dictated by a mechanical notion of picturization and composition; achieves not tempo but clockwork timing; and leaves ideas undeveloped and elements unassimilated.

CHAPTER NINE

THE DESIGN TEAM: SCENERY, LIGHTING, AND COSTUMES

THE DESIGN TEAM

Sitting in the modern theatre, we sometimes take the presence of scenery so much for granted that it is easy to forget that theatre does not have its roots in either spectacular effects or localizing settings. We have become acculturated to the presence of physical environments that so closely suit the mood and meanings of each play that we may lose sight of the fact that the theatre for a very long period used little more than the theatre space itself as environment, and that for centuries it was satisfied with stock settings that could do for many plays: a room in a palace, a garden, a forest. We live in a period of magnificent settings and superb designers; however, stage design has not always been considered fundamental to theatre or its performance.

Much the same thing is true of costume designers, although it seems likely that their art (extended to include the making of masks) is a very, very old one, whereas sound designers are so recent an innovation that most theatregoers over forty are still surprised to see them listed in the program. Creators of lighting effects may be said to go back to the Renaissance, but it is probably more helpful to think of the art of stage lighting as coming into its own when a controllable means of illumination was invented: gaslight (about 1830).

Actors, directors, and playwrights work with life as their material. Theatre designers, however, work with the *environment* of human life, and their materials are the materials of our world: light and shadow, fabric and color, wood and canvas, plastic and metal and paint. Because their materials are of this kind, the designers are far more dependent on technology than are actors, playwrights, or directors. This dependence explains the role of another theatre professional, the technical director. Advances in technology inevitably change the way in which theatre designers practice their art, and, in the case of both light and sound, technology virtually created the arts. Thus, theatre designers stand in both the world of the artist and the world of the artisan or the mechanic, and they usually must be expert in both.

WHAT IS THEATRE DESIGN?

Because the designers derive their materials and their subjects from the real world, their art is the creation of worlds on the stage. These worlds are sometimes imitations of the real world, sometimes not; in either case, they use familiar materials, but often in unfamiliar ways. The scenic and costume designers know that their products will be seen under colored light and so will look quite different on the stage from the way they look in sunlight; the lighting designer knows that the audience must see the actors, no matter what the demands of mood, color, and emphasis, and that the surfaces being lit are quite different from the things they imitate; the sound designer may be asked to create sounds that never existed in life or to amplify and distort real sounds to match the needs of an unreal world.

The world that the designers create is the world of the play, which is not at all the same thing as a literal copy of the real world. Each designer goes about his or her task differently in creating that world, but they all share a common goal: to create an environment within which the actors can create convincing life. This goal means that the designers must work as a team and that they must work in concert with the director so that a compatible world is created by all of them.

This environment begins with the play. Contemporary design is tied inescapably to the dramatic text. The world that it creates has its roots deep within that text— not merely in the stage directions, but in the lives of the characters.

Several factors, all to be found in the play, govern how the designers create their world.

Tone and Mood

Designers pay close attention to the differences between comedy and tragedy, but these two categories are simply not enough. Every play is its own category and must be approached through the range of tones that it contains: lightheartedness in several early scenes and great seriousness in a last act; both the romantic quality of a protagonist and the fragility of another major character, both funny gags and the real

FIGURE 9-1. **The Work of the Designer.** A model and finished setting by Lewis A. Crick-ard for Brecht's *Man Is Man*. *(Dartmouth College, directed by Stefan Rudnicki.)*

sadness of a central character's dilemma. *And* they must express these subtleties in the settings, costumes, lights, and sounds that are required by the scripts.

Level of Abstraction

The designers are faced with a very wide spectrum of possibilities, from literal realism to fantasy to almost pure abstraction. At one extreme, for example, could be the setting for an American tragedy, where the decision might be made to create a literal replica of a house in New England down to the last detail of the patterns in the wallpaper. At the other extreme might be one of the "space stage" settings of the 1920s—abstract constructions of stairs, ramps, and levels. In costuming, we might find real clothes, purchased in stores and dyed to look sweaty and dirty; at the other extreme, we might find the costumes of some modern theatres, which use elastic fabric, extensions of limbs, and various kinds of padding to change completely the outline of the human body.

In part, the decision about how abstract the designs will be comes from the designers' and director's interpretation of the script; in part, it comes from a decision about how much the abstraction or literalism of the play itself will be emphasized. In a realistic play, for example, the decision to create literal settings and costumes is not an inevitable one; with equal justification, the designers might decide to create a mere suggestion of a house. In the same way, the designers of a play of Shakespeare's may decide that an abstract setting is inappropriate and may go to quite literal, realistic settings.

Historical Period

The shifting of classical plays from one period to another has become common. Designers are confronted constantly with plays that do not have contemporary settings, costumes, and sound. The look and the "feel" of other periods become important aspects of design.

The lighting designer is also affected by historical period, when, for example, ideas about the direction and quantity of light and the quality of shadow come from paintings and engravings of another period. In setting and costume, some of the implications of historical period are obvious; the kinds of problems that they raise are most often handled by careful research by the designers. Sound, too, may be affected if period music is used or if certain kinds of sounds are called for—footsteps, for example, echoing from the stone walls of an old corridor instead of from modern materials; or the sound of a trumpet flourish; or the sound of *Hamlet's* "peal of ordnance."

Historical period contains a trap for the designers in the perceptions and knowledge of the audience: the designers must consider not only what things looked like in the period but what the audience *thinks* they looked like. What we know of the 1920s, for example, is conditioned by what we have seen in cartoons, old movies, and magazines—but did all women really bob their hair, and did all men really wear knickers and high collars? In the Elizabethan period, were all houses made of plaster-and-timber fronts, and did all men wear puffed-out breeches and hose? Did warriors

FIGURE 9-2. **Historical Design.** Meticulous recreation of the past is only one possible approach to historical design. Here, a sketch by the Duke of Saxe-Meiningen for Schiller's *Maid of Orleans.*

in the tenth century wear plate armor? Or, to reverse the calendar, will all people in the distant future wear tight-fitting clothes of unisex design?

And there is still another trap: contemporary fashion. Audiences are greatly influenced by their own ideas of beauty. As a result, a hairstyle that is supposed to be of 1600 and that was designed in 1930 will often look more like a 1930 hairstyle than a 1600 one; or to take a familiar example from the movies, cowboys' hats in the movies of the 1940s looked far more like 1940s' ideas of what was becoming to men than they ever looked like the actual headgear of westerners of the frontier period.

So designers must think of several things at once when confronted with historical period. It is not enough to go to a book and copy literally what is there.

Geographical Place

Like historical period, geography greatly influences design, unless the decision is made to abandon it altogether (that is, to be abstract instead of literal). The whitewashed houses of the Greek islands are different in color, texture, and scale from the adobes of Mexico or the balconied houses of New Orleans; the traditional clothes of Scotland, Morocco, and Scandinavia are distinct; the light in Alaska and Texas is very different. Sound and light are quite different outdoors from in. Even at considerable levels of abstraction, differences in geography inform some design decisions.

Socioeconomic Circumstances

Wealth and social class influence clothes, furniture, and background in many places and periods, and, therefore, their imitation on the stage. As with the other considerations, a decision may be made to ignore such matters, but a *decision must be made.* The matter itself cannot be ignored. And the more realistic the level, the more important these considerations become.

Historical period greatly complicates social and economic matters. As with other historical elements, audiences may have general or inaccurate ideas about what constituted the look of wealth or position or power or poverty in a distant era. What, for example, did a wealthy merchant wear in the seventeenth century that a noble did not? What furniture did the noble own that the merchant did not? What separated serf from artisan in the Middle Ages?

Aesthetic Effect

Put most simply, every designer hopes that the designs will have beauty. That beauty is a variable should be clear—the romantic loveliness of a magic forest cannot be compared with a construction of gleaming metal bars and white plastic plates—but that every designer aims at a goal of aesthetic pleasure seems true. Intentional ugliness may occasionally be aimed at, but even then we are tempted to say that the result is beautiful *because* its ugliness is artfully arrived at.

Composition and balance enter into aesthetic consideration, just as they enter into the considerations of the director. Teamwork is again essential, as setting, costumes, and lights are inevitably seen by the audience as a whole. Thus, unity is also an aesthetic aim, one achieved through a constant sharing of ideas by all the designers.

THE DESIGNERS AT WORK

Although many of their decisions are reached in concert (at production meetings), the designers do most of their work in solitude or with the technicians who execute their designs—the scene designer with the technical director and builders and painters, the costume designer with cutters and sewers, and so on. At this distinct stage of their work, each specializes and proceeds separately.

The Scene Designer

It is the scene designer's job to create a performing space for the actors and a physical environment for the play's action. The result is the setting, which normally has the added function of supplying the audience with clues about the play's locale.

Other important questions are the *number of settings* (Can the entire play be played in one set, or must different sets be designed and changed for each scene, or can some sort of *unit set* serve for all scenes?); the *shape and size of the stage* (Will the audience surround it or look at it through a proscenium arch? If it is small, how can it be kept from seeming cramped? Will the actors play within the setting or in front of it?); the *sight lines* of the theatre (What peculiarities of the theatre's architecture demand that the settings be built in special shapes so that every member of the audience can see?); the *means of shifting the scenery* (Is there overhead *rigging* so that scenery can be "flown," or is there an elevator stage or a turntable stage for bringing new settings in mechanically?); the *materials from which the scenery will be built* (Is it better to use traditional *flats* of wood and canvas, or will built-up details of wood or plastic be better, or will such special materials as poured polyurethane foam or corrugated cardboard or metal pipe be better?); any *special effects* that make special scenic demands (Are there vast outdoor scenes in a proscenium theatre that require large painted *drops,* or will such unusual events in the play as earthquakes, explosions, and so on require special solutions?); any decision to imitate *historical scenery* that creates special requirements (that is, if a seventeenth-century play is to be done with Italianate scenery, what will the effects be?); and the demands of *budget* and *schedule.*

All of these matters may influence the designer before pencil is ever put to paper, although preliminary doodles and sketches may attempt to catch the "feel" of the play long before any practical matters are dealt with. These early impressions will

FIGURE 9-3. The Designer's Ground Plan. Lewis A. Crickard's pencil plan for Goldoni's *The Servant of Two Masters.* (Rendering and completed setting in the color section.)

spring from early readings of the play, and they will eventually be incorporated in some form into the *rendering* of the settings that the designer gives the director. Together, they will have worked out the ground plan of each setting, and the ground plan will form the basis of both renderings and three-dimensional models. If the renderings are acceptable, the designer will proceed to elevations and scale drawings of all scenic pieces, and these, with all instructions for building and painting, will go to the production's *technical director*.

In addition, the scene designer is normally in charge of the design or selection of all *properties*, the things used by the actors that are not part of the scenery (furniture, flags, hangings, and so on), as well as such "hand props" as swords, cigarette cases, guns, and letters. Where such things must be designed, as in a period play, the designer creates, and the technical staff executes; where they are acquired from outside sources, the designer haunts stores and antique shops and pores over catalogs of all sorts. In plays done with minimal scenery, as in arena staging, the properties take on added importance, and their design and selection are carried out with great care.

The Technical Director

New York productions have large technical staffs, and they contract out such jobs as scene-construction and painting. Small community theatres may have only a single technician to do almost everything. In all kinds of theatres, however, a person exists to oversee the execution of designs and to organize and manage the technical production and its relationship with the theatre. This person is the *technical director*.

The technical director rules the theatre building around the playing area and behind whatever barrier separates audience from backstage. The job is a tangle of details and responsibilities: he or she knows the theatre building thoroughly and coordinates its maintenance with the building's owner (a university, a foundation, and so on); he or she sees that an ample stock of cables, nails, paint, and a thousand other things are kept on hand; he or she sees to the upkeep of tools, from pencils to table saws; he or she has oversight of backstage scheduling; he or she knows what scenery and properties are in storage and maintains their inventories. In short, the technical director has a huge responsibility, and a day-to-day schedule that can be crushing without the most careful planning (and an even temper).

In university theatres, the technical director usually attends meetings at which plays are first selected; even at this earliest stage, his or her advice will be needed to determine if a potential play is too demanding for the theatre's physical capabilities. Later, the technical director takes part in all production meetings, advising director and designer on the practicability of ideas and the likelihood of deadlines. Throughout, the technical director is responsible for setting and meeting scenic and property schedules. (Lighting may fall within his or her responsibility, as well; costumes generally do not.) On top of all this, in educational theatre the technical director does a great deal of the actual work of construction and painting, as well as instructing students working on the production.

Many technical directors are capable designers in their own right. When not executing their own designs, however, they must work objectively, remembering Lee

Simonson's dictum that "technology is the tail to the poet's kite." It is the technical director who causes the poet's kite to fly—but not to fly away.

The Costume Designer

The costume designer clothes both the character and the actor, creating dress in which the character is "right" and the actor is both physically comfortable and artistically pleased. This double responsibility makes the costumer's a difficult job. It is never enough to sew up something that copies a historically accurate garment; that garment must be made for a character, and it must be made for an actor. The actor must be able to move and speak and should also feel led or pushed by the costume to a closer affinity with the character and the world of the play. Generally, actors want costumes to be becoming to them personally, and costumers need tact in dealing with people who feel that their legs or their noses or their bosoms are not being flattered.

In designing for the character, the costumer must keep firmly in mind the *given circumstances* of the character, such as age, sex, state of health, and social class, as well as the focal importance of the character in key scenes (Should it form part of a crowd or stand out?), and most important of all, those elements of character that would express themselves through clothes. Is the character cheerful or somber? Simple or complex? Showy or timid? Majestic or mousy?

Other important matters are *silhouette* (the mass and outline of the costume as worn); *the costume in motion* (Does it have potential for swirl or billow or drape or curve as it moves? Does it change with movement? Will it encourage, even inspire, the actor to move more dynamically? What aspects of it—fringe, a scarf, coattails, a cape, a shawl—can be added or augmented to enhance motion?); *fabric texture and draping* (Does the play suggest the roughness of burlap and canvas or the smoothness of silk? What is wanted—fabrics that will drape in beautiful folds, like velour, silk, or jersey, or fabrics that will hang straight and heavily?); *fabric pattern* (all-over, small, repeated patterns as opposed to very large designs on the fabric, or none at all); *enhancement or suppression of body lines* (the pelvic V of the Elizabethan waist, or the pushed-up bosom of the French Empire, the pronounced sexuality of the medieval codpiece, or the body-disguising toga; and, for the individual actor, are there individual characteristics like narrow shoulders, skinny calves, or long necks that must be disguised); and, where necessary, *special effects* (such as animal or bird costumes or fantasy creatures).

In addition, the costumer must consult with both scene and lighting designer to make sure that the costumes will look as they are designed to look under stage light and against the settings. Practical considerations like budget and deadlines are, of course, always important.

The costumer's designs are usually presented as color renderings, normally with swatches of the actual materials attached, and with detailed notations indicated for the *costume shop supervisor*. From these, patterns are made, where needed; the costumer selects the fabrics and usually oversees their cutting and the construction of the costumes themselves. Most theatre companies of any size keep a stock of costumes from which some pieces can be "pulled" for certain productions, thus saving time

(Text continued on page 189.)

FIGURE 9-4. **Technical Work.** Behind the completed performance lie hundreds of hours of work overseen by the technical director. Work as a "tekkie" is the first nonaudience contact with the theatre for many students; here, a variety of tasks, and the tool area of a university theatre. *(Courtesy of the University of Maryland.)*

FIGURE 9-5. The Work of the Costume Designer. Design by Helen Huang, USAA, for Molière's *School for Wives:* Pencil sketch; rendering with fabric swatches; and photograph of the actor, Mitchell Patrick, in the finished costume. (See color section for a color rendering of the same costume.)

and money. Costume support areas of any size usually include, besides the stock, fitting rooms, cutting tables, sewing machines and sewing spaces, and tubs for washing and dyeing.

The Lighting Designer

When stages were lit by candles, attempts to control the light were very crude and seldom very successful. In those days, the lighting designer's work was largely confined to special effects, such as fire. With the introduction of a controllable light source, however, and with the demand in the nineteenth century for more and more realistic imitations of phenomena like sunrise and moonlight, the designer's task became far more challenging and the creation far richer. Very shortly, the possibilities of stage lighting expanded enormously from simple imitation of natural effects, and lighting became a design element as important and as potent as scenery itself.

The possible uses of theatre light are enormous. Through manipulation of intensity and direction, for example, a designer can change the apparent shape of an onstage object. Through manipulation of intensity and color, the lighting designer can influence the audience's sense of mood and tone. Through manipulation of direction and color, the designer can create a world utterly unlike the one in which the audience lives, with light coming from fantastic angles and falling in colors never seen in nature.

Modern equipment has made theatre lighting more flexible than early designers ever dreamed. Small, easily aimed *instruments* (lighting units) and complex electronic controls, sometimes with computerized memories, have made possible a subtlety in stage lighting that was unknown even thirty years ago.

The lighting designer works with three fundamentals: *color, direction,* and *intensity* of light. These are partly interdependent because of the nature of the light source, usually an incandescent filament. *Color* is changed physically by the placement of a transparent colored medium (usually called a *gel*) in the beam of light; this is not usually changed during a performance. *Direction* is a function of the location of the lighting instruments, of which hundreds may be used in a contemporary production. Each instrument is plugged into an electric circuit either individually or with a few others to illuminate the same scene. The location of instruments is rarely changed during performance, and so designers are limited by the number of instruments and the number of electrical circuits available to them. Light *intensity* is controlled by changes in the electrical current supplied to the instrument; this process is called *dimming* and is done by manipulating the levers on *dimmers*, of which several kinds are in use. All have the same goal of changing the amount of light coming from the instrument from zero to full intensity, with the capability of stopping at any point in between.

The lighting designer's plan is called a *light plot.* It shows the location and direction of each instrument, as well as what kind of instrument is to be set at each location— usually either a *floodlight* (soft-edged and wide-beamed) or a *spotlight* (hard-edged and narrow-beamed). The locations chosen are over and around the playing area, so that light falls on the actors and the acting space at an angle, both vertically and horizontally. (Light that falls straight down or comes in parallel to the stage floor

FIGURE 9-6. **The Work of the Lighting Designer.** A light plot and the completed lighting by Steve Gilliam: *The Merchant of Venice* at Trinity University, San Antonio.

gives very unusual effects, although both have their uses.) In addition, such subsidiary instruments as *light borders* or *strip lights* (rows of simple lights without lenses, suspended overhead for general illumination), *footlights* (at floor level along the front of many proscenium stages), and *follow spots* (very powerful spotlights that swivel so that their bright beam can constantly illuminate a moving performer) are sometimes used.

The lighting designer is usually responsible for projected scenery or projected shadows, clouds, and similar effects.

The lighting designer has the special responsibility of making everyone else's work accessible to the audience. Light determines what the audience will see. Light creates depth, for one thing, and it can make an actor's eyes seem to sink into deep sockets or vanish in a bland, flat mask. Light gives or takes color, and it can make costume colors glow with vibrancy or fade into dirty gray. Light is selective, and it can show the audience precisely what is to be seen.

In making the other artists' work accessible to the audience, the lighting designer has to consider all three elements: intensity, direction, and color. There are no hard-and-fast rules here; rather, there is need for a manipulation and an experimentation that is like putting colored paint on canvas. Although much of the lighting designer's work is done in production meetings and at the drawing board, much more of it is done in *technical rehearsals*, when, with the director, the designer experiments with colors and intensities and, frequently, makes decisions to change the locations and the plugging of instruments. Because of this experimental work that comes very late in the production period (often only days before opening), the lighting designer's work is crammed into a short time, and he or she works then at great intensity.

The Sound Designer

Sound became a theatre art with good stereo equipment and related amplification, blending, and tuning equipment. To be sure, sound was used in theatres before that time, and as long ago as Shakespeare's Globe, someone had to be responsible for rolling the cannonballs that simulated thunder, but a sound that could be shaped dimensionally and controlled in pure, correct tones was not possible until very recently. To the regret of many, the sound designer's job has been expanded in many theatres to the "miking" of performers, so that today many actors are heard through speakers rather than directly. As good as modern equipment is, it is not yet good enough to imitate in range, vibrancy, and direction the natural voice of the actor. It has proved a benefit, however, to actors who lack sufficient voice to be heard in large theatres.

As equipment becomes still more sophisticated and as expertise increases, the work of the sound designer may become as important and creative as that of the lighting designer. Limited at present to concepts of "sound effects" and "background music," the sound designer will one day be able to wrap the audience in sound as the lighting designer wraps the stage in light, and to play as flexibly with sound as the other plays with light. Rock concerts and sound-and-light shows are already pointing the way.

· MEDEA ·

FIGURE 9-7. **Good Design.** A costume sketch and a completed costume accessory by Martin Thaler. For two different plays, these show variety and creativity: the costume, creative interpretation of play and character; the hat, a great attention to detail.

WHAT IS GOOD DESIGN?

Good design is good art. It is created in terms of the production, however, and it is created within the context of other artists' decisions. Knowing what is the product of a designer and what of a director can often be difficult, however, and, especially in our director-dominated theatre, assessing each designer's work is sometimes challenging.

Good design, above all, serves the actor—giving the actor good spaces in which to act, clothing the actor, illuminating the actor.

Good design serves the production. It does not necessarily serve the "playwright's intentions"; interpretation may have greatly changed this production from those intentions. Obvious changes may have been made—in historical period, geographical location, social class—along with less obvious ones (genre, mood, style); the play may even have become the framework, in this production, for an idea the very opposite of the "intention." In serving the production, good design meshes with other elements and does not call attention to itself.

Good design, where possible, is dynamic, not static: it has the capacity to change as the performance progresses. Such change is clearest in costumes and lighting, less so in scenery, where the number of sets is limited. A set that makes a powerful statement right off the bat and never goes beyond it for the entire performance may be a bad set.

Good design is not redundant. It does not merely "state the theme." It has its own complexity.

Good design has detail and texture (variety within the whole): light is not merely a bland wash of light; a costume is not merely a wide stretch of draped and sewn fabric; a setting is not a mere painted surface.

Good design has technical finish. Designers must design within the technical limitations of their theatres, so that everything the audience sees is technically well done. Often, designers oversee the technical work or approve it; nothing second-rate should pass their eyes.

Good design is daring: it tries new technologies, avoids old solutions, and chances failure.

The good designer, then, is one who creates effective works of visual art that serve the actor, that are right for the performance, that are richly textured and dynamic, and that can be perfectly finished by the technical capabilities of the theatre. The bad designer is one who ignores the actor; who creates ugly or uninteresting things; who designs for a predetermined idea of the play, not for this production; who creates statically; who ignores the capabilities of the technical facilities and allows shoddy work to go on the stage.

CHAPTER TEN

THE MEDIATORS

Mediation surrounds the theatre, preparing the audience for the performance. Mediation informs, educates, and sometimes entertains. Although mediation includes the work of professionals connected with the theatre itself (public relations copywriters and graphics people, for example), it also includes men and women who may work at several removes from the theatre—who may even, in fact, have no direct connection with the theatre at all.

These people are not theatre artists. Their interest in the theatre is intellectual or commercial rather than artistic. Their influence can be great, although it can vary enormously from situation to situation. Their writings can be important evidence of theatrical history. These are people concerned with theory and crtiticism, dramaturgy, reviewing, and public relations.

THE THEORIST

A theory is an intellectual construct that seeks to define and explain a phenomenon. In the theatre, we have two kinds of theory:

- Dramatic theory, which deals with plays (Aristotle's theory of tragedy, for example).

- Performance theory, which deals with performance, and which has, as yet, no workable, effective example.

194

FIGURE 10-1. Mediation in the Eighteenth Century. To attract audiences and tell them what to expect, performers at London's Bartholomew Fair in 1721 used signs, barkers, and short excerpts from performances. *(Courtesy of the Billy Rose Theatre Collection, the New York Public Library at Lincoln Center; Astor, Lenox and Tilden Foundations.)*

A theory should meet three requirements:

1. It should be systematic (i.e., reasoned and orderly).

2. It should cover all cases.

3. It should agree with the evidence.

In the strictest sense, no comprehensive theory of drama or performance exists. However, Aristotle's theory of tragedy is usually accepted as a comprehensive theory of at least Greek tragedy, and sometimes of other kinds of drama, as well.

The lack of a comprehensive theory of performance is caused by the temporary nature of the evidence (the performance) and a failure to agree, as yet, on precisely what the evidence is; by the enormous difficulties in creating a systematic theory of performance; and by the bewildering number of cases that must be covered. (Shall we include dance theatre? ritual performance? improvisation?) Performance theory is further complicated by the need to include the audience in the notion of performance.

Theorists seek to answer questions like: What is theatre? and What is drama? They may seek to answer questions of genre: What is tragedy? What is comedy? Their answers may be limited to historically defined answers (Neoclassical tragedy) or political ones (social-realist drama).

Theorists mediate theatre most powerfully through education. Major theories are complex; they form the basis of university-level courses ("Aristotle on Tragedy,"

"Plato on Drama," "Suzanne Langer's Aesthetic of Drama"). They then filter into the general consciousness through the work of other mediators and artists—not always in a form that the theorists themselves would recognize.

The creation of theory is an activity of major importance. Its goal is self-justifying, and it often has nothing to do with affecting the art of the theatre. At its best, it is a branch of philosophy.

Post-Modern Theory

Theories have multiplied in the *post-modern* period (that is, the period since about 1960, when many previous assumptions about the nature of truth as "objective" and "scientifically verifiable" came under serious attack). Such multiplication is itself an expression of post-modernism: no single theory works; no single theory is universally accepted. Even within theories, elements are drawn from several disciplines.

Chief among current theories are the following:

- *Semiotics*, the "study of signs," an attempt to define how audiences make meanings of the performance's auditory and visual details.

- *Feminist theory*, an amalgam of film theory and a branch of psychoanalysis (Lacanism), with various goals: e.g., to define a feminist aesthetic; to study a historically male theatre vis-a-vis women (the theatre as an example of patriarchy); to study the theatre and gender.

- *Deconstructionism*, the close analysis of text or performance to reveal alternate, rather than its stated or its conventionally understood, meanings.

THE CRITIC

Criticism is the application of theory, but the line between criticism and theory is not a clear one. Many theorists are also critics, and many critics make theoretical statements; they may not themselves be theorists because their theoretical work is not comprehensive or systematic.

Like theory, criticism has two branches: dramatic criticism and performance criticism.

Dramatic criticism is most practiced in universities. Teaching dramatic literature is sometimes a kind of dramatic criticism. Many scholarly articles are examples of dramatic criticism, although the theories on which they are based may, in fact, not be theories of drama so much as theories of literature (e.g., new criticism, phenomenology, semiotics). The criticism of Shakespeare, for example, is a major academic industry with many theoretical branches.

Specific assumptions often underlie dramatic criticism and explain the critic's analyses. These may be political (Marxist criticism) or social (feminist criticism). The critic may choose to deal only with formal criticism (matters of form, structure, and so on) or only with content criticism (matters of idea, metaphor, and so on), although the two converge.

FIGURE 10-2. **Mediation in the Nineteenth Century.** A poster from London's Covent Garden in 1829 announces the evening's entertainment and provides the audience with the cast for each event.

Because we have no adequate performance theory, we have no adequate performance criticism; nonetheless, we have many performance critics—men and women who are trying at least to describe performances seriously. At this stage, most performance criticism is purely descriptive and seeks to record the complex impacts of the many discrete moments of performance. Performance specialists are working hard to create theories of performance, but they have the difficulties we have already noted in even talking about performance systematically. (For example, the vocabulary of dramatic criticism is not adequate: the concept of dramatic action does not suffice for the actor-playing-character-in-costume-making-decision at a moment that is only one of thousands of moments. And what is a moment?)

A further difficulty in performance criticism is the intervention of the critic: the act of criticism appears to change what is going on in the performance.

Criticism, whether of drama or performance, is a serious intellectual undertaking. Its need for reflection militates against deadlines and pressure. Probably as a result, most of the best modern critics have had academic connections and have published their work as books. A few critics have been theatre artists.

FIGURE 10-3. **Mass Marketing, Nineteenth Century.** This poster advertising *Humpty Dumpty* depicts well-known scenes from the play and leaves a blank space, center, where individual theatres could provide information about times, dates, prices.

THE DRAMATURG

Long a recognized figure in European theatres, the dramaturg has only recently appeared in America. The dramaturg is a specialist in dramatic literature and dramatic and theatrical history. Dramaturgs now have places on the staffs of some resident theatre companies; their functions include:

- Assisting in the selection of plays.

- Reading and evaluating new plays.

- Providing historical and literary background to directors, designers, and actors.

- Providing program notes.

- Assisting directors, sometimes by advising on the production.

- Working on plays—adapting, restructuring, translating.

A dramaturg is not a theatre artist but may be called on to act as one, particularly as a playwright. The historical and theoretical knowledge needed, however, and the knowledge of dramatic literature, suggest that university-level education is necessary. In fact, some American universities now offer graduate degrees in dramaturgy.

The dramaturg's mediation shows most obviously in program notes but may be present in public relations materials and in aspects of the production itself and the selection of plays.

THE PUBLIC RELATIONS SPECIALIST

Few productions can get along without some sort of advertising, be it only slips of paper photocopied at the local copy center. The directing student doing a one-act at lunch-time will probably be his or her own PR person; the New York star will

FIGURE 10-4. **Mediation in the Early Twentieth Century.** Posters often offered an idealized version of a play's most spectacular scenes in an attempt to lure customers to the theatre, as in this New York poster from 1904. (*Photograph used with permission of the New-York Historical Society, New York City.*)

have his or her own PR firm in addition to the producer's PR person and the advertising firm for the production.

University theatres have somebody who coordinates "front-of-house" activities (all those things that happen on the audience's side of the curtain), including publicity. This will include graphics for posters and programs; paid advertising; and arrangements for radio, television, and newspaper coverage, including photos and interviews. At all levels, publicity people will seek an "angle" or a "hook," something that will catch the attention of the media's gatekeepers: the actor who goes on, even with a broken ankle; the actress whose mother played the same role in the original New York production. With the director and (if such a person exists) the producer, the PR person will create an image or idea for the production that will come out of the director's interpretation; this image or idea will inform color, graphics, and text used in advertising the production (for a play about love, will we emphasize the rose or its thorns? a pink rose or a black one? will we use the word "love" or the word "passion"?).

The PR person's mediation is crucial in getting an audience into the theatre. It may also be crucial in preparing the audience correctly. Wise audience members remain skeptical of the claims of advertising ("An all-time laugh riot!"), but they learn to be alert to hints that will prepare them for a certain style, genre, and mood, as well as for subject matter in which they are interested.

FIGURE 10-5. **Mediation Today.** Here, favorable reviews have been reproduced, enlarged, and posted on the outside of the theatre as an enticement to prospective patrons.

THE REVIEWER

Reviewers are men and women who see plays and then write about them. Their orientation is toward consumer protection; that is, presenting themselves at best as an "ideal audience," they recommend or warn against performances on the basis of a taste shared with their readership.

Reviewers are seldom critics. They do not rely consistently on theory; they rarely pretend to objectivity. They lack the time to reflect on what they have seen, their work usually appearing in a daily or weekly publication. Often, their format is so limited (one minute on radio or television) that little can be said at all.

Reviewers are reviewers of both drama and performance. They do not attempt to tell readers or listeners what performance is or how it works, but they do tell them whether or not performance is likable within certain limits.

Some reviewers have theatrical backgrounds or education. Some do not. Experienced reviewers have trained themselves to recognize their own responses and to turn them into interesting, often witty prose, one of the functions of reviewing being to entertain.

Reviewers develop degrees of power within their communities, the New York reviewers supposedly having life-or-death power over Broadway productions. Their mediation extends beyond the review itself when quotations from the reviews are included in theatrical advertising. Because of this practice, some reviewers come to write quotable reviews, eager, perhaps, to see their names on theatre marquees with those of the actors. When this point is reached, the reviewer, although still a mediator, has crossed over from reviewing into public relations. In this way, a few reviewers become media stars in their own right.

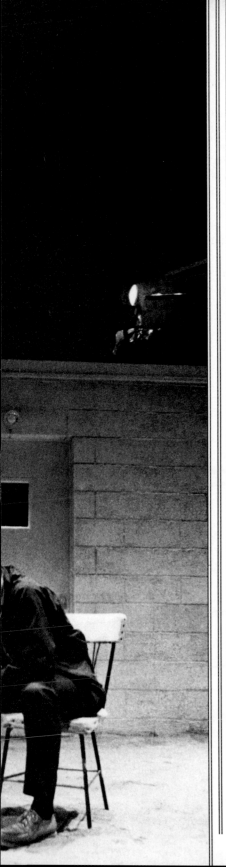

PART THREE

THEATRE
of
OTHER
TIMES
and
PLACES

THE PRESENT AND THE PAST

Because the theatre of the present is not merely a theatre of today's plays and today's techniques but is also a theatre of plays and techniques from many periods, the alert and responsive audience member will be knowledgeable about the theatre's past and its present. The prepared audience studies the past to enrich the present. It studies, too, to understand what the forces of change are and how they work and to see that audiences and artists of every age have been much like us, subject to the same pressures, glad of the same pleasures.

It is tempting, perhaps, to think of a theatre of the past as filled with people who were somehow different from us—more polite or stuffier or older or stupider or less sophisticated—but as a study of the theatre's history will show, they were not all that different. They laughed and wept, applauded and hissed, got bored by bad performances and gave standing ovations to great ones. To understand this fact—that the theatre is a great force and that its audience is a great, vital constant—is to understand why the theatre is an art that stands at the center of human concerns.

CHAPTER ELEVEN

FAÇADE STAGES: GREECE AND ROME

THE UNCERTAIN ORIGINS OF THEATRE

Scholars disagree about the origins of theatre, in part because they do not agree on what constitutes theatre and in part because evidence is too scant to permit certainty on many crucial points. Everyone agrees that theatrical and dramatic elements exist in life and therefore in all societies. Scholars do not agree, however, whether such theatrical and dramatic elements should be included within what we call *theatre*. Issues of definition are important because they have both political and artistic implications.

Two examples can clarify the political stakes. If *theatre* is understood to be one of several forms of ritual, then theatre probably originated in many cultures; if *theatre* is defined as a self-conscious work of art, then theatre probably originated in Athens. If *theatre* is understood to encompass informal, improvisational performances at community gatherings, then women probably participated in theatre from its beginnings; if *theatre* is defined as an institutional activity supported by church or state, then theatre has been an all-male event for most of its 2500-year history. Questions of definition are important, then, because they can serve to exclude or empower certain groups of people. As you will see in the following chapters, the theatre's history as traditionally taught has been the history of an institution of mostly white, European males (for whom it originated in Athens and was supported by church and state.)

Different definitions of theatre obviously predispose toward different theories of the origins of theatre. The conservative definition (and the one that we have adopted in this textbook—see Chapter 1) is that theatre is a self-conscious activity whose aim is a work of art. While acknowledging the many paratheatrical (theatre-like) activities in everyday life, this conservative definition seeks ways of distinguishing among life, ritual, ceremony, dance, music, theatre, games, and so on. In this context, the question of theatre's origin becomes, "Where, why, when, and by what means did the various theatrical and dramatic elements that are routinely found in life and in religion become transformed into activities whose primary aim is artistic (as distinct from religious or instructional)?"

Even if we can agree on this definition of theatre, we still cannot agree on the origins of theatre because evidence does not allow us to offer clear answers to central questions. In the absence of certain answers, a number of theories have emerged.

The Storytelling Theory

Some scholars have proposed that Western drama developed from storytelling. Telling and hearing stories, according to this theory, are pleasurable and natural; so too is the tendency of a narrator to elaborate parts of the telling by impersonating the various characters, using appropriate voice and movement. From here, it seems merely a short step to having several people become involved in the telling of a story; and from this, it is thought, drama and theatre arose.

The Dance Theory

Other theorists suggest that movement rather than speech was at the core of the drama. By imitating the physical behavior of animals and humans, and by donning appropriate skins or garments, a dancer first impersonated them and later embroidered this performance with sounds and words. The single dancer was joined by others who likewise impersonated and garbed themselves, and a form of theatre was born, it is supposed.

The Judicial Theory

A few scholars have sought the form of drama in the judicial system of Athens. Alluding to the many instances in which debates and arguments occur in the plays and to the instances in which judgments are required, such theorists have sought the beginnings of Greek drama in the courtrooms of its early societies.

The Ritual Theory

Probably the most fashionable, but not necessarily the most correct, view of the origin of theatre is the so-called ritual theory. A ritual is an activity that is repeated to gain a specific and predictable outcome. Religious rituals developed in all primitive

FIGURE 11-1. Dionysus. Whatever its origin, early theatre in Greece was closely associated with the god Dionysus, imagined in this drawing with a satyr who plays a flute-like instrument.

cultures as a means of affecting events, propitiating gods, transmitting information, educating the young, and so on. The ritual theory of drama proposes that from primitive religious rituals, in particular those connected with fertility and the spirits of the seasonal cycle, dramas evolved. Although few respectable scholars still accept the idea that drama "evolved" in some organic, necessary way from religious ceremonies, most acknowledge that ritual probably influenced emerging theatrical forms.

The "Great Man" Theory

Finally, some scholars view the appearance of tragedy and comedy as a supreme creative act of an unidentified artist (perhaps Thespis, perhaps Aeschylus, perhaps another). Arguing that art neither evolves like a biological organism nor happens by chance, such scholars look for the birth of drama in a revolutionary discovery made by a human being, an artist: that the synthesis of many elements already established in Athenian society (dance, music, storytelling) would produce a more sublime work of art—and thus drama was born.

Aristotle's Evidence

Two statements by Aristotle, too, bear on the question of the drama's origin. He claimed, in Chapter 4 of the *Poetics*, that "tragedy was produced by the authors of the dithyramb, and comedy from [the authors] of the phallic songs." Dithyrambs were choral odes; phallic songs were rites whose precise nature is not known. Although tantalizing, Aristotle's account does little to clarify for what reasons or in what manner the authors shifted from dithyramb to tragedy or from phallic song to comedy. He also observed that "imitation is natural to men from childhood and in this they differ from the other animals . . . and then everybody takes pleasure in imitation." Because Aristotle was writing closer to the event than any of those advocating other theories, his account deserves consideration; still, it should be remembered that Aristotle was himself writing more than two hundred years after the event he was describing.

In its essence, the argument over the origin of theatre is an argument over the most important element of theatre. To the anthropologist who looks at mimings or impersonations as different as the Mandan Buffalo Dance, the Iroquois False Face Society, and the Egyptian "Passion Play," the essence of theatre is ritual, and the ritual theory will be favored. To the critic who finds the bedrock of drama in conflict, mythmaking or legal battle will seem the most like dramatic action, and the story-telling or the judicial theory will be favored. To the artist who looks at world theatre and sees a form rich in human meaning and almost indescribable in complexity, only a nonrational leap will explain its beginnings.

In fact, we do not know how theatre began. And finally, it is not so important for us to know its beginnings as to theorize and to argue about them, for in that thinking and that argument we preserve our sense of the extraordinary richness of a great art that will not allow itself to be reduced to simple explanations.

The first phase of theatrical and dramatic history for which we have records began in the sixth century B.C. and ended around A.D. 500, a period of about one thousand years. Despite important differences, the theatres of Greece and Rome shared important traits:

1. A *façade stage,* where actors performed in front of a neutral background.

2. A *relationship with religion,* in which plays were presented as a part of larger, religious celebrations.

3. A *sense of occasion,* because performances were offered only on special occasions and never often enough to be taken for granted.

4. A *noncommercial environment,* in which wealthy citizens or the state itself bore the costs as part of the obligations of citizenship.

5. A *male-only theatre,* in which women participated only as audience.

THE GREEK THEATRE

Background

Although civilizations had existed in Greek lands for thousands of years, the civilization that produced the first recorded theatre and drama dated from about the eighth century B.C. By the fifth century B.C., the society had developed a sophisticated system of government and culture. The basic governing unit was the city-state, or *polis,* which consisted of a town and its surrounding lands. Many were important

FIGURE 11-2. **Map of the Greek World.** Athens's position on the sea gave it access to Troy to the east and Italy to the west.

(e.g., Corinth, Sparta, Thebes), but Athens emerged during the fifth century as the cultural and artistic leader of Greece. The Athenians established the world's first democracy (508 B.C.) and provided a model for the participation of citizens in the decisions and policies of government, achieving a level of participation unequaled except perhaps by the New England town meetings.

Under Pericles (c. 460–430 B.C.), Athens soared to new heights in art, architecture, and drama and headed an empire in the eastern Mediterranean, providing protection and trade outlets for other city-states in exchange for payments and other forms of tribute. Athens developed a drama that is still acknowledged as superb; buildings like the Parthenon and the Theatre of Dionysus were major achievements; and the arts in general achieved a status seldom rivaled since.

A defeat in the Peloponnesian War (404 B.C.) ended Athenian supremacy among the city-states, and an invasion of Greece by Alexander the Great (336 B.C.) changed the political and social configuration of the whole peninsula. By the time the Roman Empire encroached on the area in the second and first centuries B.C., little of the former glory of Athens remained.

Greek theatre and drama lasted for over a thousand years. Records of organized theatrical activity date from the sixth century B.C. and continue well into the Christian era. The unquestionable impact on the audiences of its day can be explained, at least in part, by four qualities that characterized this very vital theatre:

1. Greek theatre was closely associated with Greek religion.

2. Greek theatre was performed only on special occasions.

3. Greek theatre was competitive.

4. Greek drama was choral.

Greek Theatre and Greek Religion

Whatever the theatre's origin, Greek theatre was closely associated with Greek religion, which, unlike Judaism and Christianity, had many gods: Zeus, the king of the gods; Hera, his wife; Athena, goddess of wisdom; and so on. Private worship was interwoven into the daily lives of the people, but public worship occurred at festivals dedicated to a particular god. The festivals might last several days, and each *polis* had several festivals each year. In and around Athens, there were four festivals every year devoted to Dionysus, god of wine and fertility. At three of these festivals (the Great, or City, Dionysia; the Rural Dionysia; and the Lenaia), dramas were regularly performed as a part of the festivities.

For at least two hundred years after the first surviving records, all drama in Greece seems to have been performed only at Athens and only at religious festivals devoted to the god Dionysus.

The close association of Greek religion and Greek theatre is further shown by the presence of an altar within the playing area and, later, by places of honor in the theatres for the priests of Dionysus. Although the intimate connections between religion and theatre had been loosened by the end of the fourth century B.C., their relationship persisted; for example, when an actor's union was formed in the third century B.C., it took the name "Artists of Dionysus" and drew its officers from the ranks of Dionysian priests.

The Occasional Nature of the Theatre

The fact that a festival is religious does not make it solemn; Mardi Gras and Halloween are, after all, religious festivals. Indeed, the fact that drama was performed at religious festivals in Greece seems not to have inhibited its joy or power. Experience suggests that annual celebrations often result in a more festive atmosphere and a more exuberant audience than regular affairs, simply because the event is relatively rare and therefore special. Because Greek drama was performed at festivals, it was performed only on special occasions, several times a year rather than several times a week. In trying to capture the effect of the festival arrangement, it might be well to compare it with celebrating a birthday or attending Mardi Gras, rather than with attending a play or a movie.

The Competitive Side of the Theatre

To add to the excitement of the event, dramatic works in the festivals were competitive, with dramatists competing among themselves for awards in writing and actors competing for prizes in performing. The audience was interested not only in hearing the individual plays but also in learning who had won the various contests.

FIGURE 11-3. The Chorus. This nineteenth-century production of a Greek play at Cambridge University shows an all-male chorus (in keeping with Greek practice) but a chorus without masks and similar costumes (departing from Greek practice).

Greek theatre, then, probably had some of the elements of a long-standing football rivalry, as well as those elements associated with drama and theatre.

The Choral Drama of Greece

In addition to actors, Greek drama required a chorus, a group of men who dressed alike, who were masked alike, and who moved and spoke together most of the time. The chorus often figured prominently in the working out of the play's action, and its importance to the total theatrical experience can scarcely be overemphasized.

The presence of the chorus in the performing area throughout the performance provided considerable spectacle, its costumes, songs, and dances adding to the visual experience of the production. Because the chorus danced as it spoke, chanted, and sang, its rhythms indicated changing moods and shifting fortunes. By focusing attention on certain characters and events and avoiding others, by supporting some actions and denouncing others, the chorus provided a point of view, serving often as an ideal spectator. The chorus established the ethical system operating in the play and indicated the moral universe of the characters. Finally, and perhaps most important of all, the chorus—like an actor—participated often and directly in the action of the play, providing information and making discoveries and decisions.

Whether in comedy or tragedy, the chorus was an invariable fact of the performance and influenced a number of practices. Although estimates of its size are questionable, the traditional view is that in tragedy, the number of men in the chorus was first fifty, then twelve, and then, with Sophocles, fifteen, where it remained throughout the Classical Age; in comedy, the chorus probably numbered twenty-four.

Because the chorus usually came into the performing space soon after the play opened and remained there until the end, its presence had to be considered in both the physical layout of the theatre and the action of the drama. The chorus required a space large enough to move about in; and the presence of the chorus had to be justified and their loyalties made clear when secrets were shared. Because the vocal and visual power of the chorus was great (the contribution of each chorus member was, after all, multiplied by fifteen or twenty-four), the actors adjusted their style so as not to be overwhelmed by the impact of the chorus.

The Study of Greek Theatre and Drama

Beyond the facts that Greek drama and theatre were closely associated with religion, were performed on specific occasions, and were competitive and choral, little else is certain. Evidence is scanty and often contradictory. Most of what is known comes from five kinds of sources: the extant plays; scattered dramatic records of the period; commentaries such as those of Aristotle; the archaeological remains of theatre buildings; and certain pieces of visual art, most notably vase paintings. Ironically, most of the extant plays date from the fifth century B.C., but most of the other evidence dates from the fourth century and later. The result is that for the period in which we know most about the theatre *buildings*, we know least about the *plays*; and for the years for which we have plays to study, we know very little about the buildings in which they were done or the techniques used to produce them.

Unfortunately, some have "solved" this problem by grouping all of the evidence together and speaking of the Greek theatre as though its practices remained invariable throughout its thousand-year history. But Greek theatre changed as markedly during its existence as the modern theatre has changed in a thousand years (since c. A.D. 990). And so it is necessary to identify which period of the Greek theatre is meant when considering production practices.

To simplify matters, we divide the Greek theatre into three major periods: the Classical, the Hellenistic, and the Graeco-Roman. Because most of the extant dramas date from the Classical Age, its practices will be described first and in greatest detail.

FIGURE 11-4. **Time Line: Greek Theatre and Drama.** Extant dramas date from the Classical period, but architectural evidence dates from the Hellenistic and Graeco-Roman periods.

The Classical Period (c. 534–336 B.C.)

The Theatre

The Theatre of Dionysus, Athens' first important theatre, was situated on a hillside, with a circular playing area at its base and the audience seated on the slope looking down. The first documented production occurred there in 534 B.C., and tradition holds that the winner of the contest was Thespis, who both wrote and acted in the winning tragedy. For a time, the playing area (*orchestra*), the audience area, and the corridors separating the two may have been the only parts of this theatre.

By 458 B.C., however, a scene house (the *skene*) had been erected adjacent to the orchestra. Although its exact appearance remains a matter of conjecture, it probably had two or three doors and was used first as a place for the actors to change costumes and masks, later becoming a background for the play's action, representing variously a palace, a temple, a home, or even a cave. If a raised stage was present (scholarly opinion is divided on this point), it probably ran the length of the scene house and was low enough to allow easy access from the orchestra, thus permitting the necessary mingling of actors and chorus. So long as the scene house was built of wood, it was temporary and may well have been remodeled often. Once built in stone, the scene house must be considered permanent and inflexible. Thus, Greek theatre early adopted a *façade stage*, a convention in which actors performed in front of a neutral façade, with the audience facing or arcing to three sides.

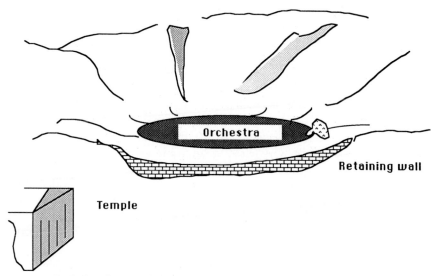

FIGURE 11-5. **Early Theatre of Dionysus.** An imaginative reconstruction of the early theatre where audiences, seated on the hillside, presumably looked down on a circular performance space and its adjacent temple.

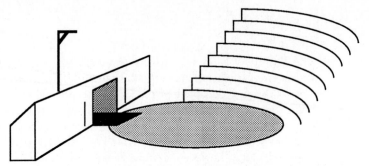

FIGURE 11-6. **Greek Stage Machinery.** The eccyclema and the mechane, imaginatively reconstructed here from evidence gleaned from extant plays. The mechane resembles a large crane; the eccyclema is a platform that can be rotated or rolled into the performing area from the skene.

The Audience

That the theatre was out-of-doors meant, of course, that the audience, numbering perhaps as many as fourteen thousand, was subject to the caprices of the weather. Being outside also meant that the audience was as visible as the performers, an attribute shared by modern football games but not by modern theatres. Laws passed in Greece making violence in the theatre punishable by death suggest that theatrical audiences of the time were sometimes unruly.

Production Practices

The basic setting, at least after 458 B.C., was the scene house. Whether or not its appearance was altered in an attempt to suggest changes in locale is not known. Something resembling modern-day flats existed, but their exact use is unclear. Two machines were used for special effects: an *eccyclema* and a *mechane*. The *eccyclema* was a movable platform capable of being rolled or rotated out of a door in the scene house, typically to reveal the bodies of characters presumably slain indoors. The *mechane* was a cranelike machine that allowed objects and people to be "flown" into the acting area. So often did the playwright Euripides fly in gods to bring his plays to a suitable conclusion that the Latin expression *deus ex machina* ("god from the machine") now refers to any obviously contrived ending in dramatic literature. Various properties were used in productions. Tragedies called for altars, tombs, biers, chariots, staffs, and so on; comedies often required domestic furniture. *Periaktoi*, scenic units with three faces mounted on a central pivot, may have been available during the Classical Age, but their use can be documented only for a later period.

Costumes and Masks

Costumes and masks helped to differentiate one character from another and often provided clues about the characters wearing them. For example, in some plays, references can be found to characters who are dressed in the manner of Greeks and others who are dressed as foreigners. Black was a color often worn by characters in mourning; and in a comedy, a god was dressed in yellow to make a point about his effeminacy. Although some historians have argued for a standard tragic costume, it seems more likely that costumes were a variation on the garments worn by contemporary Athenians; in the case of tragedy, probably like the elegant garments of the upper classes, and, in the case of comedy, more like the clothes of the lower and middle classes, but made laughable by having them ill-fitting, too tight, and too short. To the costume of many male characters in comedy was attached a very large phallus, intended probably as much for comic effect as for a reminder of the drama's associations with fertility and the god Dionysus.

Masks were worn by all performers (except possibly the flute player). The masks were full and carried on them hairstyles and beards as well as appropriate facial expressions. During the Classical Age, the masks, headdresses, and footwear were not exaggerated (the high boots and large-mouthed tragic masks often seen in books belong to a later period). Whereas the masks and costumes of the actors served primarily to distinguish one character from another, those of the chorus members stressed the *groupness* of the chorus by all looking alike.

Acting

Acting, like playwriting, was a competitive activity during the Classical Age, and rules governed its practice. For example, all actors were male. Apparently no more than three *speaking* actors were allowed in the tragedies and five in the comedies, although any number of extras might be used. Because the leading actor, or *protagonist*, was the only one competing for the prize, he was assigned to the playwright by lot, so that chance rather than politics decided who got the best roles. The second actor and the third actor were probably chosen by the playwright and the protagonist in consultation. With only three actors, doubling of roles was required, for the plays themselves often had eight or more characters. If the protagonist had an exceedingly demanding role, like the title role in *Oedipus Rex,* he might play only one character, but the second and third actors were expected to play two or more secondary roles. Doubling, the use of masks, and the use of only male actors suggest that the style of Greek acting was more formal than realistic; that is, although the acting was true and believable *in its own terms,* its resemblance to real life was of considerably less importance than its fidelity to the dramatic action. Given the size of the audience, the physical arrangement of the theatre, and the style of acting, it should be no surprise that vocal power and agility were the actor's most prized assets.

Plays

Of the thousands of plays written during the thousand years of Greek theatre, only forty-six survive. Most of these date from the Classical Age and can be attributed to four authors: Aeschylus (seven), Sophocles (seven), Euripides (eighteen), and Aristophanes (eleven).

THESPIS. The semilegendary Thespis supposedly wrote tragedies using only one actor and a chorus. Although none of Thespis' works survived, they probably were based on the intensification of a single event rather than the development of a story, because stories require changes to occur. With only one actor and a chorus, the opportunity to introduce new information into a scene (and thus, to introduce change into a situation) was severely limited. The continual disappearance of either the actor or the chorus to fetch new information would obviously have been awkward and was thus necessarily curtailed.

AESCHYLUS. Aeschylus (c. 525–456 B.C.) probably introduced a second actor, thereby permitting change to occur within the play. Although a second actor would also allow conflict between two characters, Aeschylus still tended to depict a solitary hero, one isolated and facing a cosmic horror brought about by forces beyond his control. With such a grand tragic conception, Aeschylus required great scope, and so he often wrote *trilogies,* three plays on a single subject that were intended for performance on the same day. One of his trilogies, the *Oresteia* (comprising the *Agamemnon,* the *Choëphoroe,* and the *Eumenides*), has survived intact along with the single plays *The Persians, Seven Against Thebes, The Suppliants,* and *Prometheus Bound.* All display characteristics for which Aeschylus is admired: heroic and austere characters, simple but powerful plots, lofty yet sturdy diction. His general tone is well summarized by an ancient commentator: "While one finds many different types of artistic treatment in Aeschylus, one looks in vain for those sentiments that draw tears."

SOPHOCLES. Sophocles (496–406 B.C.) was credited with adding the third actor (Aeschylus also used three actors in his late plays) and with changing practices in scenic painting and costuming. Less interested than Aeschylus in portraying solitary heroes confronting the universal order, Sophocles wrote plays that explored the place of humans within that order. The tragedy of Sophocles' heroes typically erupts from decisions made and actions taken based on imperfect knowledge or conflicting claims. Various aspects of the hero's character combine with unusual circumstances to bring about a disaster caused not by wickedness or foolishness but merely by humanness. For Sophocles, to be human was to be potentially a hero of tragedy.

The role of the chorus in Sophocles' plays remained important but not so central as in Aeschylus'. Conversely, the individual characters in Sophocles tend to be more complex, to display more individual traits, and to make more decisions. The result is that in Sophoclean tragedy, the actors, not the chorus, control the rhythm of the plays. Unlike Aeschylus, Sophocles did not need a trilogy to contain his tragedies; his plays stood alone. Of the more than one hundred attributed to him, seven have survived: *Ajax, Antigone, Oedipus Rex, Philoctetes, Electra, Trachiniae,* and *Oedipus at Colonnus.* Of these, *Oedipus Rex* is recognized by most critics as among the finest tragedies ever written.

EURIPIDES. Euripides (480–406 B.C.) was never very popular during his lifetime but came to be highly regarded after his death. Growing up at a time when Athens was embarking on policies of imperialism and expansionism that many patriots found repugnant, Euripides became a pacifist and a political gadfly. Although the populace viewed him with considerable distrust, the intellectual elite apparently admired him.

FIGURE 11-7. **Greek Tragedy.** *Oedipus Rex* as performed at Harvard University in the late nineteenth century.

It is reported, for example, that Socrates, one of the wisest men of the age, came to the theatre only to see the tragedies of Euripides and that Sophocles dressed his chorus in black on learning of the death of Euripides.

In comparison with the plays of Aeschylus and Sophocles, those of Euripides are less exalted and more realistic. His characters seem less grand and more human; their problems are less cosmic and more mundane. Euripides tended to examine human relationships and to question the wisdom of social actions: the purpose of war, the status of women, the reasons for human cruelty.

In keeping with Euripides' changed outlook came changes in dramatic technique. Replacing the philosophical probings common in the plays of Aeschylus and Sophocles, Euripides substituted rapid reversals, intrigues, chase scenes, and romantic and sentimental incidents of the sort later associated with plays called *melodramas*. (Euripides is said by some to be the father of melodrama.) He further reduced the role of the chorus, until sometimes it was little more than an interruption of the play's action. As the role of the chorus declined and the subjects became more personal, the language became less poetic and more conversational. Many of the changes that Euripides introduced into Greek tragedy, although denounced in his own time, became standard dramatic practice during the Hellenistic Age.

COMEDY. Comedy was introduced into the Great Dionysia in 486 B.C., some fifty years after tragedy. It seems never to have been comfortable there, perhaps because

FIGURE 11-8. Greek Old Comedy. Actors achieved comic effect in part through their costumes, which were commonly padded, often too short and too tight, and marked by a large phallus, doubtless the source of many visual gags in Aristophanes' *Lysistrata*.

the festival was an international showcase for Athenian culture and thus often visited by foreign dignitaries. The real home of comedy was the winter festival, the Lenaia, where a contest for comedy was established in 442 B.C. At both festivals, an entire day was set aside for competition among the comic playwrights, five of whom competed.

Of the twelve extant Greek comedies, all but one are by Aristophanes (c. 448–c. 380 B.C.); therefore, information about comedy during the Classical Age necessarily comes from these plays. It is possible, of course, that Aristophanes was atypical, and so the conclusions drawn from his works may be incorrect.

During the Classical Age, comedy was highly political and was filled with references to contemporary people and events. Although no two extant comedies are exactly alike, they bear similarities and suggest a highly formal structure that can be summarized briefly.

Greek "old comedy" was in two parts divided by a section during which, typically, the chorus or the choral leader broke the dramatic illusion and addressed the audience directly.

The first portion of the play generally consisted of a prologue, during which the outrageous assumption on which the comedy was based was set forth. Following the entrance of the chorus, there was a debate about whether or not the basic assumption, or "happy idea," should be adopted. The first part of the comedy ended with the decision to put the "happy idea" into practice.

The second portion consisted simply of a number of episodes and choral songs showing the "happy idea" at work. The comedies ended happily on a note of feasting and merriment. Although all of Aristophanes' comedies follow this pattern more or less, no one of them corresponds in every detail.

Near the end of the Classical Age, when Sparta defeated Athens in war, some sort of censorship was apparently imposed, and so comedy became less political. Aristophanes' later plays refrain from the numerous topical references and often vitriolic attacks that mark his earlier comedies. The change has been noted by a number of scholars, and so the early comedy is called *old comedy*, and the less political, later works are called *middle comedy*.

Contest Rules

During the Classical Age, plays were produced in Athens by the city-state in cooperation with selected wealthy citizens. (Women were not considered citizens in Athens.) At the Great Dionysia, three tragic writers (always male) competed each year for the prize. To compete, each submitted three tragedies and one satyr play (a short comic piece that followed the tragedies and occasionally burlesqued them).

FIGURE 11-9. Classical Theatre of Dionysus. An imaginative reconstruction of the Theatre of Dionysus after the appearance of the skene, which may (or may not) have had three doors, a porch (stage), and columns.

One day was set aside for the work of each tragic author; therefore, each year there were nine tragedies and three satyr plays presented at the Great Dionysia. At the Lenaia, only four tragedies competed each year, each by a different playwright. At both festivals, five comic playwrights (always male) competed for a prize, and a single day was set aside for this competition.

How the competitors were selected is unknown, but, once chosen, each author was matched with a wealthy citizen-sponsor, who was then responsible for meeting the costs incurred by the chorus. The city-state provided the theatre in which the plays were performed and the prizes that were awarded to the winners.

The Hellenistic Age (c. 336–c. 100 B.C.)

Historians mark the beginning of the Hellenistic Age with the conquests of Alexander the Great. The system of city-states was replaced with a more centralized form of government, and the seat of power shifted away from Athens. Theatres began to be built outside Athens and throughout the eastern Mediterranean. Productions came to be seen in many cities and on numerous occasions, military and social as well as religious. Indeed, in general, the civic and religious nature of the theatre eroded as its professional standing increased. Actors, all of whom were still male, became professionals and organized, along with other performers, into the Artists of Dionysus, an agency that oversaw contracts between the actors and the cities wishing to hire them. The citizen-sponsors turned over their financial responsibilities to the state.

Theatres were built of stone during this period, and so archaeological evidence remains. The primary features of the Hellenistic theatre included a two-storied scene house, to which was attached a very long and narrow and high stage. Usually, the stage could be reached by steps or ramps affixed to each end, but in some theatres the only access was apparently through the scene house. The orchestra circle remained essentially unchanged, but its use during this period is uncertain. Was the chorus there and the actors on stage? Or were they both one place or the other? Or did it depend on the play?

Tragedy appears to have declined in popularity during the Hellenistic Age. Those tragedies written seem to show the influence of Euripides' innovations, including the

FIGURE 11-10. Hellenistic Theatre. An imaginative reconstruction of a typical Hellenistic theatre, showing a raised stage and scenic units between the columns at orchestra level.

reduced importance of the chorus and the increased importance of sensational and melodramatic scenes. Satyr plays disappeared altogether.

Comedy, on the other hand, remained very popular. Its strong political flavor now gone, *new comedy*, as it came to be called, portrayed domestic situations of the Athenian middle classes; featured love, finances, and family relationships; and often included intrigues involving long-lost children and recognition scenes. The highly formal structure of old comedy disappeared, leaving behind only a series of episodes and choral songs, with the chorus often quite incidental to the action of the play. Because Greek new comedy greatly influenced the development of Roman comedy, its qualities assume an importance beyond that accorded Hellenistic tragedy. One example of new comedy, Menander's *The Grumbler* (c. 300 B.C.), survived.

Aristotle

During the Hellenistic Age, too, the world's first and probably most influential dramatic theorist appeared. In his *Poetics* (335 B.C.), Aristotle provided a theoretical definition of the form tragedy (Aristotle defined neither comedy nor mixed forms in *The Poetics*). He proposed that "tragedy . . . is an imitation of an action that is serious, complete, and of a certain magnitude . . . in the form of action, not narrative . . . producing pity and fear and the catharsis of such emotions." The meaning of the definition has been endlessly debated, especially the phrase about catharsis, which some scholars believe refers to the response of audiences (though elsewhere Aristotle said he did not intend to talk about audiences), and other scholars think refers to emotions embedded within the episodes of the play itself.

He then defined and discussed the six parts of a play (plot, character, idea, language, music, and spectacle). Of the six parts, plot was the most important to Aristotle. He therefore discussed it in the most detail, considering its wholeness (having a beginning, a middle, and an end, connected by causality); its unity (so that if any part is removed, the whole is disturbed); its materials (suffering, discovery, and reversal); and its form (complication and denouement).

He then considered the remaining parts of the play in turn. Along the way he argued that the best tragic protagonist is one who causes his own downfall through some great tragic error (*hamartia*), that the play's language should be both clear and interesting, and that spectacle is the business of the stage machinist rather than the poet.

Because *The Poetics* is so cryptic and its translation so difficult, its meaning has been hotly debated for two thousand years. Certainly, it remains the base from which most discussions of dramatic theory must proceed, through either acceptance or rejection of its primary tenets.

The Graeco-Roman Age (c. 100 B.C.–A.D. 500)

By about 100 B.C., the expanding Roman Empire was exerting pressure on Greece. Trends begun in the Hellenistic Age continued but were altered to bring them more in line with Roman ideals and practices. For example, Roman theatres were built in Greek lands, and Hellenistic theatres were remodeled to resemble Roman theatres more closely (we call these remodeled Hellenistic theatres *Graeco-Roman*). Although some records show that theatre in Greek lands persisted throughout this period, the center of influence clearly shifted to Rome around the time of Christ, and so attention to Greek theatre declined and was replaced by interest in Roman practices.

THE ROMAN THEATRE

Background

Rome was unparalleled among great Western civilizations simply because it remained intact so long. From a small prehistoric settlement, it grew to become the center of a far-flung empire that touched Asia and Africa as well as Britain and western Europe.

The city, although founded in the eighth century B.C., did not control the Italian peninsula until the third century B.C. By that time, Rome had developed a republican form of government, the leaders of which were noted for their economy, discipline, loyalty, and rhetorical prowess. In technology and military matters, moreover, Rome had no contemporary equal. By the first century B.C., its territory was vast and included much of western Europe as well as many of the lands once within the sphere of Greek influence. Whenever Romans made contact with another culture, they freely borrowed its arts, religion, technology—anything that seemed useful. Roman culture, then, in many ways, was an amalgam of attitudes and practices drawn from other lands but always adapted to the particular needs and interests of Rome and Romans.

In 27 B.C., the republican form of government was abandoned in favor of an imperial form; that is, power once vested in many representatives now resided in the person of the emperor. By that time, too, the energies of the government were becoming increasingly directed at maintaining control of the conquered territories, which were both numerous and distant. Its size and territorial complexity led in 330 A.D. to the formation of a second (Eastern) capital of the Empire, Constantinople, which shared responsibilities with Rome. That the Western Empire lasted until the sixth century A.D. is a tribute to the administrative and technological sophistication of the Romans. Internal struggles and attacks from the north led to the collapse of Rome by the sixth century. Although the Eastern Empire, centered at Constantinople, continued until 1453, Rome's influence was no longer a significant factor in the political life of Europe after about A.D. 500.

As the time line shows, Greek and Roman theatres coexisted and influenced each other for about eight hundred years. In Rome as in Greece, the periods for which we have plays (mostly B.C.) do not correlate well with the periods for which we have information about the theatre buildings (mostly A.D.).

Sources for the Roman Theatre

As with other areas of life, Romans developed their theatrical practices by adapting practices from other cultures with which they came into contact. *From the Etruscans,* the Romans learned to place theatre within a context of other sorts of entertainments (chariot racing, boxing, wrestling, gladiatorial combats), all of which took place at great civic games, the first of which, the *Ludi Romani,* were instituted by an Etruscan

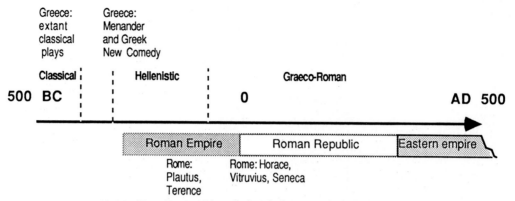

FIGURE 11-11. **Time Line.** Although Greek drama predates Roman drama by about two hundred years, Greek and Roman theatres overlap for most of their more than one-thousand-year history.

(364 B.C.). From the Etruscans too probably came the Romans' heavy use of music within plays and their use of stadium seating within auditoria. *From the Oscans*, also in the fourth century B.C., the Romans probably learned of the short, improvised plays (called *Atellan farces*), which featured recognizable stock characters whose masks and costumes repeated from play to play. Some scholars see in these plays not only the basis for some Roman comedy but also for Renaissance Italy's *commedia dell 'arte*. By the time Rome came into contact with *Greek theatre* in the third century B.C., Greece was already well into its Hellenistic period and Rome already had many of its theatrical practices established. *From the Greeks*, the Romans probably learned ways of constructing tragedies and comedies, and theories about the nature and importance of drama.

Production Arrangements

Theatre in Rome took place at *ludi*, or games, most of which were state religious celebrations devoted to the worship of any of Rome's several gods; occasionally, *ludi* were staged in celebration of birthdays, funerals, military victories, and political rallies. *Ludi* were managed by a civic or religious magistrate who received a government grant to cover the expenses of the festivals, whose complexities he was expected to oversee. Typically, among his other duties, the magistrate contacted the heads of several acting troupes and established fees for the performances. This fixed fee, paid by the state, might be augmented either by the magistrate himself (as the success of a festival reflected well on him) or by a bonus that the state awarded whenever public acclaim was unusually vocal. This bonus apparently resulted in some people's being paid to applaud wildly the work of certain troupes and in government officials' being bribed to notice such responses.

Theatre in Rome was free and open to everyone. Apparently, it was quite popular, for the number of performances of plays steadily increased, from only one in 240 B.C. to more than one hundred during the third century A.D. Typically, several troupes

FIGURE 11-12. **Roman Tragedy.** Probably a statuette of a Roman actor from the time of the Empire. Notice the exaggerated mask, the high headdress, and the platformed footwear, none of which were used in the Classical Greek theatre.

participated at each festival, and on the days set aside for performances, plays were presented continuously, without intermissions.

As in Greece, theatre in Rome was an all-male event, except for the mime, an entertainment of poor reputation that did include female performers.

Plays

Tragedy

Although no tragedies survived from the Republic, titles and fragments indicate that they resembled Hellenistic Greek tragedy: sensational and melodramatic elements took precedence over philosophical inquiry, and the role of the chorus was peripheral rather than central to the development of the action. Depending on the subject matter and the costumes worn by the actors, Roman tragedy was divided into two types: (1) those written about Greeks, in which the actors dressed as noble Greeks, and (2) those written about Romans, in which actors were dressed as upper-class Roman citizens.

SENECA. From the Empire, ten tragedies are extant, nine by Seneca (c. 5 B.C.–A.D. 65). None was intended for production in a public theatre. The importance of Seneca's tragedies rests neither on their literary excellence nor on their position among contemporary Roman audiences but on their monumental effect on Renaissance writers, who discovered, translated, and copied them (probably because they were both linguistically and physically more accessible than the earlier Greek tragedies).

Seneca's plays display characteristics assumed to be typical of Greek Hellenistic tragedy. The chorus is not well integrated into the action, and so the (usually four) choral odes (songs) serve to divide the plays into five parts. His protagonists are often driven by a single dominant passion that causes their downfall. Seneca's minor characters often include messengers, confidants, and ghosts. The language of his plays emphasizes rhetorical and stylistic figures, including extended descriptive and declamatory passages, pithy statements about the human condition (*sententiae*), and elaborately balanced exchanges of dialogue. Many of his plays feature spectacular scenes of violence and gore. Although it is now customary to scoff at the plays of Seneca, their influence on the subsequent development of tragedy in Italy, France, England, and even Germany has been incalculable.

Comedy

Comedy, like tragedy, was divided into that written about the Greek middle class and that written about Romans. Although many titles, names, and fragments remain, only twenty-seven comedies survive, all from two authors: Plautus and Terence. Both wrote during the first century B.C., and both wrote about the Athenian middle class. Both drew heavily from Greek "new comedies" for their materials and stories, and neither used a chorus. Despite these obvious similarities, however, the plays of Plautus and Terence are very different from one another and suggest a considerable range within Roman comedy.

PLAUTUS. Plautus (254–184 B.C.) made a good deal of money as an actor-manager before turning to playwriting at about forty. He become a prolific and popular author. Of the more than one hundred works credited to him, twenty-one have survived, doubtless a tribute to the esteem in which he was held.

Plautus's sense of humor was always evident. The three names by which he was officially known (Titus Maccus Plautus) translate roughly as "big, splay-footed clown," perhaps a reference to his acting the role of the clown in Atellan farces. Probably his experiences as an actor working to entertain a fickle public accounted for the *theatrical* (as opposed to literary) qualities of his comedies. Plautine comedies are noted for their loosely linked episodes, which are filled with visual gags, verbal wordplay, and characters who are ludicrous in appearance as well as behavior. Never one to pass up an opportunity for a laugh, Plautus often broke the dramatic illusion, addressed his audience directly, and incorporated references to contemporary Rome

FIGURE 11-13. Roman Comedy. Copies of the comedies of Plautus and Terence were illustrated during the middle ages. Shown here are the stock characters of a soldier and a parasite from such a copy.

in his comedies about the Athenian middle class. Among his many plays, *The Braggart Warrior, The Menaechmi, Pot of Gold,* and *Amphitryon* have provided material for Shakespeare, Molière, and others.

TERENCE. Terence (d. 159 B.C.) was less boisterous than Plautus. His use of language, for example, was so careful and elegant that his plays were used in schools throughout the Middle Ages as models of Latin eloquence. His plots, although based on those of the Greek Menander and his contemporaries, often combined two or more of the Greek comedies into a single, highly complicated dramatic action. He avoided the episodic quality of Plautus's plots in favor of more carefully contrived actions that proceeded by means of seeming cause and effect. His characters, too, appeared more normal and human, and thus more sympathetic. The result was, of course, comedies that were more elegant and refined but less robust and free, more thoughtful but less fun than Plautus's.

Finally, Terence's use of the prologue was unusual. Unlike Plautus, whose prologues contained exposition, preparation, and summary, Terence used his to argue matters of dramatic theory, to encourage audiences to behave politely, and to defend himself from the attacks of drama critics. In a prologue that is as revealing of republican audiences as of Terence's prologues, the playwright explained, "*Hecyra* is the name of this play. When it was represented for the first time, an unusual disaster and calamity interrupted it, so that it could not be witnessed throughout or estimated; so much had the populace, carried away with admiration, devoted their attention to some rope dancing."

Although comedy had always been more popular than tragedy in Rome, even its popularity waned within fifty years of Terence's death, its favor usurped first by the Atellan farce and later by *mime* and *pantomime.*

Theory: Horace

About the time that regular tragedy and comedy were disappearing from public theatres, Horace (65–8 B.C.) wrote his *Ars Poetica*, a work that exerted even more influence on the Renaissance than Aristotle's *Poetics* (on which it was loosely based). *Ars Poetica* is concerned with the standards and procedures to be followed in writing poetry, with special references to comedy and tragedy. Unlike Aristotle's work, which is a philosophical inquiry into the nature of the form *tragedy*, Horace's is a practical guidebook intended for people wanting to write. As such, it is considerably more prescriptive than Aristotle's work about such matters as the unities, the separation of the genres, and the appropriate arrangement of language. *Ars Poetica* seems to have captured the views current among theorists of the day but far afield from contemporary practice in the popular theatre of Rome; therefore, Horace's importance rests on his appeal to the erudite dramatists of the Renaissance and Neoclassical theatre, who used his work as a guide for constructing their orderly and decorous works.

Nonliterary Drama

Despite the theories of Horace and men like him, drama and theatre during the Empire became increasingly nonliterary. The two most popular forms, pantomime and mime, depended on spectacle and not language and thus can scarcely be appreciated at a distance of two thousand years.

PANTOMIME. A pantomime was a solo dance that told a story by means of movement alone. Accompanied by an orchestra and a chorus, the dancer generally enacted a serious story taken from history or mythology. Because the dancer never spoke, pantomime masks were built with closed mouths. Although pantomime for a time took the place of tragedy as a serious entertainment popular with the audience, soon it too was overwhelmed by the growing popularity of mime.

MIME. Paralleling the rise of Christianity, the rise of mime caused several changes in Roman theatre. First, from its earliest days, mime included women among its performers, the only theatrical entertainment in Greece or Rome to do so. Second, performers in the mime did not generally wear masks, and so their personal appearance was both noticeable and important. Indeed, mime performers were often successful because of their looks: the very handsome or beautiful and the extraordinarily grotesque or ugly had the best chance of success, for they could more readily appeal to the audience as sympathetic or comic characters. Some mime actresses set fashions in clothes and behavior (one married an emperor), and many actors were the Roman equivalent of movie stars and matinee idols. Mimes could be either funny or serious, simple or spectacular, but whatever their form, they usually dealt with some aspect of daily living.

Mime was both Rome's most popular and its most notorious theatrical entertainment during the Empire. Because some mimes presented violence and sex *literally* as a part of the performance and because many of the works scoffed at Christian beliefs and Church practices, Christian writers and clerics called often and loudly, if unsuccessfully, for outlawing the theatre in Rome. Even though the artistic merit of mime

FIGURE 11-14. Roman Entertainments during the Empire. Competing with mime and pantomime for public favor were gladiatorial combats, chariot races, and sea battles, all imaginatively recreated here.

was low and its performances were often offensive to the growing Christian community, mime continued to thrive for as long as the Empire survived.

It is well to remember that Roman drama and theatre were forced to compete with other forms of entertainment for public support. Perhaps many of the excesses of the mime can be explained, if not excused, by the enormous popularity of imperial athletic activities like chariot racing, gladiatorial contests, wild animal fights, and staged sea battles, where violence and death were both accepted and applauded. Although such activities were generally performed in specially constructed buildings like amphitheatres (e.g., the Colosseum) and circuses (e.g., the Circus Maximus), occasionally a theatre would be temporarily converted and appropriated for such events, serving again to bolster the arguments of those advocating theatre's abolition.

FIGURE 11-15. **Roman Theatre.** An imaginative reconstruction of a stone theatre during the period of the Empire. Such theatres (and perhaps the wooden theatres that predated them) had elaborate façades, side wings, and semicircular orchestras, unlike Greek theatres of the Classical and Hellenistic periods.

Production Practices

The first *permanent stone theatre* was not built in Rome until 55 B.C., very near the end of the Republic. Almost immediately, construction began on other theatres, until, by the end of Roman influence, more than one hundred theatres existed around the Roman Empire. Because they bore similarities to each other, a brief survey of their typical features can be provided.

Theatre Buildings

Like Greek theatres, Roman theatres were façade stages; that is, actors performed *in front of* a neutral background. Unlike Greek theatres, Roman theatres were typically built on level ground, and the seating was built up, stadium style. At the rear of the Roman auditorium was a wide, covered aisle, whose roof joined that of the scene house to form a single architectural unit. The orchestra remained, but, unlike that in Greece, was a half circle, whose diameter was marked by the front of a stage raised to a height of about five feet and extended to a depth of up to forty feet. The stage was very iong (100–300 feet) and was enclosed at each end by side wings jutting out from the scene house. At the back of the stage was the scene house, whose elaborate façade was decorated with numerous statues, porticoes, columns, and so on. Perhaps to protect this elaborate structure from the weather or perhaps to improve acoustics, a roof extended from the top of the scene house over part of the stage. The corridors between the scene house and the audience area were covered and used as audience exits.

FIGURE 11-16. **Periaktoi.** Three-sided scenic pieces that turned on a central pivot may have allowed changes in scenery, but such changes were almost certainly more suggestive than literal.

Architectural evidence suggests that in the Roman theatre, a front curtain may have been used. Its introduction may well have been Rome's most significant contribution to theatre, as its use had implications for the kinds of plays written as well as the kinds of scenic displays possible.

Accounts suggest that Roman theatres could seat between 10,000 and 15,000 patrons and that considerable care was taken to ensure their comfort. Aisles were apparently wide and numerous, permitting easy comings and goings. An awning was used as protection against the sun, and at least in one theatre, a primitive air-conditioning system was contrived that used fans and ice brought down from nearby mountains. Important people could reserve seats in the orchestra or in the special boxes atop the audience exits.

Most historians assume, perhaps incorrectly, that Roman theatres of the Republic were similar to those of the Empire, but, as evidence is limited and often perplexing, the appearance of the earlier wooden theatres remains a mystery.

Masks and Costumes

Roman masks, costumes, and scenic practices resembled those of Hellenistic Greece. Roman masks for tragedy and comedy were full and exaggerated, with high headdresses and large mouths; the costumes resembled either Roman or Hellenistic fashions, depending on the kind of comedy or tragedy being done. As in Greece, all actors in the Roman theatre wore masks except for the mime performers. Clearly, as the popularity of mime increased, the use of masks on the Roman stage declined.

Settings

The basic setting in the Roman theatre was apparently the scene house itself. For comedies, its several doors represented entrances to separate homes; for tragedies, its doors were entrances to various parts of a palace or a temple. The stage itself represented either a street running in front of dwellings (in comedy) or a gathering place before a temple or a palace (in tragedy). *Periaktoi* were used to suggest changes of place. According to one ancient commentator, they were located near the ends of the stage and could be rotated to reveal one of three scenes: a tragic scene (e.g., columns and statues), a comic scene (e.g., balconies and windows), or a satyric scene (trees, caves, and "other rustic objects"). Because the *periaktoi* could not possibly have hidden the façade of the scene house, they probably served simply to inform the audience of location, not to portray the place in a realistic way. Oddly, the mime used a back curtain that hung against the façade of the scene house; the size of this curtain increased during the Empire at about the same time that the elaborate stone theatres were being built. The seemingly contradictory trends are a mystery.

Also tantalizing are contemporary accounts of wondrous special effects. How they were achieved is unclear, but for one event there were reportedly "sliding cliffs and a miraculous moving wood," and for another, a fountain of wine springing from a mountain top just before the mountain sank into a chasm and out of sight, and for another, two large theatres that could pivot to form a single amphitheatre.

VITRUVIUS. Just as Horace influenced Renaissance dramatic theory and Seneca Renaissance tragedy, the Roman architect Vitruvius influenced the nature of Renaissance theatres. He published a ten-volume work detailing Roman architectural practices, including ways to build both theatres and scenery. He described the theatre, the scene house, and three types of scenes: tragic, comic, and satyric. Because his work was not illustrated, Renaissance artists interpreted his instructions in light of their own artistic conventions. Although (mis)interpreted, Vitruvius's work influenced both theatrical and scenic design of the Renaissance.

Decline and Fall

A series of barbarian invasions first dissipated and finally destroyed the power of Rome. The "fall of Rome" managed to accomplish what the opposition of the Christian Church could not: the end of formal and organized theatrical activity in Western Roman lands, an event usually dated from about the middle of the sixth century A.D.

For many years, it was fashionable to dismiss Roman theatre as inartistic and unworthy of serious study, but clearly it was a vital theatre and one enormously popular with its audiences. With the collapse of Rome, its theatre disappeared, only to be reborn, not in the period immediately following, but in the more distant Renaissance, whose scholars studied Roman theories and plays, imitated them, and thus ensured a Roman legacy to the theatrical world.

CHAPTER TWELVE

EMBLEM AND SIMULTANEITY: MIDDLE AGES AND GOLDEN AGES

The second phase of theatrical and dramatic history began in the tenth century and ended about 1650 (approximately one hundred years earlier in Italy). Despite important differences, the theatres of the Middle Ages and those of the Golden Ages of England and Spain shared important traits:

1. A staging convention of *simultaneous settings*, where several widely separated locations could be presented simultaneously to the audience.

2. The sharing of meaning through *emblems*, shorthand embodiments of richer content (a flag standing for a country, a crown for a king).

3. *Complicated plays* with numerous characters, many lines of action, and elastic time and place (traits seldom found in classical dramas).

4. A mostly male theatre, in which women participated mostly as audience.

THEATRE IN THE MIDDLE AGES

Background

Although civilization in the Eastern Empire was flourishing, that in western Europe was in a state of increasing confusion after the fourth century A.D. From then until the eighth century, western Europe experienced political disarray, out of which emerged a different kind of Europe, one based on new nations and diverse languages and traditions.

With the collapse of Rome in the sixth century, various forces that had before served to unify Europe weakened or disintegrated. The Roman system of roads and waterways fell into disrepair, and transportation and communication became at first troubled and at last almost impossible. Laws were ignored and order broke down, replaced by the rule of force: bands of pirates and brigands grew wealthy and influential enough to challenge kings. Without the support of a government, the monetary system failed, and barter, with all of its cumbersome trappings, was the basis of trade.

Into the power vacuum created by Rome's defeat came a variety of competitive interests, each sparring for political and economic clout. The Church exerted increasing influence, especially after the tenth century, in part because its hierarchy ensured an orderly governance, and in part because its influence in the daily lives of people gave it a substantial base. The other prevailing social organization was feudal, whose primary social unit was the manor. On the manor, each serf owed absolute allegiance to the lord, who, in turn, owed allegiance to more powerful lords, and so on. Similarly, in the Church, the priests ranked below the bishops, who ranked below the archbishops; at the top was the bishop of Rome, the pope, who spoke with authority on Church matters. Both power hierarchies were essentially pyramidal,

FIGURE 12-1. Medieval Life. Agriculture formed the basis of medieval life, with peasants at the bottom of feudalism's social pyramid.

with one (male) person at the top, relatively few (male) persons immediately under him, and so on until, at the base of each pyramid, were the peasants, that great mass of people who tilled the land and provided all those above them with the necessities and amenities of life. The two pyramids interlocked when Church leaders were drawn from the noble classes; the peasants provided goods and services for both Church lords and secular lords.

The series of crusades after the twelfth century against the Muslims and other forces served to encourage trade and the opening of new sea routes. Increased trade, in turn, encouraged the development of towns, a movement well under way by the eleventh century. These towns and the merchants and tradesmen in them existed outside the feudal structure and gradually undermined it. As tradesmen organized themselves into guilds (trade brotherhoods), they were able to confront the feudal lords and eventually to challenge them successfully. With the rise of towns and the weakening of feudalism, nations began to take shape, and kings emerged to govern them. By the fourteenth century, the domination of the Church was under attack, and its monopoly on matters of faith was being eroded.

With the decline of feudalism and the authority of the Church, and with the emergence of towns and a sense of nationhood, the era ended.

Medieval Drama

For many years, historians believed that no theatre or drama outlived the collapse of the Roman Empire in the sixth century, but it is now certain that, after the empire divided into two parts (about A.D. 330), plays continued to be performed in the Eastern Empire around Byzantium, and that, even in the West, remnants of the professional performers traveled about Italy, France, and Germany, plying their trade and eking out a living. Scattered references to *mimi, histriones,* and *ioculatores* (all words used to describe actors) surfaced periodically in medieval accounts, but the degree to which such performers engaged in actual plays, as distinct from variety entertainments like juggling, tumbling, dancing, and rope tricks, is not known. Clearly, if traditional dramas were performed between the sixth and the tenth centuries, their scale was much reduced and they no longer enjoyed the support of those two most powerful social organizations of the time, the Church and the State.

Two events in the tenth century marked the reentry of theatre into western Europe.

Hroswitha, a religious leader (and noblewoman) attached to the Benedictine monastery near Gandersheim (in modern Germany), wrote seven plays, the first recorded dramas since the early days of the Roman Empire. Based on the comedies of Terence, Hroswitha's plays sought to celebrate "the laudable chastity of holy maidens" and may (or may not) have been performed at court and at the monastery. Hroswitha is important on three counts: as the first female playwright, as the first known post-Roman playwright, and as proof of an intellectual continuity from Rome to the Middle Ages. For reasons not entirely clear (but perhaps related to the fact that men have written most histories), Hroswitha's contributions have been largely overshadowed by a different strand of theatre, one that also emerged in the tenth century and also at a Benedictine monastery.

FIGURE 12-2. Three Maries. The three Maries at the tomb seeking Jesus was the subject of the first Latin music drama. Here, the same event interpreted in painting.

Ethelwold, Bishop of Winchester in England, published in 975 the *Regularis Concordia*, a monastic guidebook which, among other things, described in detail how one part of an Easter service was to be performed. For about a hundred years before Ethelwold, the Church had been decorating and elaborating various of its practices; music, calendar, vestments, art, architecture, and liturgy all had changed in the direction of greater embellishment. One sort of liturgical embellishment was the *trope* (any interpolation into an existing text). One Easter trope was sung by the choir antiphonally and began, *"Quem quaeritis in sepulchro, o christocole."* Translated into English, the trope read in its entirety:

> *Whom seek ye in the tomb, O Christians?*
> *Jesus of Nazareth, the crucified, O heavenly beings.*
> *He is not here, he is risen as he foretold;*
> *Go and announce that he is risen from the tomb.*

It was this trope to which staging directions were added in Ethelwold's *Regularis Concordia:*

> *While the third lesson is being read, four of the brethren shall vest, one of whom, wearing an alb as though for some different purpose, shall enter and go stealthily to the place of the "sepulchre" and sit there quietly, holding a palm in his hand. Then, while the third response is being sung, the other three brethren, vested in copes and*

holding thuribles in their hands, shall enter in their turn and go to the place of the "sepulchred," step by step, as though searching for something. Now these things are done in imitation of the angel seated on the tomb and of the women coming with perfumes to anoint the body of Jesus. When, therefore, he that is seated shall see these three draw nigh, wandering about as it were and seeking something, he shall begin to sing softly and sweetly, Quem quaeritis.

Translated by THOMAS SYMONS

During the tenth century, then, two major directions for subsequent medieval drama had been pointed: religious drama and secular drama. Some religious dramas (like the *Quem quaeritis*) were part of the liturgy of the church; others, like the great mysteries and the shorter moralities, were performed outside church ceremonies. Among secular dramas, some showed clear classical influence (like the plays of Hroswitha), while others drew from medieval folk and farce traditions. Among both traditions could be found plays staged indoors and those staged out of doors; among both traditions too could be found plays staged in a fixed, single place and those staged on wagons that moved from place to place (as in a parade).

Religious Drama

Latin Music Drama

Many dramas like the *Quem Quaeritis* were performed inside monastic and cathedral churches as a part of the liturgy (and so might also be called liturgical drama). Such plays were chanted or sung (rather than spoken) and were given in the language of the Church (Latin) rather than in a national language (like English or French). They were acted by clergy, choirboys, monks, and occasionally traveling scholars and schoolboys (and, occasionally nuns); the actors, then, were almost always male (except in convents). At first the audiences for such works were probably monks and others living in monasteries, but once cathedral churches became common (during the thirteenth century), lay people were the principal audiences for the plays.

From the very short *Quem Quaeritis*, Latin music drama blossomed into many plays of varying lengths and varying degrees of complexity. The subjects of most such plays were Biblical, usually drawn from events surrounding Christmas and Easter: the visit of the three Marys to the tomb, the travel of the Magi, Herod's wrath. Other Latin music dramas, however, depicted such diverse stories as the life of the Virgin Mary, the raising of Lazarus, and Daniel in the lion's den. Almost all were serious, but at festivals like the Feast of Fools and the Feast of the Boy Bishops, the usual dignity was abandoned and in its place was substituted considerable tomfoolery.

Latin music dramas continued to be performed in churches well into the sixteenth century.

Religious Dramas Outside the Church

Why drama came to be done outside of the Church has been endlessly debated. Some argue that abuses, like those at the Feast of Fools, caused the Church to force the drama outdoors. Others argued that the appearance of drama outdoors merely

PLAN OF LINCOLN
CATHEDRAL.

SCALE 100 FEET TO
1 INCH.

A, Norman Recesses in West Front;
B, C, D, Porches in Norman Front; E,
Chapels in Early-English Wings; F, Nave;
G, H, Chapels; K, Crossing under Central
Tower; L, M, Great Transepts; N, Galilee-
porch; O, Choir; P, Q, Choir-aisles; R, S,
Minor (Eastern) Transepts; T, Retro-
Choir; U, V, X, Chantries; W, South-east
porch; Y, Cloisters; Z, Chapter-house;
28, Vestry; 33, Vestibule to Chapter-house;
34, Staircase to Library.

FIGURE 12-3. Latin Music Drama. First monastic and later cathedral churches housed Latin music dramas, which used the church's architecture as stage setting. Here, Lincoln cathedral with its adjacent cloister and chapter house.

reflected the changing needs of the plays and their audiences for more space and more freedom. Whatever the reason for the development, records of religious plays given outside of churches appear by 1200 and are common by 1350, when relatively abundant accounts describe a civic and religious theatre of magnificent proportions throughout most of western Europe.

The new tradition differed from the old in several important ways:

- The plays outdoors were spoken rather than chanted or sung.

- The plays were in the vernacular (e.g., French, English, German) rather than in Latin.

- Laymen, rather than priests and clerics, served as actors.

- The stories and themes, no longer limited to liturgical sources, became more far-ranging.

- The performances tended to cluster in the spring and summer months, especially around the new Feast of Corpus Christi, rather than spreading throughout the church year, as before.

FIGURE 12-4. **Artistic Convention: Size and Emblem.** This king in his palace shows well two artistic conventions of the period: the use of emblem to convey meaning (the king sits under the emblems of wisdom) and the use of size to denote relative status or importance (the king is larger than his palace).

Of these changes, the most significant change was the shift from a universal language (Latin) to the various national tongues, for with this shift came an end to an international drama and the beginning of several national dramas, a trend important to the future of both theatre and drama.

The plays remained decidedly religious, if not always scriptural. In general, they dealt with:

- Events in the life of Christ or stories from the Old Testament (plays often called *mysteries*).

- The lives of saints, both historical and legendary (called *miracles*).

- Didactic allegories frequently portraying the human struggle for salvation (the *moralities*).

Although the plays differed in subject matter and form, they shared several characteristics. First, they aimed to teach or to reinforce belief in Church doctrine. Second, they were formulated as melodramas or divine comedies; that is, the ethical system of the play was clear, and good was rewarded, evil punished. Third, the driving force for the action was God and His plan rather than the decisions or actions of the dramatic agents. To a modern reader, the plays often appear episodic, with their actions unmotivated, their sequences of time and place inexplicable, and their mixture of the comic and the serious unnerving.

In fact, their traits expressed well the medieval view. The plays presented the lure and strength of sin, the power and compassion of God, and the punishment awaiting the unrepentant sinner. They called for all people to repent, to confess, and to atone for their sins.

Because history was God's great lesson to humankind, the most vivid drama that could contain His plan was nothing less than the entirety of human history, from Creation to Doomsday. Any combination of events, any juxtaposition of characters, and any elasticity of time or place that would illuminate God's plan and make it more accessible and compelling was suitable drama. The great dramas of the fifteenth and sixteenth century that showed this history are called *cycles*, or *cosmic dramas*.

Secular Drama

The first records of secular dramas appeared at about the same time that religious dramas appeared outside the Church. At about the same time that these great religious plays were at their zenith, another tradition was moving tentatively toward maturity.

At court and in the homes of the very wealthy, performances were given at tournaments and on holidays (especially at Christmas and Mardi Gras). There,

FIGURE 12-5. Artistic Convention: Emblem and Simultaneity. Distant times and places are shown existing together, their identities and meanings conveyed concisely through emblems. Here, the Mirror of the World has heaven, earth, and hell coexisting, each easily identified through signs like wings, staffs, and fire.

theatre pieces might be presented within another activity—for example, between the courses of a formal banquet; such a short dramatic entertainment was called an *interlude*. Short plays might also be given in connection with gift-giving by costumed revelers, as in entertainments called *mummings* and *disguisings*. The most spectacular of the noble and court entertainments, however, was the *masque*, in which allegorical compliments to the guests of honor were framed by intricate dances involving the courtiers themselves.

Towns staged *street pageants* and *entries* in connection with various special occasions, often during the visit of an important dignitary. As a part of these events, plays were combined with elaborate processions. The plays were given for the instruction and entertainment of the visiting dignitaries, whose procession through the town constituted the major entertainment for the townspeople who watched it.

Secular plays appeared in other circumstances as well. In schools and colleges *Latin comedies and tragedies* were studied, copied, translated, and emulated during much of the fifteenth century. For ordinary people in the towns and countryside, *farces* poked fun at all manner of domestic tribulations, particularly infidelity and cuckoldry. In many instances secular *morality plays* featured classical gods and heroes rather than Christian virtues and vices; and occasionally morality plays were drawn into the religious battles of the Reformation: for example, anti-Catholic moralities costumed devils as Catholic prelates and Christian figures as Protestant ministers; anti-Protestant moralities did just the reverse. Because morality plays found expression

FIGURE 12-6. Morality Play. This fifteenth-century sketch shows a circular scenic arrangement for a production of the religious morality play, *The Castle of Perseverance.*

FIGURE 12-7. **Staging Convention: Mansion and Platea.** This diagram shows two of several possible arrangements for the small scenic structures and the generalized playing area.

in both the religious and the secular traditions, they are often viewed as an important link between the two.

Staging in the Medieval Theatre

Certain basic principles underlay the staging of medieval plays, whether the plays were given inside or outside the Church, for religious or secular purposes. Staging was *simultaneous* (several different locations were presented simultaneously to the audience); and it was *emblematic* (its meaning rested in visible signs that were understood by the audience).

Simultaneous staging depended on two uses of scenic space. *Mansions* were small scenic structures that served to locate a specific place; the *platea* was a neutral, generalized playing area. In complex plays, many mansions could be arranged around the platea. Actors might first establish their specific location by reference to the appropriate mansion, after which they were free to move about the platea.

Emblematic staging depended on a shared understanding of many signs and symbols. For example, keys that were added to a costume identified the wearer as St. Peter; hoods signified women; wings meant angels; wallets and staffs, travelers.

Among mansions, an animal mouth signified hell; a well-lit, revolving globe stood for heaven, and so on.

Within these general staging conventions, some variations occurred.

In staging Latin music dramas, existing church architecture was often used. For example, the choir loft might represent heaven, the crypt hell, and the altar the tomb of Christ. For elaborate plays, special mansions might be constructed, some small but others large enough for several persons to be hidden within. Similarly, costumes were ordinarily church vestments to which signifying elements had been added. Occasionally, clerics playing kings and prophets might wear ornate, nonclerical costumes, but these instances were unusual. Special effects required machinery capable of flying objects and actors in and out of the playing area. For example, angels and doves flew about, Christ rose to heaven, and the three kings followed a moving star that led them to the stable of the Christ child and there stopped to mark the spot.

The staging of religious plays outside the church took two major forms: *fixed staging*, which occurred throughout Europe, except in parts of Spain and England, and *movable staging*, which was used most importantly in parts of Spain and England.

In fixed staging, mansions (or *scaffolds*) were set up, usually outdoors, in whatever spaces were available (e.g., courtyards of noble houses, town squares, the remains of Roman amphitheatres). Depending on the space, the mansions were arranged in circles, straight lines, or rectangles, and the platea and the audience area were established accordingly. Although the individual arrangements varied, heaven and hell (ordinarily the most ornate mansions) were customarily set at opposite poles.

In movable staging, *pageants* (pageant wagons) allowed the audience to scatter along a processional route while the plays were brought to them and performed in

FIGURE 12-8. **Fixed Staging.** Here, mansions are arranged linearly with the platea forward of them. The large animal mouth is a common emblem for hell, the jail for limbo, and the sphere for heaven.

FIGURE 12-9. **Movable Staging.** In movable staging, wagons (whose exact appearance is not known) carried plays to audiences positioned along a processional route. Shown here, one arrangement of a wagon drawn up to a platform in front of town buildings for a performance. (*Used with permission of the Archivero de Villa, Ayuntamiento de Madrid.*)

sequence, much like a homecoming parade with floats. Each play, then, was performed several times. A common pattern was for the first play (Creation) to be presented at dawn at the first station; when it moved to the second station to perform, the second play (the Fall of Man) was presented at the first station. For most of the day, several plays were performing at once. The word *pageant* is important in a discussion of movable staging because it was used to describe the play itself, the spectacle of the plays in performance, and also the vehicle on which the presentation was staged.

The appearance of pageant wagons has been much discussed, but as available evidence is scant, few firm conclusions are possible. Only one English description, dating from slightly before 1600, has survived, and its reliability is suspect:

> *Every company had his pagiant, or parte, which pagiants weare a high scafolde with two rowmes, a higher and a lower, upon four wheeles. In the lower they apparelled themselves, and in the higher rowme they played, beinge all open on the tope, that all behoulders mighte heare and see them. The places where they played them was in every streete.*

ARCHDEACON ROBERT ROGERS

An obvious problem with the description, and one of the reasons its accuracy has been questioned, is that the wagons as described would need to be more than twelve feet tall to allow for the wheels and the two levels, yet narrow enough to be pulled by horses through the medieval streets. The resulting structure would be highly unstable and perhaps unable to turn corners as required in its trek from station to station.

The staging of secular dramas followed the same conventions: simultaneous and emblematic. Some plays, like those associated with great tournaments, might be staged out of doors; others, like interludes between courses of a banquet, were staged indoors. Movable staging might be adopted either outdoors or indoors, as might fixed staging.

FIGURE 12-10. **Indoor Staging.** A play at court shows three simultaneously displayed settings, clearly a variation of mansion and platea.

Producing Plays in the Medieval Period

Plays performed in a church were produced by the church. Dramas outside a church, however, were supported in various ways. Sometimes entire towns oversaw productions; sometimes special committees were formed and charged with the task. Most often, however, labor and religious organizations (called *guilds* and *confraternities*) assumed the financial and artistic responsibility for finding and rewarding actors, providing scenery and properties, and establishing and enforcing regulations. If a guild was weak or poor, it might combine with others to meet its obligations. Plays were often assigned to guilds on the basis of their members' particular skills; for example, plays depicting the Last Supper were given to bakers' guilds, those of the Three Kings to goldsmiths', of Noah's Ark to shipbuilders' and fishermen's. Once assigned, plays usually remained with the same guild(s) year after year.

Roles in the plays were open to all male members of the community (in France, occasionally a woman might perform) and were generally performed without compensation. As in any primarily amateur operation, the quality of the performances varied considerably, and it was probably in an attempt to upgrade the general level of acting that many cities hired "property players" to take the leading roles and to instruct the less talented in improving their performances. Although these few actors were paid, they were not looked down on as socially undesirable, as were professional actors in secular plays.

Secular plays might be supported by the court, by nobles, by towns, or even by groups of actors. Unlike religious plays, secular plays were typically performed by professional actors (after c. 1450).

The enormous complexity of some medieval dramas caused some people to be hired to oversee the production and to serve as the medieval counterpart of the modern producer. Although the responsibilities differed with the particular circumstances, the tasks of one medieval producer in France included:

1. Overseeing the building of a stage and the use of the scenery and machines.

2. Overseeing the building and painting of scenery and the construction of seating for the audience.

3. Checking all deliveries to ensure accuracy.

4. Disciplining the actors.

5. Acting in the plays whenever necessary.

6. Addressing audiences at the beginning of the play and at each intermission, giving a summary of what had happened and promising greater marvels to come.

Because mechanical reproduction and printing were unavailable, a single copy of the script, with its various directions for production, was handwritten and retained from year to year. This master copy, called a *register*, was held by a designated party, often the producing organization or church. Obviously, if any group could secure the register, they could prevent further production, as indeed occasionally happened by the late sixteenth century, when religious dramas were being censored and then banned.

Because special effects in the dramas were so extraordinary, some men, called *masters of secrets*, became specialists in their construction and workings, which included:

- Flying: angels flew about; Lucifer raised Christ; souls rose from limbo into heaven on Doomsday; devils and fire-spitting monsters sallied forth from hell and back again; cotton-covered platforms, resembling clouds (*glories*), bore choruses of heavenly beings aloft.

- Traps: appearances, disappearances, and substitutions, as when Lot's wife was turned into a pillar of salt, and tigers were transformed into sheep.

- Artistic control of fire: hell belched smoke and flames (in 1496 at Seurre, an actor playing Satan was severely burned when his costume caught fire), and buildings ignited on cue.

FIGURE 12-11. **Properties and Costumes.** Devils and dragons like those shown here were among the most elaborate properties and costumes in the medieval theatre.

The scale of these effects can perhaps be suggested by the following account of a French production:

The spectacle lasted twenty-five days, and on each day we saw strange and wonderful things. . . . Lucifer was raised from Hell on a dragon without our being able to see how. The rod of Moses, dry and sterile, suddenly put forth flowers and fruits. Devils carried the souls of Herod and Judas through the air. Devils were exorcised, people with dropsy and other invalids were cured, all in an admirable way. Here Jesus Christ was carried up by the Devil who scaled a wall forty feet high. There He became invisible. Finally, He was transfigured on Mount Tabor. We saw water changed into wine so mysteriously that we could not believe it, and more than a hundred persons wanted to taste this wine. The five breads and the two fish seemed to be multiplied and were distributed to more than a thousand spectators, and yet there were more than twelve baskets left. The fig tree, cursed by Our Lord, appeared to dry up, its leaves withering in an instant. The eclipse, the earthquake, the splitting of the rocks and the other miracles at the death of Our Lord were shown with new marvels.

CHRONICLER OF VALENCIENNES

The End of Medieval Theatre and Drama

By the sixteenth century, the Catholic Church, already weakened by internal conflicts, looked on while a series of rival factions splintered away from Roman domination. To complicate matters, the religious Reformation quickly became embroiled in various dynastic squabbles. Because each side of a controversy often cast its position and arguments in dramatic form, the religious theatre served as one focus for the religious and dynastic struggles of the period and added to the problems of rulers striving to maintain civic tranquillity. In country after country, therefore, religious plays were outlawed (in Paris in 1548, in England in 1558, and by the Council of Trent in 1545–1563).

The results were profound. No longer used to glorify God and teach Church dogma, theatre and drama now sought to justify themselves on other grounds. Deprived of the financial subsidies of Church and town, theatre and drama needed other sorts of financial support. With religious plays forbidden, secular plays proliferated to satisfy the appetites of audiences long accustomed to dramatic entertainments. New playwrights emerged to offer secular plays to paying audiences. Thus, theatre became a commercial venture, regularly (rather than occasionally) performed by professional rather than amateur actors.

THEATRE IN THE GOLDEN AGES OF ENGLAND AND SPAIN

Background

Beginning around 1300, new ideas, social organizations, attitudes, and discoveries were peeking through the medieval order of Europe. For the next two hundred years, these new ideas gradually took hold and, in country after country, heralded the arrival of the *Renaissance* (literally, "rebirth"). For reasons of politics, religion, geography, and even accident, the Renaissance did not reach all countries simultaneously, nor did it manifest itself identically in every place, but by the beginning of the sixteenth century, its power throughout western Europe was evident, and it had revolutionized many former attitudes and practices.

Humanism

For hundreds of years, the Church at Rome had defined the social and political realities of the Western world, working closely with secular princes to thwart all encroachments on their shared power and wealth. But when internal strife and external politics caused the removal of the papacy to Avignon, France, in 1305, both the legitimacy and the power of the Church as a world leader became increasingly suspect. In keeping with the doctrine of Apocalypticism, people of the early Middle Ages had supposed that within a few years the present, temporal world would be destroyed in a holocaust, that the unrighteous would be purged, and that the righteous, now purified, would be transported to a world of bliss. But by 1300, a

FIGURE 12-12. Time Line. Latin music drama continued to be performed even after vernacular religious plays and secular plays commenced. All of these medieval forms overlapped many plays of the Renaissance, including Shakespeare's.

growing suspicion had surfaced that the Last Judgment was not so imminent as had first been supposed. As the immediacy of the hereafter receded, an awareness of the joys of this life increased, and so new secular and temporal interests joined earlier divine and eternal concerns. A love of God and His ways, long the basis of human behavior, was joined by a newfound admiration for humankind, whose worth, intelligence, and beauty began to be celebrated. This new concern for people and their earthly lives was called *humanism.*

Secularism

The older theology, a complete system of thought based on divine revelation, gave way to competing philosophical systems that stressed *secularism* (that is, they advocated ethical conduct as an end in itself rather than as a prerequisite to heaven, and they argued for logical systems of thought capable of existence independent of divine revelation).

Copernican Universe

Nor was science immune to a reexamination of previously held assumptions. The church-supported cosmology of the Egyptian philosopher Ptolemy, which placed the Earth at the center of the universe, and the human, God's favorite creation, at the center of the Earth, was assaulted and finally toppled by another view (supported in the Renaissance by Copernicus) that pictured a sun-centered universe in which human beings were relegated to life on a relatively minor planet, clearly no longer at the center of things.

FIGURE 12-13. Renaissance Science. Despite the strong opposition of the Roman Church, the ideas of Copernicus gradually replaced those of Ptolemy, causing a reevaluation of the centrality of human beings in the scheme of things.

Reformation

Nor was the Church so united as before. As its wealth accumulated and its allegiance to the noble classes solidified, its worldly interests came into ever greater conflict with its spiritual pronouncements. Unable to reform its practices from within and unwilling to remain a party to its abuses, some Christians (like Martin Luther, fl. 1546) protested against the Church at Rome and launched what came to be called the *Reformation*.

In sum, although God, His Church, and His theology remained the central fact of human life in the Renaissance, they were no longer absolute and unquestioned. Humanism and secularism were competing with them for acceptance. But the emergence of new ideas and attitudes was only part of the phenomenon. Vital, too, were factors that encouraged the widespread dissemination of the new spirit. Two elements in particular were critical: the growth of trade and the arrival of the printing press in Italy.

Trading

As long as the basis of wealth and social structures was agricultural activity on an essentially self-contained manor, the exchange of goods and ideas was limited. But, by 1300, shipping and trade were joining agriculture as important means of livelihood. Towns grew and overshadowed the manors, and commerce increasingly involved coinage as well as barter. Trade, both national and international, permitted and even encouraged a flow of ideas as well as of goods, an effortless exchange not possible as long as self-contained agricultural units dominated the economic life of Europe. At the center of most of the various trade routes of the fourteenth century were the several city-states of Italy, which soon became the focus of a blossoming commerce of ideas, skills, and products. When Constantinople fell to the Turks in 1453, many scholars and artists came to Italy from the Middle and Far East, bringing with them their knowledge and their books. Thus, plays and treatises from ancient Greece and Rome, rescued from endangered libraries, arrived in Italy, where their study and interpretation began almost at once.

Printing

The introduction of the Gutenberg printing press to Italy at about the same time (1467) allowed the rapid reproduction of documents arriving from the East as well as of the interpretations and imitations of these documents. Certainly, the printing press allowed a veritable explosion of accessible information, so much so that, by 1500, numerous academies in the city-states of Italy were devoted to the study and production of Roman plays. Shortly thereafter, Italians began writing their own plays in imitation of the Roman models.

Patronage of the arts during the Renaissance was a major and acknowledged source of prestige, and because the nobles' courts engaged in rivalries over which was to become the cultural center, painters, musicians, sculptors, architects, and writers flourished.

The appearance and effects of the Renaissance were markedly different in northern and southern Europe. The impact of the northern Renaissance on the medieval theatre in England brought about a golden age of theatre, that of William Shakespeare.

The Age of Shakespeare

The reign of Elizabeth I (r. 1558–1603) brought greatness to England. With her ascent to the throne, the nation achieved the political and religious stability that permitted its arts and literature to thrive. When, in an attempt to mute religious controversies, the queen outlawed all religious drama, she opened the way for the rapid development of a secular tradition of plays and playgoing. When the queen finally agreed to the execution of Mary Stuart (1587), her chief rival for the throne and the center of Catholic assaults on the Church and throne, Elizabeth's political situation was secured, and the domination of Anglican Protestants within the Church of England was affirmed. The English navy defeated the Spanish Armada in 1588 and established itself as ruler of the seas and leader among the trading nations.

England, for the first time in generations, was at peace at home and abroad and was filled with a national confidence and a lust for life seldom paralleled in history.

Elizabethan Theatres

In 1576, two theatres opened in London, one an outdoor (or "public") theatre and the other an indoor (or "private") theatre. Thus, when Shakespeare arrived in London about fifteen years later, these two sorts of theatre were well established, and he wrote for and acted in both. Although their precise appearance cannot be known, their general features can be deduced from several kinds of evidence. First, and most important, perhaps, the architectural remains of two public theatres were uncovered in London in 1989. These newly discovered remains added to the information about public theatres that scholars had previously drawn from other sources like the extant plays, a contemporary building contract for the Fortune (public) Theatre, a contemporary sketch of the Swan (public) Theatre, a contemporary drawing of the Cockpit at Court (private) Theatre, and from various accounts taken from contemporary diaries, letters, and financial records (particularly those of Philip Henslowe).

PUBLIC THEATRES. The outdoor, public theatres (of which nine were built between 1576 and 1642) consisted of a round or polygonal, roofed, multileveled auditorium that surrounded an open *yard*, into which jutted a platform raised to a height of four to six feet. The entire yard (or *pit*) and part of the stage platform were unroofed. The audience, probably numbering as many as 2500, surrounded the playing area on three sides, some standing in the pit, and others seated in the *galleries* or the still more exclusive *lords' rooms.*

The actors worked on the raised stage and apparently awaited cues and changed costumes in the *tiring house,* located at the rear of the platform. Covering part of the stage was a roof (called the *heavens*) that was supported by columns resting on the stage and apparently decorated on its underside with pictures of stars, planets, and signs of the zodiac. From the heavens flew in gods and properties as needed by the action.

The stage floor was pierced with *traps,* through which devils, spirits, and other characters could appear and disappear. Connecting the tiring house with the stage were at least two doors, which often represented widely divergent locations (as, for example, when one led to the fields of France and the other to the shores of England). Atop the tiring house, a flag flew on days of performance, and at a level just below, in an area called the *hut,* were probably housed the various pieces of equipment and machinery needed for special effects. A *musicians' gallery* was apparently located just below the hut, at the third level above the stage.

Other points are less certain. The plays clearly required two playing levels, an upper and a lower, and some sort of *discovery space,* a place where objects and characters could be hidden from view and discovered at the appropriate time. Most scholars agree that the discovery space was located between the two doors, but some conceive of it as a permanent architectural part of the theatre, whereas others conceive of it as a portable unit to be added or deleted as required; some picture the discovery space as a recessed alcove (a kind of miniproscenium theatre), whereas others see it as a pavilion that jutted out into the stage. Obviously, any decision

FIGURE 12-14. Elizabethan Public Playhouses: Rediscovering The Globe and The Rose. In 1989, archeologists began to uncover remains from over three hundred and fifty years ago. At left, the Globe excavation; notice the signs indicating the theatre's brick foundation, timber stakes, gravel surface, and crushed hazelnuts; at right, the Rose excavation, showing foundation and timbers. *(Globe photograph courtesy of Pamela M. Adams; Rose photograph courtesy of J. Edward Neve.)*

about the conformation of the space at stage level had implications for the upper level as well. Obviously, too, the degree of permanence of the discovery space would radically affect the general appearance of the theatre. The whole problem has been made thornier by the absence of such a space in the Swan sketch and by the appalling problems with sight lines that any sort of discovery space seemed likely to introduce. Because the available evidence will not permit the issues to be resolved, ideas about the appearance of Shakespeare's playhouse must remain tentative.

PRIVATE THEATRES. About the indoor, or private, playhouses, even less is known. They were roofed, smaller, and therefore more expensive to attend than the public playhouses. Despite their name, they were open to anyone caring to pay. Initially, the private theatres attracted the most fashionable audiences of London, who came to see erudite plays performed by troupes of boy actors. By 1610, however, as the

FIGURE 12-14. (continued)

popularity of children's troupes waned, the adult troupes that performed in the public theatres in the summer took over the private houses for their winter performances. The fact is significant because it indicates that the arrangement of the stage spaces in the theatres was probably very similar.

Staging

Elaborate scenery was impossible in the Elizabethan theatres; various small properties suggested the specific (sometimes simultaneous) locations. Costuming was far more important than scenery to the visual excitement of the performance. Contemporary accounts spoke of luscious fabrics in rich colors. Although fanciful characters like devils, angels, spirits, and allegorical figures appeared in garments designed and made especially for the theatre, most roles were played in Elizabethan garments, regardless of their historic reality. Occasionally, different periods, countries, or races were signified by the emblematic addition of a drapery or a turban, but historical accuracy was never a goal of the costume. Most actors wore contemporary dress that differed from that of the audience only by being more elegant. The similarity of dress between actors and spectators doubtless served to heighten the sense of a shared theatrical experience, as did the relative proximity of the audience to the stage and the constancy of the lighting (stage and auditorium were equally visible, the plays being

FIGURE 12-15. **Map and View of the Theatre District, London.** In Shakespeare's day, the Hope, the Rose, and the Globe theatres were clustered together, with the Swan only a short distance away.

performed during daylight). Clearly, the underlying conventions of this staging were medieval.

Actors and Acting

By the time of Shakespeare, English actors (all male) had attained a satisfactory level of financial and social stability, in part because the Master of Revels, a member of the royal household, licensed acting troupes and guaranteed those licensed the right to play unhampered by threats of arrest for vagabondage, and in part because most troupes were at least nominally attached to the house of a noble above the rank of baron. Although few actors became truly wealthy, most were well paid by the standards of the day, and some (like Shakespeare) were able to retire in style and live like gentlemen.

The troupes themselves were organized as democratic, self-governing units (sharing companies) whose members shared expenses, profits, and responsibilities for production. A very few members owned a part of the theatre building itself; these were called *householders.* The most valuable members of the company held a whole share in the costumes, properties, and other company possessions; lesser members owned only half or quarter shares, with their influence and income reduced accordingly. In addition, each company hired some actors and stagehands (*hirelings*), who worked for a salary rather than for a share of the profits. Because all members were male, the roles of women were taken by men or young boys, many of whom were apprenticed to leading actors in the troupe. Among the actors, most specialized in certain kinds of roles (e.g., clowns, women, or heroes), and some were widely admired in Shakespeare's day: Richard Tarleton, William Kemp, and Robert Armin as clowns, and Richard Burbage and Edward Alleyn as tragedians.

The precise style of acting is unclear, but vocal power and flexibility were clearly prized. Plays of the period offered ample opportunity to display breath control and

FIGURE 12-16. **English Public Theatre.** The sketch is a redrawing of a famous historical depiction of the Swan theatre. The labels are translated here from the Latin of the original. The three-dimensional model, based on the Swan drawing, helps clarify the spatial relationships among stage, audience areas, and actor's house. (*Model courtesy of Richard Leacock. First published in* Theatre Notebook.)

verbal dexterity in the monologues, soliloquies, complicated figures of speech, and symmetrical and extended phrases. On the other hand, oratorical and rhetorical techniques did not seem to have overpowered the actors' search for naturalness. Contemporary accounts, including lines from Shakespeare's *Hamlet*, spoke of an acting style capable of moving actors and audiences alike. The goal was apparently a convincing representation of a character in action performed by an actor with a well-tuned vocal instrument.

By Shakespeare's day as well, the importance of drama and theatre had been argued and demonstrated by leading literary figures. In response to attacks on the theatre as an instrument of the devil, a temptation designed to lure people from useful work, Sir Philip Sidney among others had countered that drama was a most effective way of providing moral instruction and encouraging worthwhile actions in ordinary people, and this defense succeeded in pacifying many of the theatre's critics, at least for a while.

By the time that Shakespeare arrived in London about 1590, then, his was a proud and growing nation whose power wanted to be celebrated. In place in the capital

FIGURE 12-17. Elizabethan Acting. Actors (all male) here perform in *The Spanish Tragedy*, a popular revenge tragedy by Thomas Kyd. The dialogue (in balloons from the characters' mouths) suggests the story: "Alas, it is my son, Horatio;" "Murder helpe Hieronimo;" "Stop her mouth."

was a native theatre with permanent buildings, professional actors, and a legitimacy based on its own identity with capital and court.

The Drama and Shakespeare

Added to the general well-being of the nation was the vigor of the court, the schools, and the universities, where scholars were remaking Italian humanism and classical documents with an eye to English needs and preferences. In particular, university students (the *University Wits*) were applying classical scholarship to the English public stage and laying the foundations for the vigorous theatre to come: Robert Green, Thomas Kyd, John Lyly, and Christopher Marlowe developed elegant prose and blank verse, romantic comedies, and complex protagonists. These University Wits brought the erudition of humanistic scholarship to the English stage.

Kyd and Marlowe, in particular, broke new ground in tragedy; both adopted techniques from the Roman, Seneca, and Marlowe created a "mighty line" of sonorous blank verse. Kyd is remembered for the *revenge tragedy, The Spanish Tragedy,* Marlowe for *Doctor Faustus* and the *history play, Edward the Second.*

SHAKESPEARE (1564–1616). Born in provincial Stratford-Upon-Avon, a day's journey from London, in 1564, Shakespeare was a middle-class boy who grew up as the nation moved from medieval to Renaissance. Not university-educated, Shakespeare nonetheless had the solid basics of village schools: Latin, the classics, the foundation of writing style. His early life appears to have included acquaintance with powerful local families; his father, although a tradesman, was a man of position in the town.

Shakespeare married a local woman but did not stay long in his hometown. By his mid-twenties, he had gone to London to take up the perilous profession of acting, putting his father's trade behind him. He took with him, however, the rural England and the English characters of his youth, which would inform his plays and his poetry for his entire life.

When, rich and famous, he retired about 1612, it was to Stratford that he returned,

FIGURE 12-18. Shakespeare. Considered by many the greatest dramatist of all times, Shakespeare was a man of the theatre—an actor, a playwright, and a part-owner of the theatre building itself.

there to purchase a handsome house and display the gentleman's coat-of-arms his success justified.

William Shakespeare was the greatest playwright of the English-speaking world and one of the greatest dramatists of Western civilization. Between 1590 and 1613, a period now acknowledged as the golden age of English drama, Shakespeare wrote thirty-eight plays, which for convenience are customarily divided into three types: the history plays (those treating *English* history), like *Henry IV* (Parts 1 and 2), *Henry V*, *Henry VI* (Parts 1, 2, and 3), *Henry VIII*, *Richard II*, and *Richard III*; the tragedies, like *Romeo and Juliet*, *Julius Caesar*, *Hamlet*, *King Lear*, *Othello*, *Macbeth*, and *Antony and Cleopatra*; and the comedies, ranging from popular romantic works like *Love's Labor's Lost*, *As You Like It*, *Twelfth Night*, *Much Ado About Nothing*, and *A Midsummer Night's Dream*, to the darker tragicomedies like *All's Well That Ends Well* and *Measure for Measure*.

Features that tended to recur throughout his plays and those of his contemporaries include the following:

1. Shakespeare generally adopted an *early point of attack*; that is, he began his plays near the beginning of the story, with the result that the audience sees the story develop onstage rather than learning about it secondhand, through messengers or reporters.

2. Shakespeare customarily developed several lines of action ("subplots"). Early in his plays, the various lines appear to be separate and independent, but as the play moves toward its resolution, the several lines gradually merge so that by the play's end, the unity of the various lines is evident.

3. Shakespeare filled his plays with a large number and variety of incidents. The

FIGURE 12-19. **Famous Actors in Major Shakespearean Tragedies.** Three nineteenth-century stars shown here: William C. Macready as Hamlet, Edwin Forrest as King Lear, and Edwin Booth as Iago in *Othello*.

mixing of tears and laughter is not uncommon, nor is the close juxtaposition of tender scenes of love with brawling scenes of confrontation.

4. Shakespeare ranged freely in time and place, allowing his actions to unfold across several months and in several locales.

5. Shakespeare used an unusually large number and range of characters. Casts of thirty are common, and among the characters can be found kings and gravediggers, pedants and clowns, old people and youths, city dwellers and rustics, rich people and poor ones.

6. The language in the plays is infinitely varied. Within the same play are found passages of exquisite lyricism, elegant figures of speech, ribald slang, witty aphorisms, and pedestrian prose, all carefully chosen to enhance the play's dramatic action.

In sum, the art of Shakespeare was an expansive one that filled a very large dramatic canvas with portraits of a wide cross-section of humanity engaged in acts ranging from the heroic to the mundane. The texture of the plays is rich, detailed, and allusive.

Shakespeare's plays shared more features with those of the middle ages than with those of classical Greece and Rome. Whereas Classical plays like *Oedipus Rex* had late points of attack, unity of action, and relatively few characters, locations, and incidents, Shakespeare's plays told their stories from the beginning and included many rich details in several developing lines of actions, each with its own characters and often set in farflung locations. Whereas Classical plays adopted rather restricted patterns of time, place, and language, Shakespeare ranged freely among the possibilities. Whereas the power of classical tragedy rested on intensity achieved through concentration and sparseness, Shakespeare's power emerged through the wealth of detail, the range of emotion, the sweep of his vision.

OTHER DRAMATISTS. With Shakespeare's death in 1616 came a decline in the quality, if not the quantity, of drama. Although many of the playwrights were esteemed in their own day (most notably Ben Jonson (1572–1637), and John Fletcher, Francis Beaumont, John Webster, and John Ford), none has achieved the modern admiration accorded Shakespeare. Thus, the golden age of English theatre was already in decline after 1616.

The Court Masque

Not all theatre was done in the public and private playhouses, however. By invitation only, some individuals formed a courtly audience for plays and spectacles staged in royal and noble houses. Although both Henry VIII (Elizabeth's father) and Elizabeth had staged theatrical entertainments from time to time, it was the Stuart kings who followed them, James I (r. 1603–1625) and Charles I (r. 1625–1642), who perfected the splendid court *masques*. Stuart masques were allegorical stories designed to compliment a particular individual or occasion. Their texts were little more than pretexts for the elaborate scenic displays and lavish costumes that characterized the presentations. Although the major roles and all of the comic or villainous characters were portrayed by professional actors, the courtiers themselves performed the heart of the masques, three spectacular dances. Great sums of money ensured the splendor of the

Duchess
by
Helen O Huang
University of Missouri 1987
The Duchess of Malfi

FIGURE 12-20. **Other Dramatists.** Few plays by Shakespeare's contemporaries remain in today's repertory. John Webster's *The Duchess of Malfi* finds occasional production. Here, a costume design for one such production. *(Design by Helen Huang, USAA.)*

entertainments; one such masque cost a staggering 21,000 pounds at a time when the average *annual* wage for a skilled worker was about 25 pounds.

Although many leading dramatists wrote masques, Ben Jonson and William Davenant were the most significant. Jonson, perhaps the leading playwright of the period excluding Shakespeare, became annoyed that the text assumed such a clearly secondary position to the scenery, and so he stopped writing masques in 1631, leaving Davenant as the primary author of the courtly entertainment thereafter. The star of the masques, however, was neither Jonson nor Davenant but the scenic designer Inigo Jones. An Englishman by birth, Jones studied design at the court of Florence in Italy, where he learned the newest techniques of stage painting, rigging, and design. He introduced many of these into the English court when, in 1605, he staged his first masque for James I. *By the end of his career, Jones had introduced into the English courts* (but *not* into the theatres) *all the major elements of Italianate staging then developed* (see pp. 270–275).

Stuart masques, then, have a significance that exceeds the number of persons who saw them. First, they were using Italianate systems of staging during the first half of the seventeenth century, at a time when the English public and private theatres still relied on scenic practices that were essentially medieval. Second, the close association

FIGURE 12-21. **Court Masques: Inigo Jones.** Staged in noble houses throughout Western Europe, masques depended more heavily on spectacle than on language. Here, designs for masque costumes by Inigo Jones.

of the masques with the monarchy, added to the Puritans' displeasure at their expense, were major factors in the Puritans' decision to outlaw the theatre when they seized power.

The Civil War

In 1642, a civil war broke out between the Monarchists (those wishing to keep Charles I on the throne and, implicitly, Roman Catholic influence strong within the Church of England) and the Puritans (those who wished to purify the Church of

FIGURE 12-22. The Closing of the Theatres. Although the Civil War led to laws against theatre, illegal performances took place in makeshift theatres, some perhaps resembling the Old Stage and Balcony shown here. Compare with the Swan drawing, Figure 12-16.

England of all its Romish practices and to remove Charles I from power). The Puritans deposed Charles, seized power, formed a government—and closed the theatres. It took a second civil war, however, to put Oliver Cromwell in power and to bring stability to the war-torn island.

Cromwell put an end for a time to legitimate theatre in England, but, as music was not banned, William Davenant produced operas during the period, and, in these productions he introduced the Italianate system to the general public. Also, the bribery of petty officials apparently made it possible to produce plays occasionally, for contemporary records of arrests and repeated legal sanctions suggest continued, if reduced, theatrical activity between 1642 and 1660.

On Cromwell's death, no acceptable successor could be found, and so Parliament finally called Charles II, son of Charles I, from France, where he had lived in exile. For the period of the Interregnum (the period "between kings," 1642–1660), the English theatres were closed

When the theatres reopened in 1660 with the restoration of the monarchy, both the drama and the staging traditions were very different.

The Spanish Golden Age (c. 1550–c. 1650)

In the sixteenth and early seventeenth centuries, Spain vied with England for supremacy on the seas and in the New World. With a strong navy and a strong monarch, Spain sought to subdue England, first through marriage (to Mary or Elizabeth) and, failing that, through war on the seas (the Spanish Armada). Unsuccessful on both counts, Spain shortly thereafter withdrew from the mainstream of Europe to pursue its own God-centered view of life, government, and society. But during the early years of the seventeenth century, Spain had a strong and developing theatre.

Medieval religious theatre saw the rise of the Corpus Christi play in the 1540s. At almost the same time, Spanish professional actors began organizing as sharing companies and traveling to major towns, where they performed on temporary (booth) stages in whatever locations seemed suitable. Traditional religious plays, comedies and farces, school and university plays, and even court *entremeses* (similar to English interludes and Italian *intermezzi*) formed their repertory.

These companies differed from the English companies, however, in their use of women as actors. Exactly when women first appeared on the Spanish stage is unclear, but they were certainly there by the time of the first two permanent theatres in Madrid: the Corral del Cruz (1580) and the Corral del Principe (1584). Thereafter, some actors were able to settle in the city, touring only when the permanent theatres were closed.

Theatre Buildings

Spanish theatres of the Golden Age shared several features with the public theatres of Elizabethan England:

1. They were outdoors.

2. A five- or six-foot-high platform jutted out in front of a background pierced by entrances.

3. On the stage platform were two columns holding up a roof that covered part of the acting area.

4. There was a raised, secondary acting area.

5. An audience area existed slightly below and in front of the stage, with additional audience areas provided by galleries above and around it.

6. Flying machines and stage traps were available, probably remnants of the medieval stage magic.

Spanish theatres, however, had some features not encountered in England. The permanent Spanish theatres were set up in *corrales* (yards in the center of blocks of houses), over which an awning stretched as protection against the elements. Some of the audience stood in the central courtyard (*patio*) or sat on covered benches (*gradas*) along the sides. Opposite the stage at the second level was a gallery (*cazuela*) set aside for women, who were segregated from the men in the audience. The *cazuela* had its own entrance to the street, which was guarded by police. Along the side houses were windows covered with grills (*aposentos*) through which people could watch the play. Above the *cazuela* were two additional galleries, the second level divided into boxes, and the third (*tertulia*) holding the cheapest seats. The stage itself was somewhat smaller than the Globe's and had a back curtain that, when opened, revealed an additional acting area (discovery space).

FIGURE 12-23. Spanish Theatre. A speculative reconstruction of the Corral del Principe, Madrid. The numbers show: 1. the machine space over the stage; 2. the backstage area; 3. the curtained discovery space; 4. the stage; 5. the patio, with benches near the grilled windows (*aposentos*) in the wall above; 6. roof over lowest bank of seats; 7. the exterior street wall, showing one of several entrances. (*Reconstruction by Kenneth M. Cameron.*)

Staging Conventions

Spanish scenery and costuming conventions were similar to those in England, although larger scenic pieces were probably common. Large properties (e.g., a fountain, a tomb, or a ship's rigging) were sometimes set behind the curtain. Costumes were emblematic, with a mixture of contemporary garments and special dress. There was no attempt at unified "design."

Plays and Playwrights

The Spanish Golden Age produced thousands of plays, including secular tragicomedies (*comedias*), plays on religious subjects (*autos sacramentales*), cloak-and-sword plays (*capa y espada*), and farces. The earliest important playwright, Lope de Rueda, specialized in farces and religious plays. Lope de Vega may have originated the cape-

and-sword plays, swashbucklers that subsequently influenced both English and French dramatists. The author of over five hundred works, Lope de Vega is now best known for his *Fuenteovejuna*, a play that still finds occasional contemporary production. Tirso de Molina is remembered for his Don Juan play, *The Trickster of Seville*. The best-known Spanish playwright of the Golden Age, however, was Pedro Calderón de la Barca, whose *Life Is a Dream* epitomized the poetry and intellect of his best works. Calderón stopped writing for the stage around 1640; the theatres were closed shortly thereafter for a time of royal mourning (1644–1649). When they reopened, the Golden Age of Spanish theatre had passed, although the theatres remained in use into the eighteenth century.

CHAPTER THIRTEEN

ILLUSIONISTIC THEATRES I: NEOCLASSICISM AND ITALIANATE STAGING

THEATRE IN ITALY (1550–1750)

The Renaissance in Italy, unlike that in England and Spain, revolutionized theatre and drama. In their efforts to recapture the practices of Greece and Rome, Italian artists set theatres in Europe on a new path—a path toward *illusionism*. Theatre was henceforth to seek an illusion of real life.

Three contributions of the Italians were to have far-reaching effects: (1) the Neoclassical ideal in playwriting and criticism; (2) the Italianate system of staging and architecture; and (3) the popular theatre known as *commedia dell'arte*.

Neoclassicism

Neoclassicism literally means "new classicism," but in fact it was based far more heavily on Rome than on Greece. Neoclassicism, as first developed by the Italians and later adopted throughout most of western Europe, rested on five major points:

FIGURE 13-1. Renaissance Italy. Competing republics and city-states shared the Italian peninsula, whose extended coastline encouraged trade and therefore contact with, among others, Constantinople.

(1) verisimilitude, and the related decorum; (2) purity of genres; (3) the "three unities"; (4) the five-act form; and (5) the twofold purpose: to teach and to please.

Verisimilitude

Central to Neoclassical doctrine was a complex concept called *verisimilitude*—literally, "truth seeming." But the meaning of *verisimilitude* is more involved than its facile definition might suggest, for serious artists of all ages have aimed to tell the "truth."

Because the characteristics of art throughout the ages have changed, it is probably safe to conclude that the arts differed from age to age because the truth that the artists saw and sought to depict had changed. Thus, the critical problem for a student of Neoclassicism is to understand what "truth" meant to the Neoclassicist.

Truth for the Neoclassicist resided in the essential, the general, the typical, and the class rather than in the particular, the individual, or the unique. To get at truth, a Neoclassical artist had to cut away all that was temporary or accidental in favor of those qualities that were fundamental and unchanging. To be true meant to be *usually* true, *generally* accurate, *typically* the case. The humanness of one person, for example, rested in those essential qualities that he or she shared with all other people, regardless of the historical accident of place, century, or nationality of birth. Individual differences were not important because they were not essential to humanness. Such a view of truth placed a premium on classification and categorization, and *verisimilitude* had a meaning very different from that ascribed to it by our own age's view of the importance of individuality and uniqueness.

Neoclassical truth implied other matters as well. Verisimilitude in drama required the elimination of events that could not reasonably be expected to happen in real life. Although an exception was made when ancient stories or myths incorporating supernatural events were dramatized, even then the dramatist was expected to minimize the importance of such events, perhaps by putting the action offstage. Because in real life people generally talk to one another rather than to themselves, monologues and soliloquies were customarily abandoned in favor of dialogue between major characters and their *confidants*.

DECORUM. The tendency of people to behave in certain ways based on age, social rank, occupation, gender, and so forth could be observed; therefore, characters in drama were expected to display proper *decorum* (that is, they were to embody the traits normally held by members of their class) or, if they did not, to suffer ridicule or punishment for their deviations.

MORALITY. Finally, because it was believed that God ruled the world in accord with a divine plan and that He was a good God, verisimilitude required that dramatic actions be organized in such a way that good was rewarded and evil punished, in keeping with eternal truth. Although in daily life good occasionally went unrewarded and evil unpunished, such observable events were believed to be aberrational and therefore to be unsuitable subjects for drama.

Purity of Genres

From the concept of *verisimilitude* derived *purity of genres*, which meant that the two major forms, tragedy and comedy, must not be mixed. The injunction against mixing did not mean merely that funny scenes were improper for tragedy or that unhappy endings were inappropriate for comedy. Both tragedy and comedy were far more rigidly defined than today, and the rule against mixing the forms meant that no element belonging to the one should appear in the other. For example, tragedy was to depict people of high station involved in affairs of state; its language was to be elevated and poetic; its endings were to be unhappy. Comedy, on the other hand, was to display persons of the lower and middle classes embroiled in domestic diffi-

FIGURE 13-2. A Changed Way of Life. In Renaissance Italy trading replaced agriculture, cities replaced manors, and cannons ended the era of knights on horseback, as this drawing clearly captures.

culties and intrigues. Its language was always less elevated, and often prosaic, and its endings were happy. Purity of genres meant, then, that a prose tragedy or a domestic tragedy could not exist—both were a contradiction in terms. It also meant that kings and queens did not appear in comedies, nor were affairs of state suitable subjects for the comic author.

The Three Unities

Based on verisimilitude and on current interpretations of ancient commentators, the Neoclassical notion of the "three unities" (time, place, and action) developed. Although Aristotle had argued cogently for plays with a unified action, Neoclassical theorists were more concerned that their plays unfold within a reasonable time and a limited place so that verisimilitude would not be strained. No audience would believe, the Neoclassical argument went, that months had passed or oceans had been crossed while the audience sat in the same place for a few hours. Although theorists varied in the strictness of their requirements for unity (some argued for a single room, others allowed a single town; some required that the playing time of the drama equal the actual time elapsed, others permitted a twenty-four-hour time period), most Italian theorists accepted some version of the three unities after about 1570.

Five-Act Play

By then, as well, Neoclassicists had adopted the *five-act play form* as standard for drama, a norm probably derived from the theories of Horace and the practices of Seneca.

Purposes of Drama

The Neoclassicists sought a justification for drama and theatre and found it in their ability to teach moral precepts while entertaining and delighting an audience. *To teach* and *to please* were defined as the *dual purposes of drama,* and playwrights desiring critical acclaim took care that their plays did both. The idea of a drama's existing only for its own sake or as an expression of an individual artist was not accepted by major Renaissance theorists.

After about 1570, Neoclassical ideas became the standard for Italian dramas. By 1600, Neoclassical standards were being accepted in other parts of Europe, where they remained dominant for the next two hundred years among educated and courtly audiences. Neoclassicism's propriety and concentration may account for its lack of appeal to many people, who sought more spectacle than the three unities permitted. Thus, despite the acceptance of Neoclassicism as an ideal, its tenets were undercut in a variety of ways.

Italianate Staging

Italianate staging, like Neoclassicism, developed as an amalgam of ideas and techniques from classical Rome (and to a lesser extent from ancient Greece) and contemporary Italy.

Vitruvius

In 1486, Vitruvius's work on Roman architecture was printed. The dissemination of *De Architectura* was so rapid that by 1500 its major points had been accepted as authoritative, and a number of contemporary Italian interpretations of it had been undertaken. Although his books dealt with architecture and scenery, Vitruvius provided no illustrations of his ideal theatre. Because Vitruvius offered no illustrations, the Italians translated his words and ideas in light of contemporary practices in art and architecture, most notably the current fascination with *linear perspective.*

Perspective

Although known to the ancients, perspective, when it was rediscovered by the Italians around 1500, caused an artistic revolution. Artists struggled to master the intricacies of the "new" technique, and uninitiated spectators hailed its ability to trick the senses as if by magic.

Serlio

Soon the potential of perspective painting for scenic decoration was recognized, and, in 1545, Sebastiano Serlio (1475–1554) published the second book of his seven-volume *Dell' Architettura,* which became the most authoritative interpretation of Vitruvius to date. Serlio's work established the guidelines for theatrical architects and designers for the next hundred years.

Serlio's interpretation of Vitruvius's Roman theatre, however erroneous, set a model for permanent theatres built in Italy during the Renaissance. Vitruvius was obviously describing the outdoor, circular Roman theatre that he knew. Wealthy

FIGURE 13-3. **Teatro Olimpico.** Perspective vistas (two of which are shown here) receding within doorways of a façade stage were an early experiment in combining Vitruvius with Renaissance perspective.

Italians, on the other hand, were accustomed to plays produced in banqueting halls in the homes of the wealthy. When the first permanent theatres were envisioned, therefore, the task was to fit the classical theatre as described by Vitruvius into the rectangular spaces familiar to the Italians and, in some way, to accommodate the result to the current fashion for linear perspective.

An early solution was the Teatro Olimpico, whose five doors corresponded roughly to Vitruvius's description of five stage openings, except that now each door had a vista in forced perspective.

A later theatre used a permanent proscenium arch that protected the illusion of perspective and featured a series of additional arches farther back on the stage, each increasing the sense of depth and heightening the illusion.

In scenic display as well as in theatrical architecture, Serlio's interpretation of Vitruvius set the standard. From Vitruvius's scant descriptions of tragic, comic, and satyric scenes, Serlio elaborated each into detailed directions, with illustrations drawn in perspective. A brief comparison of Vitruvius and Serlio as they described one setting will suggest the differences.

Of the satyric scene, Vitruvius said, "Satyric scenes are decorated with trees, caverns, mountains, and other rustic objects delineated in landscaped style." Of the same scenes, Serlio (as translated into English in 1611) amplified, "The Satiricall Scenes are to Represent Satirs, wherein you must place all those things that be rude and rusticall." He then went on to quote Vitruvius as calling for "Trees, Rootes, Herbs, Hils, and Flowers, and with some countrey houses. . . . And for that in our dayes these things were made in Winter, where there were but fewe greene Trees,

FIGURE 13-4. **Serlio.** Interpreting Vitruvius's description in light of contemporary Italian interest in linear perspective, Serlio illustrated the tragic, comic, and satyric scenes and thus influenced practices for about one hundred years. *(Courtesy of Center for Archival Collections, Rare Books Division, Bowling Green State University.)*

Herbs, and Flowres to be found; then you must make these things of Silke, which will be more commendable than the naturall things themselves."

In the remainder of the book, Serlio provided such tips on stagecraft as the proper use of colored lights, the production of fire effects, the building of fanciful costumes, and the use of pasteboard figures on a perspective stage. After its printing in 1545, Serlio's account, a blending of the classical descriptions of Vitruvius with current Italian scenic practices, swept western Europe and became the basis of what was called the *Italianate system* of staging.

Italianate Scenery

With certain modest modifications related to the particular country and the specific date, Italianate settings shared these features throughout the sixteenth, seventeenth, and early eighteenth centuries:

1. The scenery was painted in single-point perspective, calculated from a seat toward the back of the orchestra (usually reserved for the most important noble associated with the theatre).

2. The scenery consisted of a series of wings (paired *flats*, i.e., wooden frames covered with fabric) positioned at each side of the stage, with each pair placed relatively closer to the center line of the stage than the one in front of it, so that the apparent distance increased. The setting culminated at the back of the stage in a single backdrop painted in perspective (or alternately, a shutter formed when a set of wings was shoved together and then painted in perspective).

3. The scenery was placed behind the proscenium arch and thus behind the actors, forming a background against which they played, rather than an environment for the action.

4. The stage was raked (slanted) to increase the sense of depth by forcing the perspective. Sometimes the front part of the stage, where the actors performed, was flat and only the portion of the stage behind the proscenium arch was raked; at other times, the rake began at the front of the platform and continued uninterrupted to the back wall.

5. Overhead machinery and theatrical rigging were hidden from view by a series of *borders* (fabric, framed or unframed) arranged to enhance perspective.

6. A proscenium arch (or several) framed the whole picture, thereby protecting the illusion created by the perspective painting.

Changeable Scenery

Having developed this basic system for decorating the stage, Italian artists set about almost at once to perfect it. Specifically, they investigated ways of shifting scenery in order to permit a rapid change of place. Experimentation soon revealed that quick changes required the replacement of all three-dimensional details with two-dimensional, painted settings, as well as the replacement of *angle wings* (two flats hinged together) by flat wings. By the 1640s, the methods of scenic change were well developed and were summarized in two influential works, one by Niccolo Sabattini and another by Joseph Furttenbach. But the real breakthrough came in 1645, when Giacomo Torelli (1608–1678) astonished the theatrical world with his invention of a new mechanism for changing scenery: the *chariot-and-pole system*. The name derived from the small wagons (or chariots) that ran on tracks beneath the stage and carried on them a long pole that extended from the chariots through slits in the stage floor up to a height sufficient to provide a sturdy support for scenic pieces, which were

FIGURE 13-5. **Chariot and Pole.** In order to change scenery during elaborate court masques, Torelli invented the chariot and pole system, shown here reproduced from an eighteenth-century encyclopedia. *(Courtesy of University of South Carolina Library.)*

attached to the poles at stage level. The idea was a simple one: as the chariots moved on their tracks toward the center of the stage, a piece of scenery came into view; as the chariot moved off to the side, a piece of scenery disappeared. By devising an elaborate system of ropes and pulleys, Torelli succeeded in rigging everything together so that the turn of a single winch could produce a complete change of setting. By coordinating such changes with the machinery used to produce special effects, like flying, trapping, wave making, thunder, lightning, and explosions, he was able to achieve a truly magical effect. Such tricks earned Torelli the name of the "Great Wizard."

A contradiction clearly existed between the ideals of drama, where Neoclassicism called for the unities of time, place, and action and an avoidance of supernatural events, and the ideals of scenic display, whose Italianate artists stressed increasingly elaborate splendors involving multiple scenes, instant transformations, and a variety of spectacular effects. In Italy, as elsewhere, the tension was resolved by producing dramas simply and by expending imagination and money for the production of lavish operas, dances, and *intermezzi* (courtly entertainments typically given between the acts of a play). By the mid-seventeenth century, the Italian opera had become the most popular form of dramatic entertainment in Italy. As Italian opera was exported to France, Germany, and the rest of Europe, so were many of Italy's latest scenic techniques.

Commedia Dell'arte

Neoclassical dramas and elaborately staged operas were primarily the entertainment of the noble, the wealthy, and the erudite. Among the common folk, another, very different kind of dramatic entertainment was flourishing: the *commedia dell'arte* ("professional playing"). Although neither the origins nor the sources of *commedia* are well understood, its major characteristics were well established by 1550, and Italian troupes of *commedia* players were touring western Europe by 1600.

Commedia players (both male and female) worked from a basic story outline (*scenario*) within which they improvised much of their dialogue and action. Each actor in the troupe played the same character in almost every scenario and therefore wore the same costume and mask, reused the same bits of comic business (*lazzi*), and even repeated some of the same dialogue from scenario to scenario. Most troupes had ten or twelve members, each of whom assumed the role of one of the stock characters. Each troupe had one or two sets of young lovers (*innamorati*) and a host of masked comic characters, the most common of which were Capitano (the captain), Pantalone (the merchant), Dottore (the doctor), and the several *zanni* (servants) like Arlecchino (Harlequin), Brighella, Scaramuccio, and Pulcinello. Male actors outnumbered female, but women were a recognized part of all commedia troupes.

Organized as sharing companies, such troupes toured constantly as they tried to scratch out a living in the theatre, without the protection or the financial support of noble houses. Although the influence of *commedia* extended throughout Europe, its ephemeral nature militated against its leaving a lasting record (especially scripts), and so today this popular Italian comedy is a phenomenon whose excitement and vigor cannot be recaptured.

Despite Italy's unquestioned leadership in dramatic theory and scenic display and in spite of its unique popular comedy, Italian theatre and drama did not attain lasting international prominence. By 1750, except for opera Italy was no longer a world leader in theatre. Both England and France had outstripped their teacher and had attained an international reputation by the end of the seventeenth century, and both achieved a lasting acclaim never given the Italians, from whom they drew.

THEATRE IN FRANCE (1550–1750)

The ideas and practices of the Italian Renaissance reached and affected French courts and universities early. However, France, unlike England, failed to achieve political and religious stability in the sixteenth century, and so the development of a vigorous public theatre was delayed.

Not until about 1600 did a popular playwright, Alexandre Hardy (c. 1572–1632), emerge to challenge improvised French farces performed by itinerant actors as the mainstay of French popular theatre. And not until 1625 did the first acting troupe establish itself permanently in Paris at the Hôtel de Bourgogne, a theatre built almost

Scapino.   Cap. Zerbino.

Pulliciniello.   Sig.ª Lucretia.

FIGURE 13-6. Commedia dell'Arte. Improvised comedy, which included female performers, featured young lovers (unmasked, as Lucretia here) and several masked characters like Pulcinello, Scapino, and Captain Zerbino.

Comedie ou farce de six parsonnaiges.

FIGURE 13-7. **French Farceurs.** France had a popular, partly improvised theatre not unlike Italy's *commedia dell'arte*. Molière seems to have been influenced by both.

seventy-five years earlier by a religious fraternity devoted to the production of religious plays in Paris (before they were outlawed in 1548). Thus, at a time when English theatre had already enjoyed the vigor and excellence of Shakespeare, the French public theatre was merely at the brink of its golden age.

Corneille and Le Cid

Political stability arrived in Paris following the ascent of Louis XIII to the throne (r. 1610–1643). It was then that the French public theatre began its climb to greatness. A number of educated men started to write for the theatre, among them Pierre Corneille (1606–1684), whose play *Le Cid* (produced in 1636) marked a turning point in French drama. Based on a Spanish play that depicted a welter of events strewn through several locations and many years, *Le Cid* was rewritten by Corneille to bring it into closer accord with the Neoclassical ideal. Thus, the six acts of the Spanish piece were reduced to five, the several years compressed into a single day, and the numerous locales squeezed into a single town. Still, the play departed from Neoclassical tragedy; for example, it had a happy ending, and its numerous incidents strained verisimilitude. Cardinal Richelieu, long a promoter of Italian culture, resolved to use the play as a test case in his efforts to bring France closer in line with Italian practices. He therefore submitted the play for evaluation to the recently formed French Academy, a prestigious literary society charged with maintaining the purity of French language and literature. The verdict of the academy was clear. It praised *Le Cid* wherever it conformed to Neoclassical precepts and condemned it wherever it strayed from them. French playwrights, including Corneille, were quick to conclude that critical acclaim would rest on strict adherence to the principles of Neoclassicism. And so, after 1636, Neoclassicism dominated French drama for over one hundred years.

Torelli and Italianate Staging

In 1641, Cardinal Richelieu opened the first Italianate (proscenium-arch) theatre in France, the Palais-Cardinal. His successor, Cardinal Mazarin, brought Giacomo Torelli to Paris in 1645. Already famous in Italy, Torelli installed his chariot-and-pole systems in the Palais-Royal (formerly the Palais-Cardinal, but renamed when Louis XIV appropriated it on Richelieu's death) and in the newly remodeled Petit Bourbon. Torelli's early productions marked the acceptance of all major Italianate scenic conventions in the French theatre. Henceforth, the Neoclassical plays, with their stark and simple settings, competed with lavish operas, ballets, and *machine plays* (plays written particularly for the display of scenic marvels) for the attention of Parisian audiences.

Between 1660 and 1700 under Louis XIV, France attained a glory equal to that of Shakespeare's England. The period was characterized by four major traits:

FIGURE 13-8. **Italianate Staging in France.** A proscenium arch, scenery in single-point perspective, and (after 1645) a chariot and pole system of changing scenery showed the strong influence of Italians like Torelli on French staging. Shown here, the production of *Mirame* in the French court theatre of 1641.

1. The continuing strength of Neoclassicism as the dramatic ideal.

2. The continued acceptance of Italianate staging conventions.

3. The emergence of three master playwrights: Pierre Corneille, Jean Racine (1639–1699), and Jean Baptiste Poquelin, or Molière (1622–1673).

4. The presence of five permanent acting troupes in Paris.

Major Dramatists, 1650–1700

Racine

Although Pierre Corneille wrote important plays until after 1675, his fame was eclipsed by that of Jean Racine. Born three years after the first production of *Le Cid*, Racine was raised by Jansenists, a Catholic sect with an overriding preoccupation with sin and guilt, concerns that permeated Racine's major plays. Educated in the Greek and Roman classics, Racine based his only comedy, *The Litigants*, on Aristophanes' comedy *The Wasps*, and his most esteemed tragedy, *Phèdre*, on Euripides' *Hippolytus*.

Phèdre, one of the finest tragedies ever written, was a model of Neoclassicism. Because the play's major conflicts occur within the character of Phèdre, the Neoclassical requirements for unity were easily accommodated; and, because Phèdre's passion leads to her downfall, Neoclassical commitment to the punishment of evil was amply satisfied. *Phèdre*, unlike *Le Cid*, was Neoclassical through and through, and its achievement in plot, character, and diction placed it clearly among the masterpieces of dramatic literature. In short, France accomplished what England did not: lasting and popular drama based on neoclassical theory.

Molière

French comedy found its genius in the actor-dramatist Molière. At about the time that theatres were closing in England, Molière was leaving home to form a traveling theatrical troupe in France. By 1660, he was head of the troupe, wrote most of its plays, and had firmly established it at court as a favorite of Louis XIV. Perhaps the greatest comic writer of all times, Molière used his own experiences as an actor as well as his knowledge of Roman comedies, Italian *commedia,* and indigenous French farces to develop comedies that ridiculed social and moral pretentiousness. Molière's comedy typically depicts characters made ludicrous by their deviations from decorum. Although his dialogue is often clever, verbal elegance and wit for their own sake do not form the core of his plays; instead, the comedies depend heavily on farcical business (like *commedia's lazzi*) and visual gags for their power. Of his more than twenty plays, the best known are probably *The Doctor in Spite of Himself* (1666), *The School for Wives* (1662), *Tartuffe* (1669), *The Miser* (1668), and *The Imaginary Invalid* (1673). While acting the leading role in *The Imaginary Invalid,* Molière was seized by convulsions and died a few hours later, denied last rites by the Church because of his life as an actor and granted Christian burial only through the direct intervention of Louis XIV.

FIGURE 13-9. **Molière's *Tartuffe*.** This lady's fan is illustrated with scenes from Molière's controversial comedy. Shown here, the famous scene where the husband, hiding under the table, overhears the religious hypocrite Tartuffe trying to seduce his wife.

Actors and Acting

The life of French actors (male and female—the first female actor appeared in Paris about 1610) was not easy. Some troupes were granted royal subsidies, and Louis XIII had tried to improve their reputation and social acceptability by royal edict. Nonetheless, French actors were denied civic and religious rights throughout most of the seventeenth and eighteenth centuries, a situation that led many actors to adopt pseudonyms in order to spare their families anguish and reproach. Forced to tour continuously until 1625, only the most talented actors were gradually able to settle in Paris as members of a permanent troupe. By 1660, there were five such troupes in Paris: the players at the Hôtel de Bourgogne; those at the Théâtre Marais (a tennis court converted into an Italianate theatre, as was a common continental practice); Molière's troupe at the Palais-Royal; a *commedia* troupe from Italy, which alternated with Molière at the same theatre; and at court, the opera, music, and dance troupe headed by Jean-Baptiste Lully (1632–1687). All were sharing companies, and all included women. Thus, France had women in its acting companies at least fifty years before England. Unlike England, however, France had no householders, no actors who owned parts of the theatre building.

With Molière's death came the amalgamation of his troupe with those of the Bourgogne and the Marais to form the new Comédie Française, which became France's national theatre. Membership in this sharing company was fixed; therefore,

FIGURE 13-10. **French Actors.** This frontispiece seems to show scenery in single-point perspective, two doors over which are two actors (or statuary? or audience members?), and three comic actors.

new members could not be elected until others had retired or died. Because of its financial rewards, including a substantial pension for retired members, the list of applicants was long. Many never made it, but those who did held a monopoly on the legal performance of tragedies and comedies for the Parisian public.

Lully's troupe likewise held a monopoly on the production of musical entertainments and spectacles, and the *commedia* troupe (after a brief banishment for a political indiscretion) had exclusive performance rights to comic operas. Members of these three troupes were expected to continue the traditions already established, not to initiate new techniques. The result was a highly polished but quite tradition-bound style of production.

Drama and Theatre, 1700–1750

Around 1700 in France, a new conservatism was noticeable in both theatre and drama. Louis XIV had grown old and cautious. Dramatists, perhaps intimidated by the genius of Corneille, Racine, and Molière, strove to copy their style. A modest shift toward morality and sentimentality occurred. In tragedy, for example, Voltaire (1694–1778) sought to loosen the bonds of Neoclassicism by introducing some Shakespearean features to the French stage, particularly more spectacle and a greater range of permissible subjects, but his efforts before 1750 were largely frustrated. In comedy, Pierre Claude Nivelle de La Chausée (1692–1754) pitted virtuous heroes against numerous obstacles that they finally overcame in a burst of energy and good humor. The audience was moved to tears by the expressed sentiments of the sympathetic characters and by the rewards heaped on them for their virtuous behavior. Such *sentimental* and *tearful comedies* were a far cry from Molière's works, where the frailty and stubbornness of the characters provoked hearty laughter from spectators of all social classes.

Scenic Innovations, 1700–1750

Scenic displays in the opera and the ballet, although perhaps more sumptuous than before, changed little in basic concept. Two innovations, however, did make their way to France from Italy by the first half of the eighteenth century. The first, *angle perspective,* meant that scenic artists relegated vistas to the sides, and the actors could work closer to the scenery at center stage without violating the perspective. The second, a *changed scale,* meant that only the lower portions of the scenery were portrayed. With the tops no longer visible, the scenery seemed to disappear into the overhead spaces and out of sight, thereby multiplying the apparent size of the setting and producing a sense of vastness and monumentality that dwarfed the individual actors playing before it.

Staging Practices, 1700–1750

Acting was still applauded to the degree that it was oratorically interesting and vocally sound. Costumes, in keeping with the Neoclassical view that time and place were relatively unimportant, consisted of the most splendid contemporary outfits that the actors could afford, the lavishness of the costume always being a more accurate index to the wealth of the actor than to the character being impersonated.

New Directions for Theatre, 1700–1750

With no outlet for the talents of the many actors and writers who were denied access to the Comédie Française, and with only limited satisfaction from the erudite plays of Neoclassicism, some French men and women worked in illegal theatres, that is, theatres other than the Comédie Française and the Opéra. Joining jugglers, dancers, and similar entertainers who had long appeared at French fairs, theatrical troupes began to form and play just outside the law, practicing all manner of stratagems to avoid open conflict with the monopolies held by the licensed troupes. From the experiments of these illegitimate theatres (which before 1800 moved to the Parisian "boulevards") developed the forerunners of comic opera and melodrama, forms that flourished in the great Romantic theatre of the next century.

In sum, the French theatre for the first half of the eighteenth century recalled its past glories when the genius of Corneille, Racine, Molière, and Torelli had estab-

FIGURE 13-11. **Angle Perspective and Monumentality.** By the eighteenth century, angle perspective often replaced single-point perspective, and sets appeared to dwarf actors. Both innovations originated in Italy and shortly appeared in France.

lished it as the leader of the civilized world. Changes from seventeenth-century practices were few and infrequent. When made, they were almost always in the direction of elaborating Neoclassical dramas and Italianate staging. Thus, by 1750, French theatre was tradition-bound, highly conventionalized, and perhaps out of touch with the lives of everyday French citizens. In a short one hundred years (1650–1750), the theatre had moved from a vigorous and forward-looking activity to a depressed and backward-gazing one.

THEATRE IN ENGLAND (1660–1750)

When the English monarchy was restored in 1660, theatre was reinstated almost immediately. Its conventions were illusionistic rather than medieval. Until new permanent theatres could be built, companies used whatever spaces were available

FIGURE 13-12. **Women on Stage.** Almost immediately after the theatre reopened in London in 1660, women appeared on the stage. Here, a male and female actor performing in 1673.

(spaces left over from pre-Commonwealth days or tennis courts remodeled for theatrical productions). English theatre, like the French, was organized as a monopoly in which only two troupes were licensed, originally those of William Davenant and Thomas Killigrew (1612–1683). Although these monopolies were often challenged and although they changed hands and specific regulations from time to time, they were continuously reaffirmed, most strongly in the *Licensing Act of 1737*, which allowed only two legitimate theatres in London, at Drury Lane and at Covent Garden, and at the same time forbade the presentation of any play not previously licensed by the Lord Chamberlain. Throughout the period, therefore, only two "legitimate" theatres played.

At the Restoration women were introduced to the stage and into acting companies. Their presence seems to have encouraged, fairly or not, the reputation of frivolity and even libertinism that early pervaded the Restoration playhouse. After about

1661, women assumed all female roles except those of witches and comic old women (roles that continued to be played by men).

Drama

Many plays written during the age of Shakespeare continued to be produced (usually in severely adapted versions), but the new plays, both comic and serious, were closer to continental Neoclassicism than to Shakespeare. From 1660 to about 1700, the plays tended to depict a highly artificial court society, probably influenced by life at the French court of Louis XIV.

The eighteenth century, however, brought with it a change of values. Between about 1700 and 1750, values grew steadily more conservative, middle-class, moralistic, and sentimental.

Sentimentalism asserted the basic goodness of each individual. This doctrine contrasted with the previous, Neoclassical, view that human existence was a continuing struggle between good and evil. According to the sentimentalist, evil came about through corruption; it was not part of human nature at birth. Sentimentalism thus implied that, although people might not be perfect, they were perfectible. Literature should therefore show virtuous people acting virtuously in their daily lives. Heroic behavior and ethical perfection need not be restricted to some idealized world of pastoral poetry or exotic tragedy. Sentimentalism affected both comedies and serious dramas in England (as in France).

Comedy of Manners

Most famous today are the Restoration "comedies of manners," plays whose witty dialogue and sophisticated sexual behavior reflect the highly artificial, mannered, and aristocratic society of the day. The heroes and heroines are "virtuous" if they succeed in capturing and satisfying a lover or in cuckolding a husband and avoiding detection. "Honor" depends not on integrity but on reputation, and "wit," the ability to express ideas in a clever and apt way, is prized above all. The admirable characters in the plays are those who can operate successfully within the intricate social sphere; the foolish and laughable are those whose lack of wit or upbringing denies them access to social elegance. In short, the comedies depict the mores and conventions of a courtly society where elegance of phrase and the *appearance* of propriety were more highly prized than lofty morals and sincere feelings. Among the most famous authors of Restoration comedies were William Congreve (1670–1729); George Etherege (c. 1634–1691); and William Wycherley (1640–1715).

Heroic and Neoclassical Tragedy

"Heroic" tragedies present the inevitable conflict between love and duty. In a world far removed from that of the Restoration comedies, tragic heroes are flawless and heroines chaste. The dialogue is bombastic and replete with "heroic couplets," two-line units of rhymed iambic pentameter (probably an attempt to reproduce in English the verse form of French Neoclassicists, the twelve-syllabled Alexandrine). The idealization and formality of this kind of tragedy make it unusually susceptible to parody, and so burlesques of it soon appeared.

Original

So, two kind Turtles, when a storm is nigh,
Look up; and see it gath'ring in the skie:
Each calls his Mate to shelter in the Groves,
Leaving in murmures, their unfinish'd Loves.
Perch'd on some dropping Branch they sit alone,
And Cooe, and harken to each others moan.

from *The Conquest of Granada* by JOHN DRYDEN

Burlesque

So Boar and Sow, when any storm is nigh,
Sniff up, and smell it gath'ring in the sky;
Boar beckons Sow to trot in Chestnut Groves,
And there to consummate their unfinish'd Loves;
Pensive in mud they wallow all alone,
And snore and gruntle to each others moan.

from *The Rehearsal* by GEORGE VILLIERS, 2ND DUKE OF BUCKINGHAM

Succumbing both to the onslaught of burlesque and to the changing tastes of audiences, heroic tragedies declined in public favor, their place being filled by Neoclassical tragedies like John Dryden's *All for Love* (1677), a rewriting of Shakespeare's *Antony and Cleopatra* that brought it closer to the principles of Neoclassicism.

Sentimental Comedy

The amoral tone of Restoration comedies of manners had become offensive to many by the early 1700s. In its place came the view that drama should teach morality. One result was that comedies became more sentimental. At first, the change was merely in the plays' endings: young lovers philandered and cuckolded throughout four acts of the play but, in the fifth, repented and declared their intention to lead a moral and upright life henceforth. By the 1730s, heroes and heroines were becoming the virtuous embodiments of middle-class values, struggling cheerfully against adversity until, at the end, their courage and persistence were rewarded. Prized especially were characters able to express their insights into human goodness in pithy statements (which came to be called *sentiments*). Thus, the label *sentimental hero* or *heroine* implied not only those who embodied virtues and who recognized such virtue in others but also those whose speech was rich in sentiments. The audiences of the day experienced "a pleasure too exquisite for laughter," and so the terms *tearful comedy* and *sentimental comedy* predominated in the comic literature by the middle of the eighteenth century.

Serious Drama

George Lillo's *The London Merchant* (1731) was a major break with the Neoclassical ideal. In *The London Merchant*, a middle-class hero is led astray by love and is ultimately punished. Although teaching morality by showing the punishment of evil

FIGURE 13-13. **Serious Drama.** An actor in Lillo's *The London Merchant,* a middle-class prose tragedy of enormous popularity in the early eighteenth century.

(the play was done in London for years to educate apprentices in proper working attitudes), the "tragedy" is nonetheless a far cry from strict Neoclassicism because it is written in prose, features a middle-class hero, and deals with affairs of the heart and the marketplace, rather than affairs of state.

New Forms of Drama

None of these plays, however, satisfied the English taste for scenic splendor and spectacular effects. Thus, opera and a number of so-called minor forms developed to provide outlets for visual display. Native English opera was gradually replaced in public esteem by spectacular Italian operas, whose popularity soared in the eighteenth century. But burlesques, ballad operas, and most of all *pantomimes* also grew in public favor. English pantomimes typically combined elements of *commedia dell'arte,* farce, mythology, and contemporary satire with elaborate scenes of spectacle to produce a short *afterpiece,* that is, something to be performed after the evening's play. Often, the dialogue was merely an excuse for major scenes of transformation, in which

Harlequin, by a wave of his magic wand, changed all places and people into new and dazzling locales and characters. Because new scenery was often commissioned for pantomimes, many innovations in the design and execution of settings in England can be credited to pantomimic displays.

Theatre Buildings

When English theatres opened in 1660, they seemed to combine Shakespearean and Italianate features. The auditorium of the Restoration playhouse was divided into box, pit, and gallery. In England, as in France, certain favored audience members sat on the stage itself. The stage, although still jutting out into the pit, now had a proscenium arch and a raked stage behind it, where grooves were installed to facilitate scene changes. Most of the acting took place on the *forestage*. Most of the scenery, on the other hand, was located behind the proscenium. Initially, the forestage was as large as the stage behind the proscenium, probably an attempt to synthesize earlier Elizabethan practice with currently fashionable Italian practice. As the period wore on, however, the size of the forestage decreased and the stage space behind the proscenium increased, so that, by 1750, little difference existed between English and

FIGURE 13-14. **Restoration Theatre.** A conjectural reconstruction showing a deep forestage, a proscenium arch, and scenery in single-point perspective, perhaps an attempt to combine earlier Shakespearean practice with contemporary Italianate conventions. (*Courtesy of Richard Leacock. First published in* Theatre Notebook.)

French or Italian stages. Between 1660 and 1750, both the stage and the auditorium increased in size as the composition of the audience and the repertory of the plays changed. The Restoration theatres seated about 650, whereas, by 1750, Covent Garden could accommodate about 1500.

Staging

Scenic practices were Italianate. Wings, borders, and shutters were standard. A group of stock sets appropriate for each form of drama (comedy, tragedy, or pastoral) allowed the theatres to provide scenery for most Neoclassical plays. When the theatres required new settings, which was seldom except for pantomimes, they simply commissioned them from painters of the day. Because lighting was still by candles, audience and actors were equally illuminated, although by the early eighteenth century some modest attempts were being made to dim and color lights. Costuming continued to be the major source of visual excitement, and most actors wore an elaborate and sumptuous version of contemporary fashion.

Actors and Acting

The earlier tendency of actors to specialize in certain kinds of roles became gradually more rigid until, by 1750, clearly defined *lines of business* emerged. New actors or actresses were hired as *utility players,* and gained their experience by playing a great number of small and varied roles. They then declared a specialty in a specific kind of role: a walking lady or gentleman (third line); a specialist in low comedy, or stage eccentric (second line); or a hero or heroine (first line). Once committed to a particular line of business, actors did not stray far from it, regardless of age. (Shakespeare's Juliet, for example, was often played by women in their fifties because they were "first-line" players.) Along with lines of business came a practice known as *possession of parts,* an agreement that an actor who played a role in the company possessed that role for as long as he or she remained in the company. Both practices obviously encouraged conservatism in acting and placed a premium on tradition rather than innovation. The tradition perpetuated depended heavily on vocal power and versatility and on formality and elegance rather than "truth to life." For example, some actors apparently intoned or chanted the poetic and lyrical passages of tragedies, much as the recitative of opera is delivered today, and many actors played for *points,* expecting to receive applause for passages particularly well delivered (in which case, the actor might repeat the passage).

Although some acting troupes continued to be organized as sharing ventures, some performers by the early eighteenth century preferred a fixed salary that they could augment by benefit performances. For "benefits," the actor or the group of actors received all of the profits from the evening, a sum that occasionally equaled or exceeded a year's salary.

The most famous actors and actresses of this period included Thomas Betterton (c. 1635–1710), whose portrayal of Shakespearean heroes was unrivaled at the time; Nell Gwyn (1650–1687), whose success in "breeches roles" made her almost as famous as her position as an official mistress of the king; Colley Cibber (1671–1757),

FIGURE 13-15. **Theatre in the United States.** By the time of the American Revolution, the United States had several permanent theatres. Shown here, the John Street (New York), a proscenium theatre with setting in single-point perspective.

noted for his portrayal of fops; Anne Oldfield (1683–1730), the first actress to be buried at Westminster Abbey; James Quin (1693–1766), whose oratorical and formal style epitomized the "old school" of Neoclassical acting; and Charles Macklin (1699–1797), whose prosaic readings and "natural style" anticipated the end of the old and the beginning of a new English style of acting.

THEATRE IN AMERICA, ca. 1750

Many English actors and actresses found themselves squeezed out of the profitable theatres of London by the stringent enforcement of the Licensing Act of 1737. Some sought a living in the English provinces; but one group, headed by William and Lewis Hallam, chose to go to America, instead. In 1752, the troupe arrived in Virginia and, after building a theatre, opened with Shakespeare's *Merchant of Venice.* This group (although reorganized and enlarged after the death of Lewis Hallam and renamed The American Company in recognition of America's break with England) toured the towns of the East Coast with almost no competition until the 1790s. Its repertory, acting styles, and production conventions were English, with appropriate adjustments made for the needs of almost constant touring.

CHAPTER FOURTEEN

ILLUSIONISTIC THEATRES II: ROMANTICISM AND REALISM

ROMANTICISM

Background

After 1750, the decline of Neoclassicism was rapid and pronounced. Sentimental views gained strength and joined with new views on the sources of beauty, the function of art, the nature of truth. Artists and theorists in increasing numbers rejected the rules of Neoclassicism. When the various strands of these new ideas coalesced into something resembling a system of views, it was called *Romanticism*.

Romanticism took many forms. Its extraordinary diversity caused one critic to suggest that we should always speak of *Romanticisms,* to remind ourselves constantly of its plural, shifting nature. Certainly, Romanticism as practiced by English poets like Keats and Shelley was very different from that of French playwrights like Dumas or German philosophers like Kant.

In spite of its complexity, Romanticism, as it peaked through western Europe and America between 1789 and 1843, seemed to share some basic views that can be summarized.

First, Romanticism was marked by a profound interest in nature, which took many forms. In gardening, for example, Romantics sought a "natural" look that included gnarled trees, jagged rocks, and tangled greenery rather than the previously preferred formal gardens with carefully pruned trees and symmetrical arrays of flowers and bushes. In behavior, natural feelings (instincts) were accepted as more reliable guides to proper behavior than was educated opinion. The Romantics' *distrust of reason* sprang from the view that reason was a product of civilization and education and was thus corruptible; instinct was the product of nature and was thus reliable.

The celebration of nature led to a glorification of natural people, *noble savages* whom civilization had left alone in a natural state, such as American Indians, African blacks, and South Sea Islanders. Within contemporary society, the *common people*, especially rural peasants, were most admired because they were least affected by such artificial aspects of civilization as class and etiquette.

The desire to return to nature led to *primitivism*, a belief in the superiority of a simple and unsophisticated way of life, a life close to nature. With primitivism came a desire to study old civilizations, particularly those of ancient Egypt, Greece, and the Middle Ages (thus, *antiquarianism* and *medievalism*). For the Romantics, history was a process of decline or decay, not one of progress and improvement.

Second, the Romantics believed intensely (if erratically) in human equality. Civilization had created a number of artificial and social structures to divide people into classes, and so implied that some people were better than others. Romantics braced against such an assumption. The age was thus one of revolutions: the American Revolution (1776); the French Revolution (1791); the Napoleonic Wars (1798–1815); the

FIGURE 14-1. **Age of Revolutions.** Romantic emphasis on individuality led to worldwide calls for democratization. Shown here, a painting, "The Last Victims of the Reign of Terror," about the end of the French Revolution.

Europe-wide revolutions of 1830 and 1848; and the American Civil War (1865). Antislavery societies flourished; women's rights organizations formed. Most of the political turmoils during the period can be explained as a continuing struggle between those attempting to maintain the status quo (monarchy or slavery or white male suffrage) and those striving to change society in the direction of more individual freedom and more democratic processes.

Third, Romanticism placed a premium on detail, for in the particular example rested the pathway to truth. The specific, the unique, and the particular were important because the study of any single detail could lead to a better understanding of the universe, all parts of which were related. The details (and so the study) of history and geography were important because they led to an understanding of the characteristics that separated one age from other times and places. To establish uniqueness was to affirm identity.

Fourth, the Romantics believed that truth must always be sought but that its attainment in this life was unlikely. Artists and philosophers were the people most likely to have insights into truth, but their insights were both curse and blessing because most people were unable or unwilling to see the truth. To be an artist, then, was to be out of step with society; thus, the Romantic view of the *artist as misunderstood genius.* To strive for perfection was an obligation, but to achieve it was an impossibility. The constant yearning for unattainable truth lent a *melancholy* cast to life, a trait that marked much Romantic art.

Fifth, art for the Romantics served an exalted purpose. In this world, tensions exist between the physical and the spiritual, the material and the ideal. The role of art was to lead people to perceive the underlying unity of existence, to eliminate the apparent conflict: the purpose of art was "to make man whole again." Although the artist could perceive unity amid apparent disunity, he or she might be unable to share that truth, for its perception was based on *insight* and *genius,* rather than on intellect and craft. Art could therefore not be taught; it was not subject to rules. If Romantic artists searched for truth in the myriad details of external nature, they found it often within themselves. Thus, *subjectivity* and *introspection* became hallmarks of Romantic art.

Sixth, criticism, according to the Romantics, was subjective and personal. The worth of a picture or a poem could not be determined by its social utility or its adherence to a set of external criteria. Rather, its merit lay in its ability to stimulate feeling and understanding in the spectator. In a revolutionary leap, Romantic criticism moved the basis of judgment of a work of art from the work to the perceiver of the work. An obvious effect was to democratize art, by making one person's opinion of art as good as another's.

The effect of Romanticism on theatre (and the other arts) was significant, if erratic. In general, Romantic art took as its setting the remote and exotic, either past civilizations (especially Greece and the Middle Ages) or primitive societies. Tales of children, commoners, rustics, and savages unfolded against detailed backgrounds of forests, caves, dungeons, pastures, and jungles. In plays, the appeal was more often to the spectators' emotions than to their intellects, and visually interesting episodes predominated over verbally satisfying ones. Special effects involving wild animals, natural disasters, shipwrecks, and snowstorms prefigured the disaster movies of today. While aristocrats flocked to the opera and the ballet (both arts reached

FIGURE 14-2. **Nature and the Natural.** Rugged individualists, uncorrupted by social conventions, overcame villainy in settings unspoiled by civilization.

new heights of popularity and excellence during the early nineteenth century), the middle and lower classes virtually took over the theatre.

Plays in the Theatre (1750–1850)

Revivals of Shakespeare were a mainstay of the Romantic theatre, which produced them in new theatrical settings designed to illustrate the locales mentioned in the dramatic texts and to stress the plays' exotic qualities. Some Neoclassical works remained in the repertory, but mostly new plays written to flout Neoclassical conventions prevailed.

Serious Drama

During the Romantic period, a recognizable cleavage appeared between those serious plays deemed critically important and those considered merely popular. Among the critically important works can be found plays ranging from domestic tragedies to philosophical inquiries. Among the serious plays for the popular theatre, only melodramas mattered.

DRAMES. The earliest of the plays deemed critically important were sentimental plays that dealt with the everyday problems of the middle class. In France, Denis Diderot proposed recognition of a new kind of play, which he termed the *drame* (a serious play treating domestic matters), and he provided a model for it in his play *The*

FIGURE 14-3. **Shakespeare Revived.** Renewed interest in Shakespeare led to revivals offered in proscenium theatres with illusionistic settings. Shown here, *As You Like It* at Drury Lane, London. *(Courtesy of the Department of Rare Books and Special Collections of the University of Rochester Libraries.)*

Illegitimate Son (1757). In Germany, Gotthold Ephraim Lessing translated Diderot's works and added his own pleas for domestic dramas, providing Germany's first successful one when he wrote *Miss Sara Sampson* (1755). In England, after an early surge of interest in George Lillo's *The London Merchant* (1731), only sporadic and largely unsuccessful plays of the sort appeared. Although some serious domestic plays (*drames*) continued well into the nineteenth century, their place was largely taken over by the ubiquitous melodrama, whose appeal continued to spread, engulfing most other forms of serious drama by the middle of the nineteenth century.

PHILOSOPHIC DRAMAS. Germany produced major philosophical dramas. Following the publication of Lessing's *Nathan the Wise* (1779) and a surge of dramatic experiments under a group of writers called the *Storm and Stress* (fl. 1770–1790), two authors emerged as significant: Johann Wolfgang von Goethe (1749–1832) and Friedrich Schiller (1759–1805).

Goethe. Goethe had early embraced many doctrines of the Storm and Stress movement and, under their influence, had written *Goetz von Berlichingen* (1773), a piece that required over six hours to perform and more than fifty separate scenes to contain its sprawling action. Later, Goethe sought to perfect an alternate style of production that would capture the patterns undergirding everyday life. His final work, *Faust*, in two parts (1808 and 1831), told the story of the human search for truth and fulfillment and came to epitomize for many the Romantic dilemma. Never intended for the stage, the work is an episodic presentation of a philosophical point of view and an acknowledged literary (as distinct from theatrical) masterpiece.

Schiller. Schiller, like Goethe, began as a Storm and Stress writer but later joined Goethe in seeking a new style of production that would create a distance between the spectators and the stage and thereby present them with a glimpse of the ideal world. Of Schiller's many works, the best known now are *The Robbers* (1782), whose immediate success created a vogue for other "Robin Hood" plays, and *William Tell* (1804), a celebration of individual worth and democratic government.

ROMANTIC TRAGEDIES. Less philosophical but considerably more stageworthy were French Romantic plays like *Hernani* by Victor Hugo (1802–1885). Its first production in 1830 caused a riot in the theatre. At issue was the question of whether to permit certain attitudes and practices of the Romantic authors (long accepted and popular in the commercial theatres of the boulevards) to invade and presumably sully the theatrical life of the Comédie Française. *Hernani* was written in elevated and poetic language; it portrayed rulers and nobles involved in the affairs of state and was cast in a traditional five-act form. But the play incorporated some features of Romanticism to which traditionalists objected. Common people were shown in conflict with a ruler, scenes of violence and death were portrayed on the stage, and moments of humor were tucked into an otherwise turgid story. The battle of *Hernani*, fought both in the pit of the Comédie Française and the literary circles of Paris, was resolved in favor of the Romantics, and so 1830 is the date now given for the acceptance of Romanticism into the mainstream of France's theatrical life (several years after it had been accepted in England, Germany, and America). The failure of another Romantic play by Victor Hugo in 1843 marked the end of self-conscious French Romanticism, making it one of the shortest dramatic movements in history.

CLOSET DRAMAS. Perhaps because the English found in Shakespeare the traits they most prized, English Romantics produced no new serious dramas of consequence. Although English Romantic poets and novelists (Coleridge, Wordsworth, Keats, Shelley, Byron, and Scott) all wrote plays, most were closet dramas (some intentionally, others by default), and none contributed significantly to the English or American theatre.

Melodrama

The most popular form of drama during the Romantic age was *melodrama*. Although not new (such plays have probably existed in all ages), melodrama attained new stature and significance in the theatre of the late eighteenth century and the nineteenth century.

Melodrama means literally "music drama," a name derived from the extensive use of music within the plays. Much like popular television and movies of today, nineteenth-century melodramas used *emotional music* to provide the proper mood and background for the action and to underscore moments of suspense and surprise. Music was also often used to identify characters for the audience. Such music, called *signature music,* was played when a character was about to enter or leave or to perform some astounding feat.

Melodrama presented a highly simplified moral universe in which good and evil were clearly defined and obviously embodied in easily recognizable stock characters. A physically attractive hero and heroine (often in love) possessed a kindness and virtue that were as unmistakable as they were unblemished. These characters, along with their friends and servants, represented the forces of good. Propelling the action

FIGURE 14-4. **Shakespeare Revived.** Interest in Shakespeare sometimes joined with the Romantics' exaltation of the unspoiled to offer children playing major Shakespearean roles. Here, Master Burke (acting since age five) as Hamlet.

of the play was a villain, whose physical appearance as well as behavior captured the essential attributes of evil. The remaining characters were most often friends or sidekicks of the three defining characters and almost always included at least one comic (relief) character. The villain initiated the action of the melodrama by posing a threat to the hero or the heroine; he or she escaped, and the villain posed another threat; he or she again escaped; and so on. The episodic play thus progressed by a series of threats and escapes, each reversal becoming more extreme than the last, until the final incident, when the hero or heroine might move from almost certain death to a happy marriage in a matter of minutes.

Many melodramas depended heavily on special effects—fires, explosions, drownings, earthquakes—both as threats to the sympathetic characters during the action of the play and as a means of obtaining the downfall of the villain in the final scenes. As well, many melodramas developed around the use of various animals: most common were *equestrian dramas* (horses) and *canine melodramas* (dogs). The interest of the Romantic writers in sea stories gave rise to *nautical melodramas.*

Between 1750 and 1850, two writers of melodramas were especially important: Kotzebue and Pixérécourt.

KOTZEBUE. The German playwright August Friedrich von Kotzebue (1761–1819) wrote over two hundred plays, many translated into English and French and performed throughout the world. Kotzebue was particularly successful with his *domestic melodramas,* which featured errant but repentant wives and upright but forgiving husbands. His plays titillated audiences without offending them and introduced potentially

FIGURE 14-5. **Domestic Melodrama.** The mainstay of the Romantic theatre was melodrama, both domestic and spectacular. Shown here, a scene of domestic melodrama, where poor women in the home defend against a villainous intruder.

controversial views without seeming to attack the audience's standards of propriety. Most of all, Kotzebue took the lives of common people and gave them dignity by treating them seriously. From about 1780 until his death, Kotzebue was acknowledged as the most popular playwright in the world.

PIXÉRÉCOURT. René Charles Guilbert de Pixérécourt (1773–1844) was the French author of more than one hundred plays. He set a fashion for canine melodramas and disaster melodramas, which might require a flood to sweep through the stage, uprooting a tree and bearing the heroine away on a board, or might use a volcanic eruption to foil the villain. Because the physical requirements were often so demanding, Pixérécourt insisted on directing his own plays in order to ensure their success. Pixérécourt, therefore, figured prominently in the history of French directors as well as of French playwrights.

Although some critics have scoffed at melodrama, its popularity and persistence argue that attention should be paid to it. In the nineteenth century, it was revered by many, and unquestionably it attracted to the theatre a mass audience new to the art of the stage. This audience of middle- and lower-class patrons cheered and laughed and wept openly and enthusiastically at the exploits of the heroes and heroines, and

FIGURE 14-6. **Spectacular Melodrama.** Stage machinery such as this giant see-saw made possible the spectacular effects of very popular nautical melodramas.

their support made theatre the major form of entertainment for over one hundred years.

Comedy

During the Romantic period, at least three different types of comedies competed for public favor: sentimental comedy, "laughing" comedy, and the "well-made play."

SENTIMENTAL COMEDY. Probably closest in tone to the early romantic ideas of innate human goodness were the *sentimental comedies,* those written to appeal to the audience's sense of virtue rather than to its sense of humor. Although most contained some laughable situations and an occasionally funny character, the plays' primary appeal depended on their depiction of the successful struggles of virtuous characters whose laudable goals ensured their ultimate success.

Like melodrama, sentimental comedy has been scorned and largely ignored in modern times. But in its own day, its popularity and importance were unquestionable. Leading writers of sentimental comedy were the Frenchman Diderot (1713–1784) and the German Lessing (1729–1781). Sentimental comedies' popularity eroded after about 1800 as that of melodrama increased.

LAUGHING COMEDY. Some argued strongly for abandoning sentimental comedy and returning to "laughing" comedy. Three authors in particular were associated with its increasing reputation: Beaumarchais (Pierre Augustin Caron, 1732–1799); Oliver Goldsmith (c. 1730–1774); and Richard Brinsley Sheridan (1751–1816). Beaumarchais's reputation rests now principally on *The Barber of Seville* (1775) and *The Marriage of Figaro* (1783), both laughing comedies that develop by means of intrigue while poking fun at aspects of French society. Goldsmith's most popular comedy, *She Stoops to Conquer* (1773), depicts the laughable consequences of mistaken identity and benign trickery that temporarily keep two pairs of young lovers separated. Its popularity continues even today, and the play remains in the active repertory of many English and American companies. Sheridan's *The Rivals* (1775) and *The School for Scandal* (1777) were especially prized for their witty dialogue and colorful portraits of engaging characters. It is a testament to the strength of the doctrine of sentimentalism that both of Sheridan's plays use its techniques even while objecting to its principles. Laughing comedy's importance was eclipsed after 1830 by the growing popularity of the "well-made play."

THE WELL-MADE PLAY. The most popular comic writer of the hundred years between 1750 and 1850 was undoubtedly Eugène Scribe (1791–1861), a Frenchman who wrote more than three hundred plays for the Parisian theatres. Their translation into German and English and their frequent production in those countries and in America throughout the nineteenth century caused French comedy to set the standard for the world by mid-century.

Scribe's techniques (like careful preparation and meticulous networks of relationships) were designed to give the appearance of an action tightly unified by cause and effect when, in fact, the plays were built around multiple lines of action that unfolded by chance and coincidence. The phrase *well-made play* was used first as a compliment to describe the particular kind of play that Scribe perfected, but because later scholars deplored the superficiality of his works, the term became one of derision during the twentieth century. Scribe and the well-made play exerted considerable influence on later writers, both among commercial authors (most importantly Victorien Sardou, 1831–1908) and among the later realists like Alexandre Dumas *fils* (1824–1895) and Henrik Ibsen (1825–1906). The well-made plays of Scribe and others dominated the stages of western Europe and America during the nineteenth century and, with melodrama, were probably the mainstay of that threatre.

Popular Entertainments

Other kinds of entertainments also continued to be popular. Specialty acts featured jugglers, singers, tumblers, magicians, and others. Pantomimes increased in length as their popularity grew until they provided a whole evening's fare. Short musical revues or brief topical skits using music and verse (*vaudevilles*) appealed to the

FIGURE 14-7. **Popular Entertainments.** Theatre offered variety entertainments as well as plays during the Romantic period. Here, a trapeze act in a proscenium theatre, complete with illusionistic scenery, footlights, stage boxes, and a live orchestra.

politically minded. Comic operas, whose sentimental stories were set to original music, provided entertainment for those who liked music but found opera perplexing or dull. Parodies, burlesques, circus entertainments, and water shows appealed to popular audiences.

Practices of the Theatres (1750–1850)

The major trends in the theatre between 1750 and 1850 were the following:

1. The middle and lower classes came into the theatres in increasing numbers.

2. The number and the seating capacity of theatres increased.

3. The size and complexity of stages and support areas increased (although the size of the forestage decreased).

4. The number, accuracy, and consistency of visual details (scenery, properties, and costumes) increased, as emphasis shifted from the aural to the visual aspects of production.

FIGURE 14-8. Theatre Buildings. The Park Theatre (New York) and The Haymarket Theatre (London) early in the nineteenth century. Both show proscenia, with doors opening on large aprons (forestages).

Theatre Size

Because theatre was the form of entertainment preferred by vast numbers of people and because Romantic plays stressed spectacle, new theatres built and those remodeled between 1750 and 1850 featured ever-larger auditoriums and ever-more-sophisticated stages and support areas. For example, London's Covent Garden Theatre seated fewer than 1500 people in the 1730s but could accommodate 3000 by 1793. The Drury

Lane Theatre seated only 650 in 1700 but had a capacity of 3600 during the early years of the nineteenth century. In America, the original Chestnut Street Theatre of Philadelphia (opened in 1794) was built to house 1200 but was soon enlarged to accommodate more than 2000. In France, all the major theatres were enlarged and modernized between 1750 and 1800, with particular attention given to improving sight lines, increasing seating capacity, and creating greater potential for staging spectacles. Between 1775 and 1800, more than thirty permanent theatres were built in Germany, most of which incorporated elaborate machinery to permit rapid and simultaneous changes of setting; by 1850, the number had grown to sixty-five.

Audience Arrangement

The standard configuration for the audience area was box, pit, and gallery, with boxes originally the most prized and expensive seats. As *seeing* the spectacular effects gradually became more important than *hearing* the vocal displays of the actors, the advantage shifted to the pit (later called the *orchestra*), and so box seats gave way to orchestra seats as the most favored and expensive in the theatre. The cheapest seats were always those of the upper balconies (in large theatres, there might be as many as five levels). Called the *gods,* the audience in the upper galleries were primarily working-class people who were noted for their bad manners at theatrical performances.

Scenery

About 1760, spectators were no longer permitted to sit on the stages in England and France, for onstage spectators clearly destroyed the illusion of reality and took up spaces now needed for scenery and acting areas. By the 1770s, with the spectators gone from the stage, designers were free to create a complete stage picture. Phillippe Jacques de Loutherbourg (1740–1812), England's leading designer, began to reproduce familiar English locations on the stage and thus created a vogue for "local color" settings. In France, the scenery at the boulevard theatres depicted examples of French local color as well as "authentic" reproductions of places in the Orient, the Americas, Russia, and so on.

Scenery consisted of a combination of wings, drops (large pieces of fabric suspended from above the stage and extending to the floor), borders, and ground rows (cut-away flats adapted to stand free on the stage floor), the overall arrangement being called *wing-and-drop scenery.* All scenic pieces were carefully painted to achieve the illusion of reality, and some were cut away (in the shape of leaves at their edges, for example) or layered (in gauzes or other fabrics) to enhance the illusion still more. Because many plays of the Romantic period were set out of doors, the borders often consisted of a combination of sky, clouds, and leaves, while the flats and drops were forests, trees, grasses, rocks, and similar natural scenes. For plays set in medieval castles, tombs, or dungeons, all flats, drops, and borders might be painted to resemble large stones.

Whenever required by the play's action, three-dimensional details were included; for example, a bridge would be built if characters had to walk on it. But most of the scenery was two-dimensional, with all the details painted on it.

FIGURE 14-9. Scenery. The Philadelphia playhouse shows wings set in front of a back drop, all rendered in single-point perspective. The theatre's architecture shares many features with that of the Park and the Haymarket shown in Figure 14-8. *(Used with permission of The Library Company of Philadelphia.)*

The use of scenery and special effects appeared to be governed by three overriding and interrelated assumptions:

1. The stage picture should present the illusion of reality (thus the name *pictorial illusionism* was used to describe the scenery during the period).

2. Many details should be included in order to particularize the settings.

3. Because time and place were important, historical and geographical accuracy of detail should be sought. Celebration of the remote and great attention to accurate details increasingly won public acclaim and so became increasingly practiced by theatrical managers during the nineteenth century. By 1850, even in America, whose theatre was late in getting under way, *antiquarianism* had made its mark, and historical accuracy in theatrical settings and costumes was, if not achieved, at least approached.

Although there was a considerable gap between these goals and their realization, designers moved steadily in the direction of their ideals from about 1750 to 1850.

Lighting
The scene was lit by candles or oil lamps (or, after 1830, in some theatres, by gas) placed at the front of the stage as *footlights* and behind the several sets of wings. In no case was the illumination very high, and so both scenery and actors were only dimly visible.

FIGURE 14-10. **Special Effects.** Spectacular effects were an important part of the excitement of the Romantic theatre. Here, a way of having an onstage horse race by using a treadmill, fans, and moving diorama.

Special Effects

The basic settings were enlivened by an enormous variety of special equipment and effects. Characters and objects flew about by means of elaborate systems of ropes and pulleys; they disappeared and appeared magically through various traps in the floor and, less often, through rotating wall panels. Fountains and waterfalls gushed and flowed by means of specially installed water systems. Moving panoramas and dioramas permitted designers to achieve the illusion of travel onstage. By unwinding a large painted cloth from one giant spool onto another, the landscape behind an onstage boat or carriage could be made to unroll and the vehicle would seem to move. When, late in the nineteenth century, such panoramas were combined with treadmills, even horse races and chariot races could be staged. Volcanic eruptions, fires, thunder, lightning, rainstorms, explosions—all were a part of the theatre's spectacle, and all were popular with mass audiences.

Theatre Companies

Some troupes, like the Comédie Française, continued to operate as sharing companies, but most performers now worked for a fixed salary that was supplemented by the gate receipts of one or more "benefit" performances.

For a time, the *stock company* dominated, that is, a group of actors who stayed together over a period of years, performing appropriate roles in a variety of plays and each contributing to the reputation of the company as a whole. After about 1830, however, perhaps as a consequence of the Romantics' growing attachment to the idea of "individual genius," and most certainly because of improved transportation networks (particularly the expanding system of railroads), the company system gradually declined. In its place came the "starring system," which meant that leading performers moved from stock company to stock company, where they played the plum parts, supported by resident players. The starring system, although exceedingly popular with audiences, caused numerous problems for the acting profession. One French actress, for example, demanded and received a salary equal to that of her country's prime minister, leaving little for her fellow artists.

For a time, there was a rage for child stars, who played not only Shakespearean roles like King Lear and Hamlet but also the heroes in various melodramas of the day, where they single-handedly foiled the villains. The public also relished "breeches roles," that is, women playing men's roles in men's clothing; perhaps the attraction was that the breeches revealed the actress's body far more than current fashion permitted and therefore provided a bit of titillation quite separate from the play's dramatic offerings.

Acting Style

Acting style changed between 1750 and 1850. At one extreme was the formal (or "classical") and at the other pole the emotional (or "romantic").

FORMAL ACTING. Formal acting predominated from the beginning of the period until about 1815, although its various expressions were quite diverse. The emphasis seemed to be on vocal power and on dignified, restrained interpretations of character. Such performers typically excelled in tragic roles, where poetic diction encouraged a declamatory or oratorical delivery. Perhaps the most extreme example of an accepted actor performing in this tradition was the English James Quin (1693–1766).

David Garrick (1717–1779), on the other hand, was admired for his "easy and familiar, yet forcible style of speaking and acting." Acknowledged as the greatest English actor of the last half of the eighteenth century, Garrick was, however, far from our conception of natural; for example, he persisted in playing Shakespeare's Macbeth in the dress of a military officer of the eighteenth century, complete with a tail wig, and in drawing attention to himself (to the detriment of the acting company) by "the restless abundance of his action and his gestures."

By the 1790s, the leading formal actors in England were a brother and sister, John Philip Kemble (1757–1823) and Sarah Kemble Siddons (1755–1831), who were applauded for the stateliness, grandeur, and dignity of their performances. Every country had its classical actors: in America, Thomas A. Cooper (1776–1849); in France, Talma (1763–1826); in Germany, Emil Devrient (1803–1872). And in every country, the same general patterns of changing taste were observable.

ROMANTIC ACTING. A revolution in English acting appears to have occurred when Edmund Kean (1787–1833) made his London debut in 1814. Kean abandoned dignity and intellect in favor of flamboyance and passion. To see Kean act "was to read

FIGURE 14-11. **Acting: Formal Style.** Mrs. Siddons was a major practitioner of a formal (also called Classical) style of acting in England, as was Talma in France.

Shakespeare by flashes of lightning." Apparently, passionate outbursts and novel interpretations marked the actors labeled "natural" or "romantic" during the period. Other important performers in this tradition were the English/American, Junius Brutus Booth (1796–1852) and the French Frédérick Lemaître (1800–1876).

Scarcely had Romantic acting seized the imagination of the public, however, when it, too, began to appear artificial. It was gradually replaced by yet another "natural" style after 1850, a style that came to be called *realistic* acting.

Summary

The profound changes that can be seen between 1750 and 1850 were the result of changes in what audiences would accept as "real" or "true."

In 1750, generalized scenery and costumes formed a sparse background for the actors. Audiences, still largely upper class, were unperturbed by lack of detail or by its inaccuracy, for they thrilled to the verbal displays of excellently trained and elegantly attired actors. They sought and found their artistic truth in the formal, generalized portraits of an upper- or middle-class hero that formed the basis of most of the new plays.

In 1850, carefully painted settings and historically accurate costumes provided a

FIGURE 14-12. **Acting: Emotional Style.** Edmund Kean revolutioned English acting with his highly emotional (also called Romantic) style of acting. Here, as Macbeth.

richly detailed background. The audiences, now mostly middle and lower class, sought lavish spectacle, complete with elaborate special effects. They expected reasonably authentic sets and costumes and appreciated actors who could grip the emotions. Such audiences sought and found artistic truth in the detailed representations of individual people and places.

POST-ROMANTICISM: RICHARD WAGNER AND THE BAYREUTH THEATRE

Although Richard Wagner (1813–1883) is most often associated with the fields of music and opera, he was an important theorist and practitioner of the theatre as well. Two contributions in particular assured Wagner his place in the history of theatre: (1) his call for a unified work of art and (2) his development of a classless theatre.

Wagner argued that the artist should be a mythmaker who presents an ideal world to the spectators, providing them with a communal experience that highlights for them their shared culture. The best drama, according to Wagner, was one that combined music and poetry to achieve a total art, one that fused the emotional with the intellectual.

For Wagner, the experience of the audience was the critical factor in planning and shaping a work of art. He sought a stage production so compelling that spectators would be drawn in and would believe in and empathize with the world behind the proscenium arch. Indeed, for Wagner, the success of a production was measured primarily by its ability to capture the emotions of the audience and to transport them to a new sense of shared purpose.

Master Artwork

To achieve the ideal production, one capable of entrancing an audience, Wagner proclaimed the need for a "master artwork," or "united artwork," by which he meant a work in which all elements of the drama and of theatrical production were carefully synthesized into a unified whole. Such unity could be achieved only, according to Wagner, when a single person, a supreme artist, controlled every aspect of the production. Indeed, it was Wagner's concept of the master artist, the single controlling force behind a work of art, that did much to establish the role of the director as the central artist in the theatre, a view dominating many practices of the modern theatre.

Classless Theatre

Wagner was able to build a theatre that would allow him to put some of his theories into practice. Opened in 1876, the Bayreuth Festspielhaus included features that helped Wagner establish his ideal world of the stage. Rather than one proscenium arch, the theatre at Bayreuth had several; the orchestra pit, customarily in full view of the audience, at Bayreuth extended partway under the stage and was entirely hidden from the sight of the audience. Steam jets installed at the front of the stage permitted special effects like fog and mist to help establish the mood of the production and to mask the changes in scenery. Such unusual architectural features were joined by certain new practices—like darkening the auditorium during the drama and forbidding the musicians to tune their instruments in the pit—to separate the real world of the audience (in the auditorium) from the ideal world of the drama (on the stage). This separation of the two worlds Wagner referred to as the "mystic chasm."

Unusual as some of these features were, they were less innovative and influential than changes that Wagner introduced into the auditorium at Bayreuth. Whether because of a desire to democratize the theatre or because of the increasing importance of seeing (rather than hearing) a play, Wagner eliminated the box, pit, and gallery in favor of a new "classless" theatre in which every seat had an equally good view of the stage and each ticket cost the same amount of money. The seats at Bayreuth were arranged in the shape of a fan, with the shorter rows closer to the stage and with entrances at the end of each row. This kind of arrangement came to be called *continental seating,* and some version of it was widely adopted as new theatres were constructed during the twentieth century.

Although, in fact, Wagner's productions seldom strayed far from the sort of

FIGURE 14-13. **Wagnerian Production.** Wagner relied heavily on staging techniques of the Romantic theatre to produce spectacular effects. Above, the effect seen by the audience; below, the techniques used backstage to achieve it.

FIGURE 14-14. **Wagner's Bayreuth Theatre.** A "classless theatre" achieved by abandoning box, pit, and gallery in favor of continental seating. Visible, too, are the multiple proscenium arches, but invisible is the orchestra pit, all efforts to attain a mystic chasm between stage and audience.

illusionism common during the last years of the nineteenth century, his theories and architectural innovations placed him outside the mainstream of his day and made him a precursor of later experimenters.

REALISM

After Romanticism, the split between drama considered worthy of serious attention and that considered merely entertaining persisted. From 1850 through the 1950s, the significant drama and staging were in a style called *realism*. The commercial theatre and drama, a conservative force, lagged decades behind but finally embraced a diluted and trivialized realism by the end of World War I.

Background

By the 1850s, certain problems that had grown out of society's shifting bases of wealth and its developing industrialization were becoming clear. The products of industry were being distributed unevenly, and the gap between those who did the work and those who reaped the profits was widening, a development that led Karl Marx (1818–1883) to propose an alternative method of social and economic organization for society. Urban poverty was on the rise and, with it, urban crime. Political instability gave way to political repression, which, in turn, fanned latent dissatisfactions that demanded immediate correction.

At roughly this same time, science offered new theories that threatened to undermine previously accepted views of humanness. Charles Darwin (1809–1882) proposed that human beings had evolved from simpler forms of life and that they were not a separate, special act of creation. He therefore seemed to suggest that people were more like animals than like angels and that their capacity was limited by environmental forces. Gregor Mendel (1822–1884), through his work with corn, showed that certain traits were passed from generation to generation in statistically predictable ways. From there, it was only a short step to the conclusion that people, like plants and other animals, were defined by their genes and that they were neither free agents nor special creatures. Sigmund Freud (1856–1939) proposed that people's behavior was not at base rational and so their motives were not understandable, even to themselves. His emphasis on subconscious desires and repressed responses hinted that people were trapped into patterns of behavior by forces (often sexual and aggressive) that they neither controlled nor understood. One result of such developments in science was to dislodge humankind from the philosophic pedestal on which it had rested since the Middle Ages.

Finally, revolutionary technological advances had the effects of changing both the way people lived and the way they saw the world. Impressive changes in transportation (steamboats, railroads, automobiles, and airplanes) and communication (telegraph, telephone, radio, and television) speeded up the flow of information, goods, and people. Improved vaccines, antibiotics, and surgical techniques slowed down death rates. Science and technology seemed to ensure eventual answers even to complex

FIGURE 14-15. Technological Advances. The scene from a Chicago railway station late in the nineteenth century suggests well the collision of cultures occasioned by improvements in transportation and communication.

questions. History, therefore, seemed to be progressing inexorably toward a better world.

Realism—and its more extreme relative, *naturalism*—arose in part as responses to these new social and philosophical conditions. Realists and naturalists were *materialists:* they believed that truth resided in the material objects observable in the physical, external world. They were also *objectivists:* they believed that truth could be discovered through the application of scientific observation and could be replicated by a series of objective observers.

According to the realists and the naturalists, the function of art, like that of science, was the betterment of humankind, and so the method of the artist should be that of the scientist. Because truth resided in material objects, art, to be true, had to depict the material, tangible world. Because problems could be solved only through application of the scientific method, dramatists should emulate scientists and strive to become objective observers of the social milieu. Plays should be set in contemporary times and places, for only they could be observed firsthand by the playwright. As the highest purpose of art was the betterment of humanity, the subject of plays should be contemporary life and its problems.

While sharing with realists a belief in the efficacy of science as a solver of problems and in the role of drama in the improvement of society, the naturalists differed in their definition of what problems most needed attention and their hope for the future.

FIGURE 14-16. **Materialism and Objectivism.** If truth resides in objects, then artists wishing to show the truth will include many objects in their settings. *The Grip of Iron* (1893) exemplifies just such a setting.

The naturalists stressed the problems of the poor and tended to be pessimistic about the possible solution of these problems. According to the naturalists, people were victims, not actors in life. Their destiny was *controlled* by factors like heredity and environment, factors over which they had little, if any, influence. Because the naturalists attempted to give the impression that their plays were an actual record of life, the dramas often appeared formless and unstructured, traits that gave rise to the phrase "a slice of life" to describe some naturalists' plays.

Leading Figures in Realism and Naturalism

Georg II, Duke of Saxe-Meiningen

One of the first important contributors to the *realistic staging of prerealistic drama* was Georg II, Duke of Saxe-Meiningen (fl. 1870s–1880s). In some ways, the duke was merely perfecting and popularizing ideals of staging promulgated much earlier; nonetheless, it was he who influenced the later, important realists.

Saxe-Meiningen objected to many practices of the theatrical mainstream because they resulted in productions that lacked unity (internal consistency) and that seemed artificial and unreal. For the duke, the art of the theatre was the art of providing the *illusion of reality;* he therefore sought methods of production that would lead to "an intensified reality and [would] give remote events . . . the quality of actuality, of being lived for the first time." To this end, the duke stressed lifelike acting; accurate scenery, costumes, and properties; and unity.

ACTING. In Saxe-Meiningen's group, there were no stars. Each member of the company was eligible to play any role; and each member, if not cast as a major character, was required to play in crowd scenes, something a star of the old sort

FIGURE 14-17. **The Duke of Saxe-Meiningen Directs Shakespeare.** An early realistic director of mostly prerealistic drama, the duke took great care with his crowd scenes and with the
historical accuracy of his scenery and costumes. Here, his production of Shakespeare's *Julius
Caesar.*

would never have done. Moreover, each actor in a crowd scene was given lines and
actions that were carefully rehearsed. To make the crowds seem real, the duke divided
his actors into several groups, each led by an experienced actor. To increase a sense
of realism in crowd scenes, the actors were to avoid parallel lines on stage, to make
crosses on the stage diagonally rather than parallel with the curtain line, to keep one
foot off the ground whenever possible (by placing it on a step or by kneeling on one
knee), and to be aware of each neighbor's stance so that it would not be repeated.
Variety within a crowd led to its seeming reality. All actors were told to look at one
another rather than at the audience, to react to what was said and done onstage,
and to behave naturally (even if it meant delivering a line while not facing the
audience).

STAGING. The Duke believed that all elements of a production required coordination. The setting must be an integral part of the play, and so he encouraged his
actors to move *within* the setting rather than merely playing in front of it (as was
currently fashionable). If actors were to move within an environment, the scenic
details had to be three-dimensional rather than painted, and so actual objects were
used in the settings. Simultaneously, the duke strove to provide several levels (e.g.,
rocks, steps, and platforms), so that the scenic design would not stop abruptly at the

stage floor. In these ways, he did much to popularize the use of real, three-dimensional details.

Historical accuracy in both scenery and costumes was important. Georg II designed and supervised every aspect of the physical production. To increase accuracy in the selection of details, he divided each century into thirds and even differentiated among various national groups within each period. To increase accuracy of construction, he used authentic fabrics instead of the cheaper substitutes often resorted to in the commercial houses of the day; many items were made in his own shops. Moreover, he required all actors, from the most to the least important, to wear the costumes that were designed for them, regardless of the current fashions, and to acquaint themselves with the postures and stances peculiar to the period. Even the makeup was designed according to existing portraits of the time.

Beginning in 1874 (eight years after the duke took over the theatre), the Meiningen plays began touring western Europe and Russia. From then until its last tour in 1890, the troupe gave more than 2800 performances in thirty-six cities. From these performances came the group's international reputation and its influence on people like André Antoine and Konstantin Stanislavski.

André Antoine and the Théâtre-Libre

André Antoine (1853–1943) abhorred the commercial theatres of Paris, disapproved of the way actors were trained at the Paris Conservatoire (France's leading school for actors), objected to the scenic practices of the major theatres, and decried the flimsiness of contemporary popular drama. What was needed, Antoine concluded, was a theatre where new and controversial plays could gain carefully mounted and

FIGURE 14-18. **Antoine and Naturalism.** Antoine popularized a kind of staging called *naturalism,* which stressed the problems of the underclass dislayed in settings filled with three-dimensional (rather than painted) details.

realistically acted productions. Thus, when an amateur group to which he belonged balked at producing a daring new play, Antoine undertook the production himself and, spurred by early success, became the full-time director of his own new theatre in 1887. He named it the Théâtre-Libre (Free Theatre) and described it as nothing less than "a machine of war, poised for the conquest of Paris."

THE "FOURTH WALL." Antoine believed with the naturalists that environment determined, or at least heavily influenced, human behavior. Stage setting was therefore very important. For this reason, Antoine took great care to make his stage settings as believable and as much like real life as possible. He designed a room, placing the furniture and accessories in it, only then deciding which "wall" of the room was to be removed so that the audience could see in. Antoine depended heavily on actual, three-dimensional objects rather than their painted substitutes. For one play, he brought real sides of beef on his stage; for another, real trees and birds' nests; and for another, a real student's actual room furnishings. The attention that he paid to realistic detail and his reliance on actual objects led to his being called by many the father of naturalistic staging. Jean Julien, a contemporary of Antoine's, seemed to sum up the goal of Antoine: "The front of the stage must be a fourth wall, transparent for the public, opaque for the player."

ACTING. Antoine believed that actors should appear to be real people, not actors in a play. Unfortunately, actors trained at the Paris Conservatoire could not portray real life on stage because they had been trained to use their voices in special theatrical ways, to align their bodies in unlifelike poses, and to play to their audiences directly. Antoine wanted his actors to say their lines naturally, just as one might engage in a conservation with friends and, at the same time, to move about the furniture and accessories just as in real life. Sincerity and conviction were the qualities he sought, and so he advised his actors to ignore the audience and to speak to one another in conversational tones—in short, to try to *be,* rather than to *act,* the characters in the play. Perhaps for these reasons, Antoine often used amateur actors in his theatre, actors who had not received conventional training for the commercial theatre and who were therefore more receptive to the experimental, new style of naturalistic acting.

PLAYS. Although Antoine produced a wide range of plays while at the Théâtre-Libre, he seemed most comfortable with plays in the realistic and naturalistic styles. Although many such plays had been written before Antoine opened his theatre, few had escaped the censors. Because Antoine organized his theatre as a subscription house, he was able to bypass the threats of censorship. Consequently, he was able to introduce to Parisians a wide range of French and foreign authors whose works were considered too scandalous for production in the major theatres of the day. Plays by Émile Zola, Leo Tolstoy, August Strindberg, Henrik Ibsen, and Gerhart Hauptmann were produced by Antoine even while they were forbidden productions elsewhere.

   The major contributions of Antoine and the Théâtre-Libre (1887–1896) were (1) to popularize acting techniques leading toward naturalness on stage; (2) to gain

FIGURE 14-19. **Stanislavski and the Moscow Art Theatre.** In addition to revolutionizing the training of actors, Stanislavski introduced the plays of Chekhov, in which he often acted. Shown here, *Uncle Vanya*. (*From Oliver Sayler,* The Moscow Art Theatre Series of Russian Plays. *New York: Brentano, 1923.*)

acceptance for scenic practices now known as "fourth-wall realism," with all that implies about scenic detail and literal objects; (3) to introduce a new generation of playwrights (both French and foreign) to the theatregoing public of Paris; and (4) to establish a model for a censor-free theatre.

The most significant experimental theatre of its day, the Théâtre-Libre gave rise to a number of similar theatres throughout the world. Called the *independent theatre movement,* this blossoming of small, independent theatres in several countries almost simultaneously gave the impetus to an ultimate acceptance of realism as the mainstream of the commercial theatre, an acceptance completed by early in the twentieth century.

Konstantin Stanislavski and the Moscow Art Theatre

When the Meiningen company toured Russia in 1885 and again in 1890, its impact was strong indeed, for the German troupe was presenting a kind of ensemble acting and quality of visual detail not previously witnessed in Russia.

Two men, Konstantin Stanislavski (1863–1938) and Vladimir Nemirovich-Danchenko (1858–1943) saw the Meiningen company and were impressed. They decided to establish a new kind of theatre in Moscow, an experimental theatre whose goals were (1) to remain free of the demands of commercialism; (2) to avoid overemphasis on the scenic elements of production; and (3) to reflect the inner truth of the play.

For this theatre, Nemirovich-Danchenko was to select the plays and handle the administration, while Stanislavski was to serve as the production director.

From its opening in 1898, the Moscow Art Theatre was known for its careful realistic-naturalistic productions. During its early years, the greatest attention was given to the accuracy of historical detail in all areas of the physical production, but, within ten years, Stanislavski's interest moved from a largely external realism toward finding an inner truth for actors. External realism from this time on became, for Stanislavski, merely a key to opening the inner reality of the plays, and he strove to develop techniques that would help the actors achieve an inner truth.

By 1917, he had developed, from personal experience and observation of others, his major ideas for training actors, ideas that he codified in a series of books that have since been translated into more than twenty languages (the dates are for the American editions): *My Life in Art* (1924), *An Actor Prepares* (1936), *Building a Character* (1949), and *Creating a Role* (1961). Together, these books represent what has come to be called the Stanislavski "system" of actor training, although Stanislavski himself insisted neither that his was the only way to train actors nor that his methods should be studied and mastered by everyone.

Although today Stanislavski's reputation rests largely on his contributions to actors' training, he was in his own time considered an innovative director. During the early years of the Moscow Art Theatre, Stanislavski worked in a rather autocratic fashion, planning each detail of his actors' vocal inflections, gestures, movements, and so on. But as his interest in the problems of the actor grew, and as his actors became more skillful, he abandoned his dogmatic approach and became more of an interpreter and helpmate to the actors. His ideal became for the director and the actors to grow together in their understanding of the play; therefore, he no longer appeared at rehearsals with a detailed production book containing minute directions for the actors. Only after the group had grasped the psychology of the roles and the complex interrelationships (often a three-month process) did the actors begin to work on the stage. Beginning with very small units in the play and moving gradually to acts and finally to the whole play, the actors and the director built a performance, a process often requiring six months or longer.

It was probably this careful attention to psychological detail that permitted Stanislavski's company to succeed with the plays of Anton Chekhov where others before had failed. On the other hand, it should be clear that such rehearsal procedures are seldom possible in commercial ventures.

What began in 1898 as an experiment in external realism and was by 1906 an experiment in psychological realism had become an established tradition in Russia by the time of the Russian Revolution (1917). Because a number of Russians trained in "the system" left their country after the revolution, the teachings of Stanislavski came to the attention of the outside world. Mikhail Chekhov and Vera Kommissarzhevsky worked in Europe and the United States and brought their own versions of "the system" with them. Richard Boleslavsky and Maria Ouspenskaya came to the United States and led the American Laboratory Theatre, where they had as students Harold Clurman, Lee Strasberg, and Stella Adler, founders of the Group Theatre, America's major propagators of Stanislavski's system of actor training (although by their time somewhat altered and renamed the "Method").

FIGURE 14-20. **Realistic Theatre Buildings.** Theatres built for realistic plays tended to be smaller than theatres built for romantic plays; to have some version of continental seating rather than box, pit, and gallery; and to have little or no forestage. After the 1880s, many used electricity rather than gas, like this Munich Theatre.

Theatre Buildings

Theatres that were built for realistic plays or those remodeled to improve their spaces for realistic productions tended to be intimate proscenium houses without apron or proscenium doors. Because the scenic requirements were relatively simple, few provided elaborate machinery for shifting scenery. The prized seats were in the orchestra. The auditoriums often abandoned box, pit, and gallery arrangements in favor of some modification of Wagner's seating plan. The audiences consisted primarily of the middle classes, perhaps because it was most often their problems that were being addressed. The availability of electricity for theatrical lighting after the 1880s had two major results. It made the control and therefore the artistic manipulation of lighting possible, and it extended the life expectancy of theatre buildings by reducing the number of theatre fires, a plague of theatres during the first half of the century.

Staging

As staged, realistic and naturalistic plays shared many traits. Both set their plays in the contemporary world; both included numerous details; both relied on three-dimensional objects rather than their painted representations; and both adopted conventions of acting that focused the actors' attention onstage and discouraged them from moving in front of the arch or openly acknowledging the audience (which now sat in a darkened auditorium). Both abandoned wing-and-drop scenery in favor of a *box set,* a stage "room" built of flats but with one wall missing so that the audience could look through it.

Although agreeing on these basic conventions, the two styles often looked quite different onstage, mostly because their dramatic subjects and characters differed. The realists, who treated problems of the middle class, set their plays in well-appointed living rooms with standard furnishings (e.g., lamps, ashtrays, portraits) and costumed their characters as the prosperous people they were. The naturalists, dealing with the problems of the poor and downtrodden, set their plays in places like hovels, factories, and bars and costumed their characters in the rags of poverty.

Realistic Drama

Realism in the drama began tentatively and cautiously. Although French writers like Alexandre Dumas *fils* and Eugène Scribe presaged realism, it was the Norwegian Henrik Ibsen (1828–1906) who brought the several philosophical and artistic strands into successful dramatic shape and launched realism as the major artistic movement.

Ibsen

With plays like *A Doll's House* (1879), *Ghosts* (1881), and *Hedda Gabler* (1890), Ibsen broke with the sentimentalized problem plays of earlier days and assumed his controversial role as the attacker of society's values. Structurally, his plays were fairly

FIGURE 14-21. Ibsen. The great Italian star Duse appears here in Ibsen's *Rosmersholm*. The box setting is rather typical for the time.

traditional: they told a story and moved logically from event to event just as well-made plays had done for years. But their content was shocking: when individuals came into conflict with society, they were no longer assumed to be guilty and society blameless. Indeed, social customs and traditional morality were exposed by Ibsen as a tangle of inconsistencies and irrelevancies. The problems addressed were customarily those of the middle and managerial classes. Questions like the proper role of women, the ethics of euthanasia, the morality of business and war, and the economics of religion formed the basis of serious probings into social behavior. Theatrical producers throughout the world who believed that drama should be involved in the social issues of the day applauded the Norwegian dramatist, and soon other artists began to translate, produce, and, later, emulate his plays.

Shaw

In England, George Bernard Shaw (1856–1950) became one of Ibsen's most vocal and influential supporters. A prolific writer and a (Fabian) socialist, Shaw delighted in puncturing time-honored assumptions about human behavior and exposing various forms of social posturing. In an early play, *Arms and the Man* (1894), he spoofed romantic notions of love and war and satirized the then-popular comic form, the well-made play. Later, he turned to consider contemporary social situations in plays like *Major Barbara* (1905), *The Doctor's Dilemma* (1906), *Getting Married* (1908), and *Heartbreak House* (1914–1919). Unlike many realists, Shaw always retained his sense of humor; he almost always wrote comedies, and their popularity did much to ensure the final acceptance of realistic drama in England before the close of World War I.

Chekhov

In Russia, realism took a still different turn. Anton Chekhov (1860–1904) scored his first success in 1898 when *The Seagull* was produced at the Moscow Art Theatre. Within seven years, he had contributed *The Three Sisters* (1900), *Uncle Vanya* (1889),

FIGURE 14-22. Chekhov. This production of Chekhov's *Three Sisters* at the Moscow Art Theatre shows discrete acting areas and levels incorporated into a box setting. (*From Sayler, Series.*)

and *The Cherry Orchard* (1902) to the growing literature of the realistic style. Chekhov's plays differed from those of Ibsen and Shaw in their tendency toward poetic expression and symbolic meanings. Chekhov's manipulation of language, with careful rhythms, measured pauses, deliberate banalities, and artful repetitions, produced a sense of reality based on compelling psychological truths as well as a degree of music and allusion uncommon in prose dramas. His incorporation of symbols into the texts (often the plays' titles bear clues) served to extend the plays' significance beyond the drab daily lives of the central characters. Chekhov took for his study the daily lives of people trapped in social situations. In some ways, he foretold the Russian Revolution by depicting the isolation of the aristocracy and its inevitable extinction. In another sense, he portrayed the loneliness and the comic desperation of all people who continue to hope while living in a hopeless situation, who persist in believing that help will come when none, in fact, is to be had.

Naturalistic Drama

Émile Zola (1849–1912), although a playwright, is better known today for his novels and his essays promoting naturalism. He called for "living characters taken from real life," who spoke everyday language and offered "a material reproduction of life;" he called for playwrights who scientifically analyzed and faithfully reported the social problems of the world with a view to their correction. Among the most successful playwrights in the naturalistic style were August Strindberg (1849–1912), Gerhart Hauptmann (1862–1946), and Maxim Gorky (1868–1936). Strindberg's *Miss Julie* (1888) shows two complex characters, an aristocratic woman and her male servant, who are locked in a battle of wills and whose actions derive from their heredity, their environment, and their class-conscious society. Hauptmann's *The Weavers* (1892) uses a group protagonist to show the devastation that comes to already impoverished weavers when industrialization threatens their way of life. Gorky's *The*

FIGURE 14-23. **Naturalism.** Maxim Gorky's *The Lower Depths* at the Moscow Art Theatre included Stanislavski among the actors (sprawled on the table). The style naturalism depicted a more sordid reality than did the style realism.

Lower Depths (1902), by depicting the seemingly hopeless lives of people living in a flophouse, explores whether religion or political reform offers the best chance for change.

THE COMMERCIAL MAINSTREAM
1850–1900

Commercial houses in France, England, and America during the last half of the nineteenth century continued to feature plays of the sort popularized by the Romantic theatre. The most popular of them ran for dozens, even hundreds, of nights and played to audiences of all social classes and artistic tastes.

The Repertory

REVIVALS. Shakespeare's plays were produced often and were given elaborate settings designed to reproduce faithfully the illusion of specific locales mentioned in the text. "Illustrating" Shakespeare became popular, and so *The Merchant of Venice* used real water for onstage canals, and *Romeo and Juliet* reproduced in detail the historical Juliet's tomb. Countless plays from the first half of the nineteenth century and a few from the eighteenth century were also revived. Most popular, of course, were the spectacular melodramas, which thrilled audiences by their elaborate special effects and exotic costumes.

FIGURE **14-24. Shakespearean Revivals.** Antoine applied many of his staging principles to his revivals of dramatic masterpieces of the past. Here, in Shakespeare's *Romeo and Juliet,* can be seen three-dimensional scenic pieces and historically derived motifs.

COMEDIES. The most popular playwright of the period was probably the Frenchman Victorien Sardou (1831–1908), who is best remembered for well-made plays like *A Scrap of Paper* (1860). Although less well known today, Sardou's historical spectacles set in exotic locales were applauded by contemporaries for the lavishness of their costumes and scenery and the correctness of their many details. For the famous actress Sarah Bernhardt (1844–1923), virtually a cult figure of the age, Sardou wrote plays like *La Tosca* (1887), from which Giacomo Puccini's opera was derived. Although seldom produced today, Sardou's plays swept the stages of America and England as well as those of France during the last half of the nineteenth century. Their hold on the commercial theatre caused George Bernard Shaw to denounce English theatre of his day as mere "Sardoodledom."

Two of Sardou's compatriots were particularly successful authors of farce. Eugène Labiche (1815–1888), with *The Italian Straw Hat* (1851), and Georges Feydeau (1862–1921), with *A Flea in Her Ear* (1907), set the style for plays based on a highly complicated set of adventures unfolding at rapid-fire pace amidst rooms with many doors, through which a variety of odd characters bustled on their way to and from ever greater misadventures. Because these plays often dealt with amorous misunderstandings, they were the forerunners of the still popular "French bedroom farce."

MELODRAMA. Among the most important popular writers of melodramas was the Irish-American Dion Boucicault (1822–1890). Boucicault fused sentimentality with sensationalism, letting the stories unfold against a background rich in local color. He captured large audiences on two continents with works like *The Corsican Brothers* (1852), *The Poor of New York* (1857), and *The Octoroon* (1859). The popularity of his plays gave Boucicault a degree of financial security virtually unknown at the time. He demanded and received a percentage of receipts for each performance of his plays, thus instituting the practice of *paying royalties to playwrights.* By 1886, an international copyright agreement had been instituted, in part because of Boucicault's influence.

Although none was so well known as Boucicault, a number of other dramatists of the time thrilled audiences with plays that featured heroes tied to railroad tracks, heroines trapped in burning buildings, onstage eruptions of volcanoes, chariot races, and other spectacular effects.

Probably the most popular play in the world during this period was an American melodrama called *Uncle Tom's Cabin* (1852), based on the novel by Harriet Beecher Stowe. A highly romanticized view of slavery in the Old South, the play included scenes of slaves escaping across the ice-clogged Ohio River (hotly pursued by dogs and slave traders), little Eva being carried to heaven by angels amidst the weeping of her family and friends, and Uncle Tom being cruelly beaten by that villain of villains, Simon Legree. The success of the play was unprecedented. By 1879, there were twelve different Tom companies (theatre groups producing no plays except *Uncle Tom's Cabin*) criss-crossing America. By 1899, there were between four hundred and five hundred such companies, with some actors making a life's work of "Tomming," never acting in—or even seeing—another play. Various versions played in Germany, France, and England, and twelve different American versions were in print in 1900. The play's popularity remained strong through World War I, when more than a dozen companies still traveled about performing only this one play.

FIGURE 14-25. **French Farce.** Feydeau's *A Flea in Her Ear*, a farce still popular with audiences, shown here in a 1907 production, by which time three-dimensional scenic pieces were a comfortable part of commercial practice.

MUSICAL ENTERTAINMENTS. Although operettas like those of Jacques Offenbach (1819–1889) were popular, they were eclipsed by the work of two Englishmen, William S. Gilbert (1836–1911) and Arthur Sullivan (1842–1900), whose *H.M.S. Pinafore* (1878), *The Pirates of Penzance* (1879), *The Mikado* (1885), and *The Gondoliers* (1889), among others, remain popular to this day.

In America, burlesque (and its cousin, vaudeville) were quite popular. Originally little more than parodies and variety acts, both were well established in the American theatre during the first half of the century. Burlesque became overwhelmingly a male entertainment after Lydia Thompson's "British Blondes" took America by storm in 1869. Increasingly thereafter, the popularity of burlesque depended on a combination of spectacles, song, dance, and female legs. Soon after World War I, "striptease" was added, and burlesque moved still further to the outskirts of respectability. Vaudeville, on the other hand, flourished as a family entertainment, some of its stars moving to radio and the movies in the 1930s.

Theatrical Stars

The pleasure of theatregoers was not entirely bound up with the plays themselves, for the period featured theatrical stars of the highest rank. Many leading actors traveled from city to city to play starring roles with resident stock companies; others traveled with their entire productions (cast, costumes, and scenery) across continents

FIGURE 14-26. **Major Stars.** Henry Irving was knighted in recognition of his English career in diverse roles drawn not only from Shakespeare's plays but also from melodramas, of which Mathias in *The Bells* (shown here) was his most famous; Joseph Jefferson spent a career and earned his fame with one role, Rip Van Winkle.

to satisfy audiences who thronged to the theatres to see the latest star. France, in addition to Sarah Bernhardt, produced Benoît Constant Coquelin (1841–1909). England's most famous actor was Henry Irving (1838–1905), whose performances as Mathias in a now-forgotten melodrama named *The Bells* (1871) spanned thirty-four years and eight hundred performances. That, together with his Shakespearean successes, led to his being knighted, the first English actor to be so honored. In America, the leading actors were Joseph Jefferson (1829–1905), whose fame rested primarily on his portrayal of the title role in *Rip Van Winkle;* Edwin Booth (1833–1893), regarded by his contemporaries as Shakespeare's finest interpreter but probably remembered today by more people as the brother of President Lincoln's assassin; and James O'Neill (1847–1920), who made an acting career in *The Count of Monte Cristo* (1883) and fathered America's highly regarded native dramatist Eugene O'Neill.

Commercial Producers

During this period, too, the financial organization behind commercial production began to change. The *actor-managers* (stars who also funded and administered their own productions) like Irving gradually gave way to the modern *producer,* a person not an actor—and eventually not a theatre artist at all—who undertook finance and organization. In America, early producers were Augustin Daly (1836–1899), also a playwright and director; and David Belasco (1854–1931), a playwright and director famous for his meticulous (and well-advertised) commercial realism.

1900–1960

In the United States, Broadway's theatre grew ever more commercial. In response to this increasing emphasis on big business, alternative practices arose in the areas of producing and paying, locations, staging spaces, plays, and designs.

Broadway's Decline

Broadway was still booming at the close of World War I, with two or three hundred new productions a year. Costs of production were reasonable (as low as $2000 for a small show and rarely more than $10,000 for a complex one). Ticket prices were modest—for about $3.00, a patron could have the best seat in the house. Tourists joined New Yorkers in flocking to Broadway, whose growing audiences early in the century encouraged the building of several new theatres, usually featuring a proscenium arch.

The theatre's enormous vitality, including the large number of new plays produced, included many plays that were trivial—and some were downright awful. (Such plays were called *turkeys,* because they were scheduled to open on Thanksgiving day in hopes of improving ticket sales.) But many of the plays were enormously popular and had *long runs* as producers tried to recover the costs of production and turn a profit. *Long runs* rather than rotating repertory were well established by the 1920s.

By the end of the 1930s, the vigorous commercial theatre of the 1920s was in trouble. Despite occasional bright spots, Broadway's commercial theatre continued to decline through World War II and beyond. In 1930–1931, there were 187 new productions; in 1940–1941, there were only 60; in 1950–1951, only 48. Increasingly, theatres were abandoned, torn down, or converted into homes for movies or "girlie shows," as performances featuring female beauty and body were then called. Among the theatres that remained theatres, many were dark (closed) as often as they were open.

Several causes may be given for the serious decline of the commercial theatre during the first half of this century. The Depression (in the 1930s) hit theatre hard. Not only was money scarce throughout society but also new forms of entertainment began to compete with theatre for the public's entertainment dollars, especially after sound film (1927) proved so popular. Just at the time that spectator sports and movies

FIGURE 14-27. Broadway's Decline. Rising ticket prices and declining audiences led to the decline of Broadway. Many of the once famous theatres have been closed and others have been converted to houses for pornographic books, movies, shows, and videos. The area around Broadway and Forty-second street, once a glory of the theatre district, has now become quite seedy, as this photograph shows clearly.

demanded an increasing share of the shrinking entertainment dollar, theatrical unions grew strong enough to demand higher wages—from a theatre less able than before to pay them. Soon thereafter, the price of land in downtown Manhattan soared, making theatre buildings extremely expensive—to rent or to buy. Fire regulations grew more strict, and the cost of remodeling a building to meet the new codes was almost prohibitive. As the cost of producing plays escalated, ticket prices scrambled to keep up; therefore, some former patrons found themselves priced out of the theatre—unable (or unwilling) to pay the price to attend. And just when it appeared that things could not get worse, television covered its first presidential convention (1948) and showed itself to be an important national entertainment. Clearly the commercial theatre was in trouble, and its death was regularly—if inaccurately—predicted.

Producing: Some Alternatives

As theatre's business was increasingly big business, producers and producing assumed a new importance. And as producing became more and more expensive, commercial producers grew more and more conservative, preferring sure-fire entertainments to art, profit to provocation. They spent more and more money on fewer and fewer shows and longer and longer runs. Other producers, however, sought to stress the art rather than the business of theatre and so sought producing arrangements that would allow more adventurous plays and productions. The most influential of such alternatives were the Theatre Guild, the Group Theatre, the Federal Theatre Project, the regional theatre movement, and the Off-Broadway movement.

THE THEATRE GUILD. Founded in 1919, the Theatre Guild was the earliest and most dynamic new producing organization of the 1920s. It attacked the provincialism of American theatre by staging a series of foreign works by important (and controversial) playwrights like Ibsen, Strindberg, Shaw, and Tolstoy. It supported as well the works of those American playwrights whose plays treated serious social issues, among them Elmer Rice, Sidney Howard, and most of all Eugene O'Neill (1888–1953).

Between 1926 and 1928, the Theatre Guild produced fourteen plays whose success almost persuaded Broadway that there was an audience for serious American drama. By the Depression, however, the Guild's influence waned. As its own finances became more precarious, it moved closer to the practices of other commercial producers in an attempt to improve its balance sheet. By 1940, the Theatre Guild was almost indistinguishable from those commercial Broadway producers against which it had originally rebelled.

THE GROUP THEATRE. Founded in 1931, the Group Theatre was at first a militant voice for non- or anti-commercial theatre in New York. Through its repertory it focused attention on various social causes, especially those related to poverty and

FIGURE 14-28. **The Federal Theatre Project.** Over one hundred Negro Units (as they were then called) offered new opportunities for African-American writers, actors, and directors. Shown here, *Prelude to Swing + Fifty* from the Federal Theatre Project, as produced by the Afro-American Arts Institute, Indiana University, directed by Winona Fletcher. (*Photograph courtesy of the* Herald Times, *Bloomington, Indiana.*)

oppression. It also popularized an American version of Stanislavski's acting techniques. Called the *Method*, this American style came to dominate both stage and film, especially after Marlon Brando's portrayal of Stanley Kowalski in the stage and film versions of *A Streetcar Named Desire* (see p. 335).

In production, the Group favored a kind of realism, one based more on psychological truth than on detailed settings. Perhaps as a result, the Group helped popularize a style of design called simplified (or selective) realism, a style soon associated with American design. The communist leanings of some of its members caused the Group Theatre to attract the unfavorable attention of some people in power. This attention, together with financial problems, caused the Group Theatre to fade before the end of World War II.

THE FEDERAL THEATRE PROJECT (FTP). Launched in 1935, the FTP was a program of the federal government aimed at aiding theatre artists who had been thrown out of work by the Depression. Part of the program's excitement came from its national character (units were established in almost every state); part came from its commitment to cultural diversity (there were, for example, both Jewish and black theatre companies); and part came from its innovative artistic practices. In New York, for example, the first *living newspaper* in the United States premiered. A kind of staged documentary, living newspapers soon spread throughout the country, treating society's most pressing problems: housing, farm policies, venereal disease, war. During an anticommunist government probe, living newspapers were denounced as communist plots. It is probably not surprising then that in 1939 the government failed to appropriate money for the Project and so ended the nation's first far-reaching experiment in support of the arts. Before its demise, however, the FTP introduced a number of major new artists and theatres, among them Orson Welles (1915–1985), John Houseman (1902–1988), and the Mercury Theatre.

THE REGIONAL THEATRE MOVEMENT. This movement is usually dated from 1947, when Margo Jones opened a professional theatre in Dallas, Texas. Her goal was not only to decentralize the theatre (to bring professional productions to the heartlands of America) but also to encourage the production of original and classical plays. (She nurtured the talent of Tennessee Williams, for example.) Before Jones's death in 1955 there were professional theatres in Washington, D.C.; Houston, Texas; and Milwaukee, Wisconsin. With the 1960s came a surge of such houses, in places like Minneapolis, Los Angeles, Baltimore, New Haven, and Louisville. Some (like Louisville) were devoted to developing original scripts; others (like Minneapolis) specialized in producing the classical repertory. In a departure from current New York practices, too, some of these theatres built spaces without proscenia, preferring theatres in the round (e.g., Dallas and Washington, D.C.) or thrust stages (e.g., Minneapolis). (See pp. 79–83.)

THE OFF-BROADWAY MOVEMENT. This movement is usually said to have begun in 1952, when Tennessee Williams's *Summer and Smoke* (first produced by Margo Jones in Dallas) earned critical acclaim in a production at Circle in the Square—the first major hit in a theatre located below Forty-second Street in thirty years. From then through the 1960s, Off-Broadway served as a showcase for new talent and for plays whose experimental style or controversial subjects made them unsuitable for the big business of Broadway. Off-Broadway, however, finally succumbed to the pressures of commercialism, and today it is little more than a tryout space for Broadway. (See pp. 87–88).

Repertory

Perhaps by 1900 but certainly by the end of World War I (1918), realism (somewhat trivialized and popularized) was widely accepted in the commercial theatres of France, England, and the United States. By the 1920s, the Parisian Boulevard theatres regularly played serious plays treating social problems, and audiences no longer found them controversial. Commercial theatres in London found audiences ready to accept both Ibsen and Shaw as well as sophisticated plays (both serious and comic) by authors like Noel Coward (1899–1973) and Somerset Maughan (1874–1965). In the United States, comedies and musicals dominated the commercial houses, but three playwrights of serious drama earned international reputations, the first American playwrights to do so: Eugene O'Neill, Tennessee Williams, and Arthur Miller.

COMEDIES. During Broadway's boom years before the Depression, theatre thrived with large-cast plays filled with wise-cracking characters. Such plays included *You Can't Take It With You*, a comedy of family life, by George S. Kaufman (1889–1961) and Moss Hart (1904–1961). As the costs of production soared, however, the sizes of casts shrank—and with them some of the early comic exuberance. From the Depression through the 1950s, comedies tended to become gentler and more sentimental, like Mary Chase's *Harvey*, a charming portrait of an aging man and his (imagined) six-foot tall rabbit.

MUSICALS. Musical revues like the Ziegfeld Follies had long entertained audiences with a mixture of featured skits, variety acts, and songs written by some of the United States' favorite composers (Irving Berlin, 1888–1989, for example).

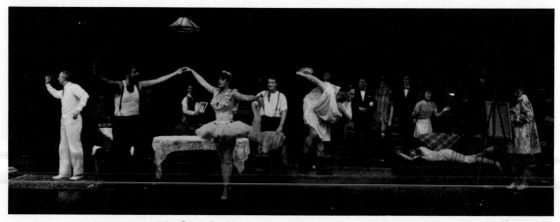

FIGURE 14-29. **Comedy.** Large casts were once common in commercial shows like *You Can't Take It With You*, shown here in production at Western Michigan University. *(Directed by D. Terry Williams, scenery By Susan Rugg, costumes by Helen Bray.)*

The form of musical theatre changed, however, when Jerome Kern (1885–1945) and Oscar Hammerstein (1895–1960) offered *Showboat* (1927), which set a fashion for musicals that integrated story line, characters, and music. Soon thereafter musicals were in their heyday, led by composers like Cole Porter (1891–1964) and George Gershwin (1898–1937). Some of Porter's songs (e.g., "Night and Day," "Begin the Beguine") are still sung, and his *Kiss Me Kate,* the musical retelling of Shakespeare's *Taming of the Shrew,* has remained in the repertory since its first production in 1948. Gershwin, in addition to his serious music like "Rhapsody in Blue" and "An American in Paris," is noted for his *Porgy and Bess* (1935), an American classic that continues to play in theatres and opera houses the world over. Gershwin's success marked the acceptance of American jazz as a legitimate musical form.

It remained for *Oklahoma!* (1943) to integrate ballet and modern dance into the American story musical (as distinct from musical revues) and to establish Hammerstein and his new collaborator Richard Rodgers (1902–1979) as major figures. Along with *Oklahoma!,* their *Carousel* (1945) and *South Pacific* (1947) remain in the repertory still.

FIGURE 14-30. **Musicals.** Cole Porter's music in *Anything Goes* invites frequent revivals even now. Produced here, at The Ohio State University. Compare the costumes shown here with their original designs, shown in the first color section. *(Directed by Robert Wharton, costumes by Dennis Parker, USAA.)*

FIGURE 14-31. Musicals. *Hello, Dolly!*, the musical version of Wilder's play *The Match-maker*, is often produced by colleges and universities, dinner theatres, community theatres, and regional theatres. Here, a production from Cockpit-in-Court Theatre in Essex Community College, Baltimore. *(Directed by Eric Potter, designs by Steve Gilliam, photo by Norma McCullough.)*

SERIOUS PLAYS. Few serious plays were commercially successful on Broadway, and even many of these have faded with the years. Few people remember *The Front Page*, *Street Scene*, or *Winterset*, although each was a major play in its day. A few more people, perhaps, remember once-admired playwrights like Elmer Rice, Clifford Odets, Maxwell Anderson, and Robert Sherwood. Some plays by Lillian Hellman (1905–1984) remain in the repertory—*The Children's Hour* (1934) and *The Little Foxes* (1939), for example; and at least two plays by Thornton Wilder (1897–1975) are still regularly produced: *Our Town* (1938) and *The Matchmaker* (1954), although the latter is best known in its later musical version—*Hello, Dolly!* (1964). William Inge's *Picnic* and *Bus Stop* are occasionally produced, as is Carson McCullers's *The Member of the Wedding*. But probably only three playwrights active before 1960 retain a prominent place in today's theatre: O'Neill, Williams, and Miller.

Eugene O'Neill (1888–1953), son of the actor James O'Neill, became America's first internationally acclaimed playwright. Nurtured by the Theatre Guild, O'Neill showed that significant serious drama could find an audience and compete with the commercial fare of Broadway. A writer not afraid to experiment with new ideas and new forms of theatre, O'Neill wrote plays that set several new directions for later writers to follow. In *The Emperor Jones* (1920) and *The Hairy Ape* (1922), he experimented with expressionistic techniques for depicting psychological disintegration. In *The Great God Brown* (1926) and *Strange Interlude* (1928), he explored the use of masks and asides as means of hiding and revealing character. In *Mourning Becomes Electra* (1931), he adapted Greek myth to American culture, and in *Long Day's Journey Into Night* (1956) he offered a searing autobiographical drama of his own family, where the mother's drug addiction and the father's weakness shaped the lives of the sons. Although certainly flawed, O'Neill's plays remain significant because of the theatricality of his visions and the intensity of his passion. O'Neill's plays are still regularly read and occasionally produced, usually in regional theatres.

Tennessee Williams (1914–1983) won the Drama Critics Circle Award for his first major Broadway production, *The Glass Menagerie* (1945), a wistful memory play vaguely reminiscent of the impressionists and Chekhov. *A Streetcar Named Desire* (1947) won both the Pulitzer Prize and the Drama Critics Circle Award and established Williams as a major American playwright. This production was significant, too, because it propelled Marlon Brando to stardom for his portrayal of Stanley Kowalski, a success that popularized the "Method" as America's contribution to the

FIGURE 14-32. **Tennessee Williams.** Stanley Kowalski and Blanche Dubois from Williams's *A Streetcar Named Desire* exemplify one of Williams's great strengths as a playwright: the construction of interesting and believable characters. Shown here from a production at the University of Wyoming. (*Directed by Gladys M. Crane, designed by Ron Steger.*)

FIGURE 14-33. **Arthur Miller.** With Williams, Arthur Miller was one of the best-loved playwrights of the 1940s and 1950s, and his plays still find frequent production. Here, a production of *All My Sons* at South Carolina State College. *(Directed by Frank Mundy, designed by Robert Osei-Wusu.)*

acting of realistic and naturalistic plays. The same production established Elia Kazan as a major American director, and selective (or simplified) realism as a major style among American designers. *Summer and Smoke* (1952), *Cat on a Hot Tin Roof* (1954), *Sweet Bird of Youth* (1956), and *Night of the Iguana* (1961) did not attain the popularity of the earlier plays, but all remain in the repertory.

Arthur Miller (b. 1915) is, like Williams, a realist of sorts, but whereas Williams's work tended toward the dreamlike and impressionistic, Miller's moved in harsher, more expressionistic ways. *All My Sons* (1947) told of an American businessman who knowingly sold inferior products to the American military in order to turn a profit. Despite the Drama Critics Circle Award, the play was banned in occupied Europe after the war and was denounced by some as a smear on the American business community. Miller was under suspicion, therefore, when he wrote *Death of a Salesman* (1947), an acknowledged American masterpiece. In this play, realistic scenes are interspersed with scenes remembered by the disordered protagonist, Willy Loman.

Death of a Salesman, as directed by Elia Kazan and designed by a major American designer, Jo Mielziner, won both a Pulitzer Prize and the Drama Critics Circle Award and further promoted the conventions of American realism. Although Miller continued to write important plays, some critics feel that he never again attained his early successes with plays like *The Crucible* (1953), *A View from the Bridge* (1955), *After the Fall* (1964), and *The Price* (1968).

CHAPTER FIFTEEN

THE AVANT-GARDE: 1890s–1960s

PROBLEMS WITH REALISM

Even before realism became the mainstream of theatrical life in Europe and America, some writers and theorists had begun to chafe under its limitations. Four questions in particular were the focus of discussion and concern:

1. *How can realistic drama be kept interesting?*

Before realism, most serious dramatists had depicted characters who were considerably removed from everyday experience—princes, kings, demigods—who participated in events that were out of the ordinary: a war, a national crisis, a cosmic struggle. The plays were set in faraway times and places, environments that were, in themselves, often mysterious and compelling. When confronting a crisis, these exalted characters burst into passages of extreme lyricism in which the full resources of the language (rhythm, rhyme, and metaphor) were marshaled to produce heights of emotional intensity.

But realistic drama, by definition, portrayed ordinary people involved in mundane situations. Their language necessarily resembled everyday conversation and their clothing reflected their middle- or lower-class status. What then, made them interesting? Audience pleasure seemed to depend largely on the factor of *recognition* alone.

Although this new factor is a very potent one, it was being asked to carry the entire weight of provoking and maintaining interest, a burden that proved too heavy for many dramas.

2. *How can realistic drama be made significant?*

Traditionally, in serious drama, playwrights depicted serious actions that were of consequence to a large range of people—a nation or even a world. But realistic dramas typically dealt with working men and women as they lived out rather humdrum lives. If no more was at stake than the happiness of a single individual or a small family, who beyond their immediate friends would find it significant?

Some realistic dramatists increased the significance of their plays' actions by having the protagonist represent something bigger, something more general. Willy Loman in *Death of a Salesman*, for example, was made to stand for all salesmen, or all working men. Such a solution, however, pulled against the very philosophical assumptions on which realism was based. Perhaps more seriously, abstractions are often undramatic. Poetry and the novel, where the reader can return time and again to study and consider the text, are usually better media for abstractions and symbolizations

FIGURE 15-1. **Problems with Realism.** To watch ordinary people in ordinary situations may become uninteresting, and the visual aspects of production (costuming, scenery, lighting), because they must resemble "real life," are denied many of the rich opportunities open to them in other theatrical styles. Shown here, a realistic production of a realistic play, Arthur Miller's A *View from the Bridge* at Center Stage, Baltimore. *(Courtesy of Center Stage. Photo by C.B. Nieberding.)*

than are plays, where the living presence of the actors encourages specificity and where the basis of the form is action rather than idea or word.

3. *What is the role of the audience in a realistic theatre?*

Even though the stage in realistic drama was a close reproduction of the real world and the actors a duplication of everyday people, the separation of the audience from the dramatic action in "fourth-wall realism" (as signified by the presence of a proscenium arch) was greater than ever before. The conventions of the style required the audience to sit in a darkened auditorium and to watch silently as a separate world unfolded behind the proscenium arch. The actors, for their part, behaved as if the audience were not there, turning their backs and mumbling lines in an attempt to reproduce the inarticulateness of everyday conversations. The result was a world on the stage quite separate from the real world where the audience sat. It is ironic that realistic drama and staging, which had seemed to bring the world of the stage closer to that of the audience, ended by separating them to a degree unparalleled in the history of the theatre.

4. *How can the theatrical event be kept probable (or believable)?*

All playwrights, of course, must construct plays that are probable, or believable, if they are to capture the interest and the commitment of an audience. But only the realist additionally required that the world in the play resemble, on a one-to-one basis, the world outside: the theatrical scenery was to be a photographic likeness of the outside world, and the actors were to be the embodiment of everyday people. To produce the familiar and to make it believable proved too demanding a chore for many realistic playwrights.

Because of these problems, a variety of alternatives to realistic plays and staging were being proposed and tested by the 1890s. The years between 1890 and 1960 saw a proliferation of *isms*: neoromanticism, formalism, symbolism, impressionism, expressionism, constructivism, futurism, absurdism, and so on. Each strove to address and solve one or more of the problems inherent in realism. As each developed, grew, and declined, the mainstream of realism shifted slightly to accommodate various attributes of the competing styles. As a result, although realism remained the mainstream of theatre from about 1900 through 1960, it shifted perceptibly throughout that period as it incorporated first one and then another new approach to playwriting or staging.

IMPRESSIONISM

Impressionism (fl. 1890s) was a style that sought to capture and reproduce the fleeting moments of awareness that were believed to constitute the essence of human existence. By reproducing faithfully these fleeting glimpses, art could provide insights into the truth that lay underneath the external world. Probably the playwright who wrote most successfully in the style was Maurice Maeterlinck (1862–1949). In short plays like *The Intruder* (1890) and *The Interior* (1894) and in longer plays like *Pelléas and Mélisande* (1892) and *The Blue Bird* (1908), Maeterlinck presented a world far removed from that of mundane reality. Introspection and subjectivity permeate the plays, which are typically moody and mysterious works hinting at a life controlled

FIGURE 15-2. Impressionism. Among the earliest alternatives to realism were the impressionistic plays of Maurice Maeterlinck, whose *The Blue Bird* is shown here in a Parisian production, 1911.

by unseen and inexplicable forces manipulating passive and often perplexed characters. The actions seem hazy, distant, out of focus; indeed, in the theatre, the plays were often played behind gauzes (*scrims*) or clouds of fog and moved between patches of light, dark, and shadow.

For impressionists like Maeterlinck, a play aimed to convey intuitions about a truth more profound than the tangible, objective, external world of the realists. Through symbols, it alluded to a significance beyond the immediate, and through its language and stories it aspired to arouse interest by its exoticism.

Impressionism in the drama was not of lasting importance, perhaps because its emphasis on internal states and spiritual glimpses was better suited to the page than to the stage. Some of its techniques, however, were appealing and so were adopted by realists like Ibsen (in his later plays), Chekhov, and, more recently, Tennessee Williams.

SYMBOLISM

The impressionists were closely allied with the symbolists, of whom the most famous were the theatrical practitioners Adolphe Appia (1862–1928) and Gordon Craig (1872–1966). Appia believed that artistic unity was the fundamental goal of theatrical production and that lighting was the element best able to fuse all other elements into an artistic whole. Like music, its auditory counterpart, light was capable of continual change to reflect shifting moods and emotions within the play. Like music,

FIGURE 15-3. **Symbolism.** Gordon Craig's designs, one of which is shown here, renounced the realists' use of many objects and details in favor of simple visual statements that depended on mass and light.

too, light could be orchestrated by variations in its direction, intensity, and color to produce a rhythm designed to underscore the dramatic action. Because he found an aesthetic contradiction between the three-dimensional actor and the two-dimensional floor set at right angles to the two-dimensional painted scenes still popular in his day, Appia sought ways to provide the stage floor and scenery with mass so that the actor could better blend with them. He solved the problem in part by devising three-dimensional settings composed of series of steps, ramps, and platforms, among which the living actor could comfortably move.

Like Appia, Craig opposed scenic illusions and favored instead a simple visual statement that eliminated inessential details and avoided photographic reproductions of specific places. His emphasis was on the manipulation of line and mass to achieve, first, a unity of design and, ultimately, a unity for the total production. Although Craig placed less emphasis on the importance of the actor and the text than Appia, they agreed on the importance of the visual elements of the production. Perhaps it would not be an injustice to designate Appia as the formulator of the theories that Craig later popularized. The theories of Appia and Craig gained a secure foothold in theatrical practice following World War I.

EXPRESSIONISM

Whereas impressionism sought to present echoes of a transitory and mysterious truth, *expressionism* (fl. 1910s–1930s) usually focused on political and social questions. If impressionism produced a dreamlike vision, expressionism created a stage world closer

THEATRE ON CAMPUS IN AMERICA

C-12. *The Revenge of the Space Pandas,* by David Mamet. Directed by Robert Hedley, designed by Lisa LoCurto and Eric T. Haugen. University of Iowa.

C-13. *A Toby Show.* Directed by Frank Mundy. South Carolina State College.

C-14. **Bread and Puppet Theatre.** Performance at the University of Vermont.

C-15. *A Midsummer's Night's Dream.* Directed by John Powell, designed by
Lewis A. Crickard and Rebecca Akins. University of Denver.

C-16. *The Ride Across Lake Constance,* by Peter Handke. Directed by Julian M. Olf.
University of Massachusetts, Amherst.

C-17. *Purlie*. Directed and designed by
Elliott C. Moffitt. Fayetteville State University.

C-18. *The Pot of Gold*. Directed by Scott K.
Strode, designed by Stephen A. Batzka; masks,
James R. Adams. Manchester College.

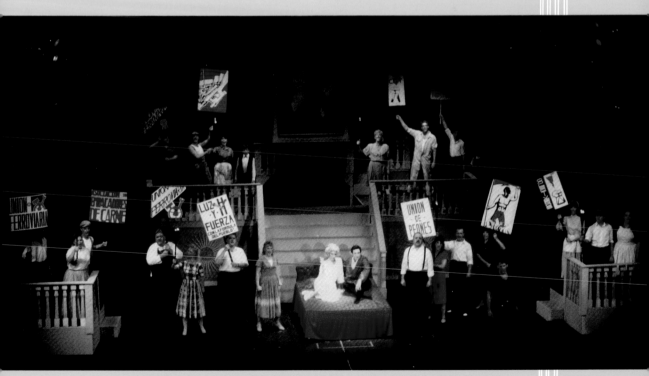

C-19. *Evita*. Directed by F. Scott Black, designed by Jan Detwiler, photo by
Norman McCullough. Cockpit-in-Court at Essex Community College.

C-20. *Man and Superman*. Directed by
Jim Patterson (photo by Keith McGraw,
Instructional Services Center).
University of South Carolina.

C-21. *Count Dracula*. Directed by
Elliott C. Moffitt, designed by Frank Whaley.
Fayetteville State University.

C-22. *Merry Wives of Windsor*. Directed by Ron Shields, designed by Robert Groff.
Bowling Green State University.

FIGURE 15-4. Expressionism. A nightmare world of trapped humanity is shown here in a production of Toller's *Man and the Masses.*

to the nightmare. The plays were often didactic and cautioned the world against the impending cataclysms to be caused by uncontrolled industrialism, rampant imperson-alization, and other threats posed by the modern industrial state. Seldom did the plays tell a simple story; more often, they developed as episodic examinations or demonstrations of a central thesis. They customarily unfolded in a world of bizarre and garish colors, jagged angles, and oddly proportioned objects (perhaps because they were often told through the mind of the protagonist, whose mental vision was distorted). Actors, often dressed identically, moved in mechanical or puppetlike ways and often spoke in disconnected or telegraphic conversations. They bore names of types rather than people: The Mother, The Son, The Cipher, and so on. Conven-tional ideas of time and space collapsed; in their place were elastic units where years could fly by as seconds crept and adjacent objects appeared as if seen through the opposite ends of a telescope.

Expressionism as a movement was most developed in Germany. Its two leading playwrights were Georg Kaiser (1878–1945), whose best-known plays are *From Morn to Midnight* (1916) and the *Gas* trilogy, and Ernst Toller (1893–1939), whose best-known works are *Man and the Masses* (1921) and *Hurrah, We Live* (1927).

Expressionistic plays are seldom produced today outside university theatres, but their influence has been substantial for three reasons. First, many of the techniques were adapted and used by the growing film industry. Second, some expressionistic techniques were adapted to the needs of important playwrights in the realistic mainstream, notably (in America) Arthur Miller, Eugene O'Neill, and Edward Albee. Third, German expressionism was an early influence on Erwin Piscator and Bertolt Brecht, whose "epic theatre" became a major force in European and American theatres during the 1940s, 1950s, and 1960s. Staging devices popularized by expressionism (and constructivism), although softened, continue to influence designers in contemporary theatre and film down to the present day.

CONSTRUCTIVISM

In Russia, the practices of Vsevolod Myerhold (1874–1940) paralleled many of those associated with the German expressionists. Although early in his career Myerhold directed experimental works for Stanislavski, during the 1920s he devoted himself to developing a theatrical art suitable for the machine age. He relied on two major techniques: *biomechanics* and *constructivism*. *Biomechanics* referred to a training system and performance style for actors: they were to be well-trained "machines" for carrying out the assignments given them, and so they needed rigorous physical training in ballet, gymnastics, circus techniques, and so on. *Constructivism* referred to Myerhold's conclusions that scenery should not attempt to represent any particular place but

FIGURE 15-5. **Constructivism.** Popularized in Russia by Myerhold, constructivist settings were conceived as machines on which actors could work rather than as representations of real places. Here, the setting for *The Man Who Was Thursday* in Moscow in the 1920s.

that it should provide a "machine" on which actors could perform. In practice, Myerhold's sets were often elaborate combinations of platforms, steps, ramps, wheels, and trapezes. The goal of both biomechanics and constructivism was to undercut the realist's emphasis on internal motivation for actors and literal representation in scenery and costumes and to retheatricalize the theatre.

ABSURDISM

Just after World War II, several new playwrights caused a temporary flurry of excitement. Not comprising a self-conscious movement, these playwrights were nonetheless grouped together and given the name *absurdists* by a contemporary scholar, Martin Esslin. *Absurdism* (fl. 1940s and 1950s) was itself a blend of earlier abortive experiments of the French avant-garde. With *dadaism* (fl. 1920s), it shared an emphasis on life's meaninglessness and art's irrelevancy and a commitment to irrationality and

FIGURE 15-6. Absurdism. Productions of Beckett's *Waiting for Godot* still occur often, but few other absurdist plays have retained their original popularity. Shown here, costumes for a recent production, designed by Martin A. Thaler, University of Vermont.

nihilism as appropriate responses to life and living. With *surrealism* (fl. 1920s), it viewed the source of insight as a person's subconscious mind. Most important, with *existentialism* (fl. 1930s and 1940s), it sought an answer to the plaguing question: What does it mean to exist and to be? Jean-Paul Sartre (1905–1980), a philosopher turned playwright and a major advocate of existentialism, sought to establish a code of life based on a consistent atheism, where the absence of absolute moral laws left human beings adrift in a world without order or purpose: each person must define his or her own value system and then act accordingly.

Absurdism stressed that the world was unreasonable, illogical, incongruous, and out of harmony. The word *absurd,* then, meant not *ridiculous* but *without meaning.* According to the absurdists, the only order in life was what a person constructed; the only moral systems were those that the individual defined. To incorporate these views into dramatic form, the absurdists abandoned telling a story in favor of communicating an experience; they abandoned a dramatic unity based on causality and replaced it with one whose source, and indeed whose very presence, was not always clear to the uninitiated. The plays were often constructed as a circle (ending just where they began, after displaying a series of unrelated incidents) and as the intensification of a single event (ending just where they had begun but in the midst of more people or more objects). Usually, the puzzling quality of the plays came from the devaluation of language as a carrier of meaning: in the plays, *what happens* on stage often transcends and contradicts *what is said* there. The tonal and rhythmic dimensions of words are often more important to the play than is their literal sense. The absurdists, unlike their most important predecessors, the existentialists, did not discuss and argue about the meaninglessness of life; they simply presented it concretely onstage, using actors to participate in apparently senseless non sequiturs amidst what seemed, on the surface, to be inarticulate and incomprehensible exchanges of dialogue.

Although absurdists like Samuel Beckett (1906–1989), Eugène Ionesco (b. 1912), and Edward Albee (b. 1928) were exceedingly popular for a time, few of their plays find contemporary production outside the educational theatre—Beckett's *Waiting for Godot* (1953) and Albee's *Who's Afraid of Virginia Woolf?* are obvious exceptions. Still, many of the techniques popularized by absurdists appear in the works of contemporary playwrights.

BRECHT AND ARTAUD

Although all of the styles described here have had an impact on today's theatre, the theories and practices of Bertolt Brecht and Antonin Artaud have probably been more influential than any others. These two theorists operated from quite different sets of assumptions about the nature of theatre and the purpose of art, but they shared a disdain for realism with all of its trappings. Although it may be a falsification, at least in part, it may be useful to regard Brecht as developing from the expressionistic German traditions and Artaud from the impressionistic and surrealistic traditions of the French theatre. Together, their theories can help account for much of the experimentation during the 1960s and 1970s.

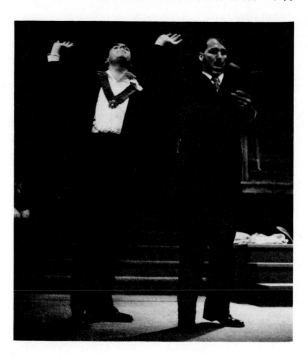

FIGURE 15-7. **Brecht and Epic Theatre.** One of the major theorists of the twentieth century, Brecht also wrote plays against which those theories could be viewed. Shown here, Brecht's *The Resistable Rise of Arturo Ui* in production at Wright State University. *(Directed by Robert Hetherington, designed by Joe Tilford.)*

Bertolt Brecht and Epic Theatre

Bertolt Brecht (1898–1956) believed that theatre should educate *citizens* (participants in a political system) in how to bring about socially responsible change. He saw theatre as a way of making a controversial topic easier to consider. His commitment to a socially responsive theatre doubtless came, in part, from his being both Jewish and leftist at a time when Hitler was rising to power in Germany.

Traditional theatres, whether those of Wagner or Saxe-Meiningen, sought an illusion that allowed the members of the audiencee to believe in and identify with the onstage actions. In such theatres, Brecht observed, audiences reached a state of self-oblivion: "Looking around, one discovers more or less motionless bodies in a curious state . . . they have their eyes open, but they don't look, they stare . . . they stare at the stage as if spellbound." As Brecht was a Marxist and viewed theatre as an instrument for change, he objected to a theatre that mesmerized its audience and made them passive. Brecht therefore strove to redefine the relationship between the theatre, its audience, and the society at large. He proposed that if he jarred audiences periodically out of their identification with the action, he would succeed in shaking their complacency and in forcing them to think about what they saw onstage. He sought, therefore, alternately to engage and estrange his audiences, a technique he called *Verfremdungseffekt* (usually translated as the *alienation effect* or, simply, the *A-effect*).

To achieve alienation required artists to work in new ways. Actors were encouraged to hold themselves distant from their roles by speaking the stage directions out loud during the rehearsal process, to think of their characters in the third person rather than in the first person, and to use the past tense rather than the present tense when talking of their work. Such procedures made an actor a commentator rather than an impersonator, an evaluator of the action as well as a demonstrator of it.

Brecht urged lighting designers to expose the instruments to remind the spectators that they were in a threatre and that the illumination was coming from a high-wattage lamp rather than from the sun. If a set was to represent a town, it should look like a town that had been built for the theatre; it should not be built with the goal of "fooling" the audience into accepting it as a real town. Theatrical elements should be juxtaposed in unexpected ways so that each could make an independent contribution and comment on the ideas of the play. Thus, if the set was to make one point, the costumes should make a different one; a grisly story of war and atrocity might be set to a lively tune with a lilting melody; the seeming incongruity would force the audience to consider the apparent conflict of elements and to draw conclusions about the absurdity of war. In short, Brecht proposed that each artist make an independent contribution to the production and to the didactic purpose of the script and that each element be used not to create an atmosphere that encouraged the audience to identify with the action (as in traditional theatre) but to reinforce the didactic purpose of the drama.

Brecht was a playwright as well as a theorist and a director. His plays typically consisted of a series of short episodes connected by songs, narratives, placards, or similar devices. The purpose was to engage the interest and belief of the audience (within each episode) and then to break the spell by forcing the spectator to think about and evaluate the meaning and implications of the episodes (by manipulating various materials between them). Brecht once described the way a play should work in this way: "Individual events must be tied together in such a way that the knots are strikingly noticeable; the events must not follow upon one another imperceptibly, but rather one must be able to pass judgment in the midst of them." Among his most successful and best-known plays are *The Threepenny Opera* (1928), *Mother Courage and Her Children* (1938), *Galileo* (1938–1939), *The Good Woman of Setzuan* (1938–1939), and *The Caucasian Chalk Circle* (1944–1945).

The whole complex of techniques of staging and playwriting used by Brecht came

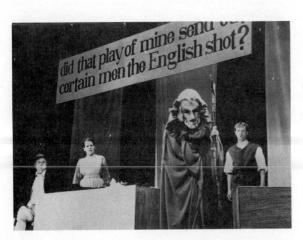

FIGURE 15-8. Brecht's Influence. Many of the techniques of Epic Theatre are now readily adopted for productions of plays by other playwrights. Shown here, a production of W. B. Yeats's poetic drama *Kathleen ni Houlihan* at the Lyric Theatre, Belfast. (*Directed by James W. Flannery, designed by Nicole Kozekiewicz.*)

to be called *epic theatre,* a term he adopted to distinguish his theatre from traditional drama of the sort described by Aristotle in his *Poetics* and from unified theatre of the kind advocated by Wagner. The name *epic,* too, captured many of the qualities that Brecht prized: the mixing of narrative and dramatic episodes, the telescoping of time and place, and the spanning of years and countries on a consequent grand scale (similar to that achieved in epic poetry).

Although Brecht was not the first to use either these techniques or the term *epic* (Erwin Piscator, 1893–1966, had been active in the same kind of experimentation several years earlier), Brecht popularized the term and the practices through his own plays, his theoretical writings (particularly the "Little Organon for the Theatre," 1948), and his productions at the Berliner Ensemble, after 1954 East Germany's most prestigious theatre.

Antonin Artaud and the Theatre of Cruelty

Antonin Artaud (1895–1948) fit the stereotype of the misunderstood and tormented artist. A visionary rather than a practical man, Artaud was an influential theorist immediately following World War II; by the 1960s, he was virtually a cult hero among the theatrical avant-garde in Europe and the United States.

Although Artaud was an actor, a director, a playwright, a poet, and a screenwriter, it was as a theorist that he made his greatest impact. *The Theatre and Its Double,* a compilation of Artaud's major essays, was published in France in 1938 but was not translated into English until the late 1950s. Because Artaud believed that important ideas came not from logical reasoning or rational thinking but from intuition, experience, and feelings, he developed his major ideas and positions by poetic rather than prosaic techniques, by means of images and metaphors rather than through traditional argument or discursive prose. For this reason, many people have found the book difficult to read and understand. Nonetheless, Artaud's major points seem clear enough, particularly if the reader attends to the major metaphors that appear: the theatre as *plague,* as *double,* and as *cruelty.*

First, Artaud called for theatre to return to its rightful place as a great force in humanity, a force for putting people back in touch with the intensity of living. Comparing theatre to a plague, Artaud attributed to both the power to release conflicts, to disengage powers, and to liberate possibilities: "It appears that by means of the plague, a gigantic abscess, as much moral as social, has been collectively drained; and that like the plague, the theatre has been created to drain abscesses collectively." He declared that theatre caused people to confront themselves honestly, letting fall their individual masks and confessing their social hypocrisies.

Second, Western theatre had lost its magic and its vibrance and had become merely a pale imitation, a *double,* of the true theatre (that is, the Eastern theatre). In order to regain its power, the Western theatre must reject logical demonstrations and causal actions and instead seize and impel its spectators toward truth, forcing them to apprehend meaning through the whole of their bodies. To this end, Artaud proposed "a theatre in which violent physical images crush and hypnotize the sensibility . . . as by a whirlwind of higher forces."

Third, Artaud wanted to remove the script from the center of his theatre, for he

THE QUEEN
THE BLACKS

FIGURE 15-9. **Theatre of Cruelty.** Jean Genet is one playwright whose works regularly show influences of Artaud. Here, masks for a production of *The Blacks*, a play in which black characters play whites in order to make the point (among several) that the races are inextricably bound as they move relentlessly toward revolution. *(Masks by Martin A. Thaler, University of Vermont.)*

believed that words, grammatical structure, and syntactical patterns were insufficient carriers of meaning. Truth came instead from spiritual signs whose meaning emerged intuitively and "with enough violence to make useless any translation into logical discursive language." Artaud wished to substitute gestures, signs, symbols, rhythms, and sounds for ordinary language; he advocated "a superabundance of impression, each richer than the next." He was convinced that theatre was neither logical, nor paraphrasable, nor rational; it was intuitive, primitive, magical, and potentially powerful.

Fourth, the audience was central to the theatre. Artaud dismissed notions of art as a kind of personal therapy for the artist. Theatre was good only when it profoundly moved its audiences, when it returned them to the subconscious energies that lay under the veneer of civilization and civilized behavior. Whereas Brecht wished to cause an audience to *think* about a social or political issue, Artaud wanted to move an audience to *feel* or *experience* a spiritual awakening, to participate in something that might be called a *communion* in its real sense of a *coming together*.

Fifth, Artaud called for a *theatre of cruelty*, a theatre that showed the "terrible and necessary cruelty which things can exercise against us. We are not free. And the sky can still fall on our heads. And the theatre has been created to teach us that first of all." Cruelty, then, was primarily psychic rather than physical.

To achieve his theatre of cruelty, Artaud developed a number of techniques seldom used in commercial productions. Because he wanted to bombard the senses with various stimuli in order to cause the whole organism (not merely the mind) to be moved, he experimented with ways of manipulating light and sound: in both, he adopted the abrupt, the discordant, the sudden, the shrill, the garish. Lights changed colors quickly, alternated intensity violently; sound was loud, sudden, often amplified. Scenery was subservient to the other elements of production, with the audiences placed in an environment created by actors, lights, sound, and the space for the production (Artaud preferred barns, factories, and the like to conventional theatres). The actors were encouraged to use their bodies and their voices to provide scenery, sounds, and visual effects and not to be bound by notions of psychological realism and character analysis. Actors were to address the senses of the spectators, not merely their minds.

Artaud's theories, in many forms and with many distortions, were appropriated and applied after 1950 by theatre artists, makers of movies, and especially modern rock music stars. Whatever one may think of his pronouncements, it is clear that, although long in coming, their acceptance has been widespread.

CHAPTER SIXTEEN

CHANGING WORLD, ECLECTIC THEATRE: 1960s–1990s

BACKGROUND

The period was one of rapid and powerful change. Space probes revealed new frontiers. Jet aircraft offered speedy travel. Computers, photocopiers, and faxes linked up to provide quick answers and almost instant contact. Satellites transformed telephones, television, and military intelligence. Such new technologies seemed to compress both time and space, and so the earth itself seemed to shrink, binding its peoples ever more closely together. *Spaceship earth* became a popular metaphor, offering an image of the earth as a closed system hurtling through space with all life on it ultimately tied together.

Shifting Alliances

Until the late 1980s there were local tensions, many left over from the two World Wars. There were limited wars in the Middle East, in Korea, in Vietnam, in India and Pakistan, in Africa. Despite their individual histories, each regional conflict

352

tended to get caught up in, and so reflect, a larger struggle, itself an aftermath of World War II: the East (Soviet, communist) versus the West (North American–European, capitalist). To be sure, not every country agreed to line up behind one or the other camp: China and Yugoslavia, although communist, would not submit to Soviet authority; India and much of Africa, although capitalist, refused to echo the United States and western Europe. Power and influence, however, lodged in one of two worlds, each led by a major superpower.

The Berlin Wall, built in 1961, became a concrete symbol of these two competing cultures. Their cold war often heated up (e.g., the Cuban missile crisis, 1961) and occasionally erupted (e.g., the Vietnam War, 1965–1972). But mostly each side warily eyed the other, each calculating the other's intentions from behind an increasingly bloated mass of military hardware. The third world, unless caught in the gaze of a superpower, remained almost invisible in the plays of power that surrounded it.

This two-sided world suddenly collapsed in 1989–1990. An economic disaster within the Soviet block and the bold vision of a new Soviet leader, Mikhail Gorbachev, ended the cold war. The world suddenly seemed more complex: the Soviet's brand of communism faded; a new, united Western Europe challenged the United States for dominance; OPEC (the Organization of Petroleum Exporting Countries)

FIGURE 16-1. **The World: War and Peace.** No sooner had the East–West struggle (the Cold War) subsided than conflict broke out in the Middle East. Shown here, pro- and antiwar protests in Washington, D.C., at the beginning of war between a United Nations alliance and Iraq.

gained new influence; and the defeated enemies of World War II, Japan and Germany, emerged as the new economic powers. It seemed that World War II had finally ended, and, as if to symbolize the new order, in 1989 the Berlin Wall was torn down and in 1990 Germany was reunited; and in 1991 the United States and the Soviet Union stood together against Iraq.

Almost at once, tentative outlines for new alliances grew visible, drawn into place by events in the war in the Persian Gulf. Some predicted that the old East–West struggle would be replaced in the 1990s by a North–South struggle, one between the relatively affluent, developed nations of Northern Asia, Northern Europe, and North America and the poor, newly developing nations of Africa and South America. Others envisioned a new world that consisted instead of a complex and interconnecting set of momentary alliances, each shifting according to specific circumstances. Although the shape of the new world remained unclear, its emergence was almost certain.

Differing Perspectives

Even while the governments of east and west had been busily threatening one another, others had begun to be struck as much by the similarities of the two superpowers as by their differences. In both blocs, the power lay with European (white) men who, it seemed, had defined the world in ways that mostly excluded blacks, browns, and females, as individuals and as cultures. For example, by the late 1950s, Sub-Saharan Africans had concluded that the best interests of European colonizers were not necessarily the best interests of Africans themselves. Consequently, the former colonies of Africa began one after another to reorganize themselves as independent nations where blacks governed. (South Africa remained an exception, with apartheid mostly undisturbed as late as 1990).

The move for racial self-determination unfolded within countries as well as between countries. During the 1960s in the United States, for example, African-American citizens began to demand those protections promised them by the Constitution but denied them by northern practice as well as southern law. In the United States as in Africa, however, dismantling the system of racial discrimination cost lives: of Martin Luther King, of Bobby Seale, of several members of the Black Panthers. Peaceful efforts toward civil and human rights turned impatient, then strident, and finally lethal, with school buses overturned and burned in cities like Boston and Louisville, and with students killed by authorities at places like South Carolina State College.

During the 1970s and 1980s, too, shifting populations and changing patterns of immigration brought increasing numbers of non-Europeans into the United States. By 1990, for the first time, Americans of European descent were in the minority in California, a harbinger of a new America. As these new immigrants chased the American dream and sought to share political and economic power, they often opened businesses in inner cities, where their close proximity to older ethnic groups caused turmoil and occasionally violence. Fleeing this volatile environment, the upper and middle classes moved to the suburbs in large numbers, taking their tax dollars with them and so accelerating both the decline of cities and the resegregation of America.

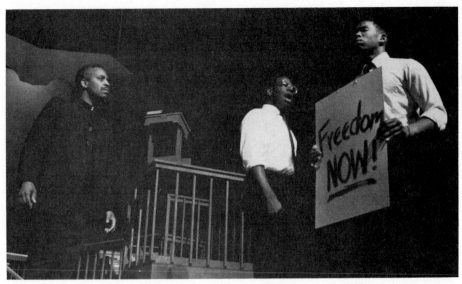

FIGURE 16-2. **Drama in the World: Race.** Along with the war in Vietnam, the drive for civil rights for African-Americans dominated the social turmoil of the 1960s. Plays by blacks called for urgent action. *Blues for Mr. Charlie,* in production by New WORLD Theatre, University of Massachusetts, Amherst. *(Directed by Roberta Uno Thelwell, designs by James MacRostie.)*

By the 1970s, conflicts over gender had joined those generated by race. A world-wide feminist movement exposed a range of discriminations against women—from physical enslavement through medical maltreatment to unequal pay. Although the inequalities varied across countries, cultures, and classes, women in every category were shown to be routinely disadvantaged when compared with their male peers. International Women's Year (1975) focused attention on strategies for securing equitable treatment for women in areas such as education, jobs, legal status, and pay.

The social and political turmoils subsided during the 1980s, when a kind of backlash set in. Thus, in the early 1990s, the end of colonialism and the equality of race and gender remained promises unfulfilled. Nonetheless, the new perspectives brought about through the struggles of the 1960s and 1970s continued to enrich political and social debate. The old ways of seeing the world now seem to be breaking down. New questions are being asked, new explanations sought. Society seems to be searching for a new paradigm, a new model by which to explain the world in which we live.

Emerging Problems

People by the 1990s were challenged by problems to which they as yet lacked solutions: How could an expanding population meet its needs for energy? How could it deal with the safe disposal of waste—human, chemical, nuclear? What could be done to eliminate acid rain, reverse the depletion of ozone, avoid climactic changes? What were the economic and political consequences of cutting down acres of trees, changing patterns of rainfall, disrupting agricultural yields, increasing erosion, and losing through extinction many plants and animals?

Medical advances outstripped ethical answers to increasingly complex issues. What were acceptable moral positions on matters like test-tube babies, surrogate mothers, organ transplants, genetic engineering, rights to life and to death? What was society's responsibility for a graying population, whose large numbers and special needs put a strain on health care systems inequipped to deal with them but whose families were no longer close enough to provide care? Medical science was challenged, too, by a worldwide epidemic of AIDS, a condition whose mysterious attack on the immune system made its cure elusive and so its prevention essential. Because its transmission was often associated with drug use and sexual promiscuity, however, educational programs aimed at teaching methods of self-protection often brought vigorous protests.

In order to solve any of these problems, resources were needed—time, money, personnel. But as the demands of a growing population pressed against limited resources, the discrepancies between rich and poor grew clearer. The gap between

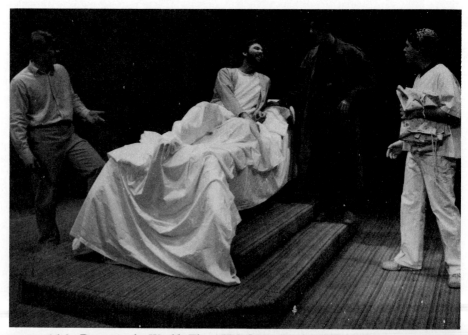

FIGURE 16-3. Drama in the World: The AIDS Crisis. By the 1980s, AIDS was recognized as both a major health and a major social problem. Several AIDS plays were offered, among the most popular, As Is, produced here at the University of North Dakota. (Directed by James B. Graves.)

the haves and the have-nots seemed to widen and in many countries threatened to tear apart the social fabric. As some clamored for the redistribution of wealth, both between and within countries, others sought to preserve the status quo. Much of the period was a see-sawing between the forces of change and those of no-change.

THEATRE, 1960s–1990s

Whenever society is uncertain about its goals and its values, art (including the theatre) is apt to display similar uncertainties. As society seeks a paradigm capable of explaining the age, its theatre will also seek a model that allows it to capture the essence of the age.

And indeed, if anything could be said to characterize the theatre during the 1960s–1990s, it was its *eclecticism*, that is, its use of many diverse styles for its own needs. The theatre buildings of the period were variously shaped and variously located. The theatrical productions were variously conceived and funded (see pp. 95–96). For purposes of discussion, however, we can divide contemporary theatres into two major groups, depending on their major goals: commercial and noncommercial. Both sorts of theatre existed in the major theatrical centers of the United States and abroad. Although reference will be made to western and eastern Europe, our major focus will remain on practices in the United States.

Commercial Theatre

Producing theatre in order to net large profits continued to be the goal of theatres on Broadway in New York, on the boulevards of Paris, and in London's West End. As costs for these productions continued to escalate, long runs grew ever more important and ticket prices rose still higher. The average ticket cost about $10 in 1975, about $30 in 1985, more than $35 by 1990. In 1981–1982 *The Life and Adventures of Nicholas Nickelby* (a dramatization of the novel by Charles Dickens) was able to command a top price of $100 per ticket. As prices rose, both audiences and repertories tended to grow more conservative. In the United States, musicals dominated the Broadway repertory, with comedies comprising most of the remainder. An occasional mystery or serious drama appeared, but none captured the attention of Broadway's audience for long.

Musicals

Early in the 1960s, the most successful musicals had an air of optimism: *Camelot* (1960), *Hello, Dolly!* (1964), *Fiddler on the Roof* (1964), and *Mame* (1966). President John Kennedy's assassination (1963), followed by an escalating war in Vietnam, darkened the public mood.

The Broadway production of *Hair* (1967) marked a turning point. Produced first Off-Broadway by Joseph Papp, *Hair* portrayed a group of impoverished but affable hippies as they lived and loved together against a background of drug use, civil disobedience, and the military draft. The show's popularity led to the acceptance in

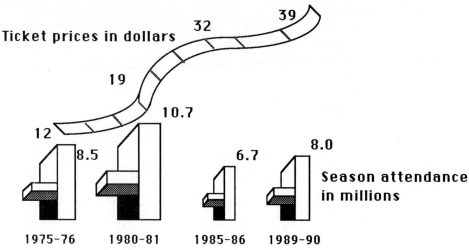

Ticket prices in dollars

39

32

19

10.7

12

8.5

6.7

8.0

Season attendance in millions

1975-76   1980-81   1985-86   1989-90

FIGURE 16-4. **Ticket Prices and Attendance.** As the graph shows, for the past fifteen years, ticket prices have risen steadily but attendance has fallen. (*Data compiled from* Variety, 6 *June 1990.*)

the mainstream theatre of practices formerly taboo: irreverence, four-letter words, and nudity, to cite the most obvious.

The musicals of the 1970s brought fame to Stephen Sondheim, whose *Follies* (1970), *A Little Night Music* (1972), *Pacific Overtures* (1975), and *Sweeney Todd* (1978) all won major awards. *A Chorus Line* (1975) epitomized the 1970s as *Hair* had the 1960s. Moved to Broadway after a successful run at Papp's Public Theatre, *A Chorus Line* told of the lives and hardships of dancers auditioning for a Broadway show. Really little more than a loosely knit series of personally revealing monologues, *A Chorus Line* dazzled audiences through the energy of its dance and touched them with the intimacy of its revelations. Somewhere between a revue and a play, *A Chorus Line* accelerated Broadway's love affair with dance and spawned many imitations. It also solidified the importance of choreographer-directors like Bob Fosse, Michael Bennett, and Tommy Tune. Indeed, by the late 1970s, with the notable exception of Hal Prince, every major director of musicals on Broadway was also a choreographer.

The 1980s echoed the 1970s, with Sondheim's *Sunday in the Park with George* winning both a Pulitzer Prize and a New York Drama Critics Award at mid-decade. Imports from England (*Cats, Evita,* and *The Phantom of the Opera*), adaptations from France (*La Cage aux Folles* and *Les Miserables*), and a rejuvenated old movie (*42nd Street*) joined *Dreamgirls* as the prize-winning musicals of the decade.

The early 1990s pointed no new directions. Revivals of earlier Broadway hits (e.g., *Peter Pan, Fiddler on the Roof*), great spectacles (e.g., *Shogun*), vividly choreographed extravaganzas (e.g., *Grand Hotel*), and tributes to the past (e.g., *City of Angels*) formed the bulk of the offerings.

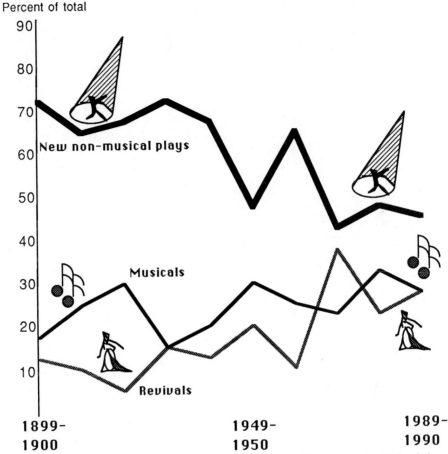

Percent of total

FIGURE 16-5. **Broadway's Repertory, 1900–1990.** During this century, the kinds of plays on Broadway have changed. Expressed as percentage of total, revivals have increased; new musicals have increased; nonmusical new plays have declined. (*Data from* Variety, 6 *June 1990.*)

Comedy

Commercial theatres also relied heavily on comedies to attract audiences and enrich box office receipts. During most of the period Neil Simon was the playwright most successful—phenomenally successful—with audiences. Major plays from the 1960s (*Barefoot in the Park, The Odd Couple, Plaza Suite*) established his reputation as the master gag writer of the theatre. During the 1970s, that reputation was solidified with works like *Last of the Red Hot Lovers, The Prisoner of Second Avenue,* and *California Suite.* In the 1980s, Simon produced semiautobiographical plays that were acclaimed by audiences and reviewers alike: *Brighton Beach Memoirs, Biloxi Blues,* and *Broadway Bound.* In 1991 he won the Pulitzer Prize for *Lost in Yonkers.*

FIGURE 16-6. Musicals. In 1967, the production of *Hair* captured qualities of the decade that delighted youth and enraged traditionalists: sexual frankness, pacifism, public nudity. (*Photograph by Martha Swope, used with permission.*)

Although no one else has come close to Simon's success in comedy, other comic writers have kept commercial comedy a moneymaker. These authors and titles may suggest the ephemeral quality of much commercial comedy: in the 1960s, Jean Kerr (*Mary, Mary*) and Robert Anderson (*You Know I Can't Hear You When the Water's Running*); in the 1970s, Bob Randall (*Six Rms Riv Vu*) and Donald Coburn (*Gin Game*); and in the 1980s, Christopher Durang (*Beyond Therapy*), Beth Henley (*Crimes of the Heart*), and Wendy Wasserstein (*Uncommon Women and Others*).

Again, the 1990s seem to echo rather than to innovate.

Serious Plays

Few significant serious pieces emerged either on or Off-Broadway. Some American playwrights from the 1950s continued writing (Lillian Hellman, Tennessee Williams, and Arthur Miller), but none achieved the acclaim formerly given their work. During the 1960s, Edward Albee won critical acclaim for plays like *Who's Afraid of Virginia Woolf?* (1962), *Tiny Alice* (1963), and *A Delicate Balance* (1966), but critics found less merit in his later plays.

During the 1970s and 1980s, critical attention shifted to David Rabe, David Mamet, and Sam Shepard. In plays like *Sticks and Bones* (1971), *The Basic Training of Pavlo Hummel* (1973), and *Streamers* (1977), David Rabe tried to make sense of America's military experiences. David Mamet attracted attention with *A Life in the Theatre* (1977), *Sexual Perversity in Chicago* (1977), and *Glengarry Glen Ross*, for which, in 1984, he was awarded both a Pulitzer Prize and a New York Drama Critics

FIGURE 16-7. **Comedy.** Although Neil Simon's comedies dominated the period, plays by several younger writers proved popular in the 1970s and 1980s. Shown here, *Beyond Therapy* by Christopher Durang, one of those promising writers. *(Directed by David Runzo, designed by P. Gibson Ralph, University of Rochester Summer Theatre.)*

Award. In plays like *Tooth of Crime* (1972), *Suicide in B Flat* (1976), *Buried Child* (1978, for which he won a Pulitzer), and *Lie of the Mind* (1985, for which he won the New York Drama Critics Award), Sam Shepard treated the effects of American popular culture on art and social structure.

Several other American playwrights have shown promise (for example, Lanford Wilson, Charles Fuller, Marsha Norman, and Ntozake Shange), but their final impact cannot yet be assessed.

Imported Successes

Despite some promising American artists, the American commercial theatre would have been seriously impoverished had it not been for imports. From the 1960s into the 1990s, some of Broadway's most prestigious—and most lucrative—productions were those whose success had already been demonstrated abroad. Early in the period, the British director Peter Brook intrigued New York audiences with his productions of *Marat/Sade* (by the German playwright Peter Weiss) and *A Midsummer's Night's Dream*, among others. England's Harold Pinter intrigued—and sometimes baffled—Broadway audiences with plays like *The Birthday Party*, *The Homecoming*, and *Old Times*. More recently, plays by English feminist Caryl Churchill (*Cloud Nine*, *Top Girls*) and English farceur Michael Frayne (*Noises Off*) have joined blockbuster musicals like *Evita*, *Cats*, *La Cage aux Folles*, and *Les Miserables*, to enrich New York's theatre. By the 1990s, few shows opened on Broadway without having first proved successful elsewhere—in England, in France, in movies, in past Broadway seasons.

Non-Commercial Theatre

The 1960s and 1970s saw the rise of a strong counterculture in the United States, one that questioned old values and traditional ways. The counterculture expressed itself in theatre through a vigorous avant-garde movement that began Off- and Off-Off-Broadway but quickly spread to many towns and cities.

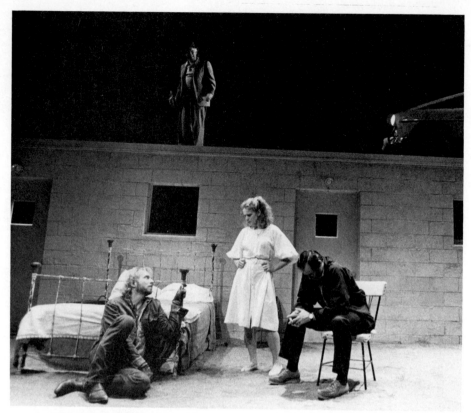

FIGURE 16-8. **Serious Plays.** Sam Shepard has been an important writer of serious plays during the 1970s and 1980s. Shown here, a production of *Fool for Love* at Center Stage, Baltimore. *(Courtesy of Center Stage. Photograph by Richard Anderson.)*

Some in the avant-garde saw theatre primarily as a weapon for political and social change and so sought through it to shake people from their complacency and convert them into soldiers for a social revolution. Such groups often took theatre out of its buildings and into the streets, parks, and even elevators of office buildings. *Street theatre* and *guerrilla theatre* were terms used to describe productions that brought theatre to people, recalling the resemblance of these theatres to street and guerrilla fighters, that is, to small cadres of well-trained, mobile, elite soldiers for the revolution.

Others in the avant-garde thought that theatre was so trivialized and demeaned by contemporary practices as to be impotent and irrelevant. Such groups sought primarily to revitalize the art, restoring its magical power, reintegrating it into the life of the community, and replacing it at the center of artistic life, a position it had once claimed.

Both sorts of avant-gardists agreed that to make theatre once again important to the social, political, and spiritual life of people and their communities would require rethinking several basic relationships: of theatre to life, the other arts, and the media;

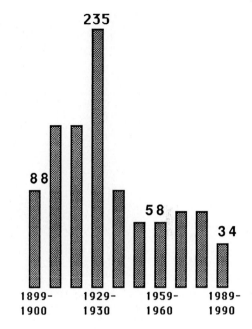

FIGURE 16-9. Broadway Openings, 1900–1990.
As the graphs show, the number of plays offered during each Broadway season reached a peak during the 1929–1930 season and has fallen thereafter, reaching an all-time low during the season of 1989–1990. (*Data from* Variety.)

of theatre to commerce; of actors to audience; of text to performance; and so on. Thus, the works of avant-gardists bore resemblances whether their primary goals were political or artistic (indeed in many groups the two goals were inextricably linked).

So long as political and social turmoil gripped society, as it did in the 1960s and 1970s, the avant-garde remained vital. In the 1980s, however, society developed a more optimistic, if less searching, vision of itself. With less inflation and more national pride, popular presidents, an invigorated economy, and three quickly successful military adventures (Grenada, Panama, Iraq), society became satisfied (some even said self-satisfied), and was disinclined to probe or to protest. In this environment, the avant-garde declined. By the 1990s, only vestiges of the once vigorous alternative theatre movement remained.

Major Non-Commercial Groups

The rise and decline of this avant-garde can be sketched through a brief summary of its major groups.

The Living Theatre (founded 1947) reorganized in the 1960s into a theatrical commune whose actors lived and performed together to promote revolution. Their international reputation came from their political agenda (benevolent anarchy), their incorporating audience members into performances (through discussions, protests, and marches), and their often shocking tactics (including nudity). The group left the United States in 1969, after which its American influence waned.

The San Francisco Mime Troupe (founded 1959) reorganized in 1966 as a collective devoted to social change and thereafter performed original pieces devised around subjects like racism, sexism, militarism, and capitalism. Playing mostly outdoors, the

FIGURE 16-10. **Bread and Puppet Theatre.** In a colorfully painted truck and bus, the actors and their large puppets travel widely to perform for audiences out of doors. See also the second color section. (*Photograph courtesy of Evelyn T. Beck.*)

company developed highly visual and aural productions marked by music, puppets, dance, and nonrepresentational acting. The group's influence declined after the mid-1970s.

The Bread and Puppet Theatre (founded 1961) renounced violence and capitalism in favor of love and community. The group toured, offering plays outside traditional theatre buildings and using common (often found) materials. The company's name came from their use of bread (which it shared with its audience) and giant puppets (who told stories that tried to recapture simple values in a complex world). The group continues to tour from its home in Vermont, but by the 1990s its influence had become mostly local.

The Open Theatre (founded 1963) explored the nature of theatre, the process of acting, and the relationship between theatre and other arts, especially narrative. The group is best known for its attention to ensemble, its use of theatre games and improvisations to build scripts, its use of transformations (actors playing several roles without changing costumes or masks and without clear transitions in dialogue), and its dependence on actors rather than scenery to build dramatic environments (by "becoming" trees, ambulances, tables). The group disbanded in 1966 after it became commercially successful, for it did not wish to change its original goals.

El Teatro Campesino (founded 1965) took short skits into the fields of Southern California in an effort to organize migrant workers. These skits (*actos*) were performed in a mixture of Spanish and English and were supplemented with signs and masks to help workers (some of whom spoke only Spanish, others only English) follow the story. After a riot-related death in 1970, the company became a religious commune devoted to revitalizing Chicano culture. It replaced *actos* with *mitos* (myths) and moved gradually toward an accommodation with the political and theatrical mainstream.

Charles Ludlam and the Ridiculous Theatrical Company (founded 1967) appealed mostly to a culturally and theatrically literate audience. Ludlam's scripts relied on "cultural recyclings": that is, he included snippets of dialogue, characters, and events from many sources and counted on the audience to recognize and appreciate the allusions. The company's performance style was highly theatrical, often camp, and noted for a kind of sexual ambiguity. Most productive in the 1970s, the theatre continued even after the death of Ludlam from AIDS in 1987, but its future is now uncertain.

Richard Foreman and the Ontological-Hysteric Theatre (founded 1968) sought to compel audiences through an accumulation of details, all controlled by Foreman himself: he wrote the scripts, designed the sets and costumes, recorded the sound track, directed the (usually untrained) actors, and ran the control boards. Foreman's goal was to cause audiences to create rather than merely to receive a performance. Important through the late 1970s, Foreman's work had lost urgency by the mid-1980s.

Robert Wilson and the Byrd Hoffman School of Byrds was heavily influenced by practices in music, dance, sculpture, painting, and cinema. Wilson sought a "theatre of images" rather than of words. Through manipulating time, space, and sound, he developed works that had an incantatory, trancelike quality and myriad sensory impressions. Although Wilson is still working, his influence was strongest during the 1970s and 1980s.

Mabou Mines, often grouped with Wilson and Foreman, shared their interest in manipulating time, space, and sound and in using techniques of film and painting. They differed, however, in their tendency to work collaboratively, to create scripts that told something akin to stories, and to incorporate both the floor and the back wall in their visual composition, thus reordering the audience's customary angle of perception. The group's major works date from the 1970s.

Major Non-Commercial Movements

Related to, but separable from, the avant-garde were two theatre movements directly tied to political movements: the black theatre movement was tied to the Black Power movement and the women's theatre movement to the feminist movement. Although these two theatrical movements shared many basic assumptions, they differed profoundly in several ways.

BLACK THEATRE. Although black performers in America date from well before the Civil War, and black theatre companies were firmly established within black communities by the end of the nineteenth century, their performers and plays seldom reached America's commercial theatres until midway in this century.

FIGURE 16-11. **African-American Theatre.** Although often neglected in standard histories of American theatre, African-Americans have a rich tradition of plays and performances dating from the nineteenth century. *The Escape,* the first play by a black ever to appear in print (1858), is shown here as produced at the University of Iowa during the 1980s. *(Photograph by Winston Barclay, courtesy of the University of Iowa, Office of University Relations.)*

Before the 1960s, most *commercial* plays featuring black characters had been written by whites, who often stereotyped blacks and placed them in inferior social positions, where they were patronized by wealthier, wittier, and more powerful white characters. Paul Green's *In Abraham's Bosom* (1926), Carson McCullers' *The Member of the Wedding* (1950), and Marc Connelly's *Green Pastures* (1930), although sensitive and thoughtful treatments of black characters by white playwrights, nonetheless displayed many of the common stereotypes.

Public images died hard, but they did die. The French playwright Jean Genet, in *The Blacks* (1959), reversed the traditions of the minstrel show and used black actors in white face to display the abuses of power. Although many American blacks rejected the play's thesis—that blacks will come to power only by adopting the tactics of their white oppressors—few failed to realize that the play represented a turning point in the portrayal of black people. In 1959, too, Lorraine Hansberry's *A Raisin in the Sun* appeared, an early portrait of black family life in which the peculiar tensions between women and men were sympathetically and sensitively sketched. When she won the Pulitzer Prize for drama, she became the first black woman so honored, and her play is now considered an American classic.

With the racial turmoil of the 1960s and the early 1970s, blacks turned in large numbers to the arts as a way of demanding change and repairing their ruptured society: "Black Art is the aesthetic and spiritual sister of the Black Power concept." The black theatre movement is dated from 1964 and the production of LeRoi Jones's first two plays, *The Toilet* and *Dutchman,* both of which presented a chilling picture of racial barriers, human hatred, and the senseless suffering that results from racism. Thereafter, the stereotypical stage Negro was increasingly replaced by more honest, if often less agreeable, black characters. Throughout the 1960s and the early 1970s, Jones (now known by his Muslim name, Imamu Amiri Baraka) remained the most militant and best known black playwright, with works like *Slave Ship* (1967) and *The Death of Malcolm X* (1965).

Alongside such antiwhite and separatist works were plays depicting the politics and economics of life within the black community. Douglas Turner Ward's *Day of Absence* (1967) poked fun at whites as they were outwitted by cleverer blacks, whose disappearance for a single day led to the collapse of the white social structure; Alice

FIGURE 16-12. **African-American Theatre.** Lorraine Hansberry's *A Raisin in the Sun* was the first play by a black woman to be produced on Broadway. Along with *Raisin*, her autobiographical *To Be Young, Gifted, and Black* remains a popular play in college repertory, as in this production at South Carolina State College. *(Directed by Frank Mundy, designed by Robert Osei-Wusu.)*

Childress's *Mojo* (1970) suggested that black men and women could work out their differences and exist happily as equals if they loved and respected one another.

By the mid-1970s, black authors felt free to criticize other blacks. Ntozake Shange's *For Colored Girls Who Have Considered Suicide/When the Rainbow is Enuf* (1976) explored the double oppression of being black and female and presented a most unflattering portrait of black males, some of whom were portrayed as brutalizing black women as they themselves had been previously brutalized. Originally staged in a black theatre, this powerful "choreopoem" eventually moved to Broadway, where it captivated audiences and earned the coveted Tony Award. With the success of *Colored Girls*, it became clear that plays once considered suitable only for black audiences could be successful in the mainstream of America's commercial theatre.

A few of the major authors and their best-known works can serve to indicate the robust state of black theatre from the 1960s through the 1980s: Ed Bullins, *The Electronic Nigger* (1968); Lonne Elder III, *Ceremonies in Dark Old Men* (1968); Charles Gordone, *No Place to Be Somebody* (1969); Adrienne Kennedy, *The Owl Answers* (1969); Charles Fuller, *A Soldier's Play* (1981); and August Wilson, *Fences* (1987).

Among the major theatres dedicated to producing black plays for primarily black audiences were the Negro Ensemble Company, the New Lafayette Theatre, and Spirit House (all in the New York area) and the Watts Writers Workshop, the Performing Arts Society of Los Angeles, and the Inner City Cultural Center (in the Los Angeles and San Francisco areas). Black theatres, like black plays, served their audiences in very different ways. In Los Angeles, for example, while one theatre specialized in revolutionary pieces, another, across town, was producing a "black version" of *Death of a Salesman*. Both believed they were serving the particular needs of their specific audiences.

With new plays and special theatres came calls for a new criticism. Some black critics took the position that their audiences saw and understood art in ways different from whites. Traditional aesthetics were at best irrelevant and at worst corrupting. Those black artists and critics sought an aesthetic that was moral and corrective, one that supported plays that, in a direct and immediate way, affected the lives of black theatregoers. A black critic explained, "The question for the black critic today is not how beautiful a melody, a play, a poem, or a novel is, but how much more beautiful [that] poem, melody, or play [has] made the life of a single black man." This attack on the accepted canon of Western drama raised issues that were still being debated in the 1990s.

WOMEN'S THEATRE. Whereas black theatre and drama arose from the social upheavals of the late 1950s and 1960s, women's theatres were a phenomenon of the 1970s, during which increasing numbers of people, mostly female, banded together into theatrical units that aimed to promote the goals of feminism, the careers of women artists, or both. By the mid-1970s, more than forty such groups were flourishing; by 1980, more than a hundred such groups had formed. Unlike black theatres, which were usually found in urban settings and amid high concentrations of blacks, women's theatres sprang up in places as diverse as New York City and Greenville, South Carolina.

The theatres ranged in size from those depending on one or two unpaid and inexperienced volunteers to organizations of professionals numbering into the hundreds. Budgets, too, varied widely, with some groups existing on a shoestring and the good wishes of friends and others displaying a financial statement in the hundreds of thousands of dollars. Organization, repertory, working methods, and artistic excellence were highly diversified, but the groups all shared the conviction that women had been subjected to unfair discrimination based on their gender and that theatre could serve in some way to correct the resulting inequities.

Like the black theatres, the women's theatres attempted to serve different audiences and to serve them in different ways. Some groups, like the Women's Interart in New York City and the Los Angeles Feminist Theatre, existed primarily to provide employment for women artists. Such groups, seeing that women had inadequate opportunities to display their crafts, served as a showcase for the works of women playwrights, designers, and directors. Because their goal was to display women's art in the most favorable light possible, artistic excellence was a primary goal of each production. Critical acceptance by the theatrical mainstream was the ultimate measure of success. But other groups, like the now-defunct It's All Right to Be Woman Theatre (also in New York), believed the problems of women to be so deeply rooted in the society that only a major social upheaval could bring about their correction. Such groups were revolutionary and tended to adopt tactics designed to taunt, shock, or shame a lethargic society into corrective action. These groups cared not at all for

FIGURE 16-13. **Women's Theatre.** Since the 1970s, many companies have formed specifically to do plays by, for, and about women. Shown here is one such company, Split Britches, performing an original play also named *Split Britches*. *(Photograph courtesy of Split Britches.)*

the approval of the established critics, because they believed that traditional theatre was a male-dominated, and hence oppressive, institution.

Two techniques in particular came to be associated with revolutionary women's theatres: a preference for collective or communal organization and the use of improvised performance material, much of it uncommonly personal. Like guerrilla theatres, many feminist groups replaced the traditional theatrical hierarchy (a director leading a team of actors, designers, and technicians) with a leaderless group working together and with the audience to create a theatrical experience. The idea seemed to be that hierarchy suggests competition, and competitiveness is a masculine trait; collectivity, on the other hand, involves cooperation, a quality to be prized in the new social order.

Perhaps this view accounts as well for the groups' frequent preference for scripts that were cooperatively developed through improvisations. The actors, occasionally aided by their audiences, were encouraged to dip into their own experiences of being women in today's society and, from these shared personal experiences, to improvise dramatic presentations. Apparently such efforts, although naive, were capable of provoking audiences to awareness and action, for, in several instances, women reported changed lives as a result of encounters with a feminist production.

During the 1970s and 1980s, three feminist playwrights attracted special attention: Megan Terry, with plays like *Approaching Simone* (1970); Myrna Lamb, for *The Mod Donna* (1970) and *Crab Quadrille* (1976); and Martha Boesing, whose best-known works included *Raped!* (1974), *The Web* (1982), and *Antigone Too* (1984). By 1990, however, these playwrights had moved to other matters: Terry, working as resident playwright of the Omaha Magic Theatre, had begun to explore "humanist" issues; Boesing had resigned her position as resident playwright of the feminist theatre At the Foot of the Mountain, in Minneapolis, to pursue new directions from the west coast; Lamb was no longer active in theatre.

By the 1990s, women's theatres were again in flux. Some, like It's All Right to be Woman, had ceased producing, and some, like Omaha Magic, had moved away from feminism. Others moved in directions being newly pointed by feminism itself—emphasizing differences among women. Through both their composition and their repertories women's theatres in the 1990s celebrated women's diversity—in age, race, ethnicity, and sexual preference. They renewed explorations of the function of gender in life and art, investigating through performance the ways in which society and theatre construct gender. These new directions (earlier pointed by Caryl Churchill) found expression in the works of playwrights like Simone Benmussa (*The Singular Life of Albert Nobbs*) and Helene Cixous (*Portrait of Dora*) and in theatre companies like Split Britches and Spiderwoman.

New Directions: Performance Art

Performance art probably began in European art circles of the turn of the century among the dadaists, and it found echoes in the happenings of the 1960s. Its resurgence in the 1980s has made performance art now the most energetic expression within the avant-garde. It is a form that defies traditional categories like theatre or dance or painting and that varies widely among its practitioners. As its name suggests, it depends on both performance and art, and despite its diversity it tends to share certain traits, among them:

- A preference for a nonlinear structure, one unified more often by images and ideas than by stories.

- An emphasis on visual and aural rather than literary elements.

- A tendency to mix elements of several arts, especially music, dance, painting, and theatre.

Although performance art includes many group works, a large proportion of the works are conceived and performed by individual artists working alone (or mostly alone).

Performance art regularly probes the boundaries between life and art and among the several arts. Its frank experimentation has made it controversial not only among those who resist blurring the boundaries of arts but also among those who resent its

FIGURE 16-14. **Performance Art.** Contemporary performance artist Holly Hughes is controversial in part because of her frank treatment of the politics of gender and sexuality. *(Photograph used with permission of © Dona Ann McAdams.)*

often graphic portrayal of (to them) repugnant ideas or activities (e.g., feminism, homosexuality, pornography). Performance artist Holly Hughes, for example, speaks of herself as "a lesbian scientist" whose work is to experiment with "polymorphous perversity." Karen Finley, another major performance artist, is known for solo performances that unfold as first-person, fragmented narratives on often painful subjects (like child abuse and rape) joined to strong visual images (like smearing food on her body).

It should not be surprising that several performance artists (including Karen Finley and Holly Hughes) were among those censured during the battles over funding by the National Endowment of the Arts during 1989 and 1990. (Both subsequently sued the NEA.)

The Avant-garde and the Commercial Theatre

Except for performance art, relatively little experimental work was still underway by the 1980s and 1990s. Some of the groups had ceased producing; some had moved toward the mainstream; some continued their earlier work, simply echoing themselves and their early experimentation. Indeed, except for the work of performance artists

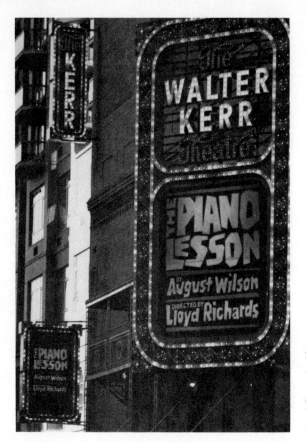

FIGURE 16-15. **Trends: Mainstreaming African-American Playwrights.** August Wilson continues to be a major Broadway playwright who now has several award-winning plays to his credit. Shown here, the marquee of a major Broadway theatre playing his *The Piano Lesson.*

and some of the women's theatres, most of the vitality of the avant-garde of the 1960s and 1970s had dissipated.

Nonetheless, several of the directions pointed by the avant-garde in the 1960s and 1970s were visible, if modified, in the commercial theatres of the 1980s and 1990s. The commercial theatre of today, unlike that of the 1940s and the 1950s

- Exercises greater freedom with respect to language, dress, and subject. Nudity and profanity are readily accepted and previously taboo subjects are now freely treated—e.g., *Torch Song Trilogy* (1983, homosexuality), *'Night Mother* (1983, suicide), and *As Is* (1985, AIDS).

- Includes and awards prizes to plays by African-American authors—e.g., *A Soldier's Play* by Charles Fuller (Pulitzer, 1982), *Fences* (Tony, 1986; Pulitzer, 1987) and *The Piano Lesson* (Pulitzer, 1990) by August Wilson.

- Includes and awards prizes to plays by female playwrights in larger numbers than before—e.g., *Crimes of the Heart* by Beth Henley (Pulitzer, 1981), *'Night Mother* by Marsha Norman (Pulitzer, 1983), *The Heidi Chronicles* by Wendy Wasserstein (Tony, 1989).

FIGURE 16-16. **Trends: Emphasis on Visual Rather Than Literary Elements.** The language of the theatre is increasingly what is seen rather than (or at least in strong addition to) what is heard. Commanding images are shown here in *A Full Moon in March* by W. B. Yeats, directed by James W. Flannery at the University of Ottawa Drama Guild.

- Offers new opportunities for diversity among performers—e.g., *Zoot Suit* (1979, Chicano), *Children of a Lesser God* (1980, hearing impaired), *Driving Miss Daisy* (1988, African-American), *M. Butterfly* (1988, Asian).

- Uses ensembles and improvisation as the basis of commercially successful scripts—e.g., in *A Chorus Line* (1976) and *Quilters* (1985).

- Continues a long-recognized trend toward less literary and more visual and aural theatre.

- Continues a trend toward mixing and merging theatre with other arts.

CHAPTER SEVENTEEN

WORLD THEATRE

It is possible to give only a brief survey of theatres outside the European tradition. The focus of this book has been the self-aware narrative theatre derived from that of ancient Greece and now the dominant theatre of Europe (including the Soviet Union), North America, and Central and South America. That theatre is now also important in most of the places to be discussed in this chapter, where a Western theatre form often exists alongside a non-Western (for them, traditional) theatre of quite different type.

International mass communication and high-speed, cheap transportation have made international cross-influences important factors in contemporary art. Cultural influence tends to follow political and economic influence. The present world position of the United States has given American culture great importance in non-Western cultures: McDonald's hamburgers appear in Moscow, Coca-Cola cans alongside roads in central Africa. With these come films and television and, with them, ideas of impersonation and dramatization and theory different from indigenous ideas. The result is sometimes a mixture.

It is not always possible, therefore, to identify purely non-Western forms in non-Western cultures: cross-influence has already had its effect. Nor is it any longer possible, especially in former colonial areas (especially Africa) to say what—if any—theatre existed before the Western idea of theatre arrived.

RITUAL

Africa, along with pre-Columbian North America, Southeast Asia, and parts of the Pacific, raises the unanswerable question of whether or not certain social and religious forms can be considered as theatre. Generally, these forms are lumped under the word *ritual*, although they include widely different activities in vastly different cultures.

Those rituals of non-Western cultures that are most often suggested as forms of theatre share certain common elements:

- Communal binding of all those present, so that the identifying characteristic is not "art" but "community."
- Overlap or eradication of lines between audience and performers.
- Purpose—to heal, to honor, to mourn—very different from the purpose usually given Western theatre (to instruct, to entertain, to make money).

In addition, such ritual events have characteristics that make them formally very different from theatre as we have defined it:

- Indifference to an established (theatre) space.
- Diffused focus; an event may take place over several miles of countryside, without audience or with audience unable to see any but flashes of the event.
- Lack of visual clues to locale or anything resembling scenery.

Some western theatre people, however, have been drawn to such rituals because of their incorporation of elements sometimes found in Western theatre:

- Masks.
- Costumes.
- Dance and music.
- "Text," although not written text; rather, an orally transmitted, sometimes improvised one.

PARATHEATRICAL FORMS

Other than these still-debated rituals, traditional non-Western forms that are related to theatre and that have received much attention from Western theatre scholars include:

- Storytelling, often with music (or at least drumming) and mime; for example, the *griot* of West Africa and the *meddah* of Turkey.

- Cultural transmission—the passing on of knowledge in cultures without writing. This varies enormously, from simple but expert pantomime of birds and animals (Botswana) to elaborate instruction in traditions through pantomime, song, and dance.

- Dance, often with narrative and elaborate theatrical effects, especially costumes and masks—for example, the elaborate temple dances of Southeast Asia.

- Puppet theatre—for example, the Karagoz shadow puppets of Turkey and the large Bunraku puppets of Japan.

Neither "ritual" nor these other forms are discussed here as kinds of theatre, although elements of them appear clearly in several non-Western theatres.

AFRICA

Africa is a huge and diverse continent. Its precolonial cultures were many and varied, and they persist as both tribal heritages and individual languages. The modern boundaries of Africa are often the boundaries of convenience set up by European colonizers. The colonial period, although relatively short, changed Africa radically; when new African nations became independent in the late 1950s and 1960s, they had to cope with the conflicting realities of old and new, of tribalism and colonialism, of Western and non-Western. By and large, they have done this well, but not without struggle and not without failures. The continent continues to have enormous economic difficulties, particularly as its populations increase and its need for industrialized goods grows. Conditions in many of these countries have not been conducive to the creation of theatre.

For our purposes, Africa can be considered in five geographical areas:

- North Africa, which is considered here with the Islamic world.

- Central Africa, whose theatre has not been a major art.

- West Africa, including both English and French former colonies.

- East Africa, particularly Kenya.

- South Africa.

The colonial influence on these last two areas was primarily British.

Many contemporary African theatre artists have theatrical or educational experience in Europe, and many are attuned to English or French as the language of criticism, and often of drama. As well, universities have commonly become theatre centers. If not specifically Western, the universities are nonetheless modern institutions with structures like those of the industrial nations' universities, which they often emulate. They frequently have departments of drama and grant advanced drama

FIGURE 17-1. **Masks.** These West African wood masks, like those of many other societies, have cultural and often ceremonial significance. Yet, masks are also an element of theatre, so that the cultural, the ceremonial, and the theatrical overlap.

degrees. Thus, even while being the main force in encouraging a native theatre, the universities exist in a Western environment. The African universities most important to the growth of theatre have been the University of Ibadan (Nigeria), the University of Ghana, the University of Dar es Salaam (Tanzania), Makerere University (Uganda), and the University of Nairobi (Kenya).

Colonialism has left a difficult heritage. African theatre artists often find themselves caught between imperfectly understood indigenous forms and imported European ones; the situation has been complicated sometimes by strong European efforts to change or stamp out the indigenous forms, whose history has thus been distorted or lost. The result in many countries has been what David Kerr has called "syncretic" drama and theatre, a mixture of the indigenous and the imported. He has identified two aspects of European theatre that are likely to be rejected, however, even in such syncretic theatre: "individual authorship, and the separation of the audience from the performance."

Because, however, most African nations are highly politicized, the use of a given form is itself a political act; and, where the government is repressive, the selection of a given form may result in the repression of that form. African governments themselves have sometimes been as repressive of indigenous theatre as the colonial governments were.

Contrarily, European influence seems to have encouraged the creation of some forms, if only as coded or masked parodies of colonialism—for example, the *malipenga* of Malawi in Southeast Africa, a blend of military marching, song, spectacle, and witty commentary.

West Africa

The francophone (French-speaking) drama of several former French colonies is vigorous, in part because of continuing ties with Paris. In the mid-1980s, one scholar identified nearly three hundred francophone plays in print since independence. Of those published after 1980, half came from only two countries, Senegal and Cameroon; another quarter came from Ivory Coast and Congo, with the remainder divided among seven nations, some of which (Zaire, for example) are more properly seen as Central than West African.

In formerly English-speaking areas, two nations stand out:

Ghana

A native theatre form, concert party theatre, emerged in the 1920s. (*Concert party* is itself a British term.) It was narrative vaudeville, sometimes funny but sometimes serious, dealing mostly in subjects from domestic life. The leading figure was Ishmael Johnson, called the first professional actor in Africa. Efua Sutherland, one of Ghana's outstanding dramatists and theatre artists, has said that "Concert Party Theatre is the only fully evolved indigenous form of theatre. . . . It enjoys a countrywide appeal."

In the 1950s, the Ghana Drama Studio (Accra) was founded by Efua Sutherland. There, she produced new Ghanaian plays, including her own *Foriwa* (1967). Ama Ata Aidoo (also a woman) is the author of *Anowa* (1970) and other plays. Both dramatists, as well as others in Ghana's theatre, have had close connections with the University of Ghana. More recently, playwrights like J. C. de Graft (*Muntu*, 1976) and Asiedu Yirenkyi have gained notice.

Nigeria

Nigeria is a very large nation with dense population centers and many universities. Out of one of its dominant languages, Yoruba, has come a traditional masked performance, the Alarinjo, on which the "father figure" of Nigerian theatre (as one Nigerian critic has called him), Hubert Ogunde, drew. Creator of a native concert party form, Ogunde wrote and produced many plays (e.g., *Yoruba Ronu*, 1964) for his own traveling troupe and was a seminal figure in an indigenous form, Yoruba opera. Rich in music, Yoruba opera is performed by touring companies that are able to create with Yoruba audiences some of the communal feeling of ritual. In part, this communality is possible because of the plays' use of traditional stories and moral ideas. Other important Yoruba-opera actor-dramatists have been Kola Ogunmola and Duro Lapido, the latter the head of the Duro Lapido National Theatre.

FIGURE 17-2. **Modern African Drama.** West Africa, particularly, has a vigorous drama with roots in both native and European forms, and a subject matter close to current events. Here, Chris Nwamuo's *The Prisoners*, the Nigerian Universities Theatre Arts Festival, 1986.

Unquestionably, however, the most important figure in Nigerian theatre has been Wole Soyinka, winner of the Nobel Prize for Literature in 1986. Soyinka's first play was produced while he was at the Royal Court Theatre in London; his later plays, like *The Trials of Brother Jero* (1964), have gained international acclaim and have (as with many African theatre people) got him into trouble with the government during periods of stress. Nigeria continues to have an active theatre scene, with theatre training at several universities; such activity has encouraged newer playwrights like Femi Osofisan (See Figure 17-3.)

FIGURE 17-3. **Modern African Theatre in the United States.** Nigerian playwright Femi Osofisan's *Farewell to a Cannibal Rage*, directed by Sandra L. Richards at Stanford University. Designed by John B. Wilson. *(Alexander Stewart photo.)*

East Africa

Kenya

Markedly different from West Africa, the East African nation of Kenya is distinct in both culture and language. Masks, for example, are virtually unknown in Kenya; the dominant language, Kiswahili, is not spoken west of the Zaire border.

The outstanding theatre figure of Kenya is Ngugi Wa Thiongo. Ngugi's plays and novels were concerned in the 1960s with the problems of independence and freedom from Western influence and, in some cases, with much earlier historical conflicts of his Kikuyu people (the education crisis of the 1920s, for example). However, plays like *I Will Marry When I Want* (written with Ngugi wa Mirii, 1980) have powerful implications for postindependence Kenya. As a result, Ngugi has had difficulty performing in recent years: his theatre company at the Kamiri Cultural Centre was forbidden to play in 1982, and he was for several years in detention outside Nairobi, the capital. He has left the country.

Elsewhere in East Africa, Tanzania has tried to encourage the growth of Kiswahili theatre, and Uganda saw the beginnings of a native theatre, but political events— particularly the waves of violence in Uganda from the late 1970s on—have muted the importance of theatre.

Characteristics of East and West African Theatre

Distinct as they are in language, East and West African theatre share certain characteristics. Their common colonial history and strong efforts at pan-African awareness have, perhaps, tended to bring them together despite obstacles.

The theatres have in common:

- Frequent connections with the universities, especially cultural centers and departments of African studies.

- Use of (mostly) amateur performers.

- Openness to various kinds of theatre space.

- A developing body of indigenous theory and criticism.

As well, certain qualities are common to their dramas:

- Extensive use of nonrealistic elements, especially music and dance.

- Extensive use of recognizable cultural elements: proverbs, drumming, cultural symbols, gestures, history.

- Didacticism.

- Openness to dramatic symbolism, including symbolic character.

- Looseness of structure and largeness of cast, idea, and scope.

- Use of both African and Western languages—typically English or French, a regional language (Yoruba, Hausa, or Kiswahili), and sometimes a tribal one.

These African plays are not as well known as they should be in the United States, perhaps precisely because of their most typical elements, which make them very different from Western commercial realism.

South Africa

South Africa remains a colonial nation in that power is vested in its white minority. As a result, its most visible art is colonial, and theatre is Western theatre in the white areas of the cities. White forms of mediation feature plays from Broadway and London and largely ignore black theatre, thus making themselves elements of white domination.

However, a black "township theatre" came into being decades ago. Originally celebratory rather than confrontational, it highlighted musicals that combined elements of Broadway with indigenous dance and music (*King Kong* had a successful international tour); the leading figure was Gibson Kente. The increasingly heated atmosphere of the sixties and seventies saw more political theatre, which was repressed by the government. Out of it, however, by way of several universities, came an integrated, multiracial theatre not associated with the white establishment; its most successful examples are the Space Theatre in Cape Town and the Market in Johannesburg.

A playwright of great international importance has appeared in South Africa: Athol Fugard. Widely produced in Europe and the United States, Fugard is the author of plays that accept the current Western idea of drama as their base. Usually realistic, these plays have made powerful presentations of the South African racial crisis on the world's stages—for example, the 1982 success of 'Master Harold' . . . and the Boys.

Although Fugard, who is white, has received by far the most international atten-

FIGURE 17-4. **Theatre in South Africa.** Matsemala Manaka is one of South Africa's important new playwrights. Here, Thelma Pooe in Manaka's *Children of Asazi*, directed by the playwright; the production was part of *Woza Afrika*, a festival of South African theatre that toured the United States in the late 1980s. (*Courtesy of the New Playwrights Theatre, Washington, D.C.*)

tion, black South African playwrights and artists like Percy Mtwa, Mbongani Nzema, and Musemala Manaka are of great importance to the new South African theatre.

THE ISLAMIC WORLD

With the appearance of the prophet Muhammed in the late sixth century A.D., a new religion, Islam, spread rapidly from the Arabian peninsula: north into the Near East; west along all of Mediterranean Africa and down the East African coast; and east into India and Southeast Asia. For complex reasons, the world of Islam was hostile to theatre (although not to storytelling, puppetry, and dance). As well, it drastically limited the public life of women, including their appearance on the stage.

Islamic peoples developed a highly sophisticated literature, especially in Persian and Arabic, along with other arts; theatre, however, was largely ignored until the nineteenth century. Turkey was an exception.

Turkey

The Seljuk Turks were Islamic but not Arabic. They conquered what was left of the Byzantine Empire, taking Constantinople in 1453. They thus became the last heirs of what was left of Rome—and perhaps of Rome's theatre.

The Seljuk rule was fairly tolerant and allowed residence by foreign enclaves, including Jews and Christians. Occupying parts of modern Rumania, Bulgaria, and Greece, as well as Turkey, the Seljuks maintained contacts with both Europe and the East. Their successors, the Ottoman Turks, founded a new empire that, in turn, weakened until, following their alliance with Germany during World War I, they were replaced by a republic under Kemal Attaturk. The new government brought about the emancipation of women, then the founding of a state theatre and conservatory in the 1930s, led by Muhsin Ertugrul. Contemporary Turkey has professional theatre companies that perform Western and Turkish plays, and Turkey has a vigorous film industry.

Traditional Turkish Theatre

Turkey also had a popular, traditional theatre that has now effectively disappeared. A popular comic form called *orta oyunu* persisted into the twentieth century. Although its origins are not known, scholars suggest that it may be a continuation of Byzantine mime, taken over by the Seljuk Turks after their conquest of Constantinople. Some similarities to Italian *commedia dell'arte*—comic regional types, improvisation, stock costumes and characters—suggest influence but may be the result of a common root or may be coincidence.

Orta oyunu was performed by traveling troupes that included actors, dancers, and musicians; at the end of the nineteenth century, there were said to be as many as five hundred such performers. At the head of each troupe was the actor who played Pisekar, the central figure; opposite him was the actor who played Kavuklu, his comic foil. Women's roles were played by men. The tone was populist, sometimes rowdy. Playing usually in the open without scenery, the *orta oyunu* actors relied on mimicry,

FIGURE 17-5. **Turkish Theatre.** The state-supported theatre in Ankara, Turkey, staged this production—M. Engin Erim's *Butun Menekseler Annem Kokar,* directed by Semih Sergen. *(Courtesy of the Turkish Culture and Tourism Office, Washington, D.C.)*

comic exaggeration, and theatrical use of the body. Important characteristics of this form of theatre were

- Freedom from established theatre spaces.
- Popularity of subject and language.
- Lack of scenery, except for an all-purpose cloth enclosure or tent.
- Continuity of characters over many years.

Nontraditional Islamic Theatre

A nontraditional theatre is known in Islamic countries, particularly since the late nineteenth century. Generally, such theatre has been the result of Western influence or of imitation of the West. The development of an Islamic theatre apparently came about because of European domination of certain Islamic areas: France in Lebanon; Great Britain in Egypt, Syria, and what is now Jordan; and Italy in Somalia. Following European example, young dramatists began to write and produce plays in Damascus and Cairo, and Cairo became the center for a theatre heavily dependent on music. An important figure early in the twentieth century was the actor-manager Hijazi.

A few women had appeared on the infant Islamic stage—most of them Christians and Jews—but after World War I, a liberal movement in Islam loosened some restrictions. In Cairo, a government-funded theatre was set up in 1948.

Modern Egyptian drama has been dominated by three people: Twfiq Al-Hakim, a pioneering intellectual playwright who showed the influence of both French and English drama; Nu'man 'Ashour, who first used spoken Egyptian, rather than classical literary Arabic, on the stage in plays like *The People Downstairs;* and Rashad Rushdy, called by one critic "the bedrock of the tragic form" for plays like *Egypt, My Love.*

Nonetheless, theatre in Islamic countries cannot yet be called vigorous, although film flourishes, especially in Egypt. Particularly since the rise of Islamic fundamentalism in the 1970s and the economic hardships of the same period, theatre has had the status of a minor, and perhaps a threatened, art.

THE EAST

Major traditional theatres have appeared in a number of cultures of the Orient. The cultures themselves have often been conservative and religious, with the result that arts—including theatre—have often been preserved centuries after their initial creative energies were gone. Elites within the cultures have often prized these arts, seeing in their preservation an expression of their own continuity. As a result, the modern nations that have emerged from these ancient cultures now typically display a dual theatrical sensibility: one track is re-creative and backward-looking, displaying the sensibility of a museum; the other is creative and forward-looking, displaying the sensibility of Western art.

Neither track is "better" than the other. Appreciation of the traditional theatres has changed; like great works of painting or sculpture, they are preserved for their beauty, even though their languages may no longer be the languages of discourse and their styles may be almost foreign. In many cases, experienced audiences for some of these traditional theatres follow performances with annotated scripts open before them, as some seasoned Western lovers of music follow orchestral concerts and operas.

As one Western scholar has pointed out, traditional Eastern theatre is an art of the "invisible world"—the world of religion, often a religion of demons, spirits, and multiple divinities. Generally, these Eastern traditional theatres are profoundly nonrealistic and share certain common elements:

- Highly stylized, dancelike movement.

- Nonrealistic makeup or masks.

- Non-Western dramatic form, meaning that they are not based on Aristotelian ideas of action, unity, and the interrelated parts of the play.

- Acting styles far removed from Western ideas of impersonation, often with radically different uses of the voice (so that Westerners have called some forms "operas"), for which years of rigorous training are required.

Despite similarities, however, traditional Eastern forms are so different from each other that one looks as foreign to an Easterner from another culture as it does to a Westerner.

The theatres that we shall consider come from three modern nations: India, Japan, and China.

India

The multilingual culture of India was already old when Alexander the Great reached the Indus River in 327 B.C. The huge Indian subcontinent stretched from the icy Himalayas to the tropical Indian Ocean coast, broken politically into many units. Dominated early by pantheistic Hinduism, India saw a major shift to Islam in the north after the twelfth century. Europeans began to set up trading enclaves in the sixteenth century, and England began the period of the "British Raj" at the end of the eighteenth, dominating the entire subcontinent from the mid-nineteenth through the mid-twentieth centuries. Independent again after World War II, the subcontinent is now made up of the nations of India, Pakistan, and Bangladesh.

It is the modern state of India that maintains an important tradition of theatre, as well as a minor modern theatre and a world-famous film industry centered in Bombay, Calcutta, and Madras.

Sanskrit Theatre

Sanskrit was the spoken and written language of India, then of its ruling and intellectual classes, until a thousand or so years ago. It was the language of an important treatise on the theatre, the *Natyasastra*, and of the drama.

THE NATYASASTRA. Probably derived from oral tradition and ascribed to the "myth-ical" authority Bharata, the *Natyasastra* was a long treatise on theatre and drama, analogous to Aristotle's *Poetics*, probably written down between 200 B.C. and A.D. 200. Its basic assumptions were those of Hinduism: a universe of unity expressed through multiplicity, therefore aesthetically an art of multiple forms—dance, song, and poetry—unified through total performance into a form that would induce in the receptive audience a state of understanding—*rasa*. The *Natyasastra* is a valuable source of theatrical evidence, revealing an ancient India of touring professional acting companies that included both men and women; of permanent theatres built of wood and stone, with elevated stages and close connections to temples; and of rigid caste limits, restricting this kind of theatre to the high and elitist Brahmin caste.

THE DRAMA. Sanskrit drama included at least a thousand plays in the period A.D. 200–800. Of these, the plays of Kalidasa are best known in the West, and his *Sakuntala*, which reached Europe in the early nineteenth century, is the most often seen. In seven "acts," it follows a highly romantic love action between a king and the modest Sakuntala and includes the intercession of gods, a curse, and a ring that is lost and then found in the belly of a fish. Like much of Sanskrit drama, it took as its source the *Mahabharata*, which, with the *Ramayana*, is the great source work of Hindu culture. *Sakuntala* is a play of many scenes, places, and moods, unified not by action but by *rasa*, the state of perception and emotion (in this case, love) induced in the audience.

POPULAR OFFSHOOTS OF SANSKRIT THEATRE: KUTTIYATAM. Sanskrit, already the language of a small elite, became archaic after about 800; popular languages took its place. In many places in India, Sanskrit theatre absorbed or was absorbed into other

FIGURE 17-6. Kathakali. One of the rich variety of theatre-dance forms of India. (*Courtesy of the Asia Society, New York. Photo by Clifford Reis Jones.*)

forms; the results were highly varied. The most important extant form is *Kuttiyatam*, still performed in the state of Kerala, in southern India. It is characterized by:

- Inclusion of part or all of a traditional Sanskrit play.

- Interpretation of and comment on the Sanskrit by a popular figure, the Vidusaka, who can be satirical, comical, and parodic.

- Performance by family troupes of the *Chakyar* lineage, traceable to the tenth century in Kerala; these actors undergo years of rigorous training.

- Creation of an indigenous theatre architectural type, the *kuttambalam*, which has a square, raised stage with a pillar-supported roof; a rear wall with two doors and two copper drums (for rhythmic accompaniment); and an audience area surrounding the stage on three sides. The *kuttambalam* is built close to a temple so that the actors perform facing the deity.

Kuttiyatam performances go on for several, sometimes many, days. Like Sanskrit theatre, they include totally integrated dance, poetry, music, story, and impersonation. Although aesthetically based in the *Natyasastra*, Kuttiyatam violates Sanskrit purity (its clowning has been called obscene, for example) but offers the possibility of adaptation and change, which pure Sanskrit drama did not.

Non-Sanskrit Theatre: Kathakali

Because of the great importance of movement, especially highly controlled and traditional movement, most Indian theatre has close affinities with dance. Certain forms are often called *dance drama* or *dance theatre* because the dance element is so important. Because they include story and impersonation, some of these forms can be included here; of them, a spectacular example is *Kathakali,* which, like Kuttiyatam, had its origins in Kerala.

Kathakali, like many Indian dramatic types, uses stories from the *Ramayana* and the *Mahabharata;* these are sung by one group of performers while others dance to the accompaniment of loud, fast drumming. No raised stage is used and there is no theatre structure: performers work outdoors on a flat earth square about sixteen feet on a side. The only light is an oil fire. There is no scenery. While the singers recite the text and the drummers pound, the dancers, in astonishing makeup and elaborate but almost abstract costumes, mime, sign, and dance, impersonating characters with intricate hand symbols, facial expressions, and body movements.

Most spectacular of Kathakali elements is the makeup, which can take all day to apply. The entire face is colored, then decorated with lines and planes of other intense colors. False "beards" of rice paste are built up; the eyes are reddened by the insertion of a special seed. In this theatre of the demonic and the divine, such utterly nonrealistic makeup is essential.

All Kathakali performers are male, and the dancers' training takes many years.

Nontraditional Theatre

British residents of India built Western theatres as early as the eighteenth century and began to perform Western plays, to which some Indians were invited. In the nineteenth century, Western theatre became one of the foci of antitraditionalism, and a Western style of Indian drama emerged. The most influential among those who bridged classical and modern Indian styles was Rabindranath Tagore (1861–1941), India's first Nobel laureate. Tagore's ideal of a native drama that would provide a modern fusion of poetry, music, and movement, however, has not been realized. The popular modern Indian form is film, not theatre, and outside cities like Calcutta and Bombay, professional secular theatre does not flourish. The Indian theatrical tradition is religious; the modern state—with its capacity for funding the arts—is secular. The gulf between the two is great.

Japan

Japan, situated on a chain of islands in the Pacific Ocean off the Asian mainland, developed early under Chinese influence and then, after about the fourteenth century A.D., rejected China and its ways. From then until the middle of the nineteenth century, Japan turned inward, deliberately turning its back on the outside, particularly the West, except for minor trading contacts. However, in the 1850s an American fleet "opened" Japan, and thereafter a pronounced political and cultural shift led to the rapid development of one of the world's great modern nations. Despite its defeat

FIGURE 17-7. **Japanese Noh.** Compressed poetic drama and symbolic, non-realistic staging typify this traditional theatre form. (*Courtesy of the Japan Information and Culture Center, the Embassy of Japan, Washington, D.C.*)

and heavy losses in World War II, Japan at the close of the twentieth century is a major technological and industrial power.

Several forces created traditional Japanese theatre: a feudal society with an emperor nominally at its top; a warrior ethic that made the samurai warrior a model and placed the military ruler at the actual head of state from the sixteenth through the mid-nineteenth centuries; and religion, including native Shinto ("the way of the gods"), Chinese Confucianism, and, above all, a form of Indian Buddhism, Zen.

Dance was probably fundamental to all Japanese theatre. Important dramatic theatre developed from or alongside it, incorporating movement forms that demanded special training. Like Indian theatre, then, Japan created an important dance form (Bugaku) and dramatic forms that were nonrealistic, preserved more or less in their ancient forms for hundreds of years.

Two of these forms are of particular interest.

Noh

Noh has been called "the oldest major theatre art . . . still regularly performed." Poetic and austere, it is a theatrical expression of Zen Buddhism. Its originators were a father and son, Kanami (1333–1384) and Zeami (1363–1444), both professional actors attached to a temple. They wrote most of the more than two hundred extant Noh plays, creating a body of work with certain rigid characteristics.

- A three-part structure of *jo, ha,* and *kyu.*
- A form based on the interaction of two characters—the *waki,* as it were an accidental confidant, and the *shite,* the protagonist—with a chorus.
- Classification of plays into five subject categories: god, man, woman, insanity, and demon.

Traditionally, a Noh performance took all day and consisted of five plays—one from each category, in the above order—and an introductory dance, the *okina,* which used an ancient Sanskrit (Indian) text. All five plays have the same active shape:

- *Jo:* the *waki* introduces himself and "travels" (to chorus accompaniment) to a destination symbolized by a pillar on the stage; the *shite* enters, and *waki* and *shite* engage in question and answer to reveal the *shite's* reason for being at that place and his or her concern.
- *Ha:* the *shite* dances; the dance is related (as expression, narrative, or symbol) to the *shite's* concern.
- *Kyu:* the *shite* appears in a new self called forth by the first two sections—for example, a possessing demon or a ghost. Resolution comes from this confrontation with hidden reality.

Noh plots are simple; their abundant exposition seems natural to a form that is concerned not with events but with the effects of past events. The protagonists are usually tormented figures—dishonored warriors, crazed women, guilty priests—whose appearance in the *kyu* section in a different form is, to a Westerner, a kind of exorcism. Profoundly influenced by Zen Buddhism, however, Noh's ideology is intuitive, not rational, and its goal is an understanding reached by a mental leap from appearance to reality.

Modern Noh performances rarely include five plays because of the plays' length and difficulty. The style and staging, however, remain largely unchanged:

- A small, raised stage, with all entrances made along a raised passage (*hashi-gakari*) at one side; at the rear is a wall with a pine tree painted on it.
- Onstage musicians (three percussionists and flute) and chorus, soberly costumed and unmasked.
- Male performers, with the male voice undisguised for female roles.
- A very deliberate tempo.
- Masks for certain characters.

FIGURE 17-8. Japanese Noh in Western Theatre.
A production of Ulick O'Connor's *Deirdre* in Noh style at the Abbey Theatre, Dublin. Directed by James W. Flannery, designed by Chsato Yoshimi.

■ Elaborate and beautiful costumes, but no scenery, and rare, often symbolic properties.

Noh had an important offshoot: Kyogen.

KYOGEN. Of later (fifteenth-century) creation but based in much earlier forms, Kyogen is a comic drama performed between Noh dramas. It seems a contradiction, for it mocks the very austerity and aristocratic spirituality that make Noh what it is. The reason usually given is that Kyogen was written by commoners at a period when commoners attended Noh performances; Kyogen expressed their attitudes. Kyogen is very funny, dealing in the universals of comedy. Its most typical character is a comic servant who serves a feudal lord and is, of course, smarter than he. Kyogen used the Noh stage but no orchestra or chorus.

Kabuki

Although it owes some characteristics to Noh, the far more robust and spectacular form of Kabuki, which appeared in the seventeenth century, quickly established itself as a different and far more popular form. Early censorship actually strengthened the form, leading to much more active and diverse texts (when music and dance were temporarily suppressed) and much more carefully defined acting (when first women, then young men, were banned from the stage).

In its developed form, Kabuki's principal characteristics are:

- Long, fully developed actions in multiact structures.

- Multiplicity of characters and scenes.

- Illusionism, with direct imitation of contemporary (seventeenth-century) life.

The Kabuki also developed its own theatre and style, which included:

- A large raised stage with a raised walkway to it, the *hanamichi,* through the audience (originally, there were two such walkways and a connecting walkway at the rear).

- Spectacular scenery, including the revolving stage, introduced c. 1750 (the first in the world); trap doors; and a front curtain.

- Elaborate but fundamentally illusionistic makeup.

- Complex, beautiful costumes, including the spectacular feature called *hiki-nuki*—costumes so constructed that at a gesture they completely change, literally turning themselves inside out to reveal, for example, a man in armor where a woman had stood.

- All-male companies, with the art of the female impersonator carried to great detail; as a result, Kabuki became above all an actor's, rather than a play-wright's, art. Great Kabuki actors have been declared national treasures, like great paintings or great buildings.

Kabuki stories were drawn from many sources and were often heroic and "ro-mantic." Whereas Noh is a theatre of resignation and withdrawal from the world, Kabuki is a theatre of confrontation and an embracing of the world.

Nontraditional Japanese Theatre

The abrupt influx of Western ideas in the nineteenth century corresponded roughly with the rise of dramatic realism in the West. The result was the somewhat exotic blossoming of several imitations of Western theatre, some of them not very well understood by their practitioners. Two important trends appeared before the end of the century:

- "Political" theatre—the use of a more or less realistic style for partisan plays as Japan encountered party politics.

- Shimpa—a melodramatic, popular form neither Eastern nor Western, using elements of both, including women in female roles.

In addition, a modern theatre that kept pace with theatrical changes in the West emerged after the turn of the century. Although not widely popular, it introduced major Western forms and encouraged a Japanese acting style distinct from Kabuki.

FIGURE 17-9. Japanese *Kabuki*. Spectacular action and gorgeous costumes mark Kabuki performances. *(Photo courtesy of the Japan Information and Culture Center, Washington, D.C.)*

Until the 1930s, leftist and proletarian theatres were important; however, censorship under the war governments of the 1930s and 1940s virtually ended modern drama for that period. After World War II, the American occupation government imposed a new kind of censorship—this one prejudicial to Kabuki and traditional forms—and modern theatres began to appear again. A new Japanese play, Junji Kinoshita's *Twilight Crane* (1950), has been called "a milestone in the history of modern Japanese playwriting"; it successfully fused Japanese art with modern concerns and was widely produced.

Recent nontraditional hits have emphasized plays as diverse as a musical version of *Gone with the Wind* and the plays of Shakespeare. Japan's large cities now have professional nontraditional troupes, but theatre is not a truly popular art; like India, Japan is in love with film.

A small avant-garde drama exists. European in influence, it has shown great concern with the theatre's ability to play on the shifting relationships between appearance and reality—the concern of such European avant-gardists as Pirandello and Genet.

China

Like India's, China's is an ancient culture that developed in a region of diverse geography and languages. Nonetheless, while Europe was struggling to create order after the collapse of Rome, China was already a stable empire whose central administration effectively governed a vast area. Invaders changed the governors but not the institutions of government, and, until the early twentieth century, Chinese society and Chinese culture existed self-sufficiently, exerting influence on Japan and Southeast Asia.

Central to Chinese society were reverence for the past ("ancestor worship") and Confucianism, a moral system based in ideas of stability and family. Social order was strongly marked. Literacy was limited to a small group. Trade and the amassing of wealth were despised. Paradoxically, then, a popular theatre developed whose actors were social outcasts and whose patrons were often wealthy merchants.

The last imperial government of China fell in 1906. Thereafter, more or less stable, more or less democratic governments held on until the Japanese invasion in 1937 and World War II, when much of the country was overrun. In 1949, a communist government under Mao Zedong (old style, Mao Tse-tung) took over. The Cultural Revolution of 1966–1976 saw much traditional Chinese culture attacked. After Mao's death in 1976, Chinese life was liberalized, but since the demonstrations of 1989, free expression is discouraged.

A civilization of many languages and many geographical areas produces many kinds of theatre. One scholar estimates that more than three hundred regional styles of Chinese theatre exist. Nonetheless, they are represented by—and to some extent are being absorbed by—one of them.

Chinese Opera

The Western designation of Chinese theatre as "opera" suggests one of its major characteristics: reliance on song and musical accompaniment. Chinese music is very different from Western music, and the style of production is very different from that of Western opera, but the name persists. Significantly, too, it accurately reflects the minor role of dance in Chinese theatre.

Early precursors included a form of theatre known as early as the ninth century A.D., for which a palace theatre school, the Pear Garden, was established. In the fourteenth-century Yuan dynasty, China's most important dramas were written. Yuan drama included:

- Performance by both men and women.

- Multiact dramatic structure, with one major song per act.

- Division of characters into four types: man, woman, and two types of clowns.

- Reliance on classical novels and history for stories and characters.

A great play of the Yuan period, still performed, was Gao Ming's *The Lute Song* (c. 1360). Hundreds of other plays were written, produced by traveling troupes of actors in temporary theatres throughout southern China.

Classical Chinese theatre as it is now understood—called *Beijing opera* after the city where it appeared (formerly called Peking)—developed in the nineteenth century on the foundation of Yuan and other forms. It is typified by:

FIGURE 17-10. **Beijing Opera.** *Princess Iron Fan.* (*Courtesy of the People's Republic of China.*)

- Multiact dramas.
- All male actors.
- Song and music virtually throughout.
- Division of characters into four major types: male, female, painted face, and clown (*painted face* referring to those using elaborate makeup, e.g., demons and warriors).
- A reliance on traditional sources for stories and characters.

Although the tradition of itinerant actors continued (troupes rarely stayed at the same theatre more than a few days, even in big cities), permanent theatres were built. Beijing opera in the nineteenth century became an enormously popular form. Leading actors moved from one theatre to another in the way that Western opera stars move; the repertory was generally so well known that without rehearsal, they could step into a part in any theatre. The performances themselves relied on centuries-old conventions, on stages all of the same type. Outstanding elements included:

- A raised, pillared stage with an audience on three sides.

- No scenery, entrances left and right, and restriction of large properties to chairs and tables (which could be used as walls, mountains, and so on).

- An acting style removed from reality, the result of up to twenty years of rigorous training in every gesture and slightest facial movement.

- An onstage orchestra and property man.

- Symbols and signs—for example, carrying a whip symbolized riding, and running with small flags symbolized wind.

- Almost unbelievable acrobatics—used, for example, in battle scenes.

Western accounts of nineteenth-century Beijing opera performances described remarkable noise—laughing, talking, and socializing; the orchestra tuning its instruments; actors in a scene but not active drinking tea or blowing noses—but these descriptions may have reflected a corrupt, late stage. However, authorities agree that Beijing opera, like Kabuki, was an actor's art: audiences came to see the great actor only at his great moments. By the late nineteenth century, the rest was a social event. For those great moments, however, there was quiet, and adulation afterward.

One name stands out in later Beijing opera: Mei Lan Fang (1894–1943). A superb actor of women's roles, he toured extensively in the West, restored some classical elements to Beijing opera, and was a force for the preservation of the form through

FIGURE 17-11. Beijing Opera. A class in clown techniques at the Beijing Opera Institute. (*Courtesy of* China Pictorial *and the People's Republic of China.*)

World War II. His memoirs are an important record of actor training and theatre history.

Nontraditional Chinese Theatre

The fall of the last dynasty loosened antitraditional feelings; antitraditionalists turned West. *Uncle Tom's Cabin* was one of the first non-Chinese plays produced (1911). Others followed, bringing disturbing innovations: popular, rather than classical, language; non-Confucian social and moral questions; all-spoken (not sung) drama; and, after 1924, actresses in female roles. The first coeducational theatre school was created in 1930. A new drama emerged, typified by Ts'ao Yu's *Thunderstorm* and his play of World War II, *Metamorphosis,* which encountered difficulties with both the communists and the anticommunists.

With the communist rise to power in 1949, Chinese theatre went into a period of change, some of it under Russian influence (evident in the introduction of classical ballet, for example). It was wrenched from any illusion of stability by the Cultural Revolution in 1966. Led by Jiang Qing, wife of Mao Zedong (and herself a former minor actress), an attack was launched on traditional theatre, and a new drama of revolutionary heroism was preached. A model opera, *Taking Tiger Mountain by Strategy,* was produced, incorporating conventions of Beijing opera but relentless in its revolutionary emphasis. The Cultural Revolution ended with Mao Zedung's death in 1976 and the arrest of Jiang Qing and the Gang of Four.

Contemporary Chinese theatre includes traditional Beijing opera and modern theatre, as well as resurgent regional theatre forms. In addition, the Republic of China (Taiwan) preserves some traditional forms, and opera companies exist in the Chinese communities of Western cities like San Francisco.

A very small avant-garde movement has appeared in China; however, the repressions of 1989 and after have endangered it. With expression rigidly controlled, avant-gardism is likely to withdraw into formalism.

GLOSSARY

(Discussion will be found on the page or pages indicated, where appropriate.)

A-Effect: See *Alienation*.

Absurdism: A style of drama popularized in France after World War II that viewed human existence as meaningless and treated language as an inadequate means of communication. Major authors include Samuel Beckett and Eugène Ionesco. (345–346)

Academy: A group formed to further a specific artistic or literary end; for example, the French Academy and the rhetorical academies of the Renaissance. (277)

Action: According to Aristotle, a causally linked sequence of events, with beginning, middle, and end; the proper and best way to unify a play. More popularly, the single and unified human process of which a drama is the imitation. To some modern critics, an interaction (between dramatic protagonist and others).

Actor-Manager: A starring actor who is head and nominal artistic director of a company; for example, Sir Henry Irving in the late nineteenth century in England. (328)

Actors Equity: See *Unions*. (85)

Actos: Very short, politically significant playlets. Term associated with Chicano theater, particularly the work of El Teatro Campesino. (365)

Aesthetics: Study of the nature of beauty.

Agit Prop: Short for *agitation propaganda*. A kind of political drama popular in the 1920s and 1930s in America. Phrase subsequently used to describe all didactic drama whose social stance was unusually militant.

Alienation: Customary, but perhaps misleading, translation of the German *verfremdung*, "to make strange." Term now almost always associated with Bertolt Brecht's epic theatre, which aims to distance the spectator from the play's action in order to force conscious consideration of the political and social issues raised by the play. Shortened often to A-effect. (347)

Angle Perspective: Multipoint perspective; results when several vanishing points are located away from the center of the stage so that vistas appear toward the wings. (283)

Angle Wing: Wings consisting of two parts hinged together, one rectangular flat placed parallel with the proscenium arch and one (called the return) placed at an angle to it in order to increase the sense of distance. (On a raked stage, the return is not a rectangle but a trapezoid.) (273)

Antiquarianism: The study of the details of past civilizations, often with a view to reproducing historically accurate settings onstage. Movement was popular toward the end of the eighteenth century and is viewed as a precursor to Romanticism. (292)

Apron: That part of a stage that extends in front of the proscenium arch. (81)

Arena Theatre: A theatre in which the audience completely surrounds the playing area. Also called *theatre in the round.* (80–82)

Atellan Farce: A short, rustic, improvised, and often bawdy play especially popular in Rome during the first centuries B.C. and A.D. Possibly the forerunner of the *commedia dell'arte* (see entry). (223)

Audition: A session at which a theatre artist, usually an actor, displays his or her craft in order to secure a job. (135)

Autos Sacramentales: Vernacular religious plays of sixteenth- and seventeenth-century Spain. (265)

Ballad Opera: A "minor" form of musical drama especially popular during the eighteenth and nineteenth centuries in England and featuring political satire interlarded with familiar tunes for which new and topical lyrics were devised; for example, John Gay's *The Beggar's Opera.* (287)

Beat: A rhythmic unit in a play; defined variously by different actors and directors. (172)

Benefit: A performance, the profit of which is set aside for a particular actor, company member, or cause. In the eighteenth and nineteenth centuries, a primary means of supplementing an actor's annual salary. Now, any performance done for charity. (284)

Biomechanics: The concept and the complex of techniques devised by Vsevolod Myerhold to train actors so that their bodies could be as responsive as a machine. (344)

Blocking: Stage movement for actors, given in rehearsal (usually) by the director. (160)

Body Language: Communicable emotional states understood from posture and other conscious and unconscious use of the body. See also *Gesture.* (125–126)

Book: 1. The spoken text of a play or musical; early musicals with stories and dialogue were called *book musicals.* 2. Several flats hinged together and folded together form a *book of flats.* 3. To *book* a production is to schedule a performance of it.

Border: Curtain, or less often flats or cutouts, suspended at intervals behind the proscenium arch to mask the overhead rigging. Particularly important in Italianate settings. (273)

Boulevard: Historically the permanent home of the old traveling-fair theatres of eighteenth-century Paris and later of the illegitimate houses where melodrama and comic opera flourished during the nineteenth century. Now refers to the district of the commercial theatres in Paris and means roughly what the word *Broadway* implies in the United States.

Box: Historically the favored, and most expensive, seats in a theater. Made by sectioning off parts of a gallery, boxes were spacious and outfitted with armed chairs, in contrast to the crowded galleries, whose seats consisted of backless benches, and to the pit, where originally no seats were provided. (81)

Box Set: Interior setting represented by flats forming three sides (the fourth wall being the proscenium line); first used around 1830 and common after 1850. (321)

Breeches Role: Role in which an actress portrays a male character and dresses as a man, presumably adding sexual titillation to dramatic interest. (306)

Broadway: In popular parlance, the area of New York City on and adjacent to the street named Broadway, where the commercial theatre of America is concentrated. (83–86)

Bugaku: Traditional Japanese dance form. (388)

Bunraku: Traditional Japanese puppet theatre using half-life-size dolls manipulated by puppeteers visible to the audience. (376)

Burlesque: In eighteenth- and nineteenth-century theatre, a form of "minor" drama popular in England and featuring satire and parody. In America of the late nineteenth century and the twentieth century, a kind of entertainment originally dependent on a series of variety acts but later including elements of female display (including striptease) in its major offerings. After moving to the fringes of respectability by the 1940s, burlesque disappeared in the United States by the late 1950s.

Business: Activity performed by actor(s) at given points in a performance; for example, the *business* of lighting a cigarette or cooking a meal. See also *Lines of business*.

Byplay: Business that takes place alongside the primary action and that is slightly different from it; for example, in *Tartuffe*, Orgon's behavior under the table while Tartuffe is trying to seduce Orgon's wife.

Catharsis: Aristotle cited as the end cause of tragedy "the arousal and catharsis of such emotions [pity and fear]," a statement popularly understood to mean that tragedy "purges" fear and pity from the audience; but alternative interpretations suggest that tragedy arouses and satisfies such emotions within its own structure and characters. Highly controversial and elusive concept.

Causality: Belief that human events have causes (and therefore consequences); as a result, events are seen as joined in a chain of cause and effect.

Centering: Actor's term for localization of human energy source in the body, usually in the abdomen. (123)

Character: One of Aristotle's six parts of a play, the material of plot and the formal cause of thought; an agent (participant, doer) in the play whose qualities and traits arise from ethical deliberation. In popular parlance, the agents or "people" in the play. (48–51)

Chariot and Pole: An elaborate system for changing elements of the scenery simultaneously. Devised by Giacomo Torelli in the seventeenth century, the system involved scenery attached to poles that rose through slits in the stage floor from chariots that ran on tracks in the basement and depended on an intricate system of interlocking ropes, pulleys, wheels, and windlasses for their simultaneous movement. (273–274)

Chorus: In Greek drama of the fifth century B.C., a group of men (number uncertain) who sang, chanted, spoke, and moved, usually in unison, and who, with the actors (three in tragedy and five in comedy), performed the plays. In the Renaissance, a single character named *Chorus* who provided information and commentary about the action in some tragedies. In modern times, the groups that sing and/or dance in musical comedies, operettas, ballets, and operas.

City Dionysia: The major religious festival devoted to the worship of the god Dionysus in Athens. The first records of tragedy appeared at this festival in 534 B.C., and so it is called the home of tragedy. See also *Festivals*. (210)

Classical: Specifically refers to that period of Greek drama and theatre from 534 B.C. to 336 B.C. (the advent of the Hellenistic period). Loosely used now to refer to Greek and Roman drama and theatre in general (a period dating roughly from the sixth century B.C. through the sixth century A.D., about twelve hundred years).

Climax: The highest point of plot excitement for the audience. (45)

Cloak and Sword Play (*capa y espada*): Romantic Spanish plays of love and dueling—swashbucklers. (264)

Closet Drama: Plays written to be read, not performed. (43)

Comedy: A kind (genre) of drama variously discussed in terms of its having a happy ending, dealing with the material, mundane world, dealing with the low and middle classes, dealing with myths of rebirth and social regeneration, and so on.

Comedy of Manners: Refers most often to seventeenth- and eighteenth-century comedies whose focus is the proper social behavior of a single class. (285)

Comic Opera: A "minor" form of musical drama popular first in the eighteenth century and characterized then by sentimental stories set to original music. Later used to mean an opera in which some parts were spoken (in contrast to "grand opera," where everything was sung). (282)

Commedia dell'Arte: Italian popular comedy of the fifteenth through seventeenth centuries. Featured performances improvised from scenarios by a set of stock characters and repeated from play to play and troupe to troupe. See also *Lazzi*. (275)

Community Theatre: Theatre performed by and for members of a given community, especially a city or town. Usually amateur, with sometimes professional directors, designers, and business staff. (93)

Complication: Ascending or tying action. That part of the plot in which the action is growing tenser and more intricate up to the point of crisis (turning point), after which the action unties and resolves in a section called the *denouement* (see entry). (47–48)

Composition: Arrangement of visual elements for aesthetic effect. (166)

Confidant: In drama, a character to whom another leading character gives private information. (50)

Confraternity: In France, a religious brotherhood, many of which sponsored or produced plays during the Middle Ages. One, the Confraternity of the Passion, held a monopoly on play production in Paris into the 1570s. (244)

Constructivism: A nonrealistic style of scenic design associated with Vsevolod Myerhold and marked by its view that a good set is a machine for doing plays, not a representation of familiar locales. Incorporated simple machines on stage and often revealed the method of its own construction. (344–345)

Continental Seating: First devised by Wagner in the late nineteenth century for his theatre at Bayreuth; eschews a central aisle in favor of entrances and exits at the end of each aisle. (320)

Convention: A way of doing things agreed on by a (usually unstated) contract between audience and artists; for example, characters' singing their most important feelings and emotions is a *convention* of musical comedy. (31–32)

Corpus Christi: A spring festival established in the fourteenth century in honor of the Christian Eucharist at which medieval cycle plays and cosmic dramas (see entry) were often performed. Also see *Festivals*. (237)

Corrales: Spanish theatres of the late middle ages, sited in open courtyards among houses. (263)

Cosmic Drama: Long dramatic presentations popular in the Middle Ages that depicted religious events from the Creation to the Last Judgment. Short plays were combined until the total presentation could last several days or weeks and occasionally a month or more. See also *Cycle play*. (239)

Court Theatre: A theatre located at the court of a nobleman. After the Renaissance, Italianate theatre, whose perspective was drawn with the vanishing points established from the chair of the theatre where the ruler sat, making his the best seat in the house. (273)

Crisis: Decisive moment at the high point of a rising action. (48)

Criticism: The careful, systematic, and imaginative study and evaluation of works of drama and theatre (or any other form of art). (196–197)

Cue: Immediate stimulus for a line, an action, or an effect.

Cycle Play: Medieval (especially English) dramas covering the "cycle" of history from the creation of the world to doomsday. See also *Cosmic drama*. (239)

Decision: In Aristotelian criticism, the most highly characterizing trait of a dramatic agent; the trait that translates idea into action and thus, in Aristotelian terms, unites with plot (in the sense here of action). See also *Plot* and *Action*.

Declamation: A style of verbal delivery that emphasizes beauty of sound, speech, and rhetorical meaning rather than the realistic imitation of everyday speaking.

Deconstruction: A strategy in criticism for finding unintended meanings in a work. Popularized by Jacques Derrida, postmodern strategies have been adopted by feminists and Marxists for social as well as poetic analyses of scripts and performances. (196)

Decorum: In Neoclassical theory, the behavior of a dramatic character in keeping with his or her social status, age, sex, and occupation; based on the requirements of *verisimilitude* (see entry). (267–268)

Denouement: That part of the plot that follows the crisis (turning point) and that includes the untangling or resolving of the play's complications. (48)

Determinism: Philosophical stance undergirding Naturalistic drama that asserts that human behavior and destiny are determined by factors, especially heredity and environment, largely beyond human control.

Deus ex Machina: Literally, "the god from the machine," a reference to a deity who flew in at the conclusion of some Greek tragedies (particularly those of Euripides) to assure the play's appropriate outcome. Popularly, any ending of a play that is obviously contrived. (214)

Deuteragonist: In classical Greece, the second actor.

Diaphragm: Large muscle, located atop the abdominal cavity, that forces air into and out of the lungs and thus figures prominently in the proper production of sound. (126)

Diction: In Aristotle, one of the six parts of a play; also called language; the formal cause of music, the material of thought; the words of a play. Popularly the proper and clear formation of the play's words. (53)

Didacticism: "Teaching." In the theatre, plays are didactic when they emphasize ideological content rather than artistic form.

Dimmer: Instrument for controlling the intensity of light by manipulating the amount of electricity that reaches individual lamps. (189)

Dionysia: A Greek religious festival in honor of the god Dionysus. The City Dionysia and the Rural Dionysia both included drama as a part of the celebration, but the city festival was clearly the dominant one of the two. See also *Festivals*. (210)

Diorama: Distant scene viewed through a cutout or other opening in scenery. Also, a three-dimensional arrangement of figures and painted scenes. (305)

Discovery: According to Aristotle, any passage from ignorance to knowledge within a play, by means of (for example) sign, emotion, reasoning, action. Good discoveries grow out of suffering (awareness) and lead to reversal (change of direction). (47)

Discovery Space: Permanent or temporary space in the Elizabethan (Shakespearean) playhouse that permitted actors and locales to be hidden from view and then "discovered" (or revealed) when needed. Location, appearance, and even invariable existence of the space are hotly disputed. (251)

Dithyramb: A hymn of praise, often to the god Dionysus, performed by a chorus of men or boys; a regular part of the religious festival of Athens after 509 B.C. (207)

Domestic Tragedy: A serious play dealing with domestic problems of the middle or lower classes. In the eighteenth century, a reaction against "regular" or Neoclassical tragedy. See also *Purity of genres*. (294–295)

Double: 1. To play more than one role. 2. *The Theatre and Its Double*, an influential book by Antonin Artaud, calls the Western theatre merely a shadow or *double* of the (to him) true and vital Eastern theatre.

Downstage: That part of the stage closest to the front. In early Italianate theatres, the stage floor was raked (slanted) up from the front to the back; therefore, to move forward on the stage was literally to move "down the stage." (165)

Drama: 1. In the eighteenth century, a serious play (*drame*, in France) that dealt with domestic issues and thus failed to conform to the standard Neoclassical definition of tragedy. 2. Any serious play that is not a tragedy. 3. The literary component of performance, the *play*—often contrasted with the *theatre*.

Dramaturgy: Practice and study of creation of plays for the theatre; the work of the dramaturg. (198–199)

Dress Rehearsal: A final rehearsal in which all visual elements of production, including costumes, are used. Typically a rehearsal that strives to duplicate, insofar as possible, an actual performance. (173)

Drop: Backdrop. Large curtain, usually of painted canvas, hung at the rear of the stage to provide literal and visual closure for the stage setting. (273)

Dual-Issue Ending: Double ending. Ending of a play when good is rewarded *and* evil is punished. Associated with melodrama particularly. (296–297)

Eccyclema: In classical Greece, a machine used to thrust objects or people (often dead) from inside the scene house and into view of the audience. Probably some sort of wheeled platform that rolled or rotated through the *skene's* central door. (214)

Eclectic(ism): Gathering of materials from many sources; popularly a mixture of styles and methods. In twentieth-century theatre, the idea that each play calls forth its own production style.

Educational Theatre: Theatre by and (in part) for students in an elementary, secondary, or collegiate setting. (90–93)

Ensemble: A performing group. Also, a group acting method that emphasizes unity and consistency of performances.

Environmental Theater: 1. Theatre whose performance is the audience's environment, so that the performance surrounds some or all of the audience and the line between performance space and audience space breaks down. 2. Theatre done in nontraditional space.

Epic Theatre: Term originated by Erwin Piscator and popularized by Brecht to describe a theatre where the audience response is objective, not subjective, and where such narrative devices as film projections, titles, and storytelling are used. See also *Alienation*. (347)

Epilogue: A short scene that comes at the conclusion of the main line(s) of action.

Episodic plot: Plot whose incidents are connected by idea or metaphor or character, not by cause and effect. (45)

Existentialism: A philosophical system that lies at the root of absurdism (see entry) whose basic assumptions are the absence of transcendental values, the isolation of humans and their acts, and the lack of causality in the universe. (346)

Experimental Theatre: Any theatre whose methods or goals depart markedly from the mainstream of its day; thus, in the eighteenth century, Romanticism was experimental; in the heyday of American Realism, Absurdism was experimental.

Exposition: Necessary information about prior events, or a part of a play given over to communicating such information; because it is a "telling" and not an enacting of narrative, it is usually nondramatic. (45–46)

Expressionism: A style of theatre popular in Europe after World War I and typified by symbolic presentation of meaning, often as viewed from the standpoint of the main character; distortions of time, space, and proportion are common. (342–344)

Façade Stage: One that puts the actors in front of a neutral (nonrepresentational) surface. (208)

Farce: Form of comedy "stuffed" with laughs that arise not from verbal wit or humane profundity but (usually) mechanics: business, mix-ups, mistaken identities, etc. (55)

Feminist Criticism: Analyses of plays and productions in terms of gender and the consequent effects on audiences and society. (196)

Feminist Theatrical Theory: An attempt to explain the effects of gender in the workings of theatre and drama and, through them, on society and culture. (196)

Festivals: In Greece, religious worship took place in private and at major public festivals. In and around Athens, there were four festivals devoted to the god Dionysus. At three of these, records of drama appeared during the fifth century B.C. At the festival of no other gods can such records be found. See *City Dionysia, Rural Dionysia,* and *Lenaia.* During the Middle Ages, there were Christian festivals at which dramas were often produced. See also *Corpus Christi.*

Flat: A structure upon which scenery is painted, consisting of a wooden frame and canvas covering; usually of a size to be carried by one or two persons for shifting. Used in both Italianate staging and box sets (see entries).

Floodlights: Broad-beam stage instruments that "flood" a large area with light. (189)

Flying: Method of handling scenery for quick shifting by raising it out of sight over the stage with one of various systems of ropes, pulleys, counterweights, machines, and so on. Also, the illusion of flight in actors and properties through the use of concealed wires and the same system of ropes and pulleys.

Focus: The point or object that draws the eye of the audience to the stage picture. (166)

Followspot: Powerful, hard-edged lighting instrument mounted so that an operator can "follow" action with the light. (191)

Footlights: Light sources arranged along the front of a stage (between actors and audience) to throw light upward from stage level to eliminate shadows from harsh overhead lighting. Rarely used with modern lighting systems, but standard equipment with candle, oil, gas, and early electrical systems (c. 1650–1920). (191)

Forestage: That part of the stage in front of the scenery, especially in Renaissance stages, using a slanted floor for forced perspective in the scenic area. See also *Apron.* (81)

Formalism: 1. Strict adherence to established ways (forms) of doing things. 2. In scenic design, use of nonrepresentational shapes and forms as the design base. 3. In criticism, attention to matters of dramatic form and structure as distinct from philosophical and sociological issues, etc.

Front of House: Activities relating to production that transpire in front of the curtain: e.g., promotion and publicity for performances, house management, box office sales.

Functionalism: Aesthetic or artistic method that focuses on the function of objects (scenery, for example) instead of on prettiness.

Gallery: The highest audience areas in nineteenth-century theatres (box, pit, and gallery), hence, the cheapest seats; the balconies. (61)

Genre: In dramatic criticism, a category of plays: comedy, tragedy, melodrama, farce. Popularly, any category. (55)

Gesture: In one sense, any human act that conveys meaning (i.e., a speech is a gesture). In a more limited sense, a planned physical movement that conveys meaning, like waving a hand or pointing a finger.

Given Circumstances: In Stanislavskian vocabulary, those aspects of character that are beyond the character's or actor's control: age, sex, state of health, and so on. (134)

Glory: In medieval and Renaissance art, a cloud or sunburst in which divinities appeared. In the theatre of those periods, a flown platform made to look like a cloud or sunburst.

Gradas: Covered bleacher-style seats at ground level in the Spanish *corrales* (which see). (263)

Graeco-Roman: That period in Greece and Greek lands when Roman domination had arrived, usually dated from c. 100 B.C. to the fall of the Western Roman Empire, c. A.D. 550. In theatre architecture, those Greek theatres that were remodeled to bring them in closer accord with the Roman ideals of beauty. (Not to be confused with Roman theatres built in Greek lands.) (221–222)

Griot: West African storyteller. (375)

Groove: A shallow channel in the stage floor in which a flat rode, for quick scene changes; a bank of several grooves would allow one flat to be pulled aside while another was pushed on in its place, seemingly in the same plane. (288)

Ground Plan: The "map" of the playing area for a scene, with doors, furniture, walls, and so on indicated to scale. (154–156)

Ground Row: A piece of scenery at stage level, often used to hide stage-level machinery or lights or to increase the sense of distance. (303)

Guerrilla Theatre: Didactic political theatre done in nontheatrical spaces—streets, factories, subways—without previous announcement; hit-and-run performances like guerrilla attacks. (362)

Guilds: Religious and, sometimes, trade or professional organizations in the Middle Ages that became the producers of civic medieval theatre. (244)

Hamartia: Aristotle's concept of error or failure of judgment by the tragic hero (sometimes translated inaccurately as "tragic flaw"). (221)

Hanamichi: In the Japanese Kabuki theatre, a walkway through the audience used by actors to get to and from the stage. (391)

Happy Idea: The basic premise on which a particular Greek old comedy was based. For example, the *happy idea* in *Lysistrata* is that women can prevent war by withholding sex. (219)

Hashigakari: In the Japanese Noh theatre, a walkway at the side of the stage for the actors' entrances and exits. (389)

Heavens: 1. Area above the stage: in the Elizabethan theatre, the underside of the roof that extended over the stage. 2. In the nineteenth century, the highest gallery. (251)

Hellenistic: 1. That period of Greek history dating from the coming of Alexander the Great (c. 336 B.C.). 2. In theatre architecture, those Greek theatres built during the Hellenistic period. (220–221)

Hero, Heroine: 1. A figure embodying a culture's most valued qualities (for example, Achilles in *The Iliad*) and hence the central figure in a heroic tragedy. 2. Popularly the leading character in a play or, more precisely, the leading male character in a play. 3. In melodrama, the male character who loves the heroine. See also *Protagonist*.

Heroic: Of or relating to a hero; by extension, exalted. *Heroic couplets* are two lines of rhyming iambic pentameter, probably an English attempt to reproduce the French Alexandrine, the approved verse for Neoclassical tragedy. *Heroic acting* stressed the vocal and physical grandeur of the actor. *Heroic tragedy*, popular during the seventeenth and eighteenth centuries, customarily treated the conflict between love and duty and was written in heroic couplets.

High Comedy: Comedy of intellect and language, usually emphasizing upper-class characters and concerns. See also *Comedy*.

Hireling: In professional companies of the Renaissance and after, an actor or technician hired by the shareholders to work for a set wage at a set task. (254)

Hikinuki: In Japanese Kabuki performance, the sudden transformation of a costume into a completely different one. (391)

Householder: Member of a professional company who owns a share of the theatre building itself. (254)

Humanism: That philosophy that believes that people should be at the center of their own deepest concerns. (247–248)

Idea: In Aristotelian criticism, the moral expression of character through language; more generally, the intellectual statement of the *meaning* (see entry) of a play or a performance. (51–53)

Identification: Audience attitude in which the audience member believes that important elements of himself or herself are to be found in a dramatic character; the audience "identifies" with the character. A suspect theory. (67)

Illusion of the First Time: An expression used by an English critic (late nineteenth century) to describe the effect of good realistic acting: that is, the event seems to be happening for the first time *to the character*.

Illusionism: Scenic practices (with analogs in acting, directing, and other theatre arts) that rely on a belief in the theatrical imitation of the real world. (304)

Imagination: In acting, inventive faculty of the actor. (See also *Instrument*.) More generally, that faculty of mind or feeling, usually thought to be nonlinear, imagistic, metaphorical, and playful.

Impressionism: A style of art that sought truth in the fleeting moments of consciousness. Prevalent in the drama and theatre of the 1890s, Impressionism was noted for its moody and mysterious quality. (340–341)

Improvisation: Acting technique or exercise emphasizing immediacy of response and invention rather than rehearsed behavior. (340–341)

Instrument: The actor's physical self. See also *Imagination*.

Interlude: A kind of dramatic fare performed between other events, as between the courses of a banquet. Important during the Middle Ages and the Renaissance and connected with the rise of the professional actor. (240)

Intermezzi: Italian entertainments usually given at courts and presented between other forms of entertainment. See *Interlude*. (240)

Interregnum: "Between the kings"—that period of English history (1642–1660) after Charles I was removed from the throne and before Charles II was restored; with a Puritan government in power, theatres were closed. (262)

Italianate Staging: A kind of staging developed during the Renaissance in Italy and marked by a proscenium arch and perspective scenery arranged in wing and drop. (270–275)

Kuttambalam: Theatre type used by an Indian *Kuttiyattam* (which see): square, roofed stage with audience on three sides. (386)

Kuttiyattam: Indian theatrical form, derived from Sanskrit drama. (385–386)

Kyogen: Japanese theatre form: comic interludes between parts of a Noh performance. (390)

Latin Music Drama: Medieval dramas performed inside churches by clergy. The dramas unfolded in Latin rather than the vernacular and were sung rather than spoken, thus the name. Also called Liturgical Drama. (236)

Laughing Comedy: Specifically, comedy dating from the late eighteenth century and intended to restore the comic (laughing) spirit to the comedies of the age—in contrast to the then-popular sentimental or tearful comedies. (See entry). (300)

Lazzi: Stock bits of business designed to provoke a particular response, usually laughter, from the audience. Associated particularly with the *commedia dell'arte* and the French farce of the seventeenth century. (275)

Lenaia: One of three major Athenian religious festivals devoted to the public worship of the god Dionysus at which drama was recorded. The home of comedy. See also *Festivals*. (210)

Lines of Business: A range of roles in which an actor would specialize for the major part of his or her acting career. Particularly important during the seventeenth and eighteenth centuries. (289)

Liturgical: Associated with the liturgy of the church; in drama, the kinds of plays that were done inside churches as part of the religious services and thus were performed in Latin, by the clergy, and were usually chanted or sung rather than spoken. Liturgical drama is also called Latin Music Drama. (236)

Low Comedy: A kind of comedy that depends for its humor primarily on situation, visual gags, or obscenity. See also *Comedy*.

Ludi: 1. In Rome, festivals or *ludi* were given for public worship of a variety of gods and on various public occasions like military victories and the funerals of government officials. As drama was often included as a part of the festivals, they are important in a history of Roman theatre. 2. Early medieval term for plays.

Mansion: The particularized setting in the medieval theatre that, together with the *platea*, or generalized playing space, constituted the major staging elements of the theatre. Several mansions were placed around or adjacent to the *platea* at once—thus "simultaneous staging." See also *Platea*. (241)

Masque: Spectacular theatrical form, especially of the Renaissance and the Neoclassical periods, usually associated with *court theatres* (see entry) or special events. Emphasis was put on costumes and effects, with much music and dancing; amateur actors frequently performed. For example, Ben Jonson's many court masques. (259–261)

Master Artwork: *Gesamtkunstwerk.* Both term and concept popularized by Richard Wagner, who argued that such a work would be the artistic fusion of all major artistic elements, including music, into a single work under the artistic supervision of a single master artist. (198)

Master of Secrets: That craftsman/artist of the medieval theatre charged with the execution of special effects in the dramas. (245)

Meaning: Intellectual content suggested or inspired by a play or a performance. All plays have meaning, however trivial, and most plays and performances have several meanings. Best thought of as "range of meaning" or "world of meaning." (153–154)

Mechane: Machine, or *machina.* In classical Greece, a crane by means of which actors and objects could be flown into the playing area (orchestra). (214)

Medieval: That period of world history dating roughly from the fall of the Western Roman Empire (c. A.D. 550) to the fall of Constantinople and the beginning of the Renaissance (c. 1450). In drama, the period between 975, the first record of drama, and c. 1550, when religious drama was outlawed in many countries throughout Europe. (233–234)

Melodrama: Literally "music drama." A kind of drama associated with a simplified moral universe, a set of stock characters (hero, heroine, villain, comic relief), rapid turns in the dramatic action, and a dual-issue ending. Leading form of drama throughout the nineteenth century. (55–56)

Method: The American version of Stanislavski's "system" of actor training. (134)

Middle Comedy: That transitional kind of Greek comedy dating from c. 404 B.C., the defeat of Athens by Sparta, and 336 B.C., the beginning of the Hellenistic age. Less topical than Greek old comedy, middle comedy dealt more with domestic issues and everyday life of the Athenian middle class. (219)

Mime: 1. A kind of drama dating at least from the sixth century B.C. in Greece in which *unmasked* actors of both sexes portrayed often bawdy and obscene stories. The first *professional* performers appeared in the mime. In Greece, the form was never permitted in the religious festivals, but in Rome, it became the most popular kind of drama after the first century A.D. 2. Form of silent modern theatre.

Miracle Plays: Medieval plays treating the lives of saints. (238)

Monopoly: Legal control or exclusive domination of a theatrical locale; the courts of both France and England in the late seventeenth century, for example, granted licenses to a limited number of theatres that thus gained *monopolies.* (284)

Morality Plays: Allegorical medieval plays, liike *Everyman,* that depict the eternal struggle between good and evil that transpires in this world, using characters like Vice, Virtue, Wisdom, and so on. (238)

Motivation: In Stanislavskian vocabulary, the dramatic justification for an action or a set of behaviors onstage. (134–135)

Music: One of Aristotle's six parts of a play: the material for diction. Popularly, the kind of art form having harmony and rhythm. (53)

Musical: An American musical comedy, a form traceable to the mid-nineteenth century and now typified by a spoken text or *book* (see entry) with songs and (usually) dances and a singing-dancing chorus.

Mysteries: Medieval plays treating events based on the Bible or the Apocrypha and performed singly or in combination to produce the so-called cycle or cosmic dramas (see entries). (238)

Myth: Story with a religious or magical base, featuring a myth hero who typifies important features of the culture, for example, the myth of Oedipus (ancient Greece) or the myth of Skunniwundi (American Indian). In a less precise sense, some critics speak of the myth behind or imbedded in a work of narrative art and even of a dream, that is, the culturally important pattern that can be found there.

Naturalism: A style of theatre and drama most popular from c. 1880 to 1900 that dealt with the sordid problems of the middle and lower classes in settings remarkable for the number and accuracy of details. Practitioners included Émile Zola, André Antoine, and Maxim Gorky. See also *Determinism*. (323–324)

Natyasastra: Ancient Indian (Sanskrit) work on theatre aesthetics. (385)

Neoclassical: A style of drama and theatre from the Italian Renaissance based loosely on interpretations of Aristotle and Horace. Major tenets were verisimilitude, decorum, purity of genres (see all of these entries), the five-act form, and the twofold purpose of drama: to teach and to please. (266–270)

Neoromanticism: Literally, "new Romanticism." A style of theatre and drama of the late nineteenth century that sought to recapture the idealism and exoticism of early nineteenth-century Romanticism. A reaction against the pessimism and sordidness of the Realists and the Naturalists.

New Comedy: That form of Greek comedy dating from the Hellenistic and Graeco-Roman periods and treating the domestic complications of the Athenian middle class. A major source for Roman comedy. (221)

Noble Savage: A manifestation of *primitivism* (see entry) that depicted a romanticized view of primitive people and led to an artistic presentation of American Indians, African slaves, and so on as major figures in art. (292)

Obie: Awards given annually to performers, playwrights, designers, and productions that made significant contributions to the Off-Broadway theatre scene. Name comes from the first letters of Off-Broadway.

Objective: In Stanislavskian vocabulary, a character's goal within a beat or scene; the goal of a motivation. (135)

Old Comedy: That form of Greek comedy written during the Classical period (see entry) and featuring topical political and social commentary set in highly predictable structural and metrical patterns. (218–219)

Off-Broadway: Popularly, those small, originally experimental but now often quite commercial theatres that are located outside the Times Square/Broadway area. Theatres with a seating capacity of fewer than three hundred that are authorized to pay lower wages and fees than are the larger, Broadway houses. (87–88)

Off-Off-Broadway: Popularly, the very small nontraditional theatres located in churches, coffee houses, and so on that fall considerably out of the commercial mainstream. Theatres with highly limited seating capacities that may be granted exemptions from a wide variety of union regulations and scales. (88)

Orchestra: 1. That area of the Greek and Roman theatre that lay between the audience area and the scene house. 2. Originally the circular space where actors and chorus danced and performed plays; later a half circle that was used as a seating space for important people and only occasionally as a performance area. 3. In modern times, the prized seating area on the ground level of a theatre and adjacent to the stage.

Organic: Suggesting growth from a definable beginning; developing naturally.

Orta Oyunu: Traditional Turkish comic theatre form. (382–383)

Pacing: Apparent rate of performance; partly a matter of speed with which the performance goes forward, but also related to intensity of action and complication and the artistic ways (actor's intensity, for example) that the action is realized. (167)

Pageant: In the medieval period, a movable stage, a wagon on which plays were mounted and performed in parts of England, Spain, and occasionally Continental Europe. By extension, the plays performed on such wagons. (242)

Pantomime: In the Roman theatre, a dance/story performed by a single actor with the accompaniment of a small group of musicians, particularly during the Christian era. In the eighteenth and nineteenth centuries, a "minor" form of entertainment marked by elaborate spectacle and often featuring *commedia* characters and a scene of magical transformation.

Paratheatrical: Related to or parallel to the theatrical. Used to refer to activities tangential to theatre: circus, parades, and so on.

Patio: Ground-level audience area in the Spanish *corrales* (which see). (263)

Performance Art: An avant-garde form that blends several arts (most often music, painting, dance, and theatre) into a visual, more than literary, expression of an often very personal truth. (370–371)

Performance Criticism: Objective analysis and explanation of performance (rather than of, for example, drama alone). (59)

Performance Theory: Objective description of the nature of performance (rather than of, for example, drama alone). (194)

Performing Arts: Those arts that depend on a live performer in the presence of a live audience, for example, theatre, dance, opera, musical concerts. (5–7)

Periaktoi: Stage machines in use by the Hellenistic period in Greece. An early method of scene changing that consisted of a triangle extended in space and mounted on a central pivot so that when the pivot was rotated, three different scenes could be shown to an audience. (230)

Period Movement: Actors' movements imitative or suggestive of the way people moved, or are thought to have moved, in another historical period. (126)

Perspective: Simulation of visual distance by the manipulation of size of objects. (270–271)

Phallus: Simulation of the male sex organ. In Greek old comedy and satyr plays, phalluses were enlarged and otherwise made prominent for purposes of comic effect. (218)

Phonetic: Relating to the human voice and human speech; symbolizing (in letters or pictures, for example) precise human sounds, as in the phonetic alphabet. (127)

Pictorialism: Directorial use of the proscenium stage's potential for creating pictures, for both aesthetic and ideological ends. (163–164)

Picturization: Directorial creation of stage groupings ("pictures") that show or symbolize relationships or meanings; storytelling through stage pictures. (164–165)

Pit: 1. Area of the audience on the ground floor and adjacent to the stage. Historically an inexpensive area because originally no seats were provided there and later only backless benches were used. By the end of the nineteenth century, a preferred seating area (now called the orchestra section). 2. Now refers often to the area reserved for members of the orchestra playing for opera, ballet, and musical comedy.

Platea: The unlocalized playing area in the medieval theatre. See also *Mansion.* (241)

Plot: 1. In Aristotle, one of the six parts of a play and the most important of the six; the formal cause of character; the soul of tragedy; the architectonic part of a play. 2. Popularly the story of a play, a novel, and so on. (45–48)

Point of Attack: The place in the story where a dramatic plot begins. Typically Greek plays, like *Oedipus Rex,* have a late point of attack, and medieval and Shakespearean plays, like *King Lear,* have an early point of attack. (46)

Political Theatre: The kind of theatre devoted to achieving political and social rather than artistic goals.

Poor Theatre: Phrase popularized by Jerzy Grotowski and referring to the kind of theatrical production that is stripped of all (to him) inessential elements (scenery, costuming, lighting, etc.) and focuses only on the relationship between actor and audience.

Possession of Parts: During the seventeenth and especially the eighteenth centuries, the practice of leaving a role with an actor throughout a career. Under the system, a sixty-year-old woman playing Juliet in Shakespeare's tragedy was not unheard of. (289)

Postmodernism: A critical approach that doubts the possibility of objectivity and that favors, consequently, the open acknowledgement of socially constructed meanings and investigates the implications of those meanings. (196)

Presentational: Style of performance and design that lays emphasis on *presenting* a theatrical event to an audience. Contrasts with representational (see entry), which stresses the reproduction of life on stage for an audience that merely looks on.

Preview: Public performance given prior to the official opening of a play, often to test the audience's response. (173)

Primitivism: Interest in life and societies of primitive people; associated in particular with the Romantic movement of the late eighteenth and early nineteenth centuries. (292)

Private Theatre: In Elizabethan and Stuart England, indoor theatres that were open to the public but were expensive because of their relatively limited seating capacity. Located on monastic lands, these theatres were outside the jurisdiction of the city of London. Initially they housed children's troupes, but later the regular adult troupes used them as a winter home. (252–253)

Probability: In drama, the internally closed system that allows each event in a play to seem likely and believable for that play (for example, the appearance of God in a medieval cycle play). (340)

Prologue: In Greek drama, that part of the play that precedes the entrance of the chorus. In other periods, a short introductory speech delivered by an actor, either in or out of character, to set the scene, warm up the audience, defend the play, or entertain.

Properties: Objects used on stage—furniture, cigarettes, dishware.

Proscenium (Theatre): Theatre building in which the audience area is set off from the acting area by a proscenium arch that frames the stage, protects the perspective, masks the backstage area, etc. The audience views the onstage action from one side only. (81)

Protagonist: In Greek theatre, the first (or major) actor, the one who competed for the prize in acting. Later, the leading character in any play (the "hero"). (50, 215)

Psychological Realism: A kind of theatre that relies on a view of human behavior as defined by late nineteenth-century and twentieth-century psychology.

Public Relations: The business of causing the public to understand and esteem an event, institution, or cause. In theatre, it usually includes activities like advertising plays, developing essays for programs, designing posters, and inducing the public to have goodwill toward the theatrical organization before and after, as well as during, a specific production. (199–200)

Purity of Genres: Neoclassical tenet that elements of tragedy and those of comedy could not be mixed. The injunction was not merely against including funny scenes in tragedy but also against treating domestic issues or writing in prose, these elements being of the nature of comedy. (268–269)

Raisonneur: In drama, a character who speaks for the author. (50)

Raked Stage: Stage slanted up from front to back to enhance the perspective. Stages began their rakes either at the front of the apron or at the proscenium line. (81)

Rasa: Important element of Sanskrit aesthetic theory—the inducing of an appropriate emotion in the audience. (385)

Realism: The style of drama and theatre dating from the late nineteenth and early twentieth centuries that strove to reproduce on stage the details of everyday life with a view to improving the human and social condition. (312–313)

Regional Theatre: Theatre outside New York City in the United States and Canada; term usually restricted to professional, nontouring companies. (88–90)

Rehearsal: The practicing of plays, either whole or in part, in order to improve their performance. (137–138)

Renaissance: Literally, "rebirth"; refers to a renewed interest in the learning and culture of ancient Greece and Rome. Beginning in Italy, the Renaissance spread throughout Western Europe from c. 1450 to c. 1650. (247–250)

Repertory: A set group of performance pieces done by a company is its repertory. Also, the practice in such a company of alternating pieces so that they are done *in repertory*. Loosely, a resident professional theatre company in the United States, called a *repertory theatre*.

Representational: A style of performance and design that lays emphasis on re-creating onstage aspects of daily life; the audience members are thought of as passive onlookers. Contrasts with *presentational* (see entry), a style that stresses *presenting* an event *for an audience*.

Restoration: The period of English history that dates from 1660, when King Charles II was restored to the throne. (283–284)

Reversal: According to Aristotle, a change in the direction of action or in the expectation of character. Reversals result in complex plots, preferred for tragedies over simple plots. (47)

Reviewer: A person who views an artistic event and then writes his or her descriptive evaluation of it for immediate publication. (85)

Rhythm: Regular and measurable repetition. (166–169)

Rigging: The combination of ropes, lines, pulleys, pipes, and so on that permits the manipulation of scenic units backstage.

Ritual: Any oft-repeated act that has a specific goal. *Ritual theory:* a theory that asserts that drama derived from religious rituals (in Greece, for example, religious rituals devoted to the worship of the god Dionysus). (14–17, 365)

Roman: A period in theatre and drama dating from c. 364 B.C. to c. A.D. 550 and customarily subdivided into the Republican period (c. 364 B.C.–c. 27 B.C.) and the Empire (c. 27 B.C.– c. A.D. 550).

Romanticism: A style of theatre and drama dating from c. 1790 to c. 1850 and marked by an interest in the exotic, the subjective, the emotional, and the individual. Began in part as a reaction against the strictures of Neoclassicism; grew out of the eighteenth century's sentimentalism (see entry). (291–294)

Royalties: Payments made to authors (and their representatives) for permission to reproduce, in text or in performance, their artistic products (plays, designs, etc.). (106, 108)

Run-Through: A kind of rehearsal in which the actors perform long sections of the play (or the whole play) without interruption, usually for the purpose of improving the sense of continuity, shaping the whole, and so on. (173)

Rural Dionysia: One of three Athenian festivals devoted to the public worship of the god Dionysus at which drama appeared. See also *Festivals.* (210)

Satyr Play: A short, rustic, and often obscene play included in the Dionysian festivals of Greece at the conclusion of the tragedies. (219)

Scaffold: In medieval staging in England, the localizing structure in or near the *platea*. See also *Mansion.* (242)

Scenario: In general, the prose description of a play's story. In the *commedia dell'arte*, the written outlines of plot and characters from which the actors improvised the particular actions of performance. (275)

Scrim: Mesh used in scenery; becomes transparent when lighted from behind, opaque when lighted from the front; useful for transformations, misty effects, and so forth. (341)

Script: Play text. See also *Text* and *Book.*

Secularism: Belief in the validity and importance of life and things on earth. Often contrasted with spiritualism, other-worldliness, or religiosity. The Renaissance period was marked by a rising *secularism.* (248)

Semiotics: The study of signs, things that stand for other things. When applied to language, art, and criticism, semiotics focuses attention on the meanings that audiences create from the words or images of a playscript or a performance. (196)

Sense Memory: Recall of a sensory response—smell, taste, sound—with both its cause and the actor's reaction; important to the creation of a character's behavior in some theories of acting. (129)

Sententiae: Pithy, short statements about the human condition. Associated with the tragedies of Seneca and with those of his successors in the Renaissance. (225)

Sentimental Comedy: A kind of comedy particularly popular during the eighteenth century in which people's virtues rather than their foibles were stressed. The audience were expected to experience something "too exquisite for laughter." Virtuous characters expressed themselves in pious "sentiments." (282)

Sentimentalism: Prevalent during the eighteenth century, sentimentalism assumed the innate goodness of humanity and attributed evil to faulty instruction or bad example. A precursor of the Romanticism of the nineteenth century. (285)

Shareholder: Member of a sharing company who owned a part of the company's stocks of costumes, scenery, properties, and so on. Sharing companies were the usual organization of troupes from the Renaissance until the eighteenth century (and beyond), when some actors began to prefer fixed salaries to shares.

Shimpa: Modern Japanese theatre form of mixed genres and origins. (391)

Shite: In Noh theatre, the protagonist. (389)

Shutter: Large flat, paired with another of the same kind, to close off the back of the scene in Italianate staging; an alternative to a backdrop; sometimes used for units at the sides. When pierced with a cutout, it became a "relieve" and showed a *diorama* (see entry). (273)

Sight Lines: Extreme limits of the audience's vision, drawn from the farthest and/or highest seat on each side through the proscenium arch or scenery obtruding farthest onstage. Anything beyond the sight lines cannot be seen by some members of the audience. (81)

Signature Music: Music associated with certain characters or certain types of characters, particularly in the melodramas of the nineteenth century. Stage directions indicate "Mary's music," "Jim's music," and so on. (296)

Simultaneous Staging: The practice, particularly during the Middle Ages, of representing several locations on the stage at one time. In medieval staging, several *mansions* (see entry), representing particular places, were arranged around a *platea*, or generalized playing space.

Skene: The scene house in the Greek theatre. Its appearance can first be documented with the first performance of the *Oresteia* in 458 B.C. Its exact appearance from that time until the first stone theatre came into existence (probably in the late fourth century B.C.) is uncertain. (212–213)

Slice of Life: Critical notion closely associated with Naturalism and used to describe plays that avoided the trappings of Romanticism and the obvious contrivance of well-made plays in favor of a seemingly literal reproduction of daily life on the stage. (314)

Soliloquy: An intensely emotional passage, often lyric, delivered by a person onstage alone.

Spectacle: One of Aristotle's six parts of a play, the part of least interest to the poet but of most importance in differentiating the dramatic form from the narrative and the epic. In everyday parlance, all visual elements of production and, by extension, particular plays, scenes, or events in which visual elements predominate. (54)

Spine: In Stanislavskian vocabulary, the consistent line that connects all elements of a character through a play. See *Through line*. (135)

Stage Left: The left half of the stage as defined by someone standing onstage facing the audience.

Stage Right: The right half of the stage as defined by someone standing onstage facing the audience.

Star: Dominant actor or actress whose name and presence draw an audience. (326–328)

Star System: Company organization in which minor characters are played by actors for the season, while central roles are taken by stars (see entry) brought in for one production; still common in opera, sometimes seen in summer theatres. (306)

Stock Company: Theatre company in which actors play standardized roles and (originally) owned shares of stock in the company. (306)

Storm and Stress: *Sturm und Drang;* a theatrical movement in Germany during the 1770s and 1780s that was marked by its militant experimentation with dramatic form, theatrical style, and social statement. (295)

Story: Narrative; coherent sequence of incidents; "what happens." A general, nontechnical term that should not be confused with *plot.* (65–66)

Street Theatre: Theatre, often political, that takes place outside traditional theatre spaces and without traditional theatrical trappings. (362)

Style: 1. Distinctive combination of elements. 2. In Aristotelian terms, the way in which the manner is joined to the means. 3. Particulars of surface, as distinguished from substance. 4. "The way a thing is done" in a time and place.

Subtext: In Stanislavskian vocabulary, action "between the lines," implied but not stated in the text. (150)

Suffering: According to Aristotle, an awareness. The material out of which discoveries are made. (47)

Superobjective: In Stanislavskian vocabulary, the "life goal" of the character. (135)

Surrealism: A style popular immediately following World War I that rejected everyday logic in favor of a free expression of the subconscious (or dream) state. (346)

Symbolism: A style of theatre and drama popular during the 1890s and the early twentieth century that stressed the importance of subjectivity and spirituality and sought its effects through the use of symbol, legend, myth, and mood. (341–342)

Technical Director: The person charged with coordinating backstage activities preparatory to production, including the coordination required to transform the scenic designer's vision into finished settings. (184–185)

Technical Rehearsal: Rehearsal devoted to the practice and perfection of the various technical elements of the show (lighting, sound, flying, trapping, and so on). (135)

Tendencies: In Stanislavskian vocabulary, aspects of an actor's performance that digress from the *through line* (see entry). (135)

Text: The written record of a play, including dialogue and stage directions; a playscript.

Theatre of Cruelty: Phrase popularized by Antonin Artaud to describe a kind of theatre that touched the basic precivilized elements of people through disrupting normal "civilized" expectations about appearance, practice, sound, and so forth. (349)

Three Unities: In Neoclassical (Western) dramatic theory, the unities of time, place, and action. (269)

Through Line: In Stanislavskian vocabulary, a consistent element of character running through a scene or a play. (135)

Thrust Stage: Dominant kind of staging during Shakespeare's time in England that is being revived in many contemporary theatres. Also called *three-quarter round* because the audience surrounds the action on three sides as the stage juts into the audience area. (79–81)

Timing: Actor's sense of tempo and rhythm. (166)

Tiring House: The building from which the Elizabethan platform, or thrust, stage extended. A place where the actors attired themselves. (251)

Tony: Annual awards made by the directors of the American Theatre Wing in memory of Antoinette Perry to recognize outstanding contributions to the current New York theatrical season.

Tragedy: In popular parlance, any serious play, usually including an unhappy ending. According to Aristotle, "an imitation of a worthy or illustrious and perfect action, possessing magnitude, in pleasing language, using separately the several species of imitation in its parts, by men acting, and not through narration, through pity and fear effecting a catharsis of such passion." At this point in theatrical history, almost indefinable.

Transformation: 1. Technique popularized in the 1960s whereby an actor portrayed several characters without any changes in costume, makeup, or mask, relying instead on changing voice and body attitudes in full view of the audience. 2. In medieval and Renaissance theatre, seemingly magical changes of men into beasts, women into salt, and so on.

Trap: Unit in stage floor for appearances and disappearances; varies from a simple door to complex machines for raising and lowering while moving forward, backward, and sideways.

Tritagonist: The third actor in Greek tragedies. Typically played a series of minor and bit parts.

Trope: An interpolation in a liturgical text. The medieval drama is believed to have been derived from medieval troping. (235)

Union: An alliance of persons formed to secure material benefits and better working conditions. Major theatrical unions are USAA (United Scenic Artists of America, for designers); Equity (Actors Equity Association, for actors); IATSE (International Alliance of Theatrical Stage Employees, for theatre technicians). (85)

Unit Set: A single setting on which all scenes may be played.

Unity: Cohesion or consistency. When applied to a text, it refers to the method of organizing: unity of plot, unity of character, unity of action. When applied to design, it refers to how well all the visual elements fit together to achieve an artistic whole.

Upstage: The sections of the stage closest to the back wall. Comes from a time when stages were raked, or slanted, from the front to the back, so that upstage meant quite literally walking *up* the stage toward the back wall. (165)

Vaudeville: 1. In America in the nineteenth and twentieth centuries, vaudeville was popular family entertainment featuring a collection of variety acts, skits, short plays, and song-and-dance routines. 2. In France in the eighteenth and nineteenth centuries, *vaudeville* referred to *comédie-en-vaudeville*, short satiric pieces, often topical, that were interspersed with new lyrics set to familiar tunes and sprinkled with rhyming couplets (*vaudevilles*). The form in France is roughly equivalent to the *ballad opera* (see entry) in England.

Verisimilitude: Central concept in Neoclassical theory and criticism. Literal meaning is "truth-seemingness," but used historically, at a time when *truth* referred to the general, typical, categorical truth. Not to be confused with "realism." (267–268)

Via Negativa: "The negative path." Popularized by Jerzy Grotowski in actor training; the necessity to strip away all disguises, masks, or protections of the performer so that he may begin work at a very basic and truthful level.

Vidusaka: Ironic commentator in Indian *kuttiyattam* (which see). (386)

Villain: Character in melodrama who opposes the forces of good (represented by the hero and the heroine) and who, at the play's end, is punished for his evil ways. Typically the villain propels the action of a melodrama. (297)

Vocal Folds: Tissue in the throat over which air passes to make sound; incorrectly called *vocal cords.* (126)

Wagon: Wheeled platform that moves on and off a stage, particularly a proscenium stage; also, in medieval theatre, a movable scenic unit and playing area, or pageant (which see).

Waki: In Noh theatre, the second character, usually a confidant. (389)

Well-Made Play: A play written by or in the manner of Eugène Scribe and marked by careful preparation, seeming cause-and-effect organization of action, announced entrances and exits, and heavy reliance on external objects or characters to provide apparent connections among diverse lines of action. Now often used as a term of derision. (300)

Wings: 1. Scenic pieces (*flats*) placed parallel to the stage front, or nearly so, on each side of the stage; combined with overhead units for "wing-and-border" settings. 2. The offstage area beyond the side units of scenery—"in the wings." (From which is derived *wing space*, the amount of room offstage at the sides.)

Yoruba opera: Nigerian theatrical form. (378)

Zanni: In *commedia dell'arte*, the group of comic servants that includes Arlecchino, Trufaldino, etc. (275)

INDEX

Page numbers in italics refer to illustrations.